OLD LONDON
Strand to Soho

THE
'VILLAGE LONDON'
SERIES
from
THE ALDERMAN PRESS

THE VILLAGE LONDON SERIES

Other titles already published in hard back are:

VILLAGE LONDON Volume I
VILLAGE LONDON Volume II
LONDON RECOLLECTED Volume I
LONDON RECOLLECTED Volume II
LONDON RECOLLECTED Volume III
LONDON RECOLLECTED Volume IV
LONDON RECOLLECTED Volume V

Other titles already published in paperback:

VILLAGE LONDON Pt. 1 West and North
VILLAGE LONDON Pt. 2 North and East
VILLAGE LONDON Pt. 3 South-East
VILLAGE LONDON Pt. 4 South-West

OLD FLEET STREET
CHEAPSIDE AND ST. PAUL'S
THE TOWER AND EAST END
SHOREDITCH to SMITHFIELD
CHARTERHOUSE to HOLBORN
STRAND to SOHO
COVENT GARDEN and the THAMES to WHITEHALL

The above seven titles are extracts from the
hardback edition of London Recollected.

OLD LONDON

Strand to Soho

by

EDWARD WALFORD

THE ALDERMAN PRESS

British Library Cataloguing in Publication Data.

Walford, Edward.
   Old London: Strand to Soho
   1. London (England)_____History
   I. Title II. Walford, Edward. Old and
   new London
   942.1   DA677

ISBN 0-946619-31-X

This edition published 1987.

The Alderman Press, 1/7 Church Street,
Edmonton, London, N9 9DR

Printed and bound in Great Britain
by Robert Hartnoll (1985) Ltd., Bodmin.

CONTENTS.

WESTMINSTER AND THE WESTERN SUBURBS.

CONTENTS.

CONTENTS.

LIST OF ILLUSTRATIONS.

———◆———

LONDON.

◆

WESTMINSTER AND THE WESTERN SUBURBS.

"I began to study the map of London."—R. Southey.

N the first two volumes of this work we
have dealt with the antiquities, the buried
history, the traditions, the folk-lore, and
the anecdotes of what we may term the
eastern hemisphere of London, and if a like
success can be achieved in our treatment
of the corresponding world which lies west
of the above-mentioned line, we shall have accomplished a task of no ordinary difficulty. With
the world of Westminster and its surrounding
districts—the "old court suburb" of Kensington,
Chelsea, Marylebone, and the suburban regions
of Lambeth, Bayswater, and Hampstead — we
have henceforth to discharge the duty of a topographer and a chronicler in one, describing their
features, "old and new," pointing out the spots
which they contain rendered sacred by old traditions and haunted by ancient memories, and
contrasting their present with their former state.
In the performance of this pleasant task, we shall
indeed be much wanting to our subject and to
the public too, if we cannot wake up again into
life and being the ghosts and the shadows of

departed greatness, and summon up before the reader's eyes some of the illustrious characters who have been identified with western London, especially during the past three or four hundred years, during which it has mainly grown into being. In this western hemisphere there are no Roman walls to tell of, no mention to make of Julius Cæsar, or of Boadicea, with her scythed chariots of war; but there will be much to say of Edward the Confessor, of William Caxton, of our Norman, Plantagenet, Tudor, and Stuart sovereigns, of the statesmen of the reigns of Henry VIII., Elizabeth and James, and of the far less interesting courts of our Hanoverian kings. The records of the Georgian and the Victorian eras, as well as those of the two previous lines of English monarchs, we shall do our best to ransack, bringing their chief men and chief events before the eyes of our readers; and it will be our pride and privilege to carry the record of the last-named era down to the sixtieth year of the reign of Her Most Gracious Majesty, Queen Victoria, whom may God long preserve, to rule over a loyal people and a mighty empire!

We shall make our start, of course, from the site of that once central edifice, Temple Bar. It can hardly be allowed that the Strand, to which we shall first bend our steps, is inferior to Fleet Street, or any other street in the City proper, in old memories and literary associations. It is not merely full of them, it positively teems with them. For centuries it was a fashionable thoroughfare, lying, as it did, between the City and the Court, and many of the noblest of the land dwelt along it, especially on its southern side, on account of the then bright and clear river on which it looked down. Where now stands Essex Street, adjoining the western side of the Temple, the Earl of Essex, Queen Elizabeth's rash favourite, was besieged, after his hopeless foray into the City. In Arundel Street lived the Earls of Arundel, whose title is now merged in the ducal house of Norfolk; in Buckingham Street, further to the west, Villiers, the greedy favourite of Charles I., began to build a palace. There were royal palaces, too, in the Strand; for in the Savoy lived John of Gaunt, and Somerset House was built by the "Protector" Somerset, with the stones of the churches that he had pulled down. At Somerset House, too, dwelt Charles I.'s queen, Henrietta Maria, and also poor neglected Catharine of Braganza; and it was almost on this very spot that Sir Edmundbury Godfrey, the zealous Protestant magistrate, was supposed to have been murdered. There is, too, the history of Lord Burleigh's house, in Cecil Street, to record;

and old Northumberland House, which stood so long, recalling its noble inmates of two successive lines of the Percies. On the other side of the Strand we shall have to take note of Butcher's Row, the place where the conspirators of the Gunpowder Plot held their meeting; Exeter House, where lived Lord Burleigh's wily son, and, finally, Exeter Hall, where the poet Gay lay in state, and where the annual meeting of many "religious" societies are held. Nor shall we forget to make mention of Cross's menagerie and the elephant Chunee, or of the many eccentric shopkeepers who once inhabited Exeter 'Change. At Charing Cross we shall stop to see the Cromwellians die bravely, and to stare at the pillory, in which many incomparable scoundrels have stood in their time, and which we much regret could not be revived for the benefit of rascals of more recent date who quite as richly deserve the infliction. The Nelson column and its lions, and the statues which surround them, have all of them stories of their own; and as we press on further northward, St. Martin's Lane becomes specially interesting as the haunt and home of half the painters of the early Georgian era. Here and in Leicester Square there are anecdotes of Hogarth and his friends to be picked up; and the whole neighbourhood generally deserves a careful exploration, from the quaintness and genius of many of its former inhabitants.

In Covent Garden again we "break fresh ground." Let us turn round to our right, then, and go east again, only at a little greater distance from the silvery Thames. As we found St. Martin's Lane full of artists, and the Strand full of noblemen, so the old monastic garden and its neighbourhood will prove to be crowded with actors. We shall trace the Market of Covent Garden from the first few sheds set up under the wall of Bedford House, to the present "Grand Temple of Flora and Pomona." We shall see what was known to most of our readers as "Evans's," a new mansion inhabited by Ben Jonson's friend and patron, Sir Kenelm Digby, and then alternately tenanted by Sir Harry Vane, by Denzil Holles, and by Admiral Russell, who defeated the French at La Hogue. The ghost of Parson Ford, in which no less sober a person than Dr. Johnson believed, awaits us at the door of the "Hummums." There are several duels for us to witness in the Piazza: there is Dryden for us to call upon as he sits, the arbiter of wits, by the fireside at "Will's" Coffee-house: Addison is to be found not far off at "Button's": at the Bedford we shall meet Garrick and Quin; and then stop for a few minutes at "Tom King's," close to the portico of St. Paul's, to watch Hogarth's revellers fight with swords and shovels on that frosty morning when the painter sketched the prim old maid going forth to early service at the church. We shall look in at the "Tavistock" to see Sir Peter Lely and Sir Godfrey Kneller at work upon portraits of the frail beauties of the Jacobean and the Caroline courts, remembering that in the same room Sir James Thornhill painted, and poor Richard Wilson produced those fine landscapes which so few had the taste to buy. The old Westminster hustings, the scene of so many a memorable election contest, will deserve a word at our hands. In fact the whole neighbourhood of Covent Garden is rife with stories of great actors, painters, poets, and men of letters ; and nearly every house, if its walls and timbers could have a voice, could furnish its quota of interesting and amusing anecdote. Indeed, the history of our two principal theatres,

> "The houses twain
> Of Covent Garden and of Drury Lane,"

if carefully looked up and sifted, would supply us with an endless store of anecdotes of actors, and with humorous and pathetic narratives that would embrace the whole region both of tragedy and of comedy. Quin's jokes, Garrick's weaknesses, the celebrated "O. P." riots, the miserable ends of some popular favourites, the fortunes made by others, and, generally speaking, the caprices of genius, afford a running commentary on the words of the old Roman satirist—

> "—— voluit Fortuna jocari."

" The oddities of Munden and the humour of Liston," it was observed in a previous volume, " serve only to render the gloom of Kean's downfall the more terrible, and to show the wreck and ruin of many unhappy men, equally wilful though less gifted. There is a perennial charm about theatrical stories, and the history of these theatres must be illustrated by many a sketch of the loves and rivalries of actors, their fantastic tricks, their practical jokes, and their gay progress to success or failure. Changes of popular taste are marked by the change of character in the pieces that have been performed at various eras ; and the history of the two theatres will include, of necessity, sketches of dramatic writers as well as of actors."

Then, again turning back into the Strand, and following the line of the Thames Embankment on our left, we shall extend our "voyage of discovery" into another region of dreamland, that of the venerable Abbey which holds the ashes of our kings, statesmen, and poets. "From the night on which," according to the ancient legend, "St. Peter came over the Thames from Lambeth in the fisherman's boat, and chose a site for the Abbey or 'Minster' of the West in the midst of Thorney Island, down to the present day, Westminster has ever been a spot where the pilgrim to historic shrines loves to linger." Need I remind my readers that Edward the Confessor built the Abbey, or that William the Conqueror was crowned within its walls, the ceremony ending in tumult and bloodshed ? How vast the store of facts from which we have to cull ! We see the Jews beaten nearly to death for daring to attend the coronation of Richard I. ; we observe Edward I. watching the sacred stone of Scotland being placed beneath the Coronation Chair of his forefathers. We hear the *Te Deum* sung for the victory of Agincourt, and watch Henry VII. selecting a site for his last resting-place ; we hear, at the coronation of Henry VIII., for the last time the sanction of the Pope bestowed formally upon the accession of an English monarch. We note Charles Edward sitting disguised in the gallery while he looks on and sees the crown which might, under other auspices, have been his own, placed on the head of George III. ; we pity poor Queen Caroline attempting to enter the Abbey in order to see the like ceremony performed on her worthless husband ; and we view once more in memory the last coronation, and draw from it auguries of a purer and a happier age.

The old Hall of Westminster, too ; how could we neglect that ancient chamber in which for so many centuries, since the reign of Richard II., at the least, the Champion of England from time to time has ridden proudly to challenge all gainsayers of the Crown, or any who may refuse to promise their allegiance ? How can we forget that the very timbers of its present roof heard Charles I. sentenced to death, and soon after saw the Lord Protector, Cromwell, throned in almost regal splendour within its walls ? We must see it not merely as it stands now, but at its exceptional seasons of important public events : when the "Seven Bishops" were acquitted, and the shout of joy shook London, it is said, like an earthquake : when the "rebel Lords" were tried and condemned to death on Tower Hill by the axe. We must see the "bad" Lord Byron tried for his duel with Mr. Chaworth, and the "mad" Lord Ferrers condemned to die at Tyburn for shooting his steward. We must try and get at all events a side view of the shameless Elizabeth Chudleigh, Duchess of Kingston, and hear Burke and Sheridan pour forth their torrents of eloquence over the misdeeds of Warren Hastings.

Then, next in order, the Parks will draw us westward, and we shall see the Second Charles feeding his ducks and toying with his mistresses at St. James's, or playing at "Pall Mall" in the Mall, which still preserves the name of that once favourite sport of royalty : again, we shall saunter northwards to Hyde Park to watch the fashions and extravagancies of successive generations. "Beau Brummel" and Count d'Orsay will drive by before our eyes, and "Romeo Coates" will whisk past us in his fantastic chariot. There will be celebrated duels to describe, and strange follies to deride. We shall see Cromwell thrown from his coach, and shall witness the foot-races so graphically described by Mr. Samuel Pepys. Dryden's gallants and masked ladies will receive due mention in their turn ; and we shall tell of bygone encampments and of many events now almost forgotten by the Londoner of to-day.

Next, the sight of Kensington will summon up the memories of William of Orange, Prince George of Denmark, and the First and Second Georges ; and Holland House will become once more peopled with Charles James Fox's friends, and the Whig statesmen, poets, and essayists of the succeeding generation. We shall also have a word to say about William Makepeace Thackeray and Leigh Hunt. At Chelsea we shall come upon pleasant recollections of the great Sir Thomas More, Swift, Atterbury, and Sir Robert Walpole. Then, extending our pilgrimage to the north, we shall again cross Kensington, to find ourselves at the pleasant suburb of Marylebone, where Queen Elizabeth sent the Russian Ambassadors to amuse themselves with a stag-hunt ; and where, at a far later date, Marylebone Gardens were the afternoon and evening lounge of persons of "quality" who had a taste for music and flirtations.

But even so, we shall hastily traverse only a very small portion of the ground so full of pleasant memories over which we purpose to conduct our readers, describing it more in detail, and halting at every step to record traditions more or less long since forgotten by the multitude. The districts of Bloomsbury, of St. Pancras, and of Kentish Town, will lead us by easy stages to the "Northern Heights of London ;" and we shall endeavour to act as our readers' guides around the pleasant hills of Hampstead and Highgate, leading them about the "wells" of the former, and the old park of Belsize, and the "Spaniards" Inn, and "Jack Straw's Castle," and the haunts of Akenside, Johnson, and Sir Richard Steele, and of Clarkson Stanfield and young Edwin Landseer. Then away, past Caen Wood, we shall take them on to the "High Gate" of the Bishops of London, to the home of Samuel

Taylor Coleridge, and the stone where Dick Whittington listened to "Bow Bells" as they prophesied his future fortune.

Then again, after a night's rest in London, we purpose to join them in one or more excursions over Westminster Bridge to Astley's, where the name of Ducrow still lingers, to Lambeth Palace, full of the religious associations of six centuries, and to Vauxhall, with its Gardens, now, alas ! blotted out and built over ; and we shall try to recall the days when Horace Walpole went thither with Lady Petersham, and helped to stew chickens in a china dish over a lamp. Then, trudging on, our pilgrim staff in hand, we shall make our way to Wandsworth and Putney, and cross the wooden bridge to Fulham, where successive Bishops of London have had their palace for several centuries ; and thence we may be led to extend our journey to Chiswick, to see Hogarth's old house, and the burial-place of his dogs, and even as far as fair "Shene" and Richmond, still redolent of Thomson and Swift, and Bluff King Hal, and (in more senses than one) of "Maids of Honour."

But the task that is before us is no light one. Mr. Ritchie says, in the opening chapter of his "Night Side of London,"—"One of the first things we are told Sir Walter Raleigh did when he was liberated from the Tower, was to take a promenade around London, to see what wonderful improvements had been effected during his incarceration. For this purpose his biographer calculates two or three hours would have sufficed. Times have altered since then. The man who now makes the tour round London would find he had no easy labour. It is hard to say where London begins or ends." The "City" of London, properly so called, is but a fraction, and geographically only a small portion of that great unit, the Metropolis, and is in reality little more than its counting-house. If we choose to take London in its widest sense—the London of the Metropolitan Police district—our capital now numbers nearly six millions of inhabitants, while in 1896 the Registrar-General's district, virtually identical with the County of London, was found to contain nearly four-and-a-half million souls. By the Local Management Act of 1856 the entire Metropolitan District was made to consist of no less than 122 square miles ; and if we regard London in its widest sense as co-extensive with the district under the charge of the City and Metropolitan Police, our readers may be astonished to hear that it covers 690 square miles.

Dr. Johnson has observed *àpropos* of the London of his day, "Sir, if you wish to have a just idea of the magnitude of this city, you must not be satisfied with seeing its great streets and squares, but must survey the innumerable little lanes and courts. It is not in the showy construction of buildings, but in the multiplicity of human habitations which are crowded together, that the wonderful immensity of London consists." If the worthy Doctor could behold the Mammoth City at the present time, with its additional century of growth and of population, he would be hardly able to find a word in his dictionary long enough to express adequately his idea of its enormous proportions !

As we, however, mean to take our time, pausing at every striking object which meets our view, to rest and to admire, the extent of ground which we have to explore need not alarm us, while in leisurely sort we roam from flower to flower over a garden as varied as the imagination can well conceive. There have been others who have essayed this flight before us, and we shall hope to profit largely by their experience. There have been brave and learned workers in this field. We shall therefore be able to build on good foundations any structure that we may endeavour to rear up. We shall hope to be wide and catholic in our selection, and to supply a variety of dishes, all suited to the taste of some one section of our numerous and varied body of readers. We shall endeavour to choose all that is of local, personal, and, above all, of human interest, pruning away what is dull and superfluous : we shall select our anecdotes with care, culling such only as will bring no blush to the cheek of maidenhood, while we trust to tell the rest in a way which at least shall be pithy and racy. At all events, we will pass knowingly by no fact that is of interest, but do our best to blend together in one consistent whole all that Time can give us bearing on old and new Westminster. Street by street, we shall delve deep into the soil for stories illustrative of the spot on which we stand, despising no book, however humble, if only it throws some light on the topographical history of London, and its ancient and modern manners and customs.

Such is the brief outline of our plan ; and it is with a good heart that we shall sally forth to realise it. We have before us a large variety of men and women, as well as of places, to portray. From the day when painted savages roamed about the forest now occupied by Hyde Park and Mayfair, down to the day when Queen Victoria drove from Paddington to Buckingham Palace, and thence to the Abbey Church of Westminster, to celebrate the Jubilee of her accession, in June, 1887, is indeed a long period over which to range. Nevertheless, we will endeavour to call up, by our wizard spells, the various generations of the human family who have had their haunts in and around Westminster, and the "Old Court Suburb," and see what we can find worth the telling about each in succession. Long lists of mere names, dull rows of dates, and dry rolls of pedigrees, we shall leave to the learned antiquary and the scientific historian, content if we can follow humbly in the steps of such chatty and gossiping chroniclers as dear old Herodotus and Livy were of old, and as Pepys and Evelyn, as Horace Walpole and Sir Nathaniel Wraxall have been in more recent and historic times. In a certain sense, too, it may be taken for granted, that the reminiscences of Westminster will prove in no way inferior to those of London proper, inasmuch as they are so closely interwoven with the histories of those successive dynasties of Tudor and Stuart sovereigns whom, in spite of all their faults and failings, and of our fealty to the crown of Victoria, we are too loyal to the past greatness of England to wish to see struck out from the history of our country.

CHAPTER I.

WESTMINSTER.—GENERAL REMARKS.—ITS BOUNDARIES AND HISTORY.

" Strange shadows from the midst of death
Are round our being strangely cast :
Thus the great city, towered and steepled,
Is doubly peopled,
Haunted by ghosts of the remembered Past."—*London Poems.*

Origin of the Name—Its Early History—Antiquity of the See—Foundation of the Abbey—The Palace at Westminster—Present Size and Importance—Extent of its Boundaries.

BUT before we start off upon our pilgrimage, that we may not stray hither and thither at random, it will be necessary to have before us, if not a map of, at all events some few general notes upon, the district over which we shall wander, together with a brief and general outline of its history as a city.

The origin of the name of Westminster is clear to the veriest child in such matters. The city must have taken its name from the noble Abbey Church of St. Peter's, the "Minster" in the "West," as doubtless it was called by the citizens of London in the days when London ended at the gate of "Lud," or, at the farthest, at Temple Bar. Stow tells us that it obtained this name all the more easily as "there was another Minster eastward of the City, and not far from the Tower, called 'Eastminster;'" but the honest old annalist has forgotten to tell us where it stood precisely, though

justified the bestowal of such a dignity ; and to the Marquisate was added a Dukedom in the person of the third and present Marquis of Westminster, by Her Majesty, on the retirement of Mr. Gladstone from office in the early part of the year 1874. It is also worthy of note that by an act of Pope Pius IX.—which, however, is not recognised as valid for legal purposes in England—Westminster was created a Roman Catholic Archbishopric, Cardinal Wiseman being appointed to fill it. On

SUFFOLK HOUSE. *After Hollar.* (*See page* 136.)

a modern writer places it on Tower Hill. For ourselves we can only say that we have not been able to verify the assertion.

Westminster appears to have been only a town down to the reign of Henry VIII., who raised it by royal letters patent into an "Honour." The Abbey Church being erected into a bishop's see in 1541, it of course became a "city," and when, ten years later, the bishopric was suppressed, the good people of Westminster did not feel called upon to resign the title, nor did the king reclaim it, so a city it remained. Its "Honour" was raised into a Marquisate by William IV. in 1831, in favour of the then head of the Grosvenor family, whose property, within the limits of its several parishes, fully

his death in 1865, the mitre was bestowed on Dr. Manning, who was succeeded by Dr. Vaughan. Under his auspices a grand cathedral is being reared.

As for the early history of Westminster, we fear that it is a little mixed up with fable. It owed its first beginning as a place of importance, no doubt, to its Abbey, or Minster, already mentioned. The first historical church was erected here during the Heptarchy, by Sebert, King of the East Saxons, or (according to Camden) of the East and Middle Saxons. Sebert, who, under his uncle Ethelbert, had been Bretwald, or Lord Paramount of the Anglo-Saxons, and like his uncle, had been converted to the Christian faith by the preaching of Melitus, one of the companions of St. Augustine, the Roman

LONDON—FROM TEMPLE BAR TO CHARING CROSS. *From Van der Wyngarde's View*, A.D. 1543.

missionary, is by some writers said to have destroyed a pagan temple on Thorney Island, and to have erected on its site a church which he dedicated to St. Peter. As Ethelbert died in A.D. 606, and Sebert followed him to the grave soon after, we can fix the date of the foundation of the church with tolerable accuracy, for we read that Sebert and his wife were buried in the Church of St. Peter in the Island of Thorney. Some writers have sought to carry the antiquity of the church to a much earlier date, and with that object in view have affirmed that St. Peter himself visited Britain, and erected here a small chapel or oratory. Others, contenting themselves with a more moderate draft upon the faith of their readers, ascribe the first sacred building on this spot to King Lucius, who reigned here in the second century, and who is said by tradition to have built here a church out of the ruins of a heathen temple, which had been overthrown by an earthquake. The existence, however, of any church here previous to that built by Sebert, is, to say the least, most doubtful; and at the time when he erected his Minster, the site was so rude and uncultivated that it was known to the Saxons as "Thorney," that is, the isle of thorns. Thorney, it appears, was at that time an island, formed by an arm of the river, called "The Long Ditch," and by brooks which flowed down from Hampstead and Kilburn; and there can be little doubt that it was on the higher and former ground, which rose up slightly in the centre of this marshy spot, that the church was built which ultimately developed into the noble Abbey or Minster of the West.

In the charter of Edgar, the Minster is alluded to as "The church of St. Peter, said to be built, pursuant to the directions of King Ethelbert, by his nephew Sebert, under whose government London then was, in a certain terrible uncultivated place called 'Thorney,' from the thorns growing there." Sebert is also mentioned as the founder in the charter of Edward the Confessor; and these records, combined with the facts of his burial in the church, and the anniversary of his death being observed, seem to confirm his right to the honour of being considered its founder.

After the Conquest, "our palace at Westminster" continued to be the usual town residence of our Norman kings, and St. Peter's Abbey the usual place of their coronation. The same was the case under the Plantagenet sovereigns, under those of the houses of York and Lancaster, and under the Tudors and their successors, many of whom were not only crowned but buried within its walls. Their palace here adjoined the Abbey and the Houses of Parliament. In the reign of Henry VIII. the splendid palace of Whitehall, which had for ages past been an appendage to the see of York, was, on the downfall of Cardinal Wolsey, granted as a royal residence to the king, and directed to be called "the King's Palace at Westminster" for ever, because, as the Act of Parliament stated, "the old palace nigh the monastery of St. Peter's was then, and had long before been, in utter ruin and decay." In the same act its limits are defined to be "as well within the soil and places before limited and appointed, as also in all the street or way leading from Charing Cross unto the Sanctuary Gate at Westminster, and to all the houses, buildings, lands, and tenements on both sides of the same street or way from the said cross unto Westminster Hall, situate, lying, and being between the water of the Thames on the east part, and the said park-wall on the west part, and so forth, through all the soil, precincts and limits of the said old palace."

In consequence, as the sun of royalty has shone here almost without interruption for upwards of eight centuries, it is not to be wondered at that the little town which rose on and around the Isle of Thorney should have grown into a population of upwards of 108,000, occupying 15,445 houses (as calculated by the historian Malcolm) in 1734. Rickman, indeed, estimates the population at even a higher figure, at the beginning of the eighteenth century; but as he gives no account of the data on which he bases his calculations, we can hardly accept them as sound. In 1801, however, the census returns show that Westminster numbered 158,210 souls; in 1811 these had increased to 162,085; to 182,085 in 1821; and in 1831, to 202,460. Its population in 1881 was no less than 248,000, but this was the last time it was recognised as a city, for in the Return of 1891 it has to content itself with the status of a parliamentary borough, of which the population is given as 55,774. The parish of St. James is credited with 24,995 inhabitants, those of St. Margaret and St. John (united) with 55,539, and that of St. Peter with 235.

Around this spot, so rich in sacred traditions, if not in actual memories, it was but natural that a town should gradually spring up. The Saxon monarchs, for the most part, loved the chase, and were devout adherents of the faith; for the one reason, they were likely to prefer living outside of their city walls in a time of peace; and for the other reason, they would wish to take up their abode under the shadow of the tower of a church where the rites of their religion were daily performed with something of solemn state. Most naturally, therefore, did Westminster, in the Saxon times, come to share with Winchester the honour of being the home of royalty. At all events, long before the reign of Edward the Confessor such was the case; and the statement is corroborated by the fact that the name of Scotland Yard, between Charing Cross and Whitehall, was so called from the Scottish king, who had that place assigned to him as a residence, when he came on a visit to the English court to do homage for his crown. Wherever the king and the court fixed their abode, the courts of law and the meetings of the nobles and chief earls and thanes for the purpose of legislation would be held, at the time when the sovereign took an actual part in such affairs, and did not discharge his functions by deputy. The result of this would of course be the steady growth of residences around for the reception of his courtiers, their families, and dependents. To supply the daily wants of these residents other and smaller tenements would be erected, and in due course a market would be held, and the formation of a town would follow as years rolled on.

It is on record that Edward III., in 1353, imposed certain duties on wool, leather, and other commodities carried either by land or by water to the staple of Westminster, in order to pay for the repairing of the highway along the Strand. The establishment of this staple, or market, it is added, raised the rents of the residents along the road so far, that the latter were ordered to pave the rest of the way at their own cost, while the surplus was to be applied to the erection of a bridge, or pier, near the palace and staple of Westminster. And, doubtless, it was by this conjunction of a monastery, a palace, and a market on the spot, that Westminster gradually became "a place of some consideration."

Such, then, in the main, we may readily believe, was the origin of the City of Westminster, the "Liberties" of which appear, at first, to have been co-extensive with the parish of St. Margaret's. These "Liberties" afterwards comprehended nine parishes more — St. Martin's-in-the-Fields, St. James's, St. Anne's, St. Paul's (Covent Garden), St. Mary-le-Strand, the Precinct of the Savoy, St. Clement's, St. John the Evangelist, and St. George's (Hanover Square). These were divided into twelve several wards, subject to a government partly ecclesiastical and partly civil, the former being exercised by the Dean and Chapter of Westminster, the latter by lay officers of their choosing. The boundaries of this parish in general, following in the main the line above indicated, are given as far back as A.D. 1222, by Cardinal Langton, Archbishop of Canterbury, and other arbitrators, on the occasion of a dispute arising between the Bishop of London and the Abbot and Monks of Westminster, as to whether the Abbey was subject or not to the Bishop's jurisdiction. The judgment itself may be seen in Wharton's "History of the Bishops and Deans of London, &c." The parish, at the time of which we speak, comprised several *villæ* beyond the actual city limits, such as "Knightebrigge," "Westburne," and "Padyngtoun," each with its chapel.

As to the exact limits and boundaries of the old city of which we have so much to say presently in detail, we may state briefly that on the southern side they were fixed by the left bank of the Thames, from which they ran up northwards, between Essex Street and the Temple, past Temple Bar, and up Shire Lane, which bounded it on the east. The boundary line then passed off in a north-western direction, keeping along the south side of Lincoln's Inn Fields, till it reached Drury Lane; thence it followed to the north-west, as far as Castle Street, West Street, and Crown Street, Soho, which brings us to the eastern end of Oxford Street proper. Thence the northern boundary of the city went due west along Oxford Street, the Bayswater Road, by the north side of Hyde Park—making, in one place, a small *détour* so as to include St. George's burial-ground—and so to the northern end of the Serpentine. From this point the western boundary-line of the city followed the course of the Serpentine, and of the stream which trickles out of its south-eastern extremity, by Wilton Crescent, Lowndes Street, Chesham Street, and the Commercial Road, and so down to the Thames, just to the east of Chelsea Hospital.

The antiquary and statistician may be interested in learning that the limits of the city enclosed an area of about 2,500 acres, exclusive of the Duchy of Lancaster, and the Chapelry or Precinct of the Savoy, which would include about ten more.

Over this area we shall wander, first exploring the Strand and its tributaries, as far as Lincoln's-inn Fields and Drury Lane on the north, and the new Embankment on the south; then we shall come to Charing Cross and Whitehall, taking St. Martin's Lane in our way; then we shall reconnoitre the Abbey, and the Houses of Parliament, and St. James's Park and Palace; then along the Green Park, Piccadilly, Hyde Park, and Tyburn, and so to Marylebone, where we shall turn back again eastwards, and, crossing Regent Street, or Portland Place, make our way as best we can to the regions of Soho, and Bloomsbury, and High Holborn. At the end of this our home tour, we purpose, if time and space allow us, to make other tours further abroad, and to take our readers with us on sundry excursions to Kensington, Chelsea, Lambeth, Putney, Southwark, and Fulham, our walk, perhaps, extending also to Hampstead and Highgate.

If we are able to make good these professions, at all events we shall find no lack of matter, "new and old," with which to light up the dull and somewhat musty records of antiquity. If we shall be found to have woke up the past into life, to have made its "dry bones" live once more, we shall have done our duty, and be quite contented. And now, having settled our line of march; and having pledged our faith in our character of cicerone, to clothe the body of dry facts with all of becoming drapery, in the way of anecdote, tradition, and folk-lore, which we are able to collect, let us, without further preamble, return to our original starting point, and take up our parable as we turn our faces towards the city of the west.

CHAPTER II.

BUTCHER'S ROW.—CHURCH OF ST. CLEMENT DANES.

" By Temple Bar I lean again,
  Haunted by many a famous face,
With oddest pictures in my brain,
  Jumbling together time and place.
The night drops down, the moonlight fades
  Along the filmy City sky ;

With draggled hose and broken blades
  The Mohawks come with shriek and cry ;
And in the light the dim street clothing
I see with loathing
  Two hideous rebels' heads that rot on high."
  London Poems.

Temple Bar and Johnson—Butcher's Row—The " Straits "—Shenstone—The Gunpowder Plotters—The Old Fish Shop—" Bulk Shops " and their Occupants—Churchyard and Church of St. Clement Danes—Johnson's Pew in the Church—Great Men Buried at St. Clement's—The Registers—Two Noteworthy Entries.

IF you and I, dear fellow traveller, could imagine ourselves our own great-grandfathers ; could we, in fact, transport ourselves a century back, and, emerging together from the busy thoroughfare of Fleet Street, pass through the narrow, frowning gateway of Temple Bar, we might perchance meet the ungainly form of Dr. Johnson, rolling up the Strand, arm in arm with Boswell, to "take a walk down Fleet Street."

But should no such good luck befall us as an encounter with the great lexicographer, at least one striking object would meet our eyes, as we looked straight before us, towards the Church of St. Clement's, namely, the stocks, a spectacle of wholesome awe to evil-doers in general, and to unruly City apprentices in particular. Beyond these, we should find the lower portion of St. Clement's suffering eclipse from a range of dull and rather squalid-looking buildings known as Butcher's Row, from having formerly served as shambles. These houses, which were almost entirely built of wood, and were several storeys in height, interfered greatly with traffic, the passage on either side of them being scarcely wide enough in any part to allow vehicles to pass each other. The Row was removed early in the present century through the exertions of Alderman Pickett, after whom Pickett Street (removed for the Law Courts) was named.

Mr. John Timbs describes the houses in Butcher's Row as having been mostly built in Queen Elizabeth's time, and constructed of wood and plaster, with overhanging eaves. " They were," he writes, " wretched fabrics, the receptacles of filth in every corner, the bane of old London, and a sort of nestling-place for the plague and fevers. The ceilings were low, with large unwrought beams, and lighted by small casement windows. The cant name for the place among coachmen in the days of the *Spectator* was the ' Pass,' or the ' Straits of St. Clement's.' "

In one of these uninviting edifices, however, as we learn from the date of some of his letters, William Shenstone, the poet, resided, on the rare occasions of tearing himself away from his "beloved Leasowes " for a stay in London. In another was born, in 1787, Dr. Andrew Reed, the benevolent founder of Reedham, the Asylum for Fatherless Children at Clapton, and the Idiot Asylum, at Earlswood. His father was a watchmaker in the Row.

Hereabouts, too, according to the confession of Thomas Winter, was concocted the Gunpowder Plot in 1605. He says, " So we met behind St. Clement's, Mr. Catesby, Mr. Percy, Mr. Wright, Mr. Guy Fawkes, and myself, and having, upon a primer, given each other the oath of secrecy, in a chamber where no other body was, we went after into the next room and heard Mass, and received the blessed Sacrament upon the same."

In a view of London and Westminster, drawn by A. Van der Wyngarde (A.D. 1543), now in the Bodleian Library, at Oxford, the Bars at the junction of Fleet Street and the Strand are flanked on the north by a row of quaint old houses, which were probably erected for the benefit of such traders as were not qualified to carry on their business in the City, and may possibly have been of the reign of Henry VIII.

"These," says Mr. J. Wykeham Archer, in his "Vestiges of Old London," "appear to have preceded the buildings of Butcher's Row, which, with Middle Row, extended from Temple Bar to St. Mary-le-Strand, the houses on the south side of Holywell Street forming their western extremity." The old house with its bulk-shop, which adjoined Temple Bar, and which had remained a surviving vestige of the sweeping measures of Alderman Pickett in the beginning of the century, stood in its original condition down to 1846, when it was modernised by the removal of the heavy pents which surmounted its ground-floor. The house bore on its front a notice to the effect that it was "established in the reign of Henry VIII.," and was occupied by "Short and Son, late Creed, Fishmongers." An engraving of it, in one of its last stages, will be found in the above-mentioned work of Mr. Archer, who explains the term "bulk-shop" as a word of Flemish origin, signifying a stall before a shop, and also associated with the idea of strength or substance. Thus deprived of its pents, it became finally the bookshop of Messrs. Reeves and Turner. The house was a mere timber frame, filled up with lath and plaster. It was pulled down in 1865 to make room for the new Law Courts.

It will be remembered that Shakespeare speaks of misery making men acquainted with "strange bedfellows." It is probable that in these words he is alluding to his experiences, where he must often have seen the heavy canopies of these parts projecting over the pathways, with their wood or leaden coverings turned up at the edge like some old-fashioned beaver, the ends being sunk a little so as to let the rain pass off. "The bulk-shops," writes Mr. J. W. Archer, "besides their connection with the thrift of olden time, have associations which invest them with a degree of poetic interest, arising from the practice of erratic and destitute authors appropriating their ledges for the purpose of a dormitory, in common with other homeless wanderers and belated roysterers. . . . The gifted but wayward poet, Savage, is said to have frequently had recourse to such shelter during his moody night wanderings; and Nat Lee, as we know, expired upon a 'bulk' in Clare Market, when overcome by wine in returning from an orgie at the 'Bear and Harrow,' in Butcher's Row, to his lodgings in Duke Street. In a pleasanter vein it is related of an inferior bard, Derrick, that, being discovered by Floyd, another poor author in each sense of the term, on one of these ledges, and being suddenly awakened, he started up, exclaiming, 'My dear Floyd, I am sorry to see you in this destitute state; will you go home with me to my lodging?'"

Close to Butcher's Row, at the date to which we refer, we should have come upon a stone cross, or rather its remains, for Strype, in his edition of "Stow's London," in 1755, speaks of it as "now headless," a decapitation which it probably owed to an effort of Puritan zeal in the days of the Great Rebellion. It is probable that at the time of the demolition of Butcher's Row all vestiges of the mutilated cross were swept away.

In Malcolm's "Anecdotes of London," published early in the present century, he says, "A stranger who had visited London in 1790 would, on his return in 1804, be astonished to find a spacious area (with the church nearly in the centre) on the site of Butcher's Row, and some other passages, undeserving of the name of streets, which were composed of those wretched fabrics overhanging their foundations—the bane of ancient London—where the plague, with all its attendant horrors, frowned destruction on the miserable inhabitants, reserving its forces for the attacks of each returning summer."

Passing on, we reach the churchyard of St. Clement Danes, so called, as antiquaries affirm, "because Harold, a Danish king, and other Danes, were buried there." One story commonly told is to the effect that to avenge an insult to his own mother, Hardicanute ordered his half-brother's body to be torn out of its grave and thrown into the Thames, and that, being cast ashore, a fisherman took it up and gave it decent burial in this place, which was consecrated to receive it. Another account states that in the reign of Ethelred, the Danes having pillaged the fair abbey of Chertsey, were here met on their return, and slain by the Londoners. And there is yet a third version, which is told by Lord Burleigh (who lived in this parish), on the authority of Fleetwood, the antiquary, to the effect that when the Danes were driven out of England, a few were left behind, being married to English women; and that these were ordered by the king to dwell "between the Isle of Thorney, which is now called Westminster, and Caer Lud, now Ludgate, and that there they built a church.

In "A Survey of St. Clement Danes," made in 1732, we are told, "The old church was built 730 years ago, and between 1608 and 1633 the repairs cost £1,586."

The body of the old church was taken down in 1680, and the present fabric was built in 1682 by

Edward Pearce, under the direction of Sir C. Wren, who superintended the work gratuitously, as recorded on a marble slab in the north aisle. The present tower and steeple were added in 1719, and underwent extensive repairs and restorations in 1839. The tower contains a peal of ten bells, of

indeed, the chimes of St. Clement's Church may still be heard as Falstaff describes having heard them with Justice Shallow.

The present Church of St. Clement Danes stands a little to the south of the ancient church or chapel of St. Clement, which had existed from the

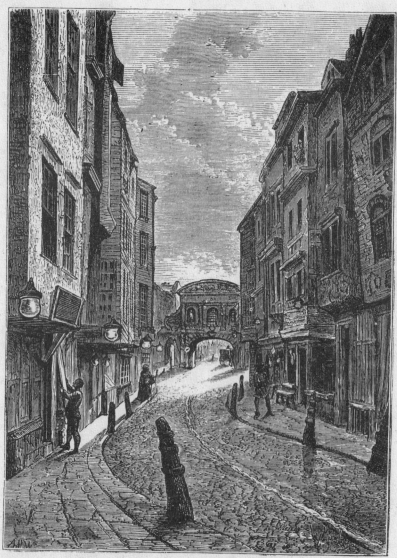

BUTCHER'S ROW IN 1800. (*See page* 11.)

a particularly musical sound, cast in 1693. The clock strikes the hours twice; "the hour being first struck on a large bell, and then repeated on a smaller one, so that when the first has been miscounted, the second may be more correctly observed." (Thomson's "Time and Timekeepers.") Besides the clock, there is a set of chimes which play the "Old Hundredth" Psalm. The bells also chime the tunes of "Hanover," and the "Lass o' Gowrie," at nine, twelve, and five o'clock, daily;

Conquest till long after the Reformation, occupying a part of what then was a rather large churchyard. It probably covers, as nearly as possible, the grave of Harold Harefoot, the mound over which was levelled by order of his vindictive and besotted brother. The church has always kept a marked position among those of the metropolis; and as it stands at once close to the City boundaries and on the high road to Westminster, all public processions, from the days of the Plantagenets to those of Victoria, have passed the building. When the Princess Alexandra of Denmark passed by it, on the 10th of March, 1863, the address presented to her by the parishioners on that occasion must have suggested to her mind a pleasing contrast to the traditionary feuds of eight hundred years ago

ing the Strand was formerly a spacious circular portico, supported by Ionic pillars. The interior of the edifice is commodious and handsome of its kind, and the roof inside is "camerated," and highly ornamented. The pulpit and altar are richly carved in the Tuscan style, and the top of

OLD HOUSES FORMERLY STANDING IN BUTCHER'S ROW, ABOUT 1800. (*See page* 11.)

between the country she had left and that to which she had come.

The present structure, like its predecessor, is dedicated to St. Clement, the patron saint of felt-workers, and also of sailors; and the symbolic anchor of St. Clement is still to be seen on nearly all the public buildings in the parish. The church is built of a white stone, both beautiful and durable; the architecture is of the Corinthian order. Front-

the communion-table is of ancient and valuable marble, supposed to have belonged to the old church. The organ is one of Father Smith's. The lofty tower and steeple, 116 feet high, which were added to the church in 1719, exhibit in succession Ionic, Corinthian, and Composite tiers of architecture.

In the north gallery of this church there is a pew which is more revered and respected than the "squire's pew" in many a country parish church.

Men of all parties and creeds cordially agree in this feeling. The lover of old times and old principles reveres the spot, and the admirer of what is new respects it while criticising the man who has made it famous and historical. Over a century has passed away since the death of Dr. Samuel Johnson, but in spite of all the changes that have since come over the world, there still stands here the simple memorial of his former presence as a worshipper within these walls. A plain plate of brass, fixed to the back of the pew, reminds us that here the great essayist and lexicographer used to kneel in worship. "Westminster Abbey can show his grave, and St. Paul's his monument; but here is preserved the memory of the sacred place where the rugged but sensitive man used for many a long year to ask for strength and grace." It has been remarked that "Boswell shows us Johnson in his chambers, in the club, and in the streets; but his own confessions enable us to understand him at church." And the remark is true. While listening to him on a Saturday night, at the "Mitre," or the "Turk's Head," we mark his rude and even fierce replies, his vehement prejudices, his domineering and despotic intellect, we should scarcely deem him a man of deep religious feelings. But when the bells of St. Clement's were heard next morning in the Inner Temple Lane, the porter regularly opened the gates to let out the well-known scholastic, large-wigged "Mr." Johnson. The man knew that, in spite of his wig, he was not a member of the Temple; but some notion of his rising fame had reached even the porters, and his rough generosity had won their respect. On by the posts of Fleet Street, touching each as he goes along, rolls rather than walks, "Mr. Johnson, the dictionary-maker." He seems more solemn than usual, and the sound of the church bells deepens his passiveness into melancholy. How is this? one who did not know the man might ask. Who was more merry than he last night at the "Mitre?" how ready were his quotations! how apt his illustrations! how overpowering his arguments! He seems quite another man to-day. No, he is just the same man, but in another mood. He enters the church as though anxious to avoid notice, and shows that with him, at least, the service is a reality. He tells us that he strove, like many another brave and good man, honestly to solve the great problem, "how to purify and fortify his soul, and hold real communion with the Highest," and that he did this in St. Clement's Church. That pew in the north gallery, as the brass plate tells us, was the actual scene and arena of this struggle. Here he sat after his good resolution to go to church every Sunday, and to read the Scriptures; and hither he repaired in the last year of his life, at the age of seventy-five, to return thanks to God for his recovery from an illness of a hundred-and-twenty-nine days. The following is the inscription to which reference is made above:—

"In this pew and beside this pillar, for many years attended divine service the celebrated Dr. Samuel Johnson, the philosopher, the poet, the great lexicographer, the profound moralist, and chief writer of his time. Born 1709, died 1784. In the remembrance and honour of noble faculties, nobly employed, some inhabitants of the parish of St. Clement Danes have placed this slight memorial, A D. 1851."

The parish is so well endowed with charities that the paupers of other neighbourhoods used to flock into it at the commencement of winter, for the sake of all they could get, and the vestry were obliged to limit their gifts to those who had resided for the space of a year.

There were almshouses for poor women in the upper and lower churchyard, at the time of the parish survey in 1732. "In the upper churchyard are six almshouses, with six rooms, and twelve poor women in each house, who are allowed 2s. per week; and in the lower churchyard are five rooms for poor women, each of whom has 2s. 6d. per week; they have also coals at Christmas, if they can make interest to get them."

The vaults beneath the church were crowded to excess. On the receipt of an Order in Council for closing them in 1858, the coffins were all placed together in one part of the vault and hermetically sealed, the whole being enclosed with a strong brick wall. Mr. Diprose tells us that towards the close of the last century "the vaults were discovered to be on fire, and continued burning for some days, many bodies being consumed."

In the church lie buried some few individuals whose names the world would not wish to forget; among others, Thomas Rymer, who compiled the "Fœdera," and the dramatic poets, Nathaniel Lee and Thomas Otway, and Bishop Berkeley, the philosopher, and friend of Pope, who attributed to him "every virtue under heaven." Sir John Roe, who died in Ben Jonson's arms, of the plague, 1606; Dr. Kitchener, and the Oxberrys, father and son, are also buried here. Among other monuments are those of Hippocrates de Otthen, who was physician to the Emperor of Germany, and was sent over to England at the request of Queen Elizabeth (in whose service, and in that of the Earl of Leicester, he was long employed), and of John Arundel, Bishop of Exeter, who died in 1503. In this church was solemnised, two centuries ago, that marriage of Sir Thomas Grosvenor with Miss Davies, the wealthy heiress of Ebury Manor, which brought into the family of the Duke of Westminster their property in Pimlico and what is now Belgravia.

The registers of St. Clement's commence with the year 1558, and are kept in far better order than in most parishes. They record the deaths of some hundreds of parishioners in 1665, the year of the Great Plague, which made great havoc in the close streets near Temple Bar, and also in Milford Lane.

One of the earliest entries of baptism is as follows:—"June 6, 1563, Master Robert Cicill, the sonne of ye L. highe Threasurer of England." Some nineteen years afterwards, the subject of this entry earned "honorable mention" for the gracious courtesy and politeness of his manners towards his inferiors.

DR. JOHNSON'S PEW IN ST. CLEMENT S. (*See page* 14.)

The neighbourhood of St. Clement Danes Church appears to have borne anything but a good reputation so far back as three centuries ago, by reason of "the unthrifts of the Inns of Chancery," who made so much disturbance in the streets by night that the inhabitants, we read, were fain to keep watches for the sake of mutual protection. Thus, "in 1582," says honest John Stow, "the Recorder himself, with six more of the honest inhabitants, stood by St. Clement's Church to see the lanthorn hung out, and to observe if he could meet with any of these outrageous dealers. About seven of the clock at night they saw young Mr. Robert Cecil, the Lord Treasurer's son, who was afterwards Secretary of State to the Queen, pass by the church. As he passed, he gave them a civil salute, at which they said, 'Lo! you may see how a nobleman's son can use himself and how he putteth off his cap to poor men; our Lord bless him.' This passage," adds Stow, "the Recorder wrote in a letter to his father, adding, 'Your lordship hath cause to thank God for so virtuous a child.'" We may draw an obvious inference from the story of Mr. Robert Cecil's conduct in this instance as to the usual habits of the fast young noblemen of Elizabeth's time.

CHAPTER III.

ST. CLEMENT DANES (*continued*):—THE LAW COURTS.

"Where do stand forth the laws of state sublime."—*Sophocles.*

Early Courts of Law—Inns of Court—Want of a Central Building—New Law Courts Projected—Selection of Architect—Discussion about the Site—Plan and Design of the New Building—Temple Bar Memorial—Old Buildings Swept away—The Old Fish Shop—Holloway's—Shire Lane and its Inhabitants—Sir C. Sedley—The Well of St. Clement's—Bell Yard—Plough Alley—Boswell Court: a Relic of Old Times—Clement's Lane: its Decline and Fall—A Grand Clearance.

IT is scarcely necessary to remind our readers that in theory it is the sovereign who sits in his (or her) right in England to administer justice to all, and hence the place in which the law is administered in this country has always been styled a "Court." And, as in early times, when law was rude and simple, the king used often to sit in his own court to administer justice, it was the custom for the seat of law to be within the palace of royalty. Hence, very naturally, when, in the Saxon and Norman times, the king's palace was at Westminster, it was a matter of course that the courts of law should grow up around the very person of the sovereign, though occasionally they were moved wherever the king travelled and took up his abode ; in this case they were said to be held *in banco regis*, that is, in the presence of the king himself.

A great impetus to the concentration of the courts of law in the metropolis was doubtless given by Henry VIII. ; for, whereas down to his day courts of arbitration had been held from time immemorial to decide cheaply and simply small matters in dispute in the several baronies, such as questions between landlord and tenant, between master and man, he ordered these and other like cases to be brought up to London, and, as Mr. Froude tells us in his " History of England," " country people found themselves compelled to take journeys to the metropolis, and to sue or be sued at his Courts at Westminster."

Gradually, however, as the English law shaped itself into a system and a science, which demanded a legal education in those who actually followed it as a profession, other "courts" of law arose nearer to the Inns of Court and the abodes of the gentlemen of the long robe ; and down almost to this day, one portion of both law and equity had been administered in the rooms adjoining Westminster Hall, and another in other courts at Lincoln's Inn. But this division and distribution of the headquarters and fountains of English justice between two localities, a mile at least apart, had long been a matter of complaint among most practical Englishmen ; and from time to time, especially during the present century, there had arisen murmurs "not loud, but deep," on account of the loss of time involved to both judges and counsel by this unhappy local severance. And it can be no matter of surprise that, from time to time, various proposals were made to concentrate in a single spot the scattered forces of the law. With a view to carrying out this national undertaking—as far back as the year 1841, as we learn from the evidence printed by order of the House of Commons—the late Sir Charles Barry designed a large building of Grecian architecture, which he intended to have placed in Lincoln's Inn Fields. It was to have contained a great Central Hall, about equal to Westminster Hall in size, around which twelve smaller courts should cluster ; the entire group of buildings, if it had been carried into effect at that time, would have covered a third of the area within the rails of Lincoln's Inn Fields, and have been surrounded by a belt of plantations, in order to keep up the delusion of rurality. Funds, however, were most fortunately wanting ; and great objections were made to the

plan of blocking up so large an open space, where open spaces were so rare ; in fact, persons who lived about Fleet Street, the Strand, and Holborn, had long considered this open area, though enclosed, as their "country walk," and seriously asserted that to all intents and purposes they had been in the country when they had completed their early morning tour round " the Fields."

At length, when the patience of the lawyers and of the rest of the public had been nearly worn out, and when attention had been frequently called to the subject in Parliament, Her Majesty was pleased in 1858 to order a Royal Commission to be issued, " for the purpose of inquiring into and reporting on the expediency of bringing into one place, or at all events into one neighbourhood, all the superior Courts of Law and Equity, the Divorce and Probate Court, and those of the Admiralty, Bankruptcy, &c., as well as of suggesting means for providing a fit site, and erecting a building suited to the purpose in hand." The Commission accordingly recommended the selection of the site on the northern side of the Strand, between Temple Bar and St. Clement's Church. In 1861 a Bill was introduced in order to carry this recommendation into effect ; but it was thrown out by a narrow majority, and the question slumbered until 1865, when the urgency of some such provision for the due administration of the law had again made itself practically felt. Two Acts of Parliament were passed in consequence, to carry out the recommendations already mentioned. The one Act empowered the Commissioners of Works and Public Buildings to acquire the site which had been recommended, and the other provided the funds necessary for the cost of the building itself, partly by a contribution of £1,000,000 of unclaimed interest on stock standing to the credit of suitors in the Court of Chancery, and partly by a small tax to be imposed on litigants in the other courts.

Another body of Commissioners was next appointed, consisting of forty eminent members of the legal profession, including Lords Cranworth, Hatherley, Cairns, and Penzance, Vice-Chancellors Stuart, Malins, and others, in order to advise the Treasury in its choice of an architect and plans for the new " Palace of Justice." The next step was to nominate a smaller body, consisting of five individuals of high standing—Mr. Gladstone, Sir W. Stirling-Maxwell, Lord Chief Justice Cockburn, Sir Roundell Palmer (afterwards Lord Selborne), and Mr. William Cowper (later Lord Mount-Temple), along with two professional architects—Mr. John Shaw and Mr. G. Pownall, who were to act as "Judges of Designs;" and a competition among the best architects of the day was invited. Eleven designs were sent in, and these were exhibited to the public, in 1868, in a temporary building put up in New Square, Lincoln's Inn ; and in the end the design of Mr. G. E. Street, R.A., was accepted— not, however, until after a very strong feeling had been shown in favour of that of Mr. E. M. Barry, a son of the architect of the Houses of Parliament.

Even after the architect, however, had been chosen, a further delay arose, as a large number of the public, and some of the competitors—Mr. Street himself among the rest—expressed an opinion that a space between the Strand and the Thames Embankment, to the east of Somerset House, would be a preferable site to that already chosen, and which had been prepared and cleared by the removal, in 1866–8, of no less than thirty close, foul, and filthy courts, yards, lanes, and alleys. And at last, after all the above-mentioned delays had come to an end, the first brick of the "Law Courts of the future"—the great central National Palace of Justice—was actually laid, on the last day of April, 1874, at the north-east corner of the chosen ground, at the junction of Bell Yard and Carey Street. The site, which had then been cleared for several years, comprised the surface of nearly eight acres, extending from Bell Yard on the east to Clement's Inn on the west, and from Carey Street on the north to the Strand and Pickett Street on the south. The substratum of solid concrete, which had been laid two or three years previously, covered about six acres and a half of this space, the remainder now forming what is known as St. Clement's Gardens, separating the Courts from Clement's Inn, and pleasantly laid out.

The buildings themselves are thus minutely described in the *Times* of May 19th, 1874 :—

"They are of Gothic design, and, viewed by non-professional eyes, might be set down as somewhat irregular examples of the Decorated or Second Pointed style. But their architect has embodied in his designs so much of modern improvements, and has so thoroughly studied the adaptation of the architecture of the Edwardian period to the requirements of our age, that we fancy he would prefer to call the structure a specimen of the 'Victorian style.' The whole building forms, approximately at least, a somewhat irregular square, the Strand front being 483 feet in length, while the depth from the Strand to Carey Street is about 460 feet. The southern, northern, and western fronts will be of Portland stone, while the eastern front will present a combination of Portland stone interspersed with red bricks, as will be the case with the interior courts and quadrangles. The entire pile of buildings will be divided into two blocks—the eastern and lesser one, which will be erected, under the contract, in three years ; and the larger block to the west, which it will take six or seven years to complete. Each front is to be relieved by dwarf towers, arches, and other features ; and there will be two high towers, one at the south-east angle, and one at the eastern end of Carey Street. The former will be 170 feet in height, or nearly four times the height of Temple Bar.

"The whole edifice will be three, four, and five storeys in height in different parts ; and its lofty pitched roofs will be relieved by the insertion of gables, dormers, and pinnacles, in great variety. The general height of the building up to the ridge of the roof will be about 90 or 95 feet ; and over the rest will rise the Central Hall, in the main or western block, to which the rest of the building will be subordinate. This Central Hall will be about 140 feet to the top of its roof, or 90 feet measured inside up to the crown of the stone-vaulted ceiling. Underneath it will be a large lower chamber, which, if it were underground, might be termed a crypt.

"The ground plan, as it stands at present, shows that the architect has given accommodation to no less than 18 distinct courts, each with its own entrance and staircase, with separate approaches and doors for the judges, the jury, the witnesses, the Bar, and the public, together with rooms for clerks, secretaries, and registrars, and also waiting-rooms.

"On the western side, towards Clement's Inn, there will be left a large, open space. This will probably be used as gardens, and there will be a flight of broad stone steps, leading up into the western end of Carey Street. It will be possible, if required, to erect here a western block of buildings, corresponding with that on the eastern side.

"The cost of the building, if the estimates allowed by the Commissioners should not be exceeded, will be three-quarters of a million. The structure will absorb no less than 62,000 tons of Portland and 18,000 tons of other stone, and also about 35,000,000 of red and white bricks. It will be remembered, in conclusion, that, about two years ago, Mr. Street proposed the removal of St. Clement's Church to a site on the vacant space on the west side of the new building—a proposal which met with the approval not only of Mr. Lowe, but also of the then Lord Chancellor. The Metropolitan Board of Works, however, declined to entertain the idea, although the Government offered to provide the site free of cost."

Mr. Street, in a printed minute, dated May, 1869, thus sums up the chief "æsthetical advantages," of the Carey Street site :—

"The elevation above the river is considerable. The entrances to the Central Hall will be exactly on the same level as the courtyard in front of the western entrance of St. Paul's Cathedral, and the floor of the Central Hall will be 22 feet higher here than it would be on the Embankment. To

The stately pile was opened by the Queen on the 11th of December, 1882, but the gifted architect who had designed it was no longer living to rejoice in the completion of his *magnum opus.*

It is unquestionably true that any great public good can only be achieved at the cost of much

THE OLD FISH SHOP BY TEMPLE BAR, 1846. (*See page* 11.)

this extent, therefore, it will in all distant views rise higher and be better seen than on the lower site. And I think that the position will be an important one, crowning the hill opposite St. Paul's, and supplying what the views of London at present much want,—namely, some very marked architectural feature in the long expanse of building between St. Paul's and Westminster."

private inconvenience; and the New Law Courts cannot claim to be any exception to this general rule. No sensible man can doubt that the destruction of so many filthy slums must ultimately prove a gain to the community at large; yet it is also undeniable that the first effect of the work of demolition was to render 4,000 persons homeless, and subsequently to drive three-fourths of them into other courts and alleys not far away, which, being previously well filled, were speedily, from the overcrowding consequent upon so enormous an influx, rendered as unhealthy

SERLE'S PLACE. *From a Drawing taken shortly before its Demolition.* (*See page* 21.)

in the case of this class, who live from hand to mouth, the unwonted possession of so large a sum was not rather the reverse of a benefit. We are told that about £20 was paid to each weekly

as the squalid dens from which the immigrants had been routed. It is also true that a liberal compensation was awarded by Government, even in cases were no legal claim could have been made, and that the utmost kindness and forbearance was shown by the Commissioners and officials entrusted to administer that compensation; but it may be doubted whether,

tenant, and this being in many instances squandered in the course of a few days, the recipient appeared, with drunken imprecations, before the distributors to demand more.

Many ingenious plans have been mooted, by philosophers and philanthropists of all ages, for the effectual cleansing of certain Augean stables; but the summary one of pulling down the building, and turning its 4,000 denizens adrift to seek shelter where best they may, is a bold stroke, which has at least the advantage of novelty, if even it savour a little of the line of policy familiarly known as "robbing Peter to pay Paul."

And now, having given some slight idea of the appearance which these eight acres—once suggestive of "the abomination of desolation"—present now that Mr. Street's stately fabric rises from their surface, let us take a brief retrospective view of them as they were not only in their last stage of decay, but in their palmy days, when St. Clement Danes was a favourite abode of "the quality."

The truth of the old proverb, "Threatened folk live long," was proved by our old acquaintance Temple Bar, which remained *in statu quo* down to the year 1878. The stones, having lain in a builder's yard for about ten years, were set up in 1888-9, at an entrance to Sir H. Meux's Park, at Theobalds, in Hertfordshire. Of this relic of the past we have already given, in a previous volume, a full and exhaustive history, which leaves nothing to be added or desired further than that since its removal its site has been marked by a column, set up at the cost of the Corporation of London. The pedestal of the "memorial" is adorned with appropriate bas-reliefs, above which on either side are statues of the Queen and the Prince of Wales, and the whole is surmounted by a bronze griffin supporting a shield bearing the city arms. The memorial, the object of much hostile criticism, was erected from the designs of Sir Horace Jones, the statues being the work of Sir J. E. Boehm, R.A.

It would be equally tedious and unnecessary to give a minute description of all the lanes, courts, and alleys which have been swept away in the process of clearing these eight acres, many of them being remarkable only for the generally unwholesome atmosphere, both moral and physical, which pervaded them ; we must, therefore, be contented to particularise such among them as are sufficiently interesting, from historical associations, to make their memories and names worth preserving.

On the north side of the old gateway stood, a few years ago, a quaint, narrow wooden house with projecting gables, and a physiognomy all its own. Here generations of fishmongers had plied their scaly trade, and here a certain Mr. Crockford, erst dealer in shell-fish, and subsequently gambling-house keeper and millionaire, laid the foundation of his fortune. During his life-time he refused to allow the old house in the Strand to be altered ; but after his death, which occurred in 1844, the gable roof and pent-house were removed. The

fishmonger's shop afterwards became that of a hairdresser, and finally, reversing the old saying about "coming to vile uses at last," it passed—as we have stated—into the hands of the well-known second-hand booksellers, Messrs. Reeves and Turner, who owned it when it was doomed to come down to make room for the New Law Courts, in 1865 (see page 11).

A few steps farther on, between Temple Bar and the entrance of St. Clement's Lane, nearly opposite to Messrs. Twining's bank, stood the house of Messrs. Holloway, the great wholesale manufacturers of the pills which bear their name. It is said that for many years the firm spent upwards of ten thousand pounds a year for advertisements in the town, country, and foreign newspapers.

As near as possible on the site of the shop of Messrs. Holloway stood, formerly, an old house with gable roof and an ornamental front, engraved in Smith's "Antiquities of Westminster." It was famous as being the reputed residence of the Duc de Sully, when ambassador here, before he could be accommodated at Arundel House.* At that time it is said to have been inhabited by Christopher Harley, Count de Beaumont, ambassador from France in 1605. In another house, a few steps still further westward, the *Daily Telegraph* (the first of the penny daily papers) was originally published, by its founder, Colonel Sleigh.

Returning to Temple Bar, we now make our way northwards, following the eastern side of the new block of buildings, and—with some latent suspicion that we may even meet with foul play from the ghosts of its former inhabitants—up Shire or Shere Lane, from which many of Addison's and other papers in the *Advertiser* are dated.

The western side of Shire Lane was in the parish of St. Clement Danes ; and therefore the meetings of the "Kit Cat" Club at the "Trumpet," which were noticed in the early part of this work, belong properly, and strictly speaking, to this place ; but it will be sufficient here to note the fact, and to refer our readers to the description previously given for fuller details on the subject. We may mention, however, that it was a thoroughfare for foot-passengers only, very narrow and filthy, and well deserving the character given of it in the *Quarterly Review* (No. 143), as "a vile, squalid place, noisy and noxious, nearly inaccessible to

---

* With reference to this assertion, Malcolm states that such a report arose from the fact of one of the houses in that narrow street bearing on its front the *fleur-de-lys* of France, and suggests that this was put there, not to commemorate Sully's arrival, but in compliment to our Henry V., the conqueror of France.

both light and air, and swarming with a population of a most disreputable character." On the left side especially the houses were of "bad repute;" and Mr. Diprose, in his "Walk round St. Clement Danes," informs us that many years ago there existed a communication from one of them with a house on the north side of the Strand, a few doors from Temple Bar, through which thieves used to escape after ill-using their victims. Higher up on the same side were three houses which were made into one by connecting passages, almost like a rabbit warren ; this was known by the name of "Cadgers' Hall," being the *rendezvous* of beggars. A few doors higher up still was another double house, called the "Retreat," through which, we are told, there was a way for thieves to pass through into Crown Court, and so into the Strand. It is worthy of record that this lane retained its old character to the last, a man being prosecuted for a robbery committed in it as late as the year 1865.

Shire Lane must have achieved an undesirable reputation at an early stage of its existence, as even in the reign of James I. it was called "Rogues' Lane," and in our own day the very name of Shire Lane had, in 1845, become such an abomination that it was ordered to be henceforth known as Upper, Middle, and Lower Serle's Place. This change of name appears to have had, to some extent, a salutary effect, as we are told by Mr. Diprose that "portions of this lane have of late years much improved in character, particularly the upper end, where Isaac Bickerstaff lived."

In Shire Lane, in the year 1639, the delightful song writer, and oracle of the licentious wits of his day, Sir Charles Sedley, first saw the light. He was baptised in the old church of St. Clement's.

Ship Yard adjoined Shire Lane on the left. "The houses in it," says Mr. Diprose, "were built very high and close together, the upper part projecting over the lower, thus admitting very little air or light." Some of them also were of great age and unhealthy, the entire locality being made up of such "courts" without any roadway. This locality was a colony of thieves ; and Mr. Diprose tells us, on the authority of a "very old inhabitant" of it, that the latter remembered a time when capital punishment was constantly inflicted for robbery, and when an execution at Newgate seldom took place without someone from this spot being amongst the number. "At the back of this court," adds the same writer, "there stood formerly a block of houses, from four to five storeys in height, which were let out to vagrants, thieves, sharpers, smashers, and other abandoned characters. Throughout the

vaults of this rookery there existed a continuous communication or passage, so that easy access could be obtained from one to the other, facilitating escape or concealment in the event of pursuit, which, from the nature of the nefarious traffic in practice, very often occurred. The end house of this block of buildings was selected for the manufactory of counterfeit coin, and passed by the name of the 'Smashing Lumber.' The ingenuity employed in the construction of the apartments may be mentioned. In the first place, every room had its secret trap or panel, that a free entrance or exit might be quickly effected from one place to the other ; and from the upper storey, which was the workshop or factory, there was a shaft or well constructed, in direct communication with the cellar before noticed. The whole of the coining apparatus and the *employés* could be conveyed away as by a touch of magic, being lowered in a basket by means of a pulley. This secret gang must have had a prosperous run for many years, and the master of it, after amassing a large sum, wisely disappeared at the right moment ; for not long after the introduction of the new police, and the appointment of detectives, this den was discovered and abolished."

We are told, in the "Life and Times of Sir Christopher Hatton," by Nicholas, that "an inn near Temple Bar, called 'The Ship,'" was granted to him ; and Chambers tells us, in his "Book of Days," that "Ship Yard denotes the sign of the 'Ship,' a house established in honour of Sir Francis Drake, and having for its sign the bark in which he circumnavigated the world."

It is difficult to associate the neighbourhood of Shire Lane with pilgrims, clear springs, and running brooks, but we read in the *Times* of May 1st, 1874: —"Another relic of old London has lately passed away ; the holy well of St. Clement, on the north of St. Clement Danes Church, has been filled in and covered over with earth and rubble, in order to form part of the foundation of the Law Courts of the future. It is said that penitents and pilgrims used to visit this well as early as the reign of Ethelred, and it was known from time immemorial as 'St. Clement's Well.' Charles Knight, in his 'London,' published in 1841, mentions the well as 'now covered over with a pump,' and he adds that 'the well still remains flowing as steadily and as freshly as ever.' It has often been supposed that this well supplied the old Roman bath in Strand Lane, but this is a mistake, the water which feeds that bath springing up out of the London clay below on the spot with perfect regularity."

Round this holy well, in the early Christian era,

newly-baptised converts clad in white robes were wont to assemble to commemorate Ascension Day and Whitsuntide ; and in later times, after the murder of Thomas à Becket had made Canterbury the constant resort of pilgrims from all parts of England, the holy well of St. Clement was a favourite halting-place of the pious cavalcades for rest and refreshment.

In the "Beauties of England and Wales" (Middlesex, vol. x., published in 1815), Mr. Nightingale says, "A pump now covers St. Clement's Well. Fitzstephen, in his description of London, in the reign of Henry II., informs us that "round the City again, and towards the north, arise certain excellent springs at a small distance, whose waters are sweet, salubrious, and clear, and whose runnels murmur o'er the shining stones. Among these, Holywell, Clerkenwell, and St. Clement's Well may be esteemed the principal, as being much the most frequented, both by the scholars from the school (Westminster), and the youth from the City, when in a summer's evening they are disposed to take an airing. This well was also much resorted to on account of its being supposed of peculiar efficacy in the cure of cutaneous and other disorders, and was consequently a place of importance to devotees. The estimation of its efficacy and sanctity have long ceased."

Bell Yard, occupied principally by law publishers at the northern extremity, and towards the Strand by a medley of small, uninviting-looking shops, was more than a century ago the abode of Fortescue, who lived in a house at the upper end of the yard, which is further honoured by being described by Fortescue's friend, Pope, as "that filthy old place, Bell Yard." Several of the small passages in this vicinity are worthy of no more particular mention than is contained in Seymour's "History of the Parishes of London and Westminster," written in 1734.

"A little above St. Clement's Well, of note for its excellent spring water, is Plough Alley, which, with three turnings, goes into a street by the Plough stables, which fronts the playhouse by Lincoln's Inn Grange, in Little Lincoln's Inn Fields. More towards Clare Market is Horseshoe Court, a pretty handsome place, with a freestone pavement, having a prospect into St. Clement's Inn Gardens. And opposite to this court is Yates' Court, not over good nor large. Between Temple Bar and the turning into St. Clement's Inn, on the north side of the Butcher's Row, are several courts, most of which are but small. The first is Ship Yard, a thoroughfare into Little Shear Lane, with a pretty broad passage ; on the east side is an open place

going into a small court called Chair Court, with a fair freestone pavement. Next to Ship Yard are these courts : Swan Court, very small ; Star Court, indifferent, good, and large, with an open air ; White Hart Court, long but narrow ; Lock Alley, long, but small ; Windmill Court very small and inconsiderable : Crown Court hath an open air about the midst, and leadeth into Little Shear Lane. Bear and Harrow Court is so called from such a sign, belonging to a noted eating-house, at the entrance into it. This court (or rather alley, from its length and narrowness) runs into Boswell Court."

It is a common mistake to suppose that Boswell Court owed its name to the biographer of Dr. Johnson. Its age and its name are at least as old as the times of the Tudors, in whose day, and in those of the Stuarts, as we are told, it was the abode of "the quality." "Here lived," says Mr. Diprose, "Lady Raleigh, the widow of the unfortunate Sir Walter." Another distinguished resident was Sir Edward Lyttleton, successively Solicitor-General, and Lord Chief Justice of England, in 1639. From Boswell House, Gilbert Talbot wrote a letter of "London gossip" to his father, the Earl of Shrewsbury, in the reign of Elizabeth, a letter which is printed in Lodge's "Illustrations." Among the other eminent inhabitants of this court was Lady Fanshawe, as we learn from her "Memoirs," where she says, "In his" (her husband's) "absence, I took house in Boswell Court, near Temple Bar, for two years, immediately moving all my goods thereto."

Ascending northwards towards Carey Street was a flight of steps which led into New Boswell Court, a dreary-looking enclosure, although described by Hatton in 1708 as "a pleasant place." At the side of these steps might be seen to the very last a curious relic of other days, a watchman's box, the last box of the old "Charlies," which was drawn up from the pavement during the day-time.

This ancient order of watchmen was instituted about the middle of the thirteenth century, and carried on its functions, growing yearly more feeble and inefficient, until, in 1829, the "Charlies," as they were termed in the slang of the day, found themselves superseded by the new police, organised by Sir Robert Peel. These midnight guardians of the peace—and it may be observed *en passant* that the only qualifications necessary for the post would appear to have been extreme old age, and general incapacity — suffered many things at the hands of the young "bucks" and "bloods" of the Regency. A watchman found dozing in his box in the intervals of going his rounds to utter his monotonous cry, was apt to be overturned, box and all, and left to kick and struggle helplessly, like a turtle on its back, until assistance arrived. Or he would be kindly offered a dram to keep him awake, and this dram being drugged, quickly sank him in deeper sleep than before, in which state "Charley" and his box, being transferred to a truck, were forthwith trundled into another quarter of the town, and left to awake at leisure.

Old Boswell Court, from having been the chief abode of the "quality," gradually came to be let out in chambers and apartments. The houses were mostly of red brick with carved doorways. The house at the southern end was, for the last twenty years prior to its demolition, the printing and publishing office of Messrs. Kelly's "Post Office Directories" of London and of the several counties of England.

The old entrance to St. Clement's Lane from the Strand was through an open gateway flanked by massive pillars of stone. This archway was erected by the Corporation of London, as a tribute of respect for Alderman Pickett, through whose exertions the thoroughfare of the Strand was widened, at an expense of more than a quarter of a million sterling. The new thoroughfare was named Pickett Street, after the public benefactor, but the name never became popular, and soon passed away, the houses being reckoned as part of the Strand. .A little beyond the gateway the lane bore off to the left, and led to the back of King's College Hospital, merging in Gilbert (now Twining) Street, and thence being continued through Portsmouth Street into the south-west corner of Lincoln's Inn Fields. The line of this lane—what is left of it—runs north from the north-west end of the Law Courts, and it will no doubt soon be superseded by a wider thoroughfare, for as these pages go to press, the dark and obscure outlets by which it still communicates with Clare Market and its neighbourhood are being swept away.

Among the other residents in this lane was Sir John Trevor (a cousin of the infamous Judge Jeffreys), at one time Speaker of the House of Commons, and twice Master of the Rolls; the same who was expelled from the House for bribery, though he had the good sense to warn James II. against his arbitrary conduct. He died here in May, 1717, and was buried in the Rolls Chapel on the east side of Chancery Lane. Another distinguished inhabitant was Oliver Cromwell, in his early days. The Lords Paget also had their town mansion here, as appears by the parish registers.

In the course of time, however, the lane, " from being the polished abode of wit, genius, and fashion, was converted by the ruthless hand of Time into a huge overcrowded den, where blasphemy, rags, gin, hollow-eyed poverty, and stinted industry, were all fearfully huddled together. Where noble dames once moved with costly and flowing trains, a short time since women in rags rocked to sleep the children of misery, to whom hunger gave a fearful vitality; and where courtiers used to exchange the bow of recognition, fearful and brutal collisions between man and man took place. Upon the once polished floor, now broken and filthy, where stately revelry held its court, human beings lay stretched in that association which extreme misery only knows; and the once elegant boudoir of some dead duchess was inhabited by seven or eight wretched human beings. Doors stood ajar with the gaping look of poverty and desolation, where the loud resounding knocks of some tall, gold-laced menial were once heard; and where the flaxen-haired daughters of wealth once sported, neglected children in filth and rags dozed out their wretched existence.

" In this sun-forsaken, dreary region lived, among the rest, a very large colony of the poorest and wildest of the Irish, attracted in the first instance, no doubt, by its nearness to the Catholic chapel in Lincoln's Inn Fields; but these, though equally poor, dirty, and drunken with the tenants of the adjoining courts, were never actually absorbed by their English neighbours. To the last they remained *ipsis Hibernis Hiberniores*, and when the rookery was broken up they migrated, if we are rightly informed, to Drury Lane and the Seven Dials.

" As a proof that the locality was as demoralised as it was poor, we may add that when wholesale executions occurred at Newgate or Tyburn, as they did occasionally occur 'when George III. was king,' it was rare indeed for this locality not to have its representative amongst those unhappy wretches who paid the last penalty of the law."

It has been very appositely observed that "Charles Dickens might well have placed the scenes of his quaintest stories of low Cockney life in the midst of this doomed quarter of London, which was the haunt of gaiety and pleasure in the reign of Charles II., and is associated with the memories of the 'bloods' and the 'bucks' of the Restoration, and the wits of the days of Queen Anne."

Mr. Diprose—who, as an old inhabitant of the parish, is well qualified to speak on the subject —gives a list of the courts, alleys, and streets which were quietly removed and effaced, in order to furnish a site for the Palace of Justice.

They are as follows, nearly thirty in all :—Bailey's Court, Bear and Harrow Court, Bell Yard, Old and New Boswell Courts, Boswell Yard, Brick Court, Chair Court, Clement's Court, Clement's Inn Foregate, Clement's Lane, Cromwell Place, Crown

attaching to them, although all traces of them have disappeared, and their place knows them no more.

The demolition of so many small tenements, in order to make a site for the Palace of Justice,

BOSWELL COURT. (*From a Sketch taken shortly before its Demolition.*)

Court, Crown Place, Hemlock Court, Great and Little Horseshoe Courts, New Court, Pickett Place, Plough Court, Robin Hood Court, Upper, Lower, and Middle Serle's Place, Ship Yard, Ship and Anchor Court, Shire Lane, and Star Court, all of them more or less dirty and overcrowded.

Besides these, however, there have disappeared a considerable part of the Strand (Pickett Street), Carey Street, Yates' Court, and St. Clement's Lane, nearly all of which have histories still

did not have so great an influence as might have been supposed upon the people living in the parish of St. Clement's, which continued to swarm with a poor population. Previously it stood at about 16,000, and immediately after this clearance it was about 15,000, a great number of the inhabitants of the old lanes and alleys having removed only into the neighbourhood of Clare Market, which, even before the influx, was almost equally close and filthy, and sadly overcrowded.

In the reign of Queen Anne Clement's Lane was the Bond Street of London, and several of its houses were the haunts of those royal and noble intrigues which figure so largely in the anecdote-memoirs of the time. "Here," says Mr. Diprose, "Steele used to show his gaudy attire, Bolingbroke his stately presence, and Pope that decrepit form which was yet the tabernacle of a noble soul within. Here Swift, with downcast head and scowling steamers. Gone, too, are the 'smashers,' and the 'Charlies;' gone, too, is that little court to the north of St. Clement's Church, of which we have already seen what Winter had to say with reference to the concoction of the fiendish Gunpowder Plot. Gone, too, now are the once fair gardens of Essex House and Norfolk House; gone are the wild beasts which once were kept in Holywell Street; gone is the last of those stocks which once held

THEATRE, PORTUGAL STREET. (*See page* 27.)

visage, used to growl to himself as the mighty satirist made and unmade cabinets; and the gentle Addison here turned some of those polished periods which have called forth the envy and admiration of after ages."

We will conclude this chapter with a few words quoted from an article in *Cassell's Magazine* in 1870, styled, "A Walk Round St. Clement Danes" :—

"Gone now are the glories of St. Clement Danes. Gone are the sedan chairs and coaches that once had here their favourite and (it is said) their earliest stands. Gone are the 'Thames watermen,' whom our fathers and grandfathers knew so well, resplendent in their scarlet coats and badges, but who were driven out by the penny in awe the roguish apprentices and youthful roughs of the parish; gone is the 'Denzil Street gang,' and the 'Alphabet' public-house, whilom so well known to the theatrical profession; gone is the far-famed Norfolk Giant, who once kept the 'Craven Head' in wretched Drury Lane; and gone is 'Joe Miller;' gone, too, are his 'jests,' and possibly his grave.

"But in the place of these and other relics of past ages we shall shortly see rising on the now bare site a stately building, the like of which Londoners have not seen reared in modern days, save only at the river-side at Westminster—a palace in which it is our earnest prayer, as Englishmen, that Justice may long sit to hold evenly the scales of law."

CHAPTER IV.

ST. CLEMENT DANES (continued).—A WALK ROUND THE PARISH.

"Sacer est locus; ite profani."—*Virgil.*

Carey Street—Its Reminiscences—Residences of Benjamin Franklin, Sir William Blackstone, and Mrs. Chapone—The "Grange" Inn—The "Plough" Tavern and Gully the Prize-fighter—The "Seven Stars"—Serle's Court, now called New Square—Ravenscroft's Wig-shop—Serle's Coffee House—Portugal Row—Playhouse Street—The Duke's Theatre—Origin of the Sergeant's Guard at the Theatre Royal—Curious Playbills of the Last Century—Portugal Street—King's College Hospital—Burial-place of Joe Miller—Enon Chapel and the Modern "Golgotha"—The "Old Black Jack."

LEAVING the Palace of Justice upon our left hand, we will now continue our way westwards from the top of what was once Shire Lane, but which, as before mentioned, gradually developed into Serle's Place.

At right angles to Serle Street, and running from east to west, is Carey Street, the south side of which was demolished to form the north side of the New Courts of Law. These houses, at the time of their demolition, were almost all tenanted by solicitors and law-stationers. Although, as compared with the rest of the neighbourhood, markedly wanting in memories of the past, Carey Street has its reminiscences. The heroic Lady Fanshawe tells us, in her "Memoirs," that in 1655-6 she and her family spent a twelvemonth in it, as tenants of a house belonging to Sir George Carey, from whom apparently the street was named. It is said by Mr. Diprose that at No. 19 Benjamin Franklin is supposed to have lived whilst working as a journeyman printer in the neighbourhood. Sir William Blackstone lived in this street in 1761; and the celebrated Mrs. Chapone, authoress of "Letters on the Improvement of the Mind," and an ardent disciple of Richardson, also resided here until her husband's death.

It is difficult to imagine any levity of conduct in a street once inhabited by this most decorous lady; indeed, Carey Street, to its credit be it spoken, seems, in spite of its surroundings, to have been

"Content to dwell in decencies for ever,"

which is perhaps the reason why its name is scarcely mentioned by Stow, Pennant, Northouck, or Malcolm, or even by such modern writers as Peter Cunningham and John Timbs. If there be truth in the old adage, "Happy are the people whose history is a blank," the denizens of Carey Street are much to be congratulated.

Though the street was dull and sober in outward appearance, yet it may probably have been the scene of more than one gay frolic in other days. The "Grange" Inn — removed in 1853 to make room for King's College Hospital — with its picturesque yard and offices, was much patronised in its day by the actors of the Duke's Theatre hard

by, and of other places of the same kind. It is mentioned by Sir W. Davenant, in his "Playhouse to Let." The "Plough" Tavern, also in this street, —kept at one time by Mr. John Gully, the prize-fighter, afterwards M.P. for Pontefract — was an ancient hostelry of good repute, as among those who made it their head-quarters in London was the antiquary, Browne Willis. Another inn in the street was the "Seven Stars," formerly the "Leg and Seven Stars," a corruption of the "League and Seven Stars," denoting the Seven United Provinces.

Little is known of the family of Serle, after whom this street is named, except what Mr. P. Cunningham tells us in his "Handbook of London," namely, that it was called after a Mr. Henry Serle, one of the benchers of Lincoln's Inn, who died about 1690, having bought some property in this parish from the executors of Sir John Birkenhead, the writer of "Mercurius Aulicus," during the Great Rebellion.

The early name of New Square, Lincoln's Inn Fields, which lies on the north side of Carey Street, was Serle's Court; and the arms of Serle were quartered with those of the Inn over the gateway, which still leads into Carey Street, and was formerly known as Serle's Gate.

New Square is so called on account of its comparatively recent erection (about 1725). Seymour, in his "Survey of London and Westminster" (1735), speaks of the centre of the Court being "spacious and nicely kept, and covered with gravel, raised low, the middle to cast off the rain when it falls. In the middle of the court," he adds, "is a curious stone pillar artificially wrought, on which is a dial-clock, with four boys who used to spout water out of Triton shells, and at the bottom is a basin, that receives the said streams of water falling down from the shells, all incompassed with handsome iron bars." The garden in the centre was not railed in until about the year 1844. In 1867 a temporary building was erected in it for the purpose of exhibiting the various architectural designs for the New Law Courts.

In Serle Street was the old shop of Messrs. Ravenscroft, the famous wig-makers, which had been for a century a rendezvous of legal celebrities. Here might be seen on the walls of the shop a series of portraits of big-wigged lawyers, from Judge Black-stone downwards, and a book of legal autographs was kept in the shop with an almost religious veneration.

At the corner of Serle Street and Portugal Street stood the celebrated coffee-house, so long known to law and to literature as " Serle's." The entrance, flanked with two massive doorposts of a classical design, remained to the last unaltered from what it must have been in the days of Akenside and his friend and patron, Jeremiah Dyson, who used to make this his head-quarters. Addison frequented it in order to study the humours of the young barristers who met there of an evening, and it is not difficult to imagine him seated in a quiet nook, and watching all that is said and done. He thus mentions the house in No. 49 of the *Spectator*: " I do not know that I meet in any of my walks objects which move both my spleen and laughter so effectually as those young fellows at the Grecian, Squire's, Searle's, and all other coffee-houses adjacent to the law, who rise early for no other purpose but to publish their laziness."

The author of "London Poems" writes very graphically in allusion to this neighbourhood—

" Beneath the shade of Temple Bar
. Walk shabby wits who serve the state;
Steele, with mad laughter steeped in war,
   And Addison with smile sedate,
And Swift, the bilious English Rabelais,
   Plods westward shabbily,
On my Lord Bolingbroke alone to wait."

The whole of the space bounded by Carey Street, Serle Street, and Portugal Street, has recently been cleared, and a block of buildings used as the Bankruptcy Court has been erected on the site.

But it is time that we took up our walking-sticks and pursued our journey a little further to the north and north-west, and entered Portugal Street.

In spite of the levelling of the burying-ground on its southern side, and the erection of King's College Hospital on its site, it must be owned that Portugal Street has a dull and dingy look, as if it had met with misfortune. The blank dead wall presented by the back of the museum of the Royal College of Surgeons on the northern side con-tributes to this effect, and the few shops which it contains are mostly those of law-stationers and printers. Its very name, suggestive of the un-happy wife of Charles II., would seem to have cast a blight on it; and we are told that it inherited the name when the south side of Lincoln's Inn Fields ceased to be called Portugal Row. Yet, in olden days, it must have been lively and gay; for did not

the " Lincoln's Inn Theatre" once cover the site of the museum just named? and was not the " Duke's Playhouse " hard by?

In Strype's time the street was without a name; and that venerable antiquary, with good reason, proposed to call it " Playhouse Street," though his suggestion fell on dull and heedless ears.

" On the back side of Portugal Row," says a writer in 1734, "is a street which runneth to Lin-coln's Inn Gate, which used to pass without a name; but since the place is increased by the new buildings in Little Lincoln's Inn Fields, and the settling of the playhouse, it may have a name given it, and not improperly, Playhouse Street. Fronting the playhouse is a street which goeth to Plough Stables, which also had no name, unless one may call it Grange Street, from the 'Grange' Inn, a place of good note; nigh to which is the parish roundhouse, on the back side of which is a churchyard also belonging to the parish."

We have said that in this street there were formerly two theatres; but in reality there have been three, as "honest John Timbs" is careful to remind us. He writes, "The first theatre here (named the Duke's Theatre, from the Duke of York, its great patron, and the opera, from its musical performances), was originally a tennis-court. It was altered for Sir William Davenant, and opened in 1662 with his operatic *Siege of Rhodes*, when regular scenery was first introduced upon our stage." Here Pepys, in 1662, saw acted *Romeo and Juliet* (for the first time), *Hamlet*, and *Macbeth*, adding, on the last occasion, that he saw "a mighty company of citizens, ordinary 'prentices, and mean people in the pit." Here, too, as he tells us, he first saw, and sat next to, "pretty, witty" Nell Gwynne, when King Charles and Lady Castle-maine were there to see Lord Orrery's *Mustapha* performed. It is said also, that in this theatre female characters were first played by women, among whom the most famous were Elizabeth Davenant, Mary Saunderson (afterwards Mrs. Betterton), Mary (or Moll) Davis, Mrs. Long, and Mrs. Barry. Davenant having acted musical pieces before the Restoration, Pepys frequently calls this theatre "the Opera," though, in fact, tragedies and comedies only were performed there. It should be added that among the principal actors here was Thomas Betterton, "the rival of Burbage and Garrick, and the last survivor of the old school of English actors." Sir William Davenant made this theatre his head-quarters, if not his home. Early in 1671-2 the players of the Duke's Theatre re-moved to Dorset Gardens; and the King's Com-pany, being burnt out from Drury Lane, made use of it for about a year, when it was again turned into a tennis-court. The rest of its history shall be told in the words of Mr. Timbs :—"It was refitted and reopened in 1695, with Congreve's comedy of *Love for Love*, which was then played for the first time. This second theatre was taken down and a new house built for Christopher Rich, and opened by John Rich in 1714. . . . . Here Quin played his best parts ; and from a *fracas* in which he was embroiled originated the Sergeant's Guard at the Theatre Royal. The first English opera was performed here in 1717-18 ; here was originally used the stage motto, *Veluti in Speculum;* and here in 1727-28 the *Beggar's Opera* was produced and acted for sixty-two nights, "making Gay rich and Rich gay." In 1732 Rich removed to Covent Garden, which he had lately built, and the Portugal Street house was let by turns for Italian operas, oratorios, balls, concerts, and exhibitions."

In 1735 Mr. Gifford, who had opened another place of amusement in Goodman's Fields, took this theatre, lately vacant by the withdrawal of Rich and his company to Covent Garden, but gave it up at the end of two years, when it was closed. Having undergone several vicissitudes, it became at length the pottery and china warehouse of Messrs. Spode and Copeland. It was here that in 1735 Macklin killed Mr. Hannam; and Nightingale, in the tenth volume of the "Beauties of England and Wales," gives the following strange account of its last performance : " The shutting up of this structure has been whimsically accounted for by vulgar tradition. Upon a representation of the pantomime of *Harlequin and Dr. Faustus*, when a tribe of demons, necessary for the piece, were assembled, a supernumerary devil was observed, who, not approving of going out in a complaisant manner at the door, to show a *devil's trick*, flew up to the ceiling, made his way through the tiling, and tore away one-fourth of the house; which circumstance so affrighted the manager, that the proprietor had not courage to open the house ever afterwards."

With regard to the *Beggar's Opera* we find the following remonstrance in the *Gentleman's Magazine*, September 15th, 1773 :—"This day Sir John Fielding informed the bench of justices that he had last year written to Mr. Garrick concerning the impropriety of performing the *Beggar's Opera*, which never has been represented on the stage without creating an additional number of real thieves; he begged, therefore, the gentlemen present would join with him in requesting Mr. Garrick to desist from performing that opera on Saturday

evening. The bench immediately consented to the proposal ; and a polite card was dispatched to Mr. Garrick for that purpose. To which Mr. Garrick returned for answer, that his company was so imperfect and divided (many of his performers being yet in the country), that it would be impossible for him to open with any other piece ; but added, that he would in future do everything in his power to oblige them."

Here is the copy of a playbill of this theatre a century and a half ago :—

"The Sixth day, 1720, for the benefit of the author, by the company of comedians, at the Theatre in Little Lincoln's Inn Fields, this present Saturday, being the 16th of January, will be presented a new farce of three acts, call'd *The Half-pay Officers*. A principal part to be perform'd by Peg Fryar, it being the 6th time of her performance on any stage since the reign of King Charles II. To which will be added the new farce of two acts, call'd *Hob's Wedding*, being the sequel of the *Country Wake*. With entertainments of dancing by Mrs. Fryar, particularly the Bashful Maid, and an Irish Trot. Boxes, 5s. Pit, 3s. Gallery, 2s. N.B.—The author's tickets, · which could not come in on the third night, will be taken to-day."

This performance was patronised by royalty, as we find that on Monday, the 11th January, 1720, " His Royal Highness the Prince came to the New Playhouse in Little Lincoln's Inn Fields, and saw a new farce of three acts, call'd *The Half-pay Officers*, with another new. farce of two acts, call'd *Hob's Wedding*."

To this we cannot resist appending a playbill culled from Mr. Diprose's "Anecdotes of the Stage and Players" :—

By his Majesty's Company of Comedians.
Kilkenny Theatre Royal.
(Positively the last night, because the Company go to-morrow to Waterford.)
On Saturday, May 14, 1793,
Will be performed by desire and command of several respectable people in this learned Matrapolish, for the benefit of Mr. Kearnes, the manager,
The Tragedy of
HAMLET, PRINCE OF DENMARK.
Originally written and composed by the celebrated Dan Hyes, of Limerick, and insarted in Shakespeare's works.
Hamlet, by Mr. Kearnes (being his first appearance in that character, and who, between the acts, will perform several solos on the patent bag-pipes, which play two tunes at the same time). Ophelia, by Mrs. Prior, who will introduce several favourite airs in character, particularly "The Lass of Richmond Hill," and "We'll be unhappy together," from the Rev. Mr. Dibdin's oddities. The parts of the King and Queen, by directions of the Rev. Father O'Callaghan, will be omitted, as too immoral for any stage. Polonius, the comical politician, by a young gentleman, being his first appearance in public. The Ghost, the Grave-digger, and Laertes, by Mr. Sampson, the great London comedian. The characters to be dressed in Roman shapes. To which will be added, an interlude, in which will be in-

troduced several slight-of-hand tricks, by the celebrated surveyor Hunt. The whole to conclude with the farce of

MAHOMET THE IMPOSTER.

Mahomet, by Mr. Kearnes.

Tickets to be had of Mr. Kearnes, at the sign of the "Goat's Beard," in Castle Street.

The value of the tickets, as usual, will be taken out (if required) in candles, bacon, soap, butter, cheese, potatoes, &c.—as Mr. Kearnes wishes, in every particular, to accommodate the public. N.B.—No smoking allowed.—No person whatsoever will be admitted into the boxes without shoes or stockings.

In 1726, George I. paid a visit to the theatre in Lincoln's Inn Fields, and the event is thus recorded in one of the newspapers of the day :—

"March 18.—Last night His Majesty went to the Theatre Royal in Lincoln's Inn Fields, to see the play of the *Country Wife*, and the entertainment of *Apollo and Daphne*, in which was performed a particular flying on that occasion, of a Cupid descending, and presenting His Majesty with a book of the entertainment, and then ascended—at which new piece of machinery the audience seemed much pleased."

The after history of the place is curious. Having been used first as a barrack and then as an auction room, it was bought by Messrs. Copeland and Spode, as a repository for their china-ware ; and finally the premises were taken down in 1848, or the following year, to make room for the enlargement of the museum of the College of Surgeons, which was finished in 1854.

By the rate-books of St. Clement Danes for 1668 we find Portugal Street to have been the residence of many distinguished personages in the seventeenth century. The Earl of Rochester lived "in the house next to the Duke's Theatre," from whence he gives notice to a correspondent, "If you write to me, direct to Lincoln's Inn Fields, the house next to the Duke Playhouse, in Portugal Row, there lives your humble servant,—ROCHESTER."

John Timbs tells us that Portugal Street was the last place where the stocks were set up in London, those of St. Clement Danes, which had formerly stood in the Strand, near Temple Bar, having remained here until about the year 1820. He adds that they were on the north side, facing the hospital. He also reminds us that even in recent days the street enjoyed "a sort of cant notoriety," from the fact of the Insolvent Debtors' Court being in it.

On the south side of Portugal Street, near the centre of the few small courts that have not been swept away, stands King's College Hospital, which owes its existence mainly to the exertions of Dr. R. B. Todd. It forms a plain, substantial, and unpretending block of buildings, four storeys in height, and is hardly old enough as yet to have a history,

having been founded only as far back as the year 1839. It grew naturally out of the wants of the Medical Department of King's College in the Strand, of which we shall have more to say in another chapter. It stands on the site of the old workhouse of St. Clement Danes, and of one of the burial-grounds already mentioned. Its design was twofold : to offer the medical students of the college the advantage of witnessing medical and surgical practice, and receiving clinical instruction from their own professors; and secondly, to afford medical and surgical aid to a poor neighbourhood, at a distance from any other hospital. The architect was Mr. T. Bellamy. The patients relieved by the hospital in 1840 were about 4,000, a number which, in a quarter of a century, was multiplied nearly tenfold. New buildings on an extensive scale were added in 1852, and more recently the building has been still further enlarged. The medical staff of the College comprises four "consulting" physicians, seven physicians, besides "assistant" physicians, a "consulting" surgeon, three surgeons with "assistants," a surgeon-dentist, &c. ; and the syllabus of its lectures embraces about twenty different subjects. It will accommodate about two hundred patients. The medical students attending hospital practice within its walls average upwards of three hundred. It is under a committee of management, and is but slenderly endowed. The hospital has appended to it a medical library, several museums, a chemical laboratory, and other appliances. The usual course extends over four years, though some few students complete it in three. Though so recently established, it can already boast of a long list of distinguished names among its professors and lecturers.

A part of the buildings of this hospital stands on ground which, up to about the year 1850, was one of the burial-places belonging to the parish. It was about the third of an acre in extent, and called the "Green Ground," as if in mockery. From a report of a parochial committee in 1848, we learn that upwards of 5,500 bodies had been interred within it in the previous quarter of a century. The scenes witnessed here were of the most offensive character. In it was interred, among other lesser celebrities, Joe Miller, the author of the "Jest Book" which bears his name, who died in 1738. A monument was erected to his memory, with an inscription, said to be by Stephen Duck, who began life as a thresher, but afterwards entered the Church, and wrote some poems, which incurred the satire of Dean Swift. This monument, having become decayed and almost illegible, was renewed in 1816, and is to be seen leaning up against the wall of one of the offices of the hospital. The inscription on it ran as follows :—

> "Here lie the remains of honest Joe Miller,
> Who was a tender husband, a sincere friend,
> A facetious companion, and an excellent comedian.

He departed this life the 15th day of August, 1738, aged 54 years."

in his day as an actor for his excellent personations of some of the characters in the comedies of Congreve, and as a gleaner and compiler of other men's witticisms he has enjoyed a reputation for wit and humour which in all probability he never deserved. Allibone's "Dictionary of Authors" tells us that

OLD HOUSES IN WYCH STREET, 1876. (*See page* 34.)

> "If humour, wit, and honesty could save
> The humorous, witty, honest from the grave,
> His grave had not so soon its tenant found,
> With honesty, and wit, and humour crowned !
> Or could esteem and love preserve our health,
> And guard us longer from the stroke of death,
> The stroke of death on him had later fell,
> Whom all mankind esteemed and loved so well."

Of "Joe Miller" little is known except what may be gathered from his tombstone. He was famous

"his 'Jest Book' was originally published in 1730 as the compilation of his friend, Elijah Jenkins, but the real editor (and author, as it is asserted) was John Mottley, the author of a 'Life of Peter the Great.' The book itself appears to have gained a sudden celebrity, second only to that of 'Ingoldsby Legends' and 'Pickwick,' three separate editions of it having appeared in 1739, and seven editions being disposed of in as many years."

Mr. Peter Cunningham, in his "Handbook of London," published in 1850, speaks of Joe Miller's headstone as standing in the old burying-ground "half concealed in summer by a clump of sun-flowers," and draws the special attention of his readers to "the 'Grange' public-house, with its old and picturesque inn-yard." It may be remembered building stood till 1889 at the eastern entrance to Clement's Inn, the access to it being through a gateway leading into a narrow and extremely dingy court, which opens out into Carey Street. It was converted from secular to religious uses in 1823, by a Dissenting congregation, of whom Mr. Dip-rose writes—

LYON'S INN. *From a View by S. Ireland, published* 1800. (*See page* 34.)

that Sir William Davenant, in his "Playhouse to Let," mentions this hostelry in a way which implies that it was a haunt of players. "Let him enter and send his train to our house-inn, the 'Grange.'" But alas! for the progress of modern improvements, the "Grange" and its yard are gone. It was taken down in 1853, and its site is now covered by a part of the hospital.

But far worse than the graveyard alluded to above, was another place of burial within the limits of this parish, long known as Enon Chapel, but afterwards converted into a chapel of ease to St. Clement's, and called Clare Market Chapel. The

"These pious people, looking very naturally to ways and means, turned the vaults beneath their meeting-house into a burial-place, which soon became filled with coffins up to the very rafters, so that there was only the wooden flooring between the living youth and the festering dead, for a Sunday-school was held in the chapel as well as the congregational meeting. This state of things was allowed to continue till 1844, when a new sewer having to be carried under the building, the Commissioners of Sewers discovered the loathsome charnel-house, and had the place closed, but left the bodies to lie there and rot, heedless of all consequences. The upper premises then became tenanted by a set of teetotallers, who, amongst other uses, turned it into a dancing-room, where the thoughtless and giddy went to 'foot it' away over the mouldering remains of sad mortality, part of the bygone generation turning to dust beneath the dancers' feet." This loathsome abomination ceased in 1847-8, when a surgeon, Mr. G. A. Walker, gained possession of the chapel with the intention of removing the remains from the vault, or "dust-hole," as it was usually called, to a more appropriate place. The work of exhumation was then commenced, and a pyramid of human bones was exposed to view, separated from piles of coffin wood in various stages of decay. This "Golgotha" was visited by about 6,000 persons, previous to its removal, and some idea may be formed of the horrid appearance of the scene, when it is stated that the quantity of remains comprised four up-heaved van loads. The whole mass of bodies was decently interred by Mr. Walker, at his own cost, in one pit in the cemetery at Norwood, the coffin-wood being piled up and burnt. It is indeed

strange to think that such foul abuses were not swept away until the reign of Victoria.

Was it in jest and scorn, or in a fit of royal pleasantry, that the little thoroughfare which joins the west end of Portugal Street to the south-west angle of Lincoln's Inn Fields was called Portsmouth Street? At all events it is not a little strange that this should have been the case when the Queen of Charles II. was Catharine of *Portugal*, and one of his court favourites the Duchess of *Portsmouth*. It is a short, narrow, and not very interesting street, though it still contains one or two of the few surviving wooden houses of the Stuart times. Mr. Peter Cunningham tells us that the "Old Black Jack," in this street, demolished in 1896, a famous hostelry of Joe Miller, was long known as the "Jump," on account of the fact that another of its frequenters, "Jack Sheppard," that hero of our town-bred urchins, once jumped out of its first-floor window, to escape the emissaries of Jonathan Wild. John Timbs tells us that here used to meet, until the year 1816, the members of a club known as the "Honourable Society of Jackers."

CHAPTER V.

THE STRAND (NORTHERN TRIBUTARIES).—CLEMENT'S INN, NEW INN, LYON'S INN, ETC.

"He must to the Inns of Court. I was of Clement's once myself, where they talk of Mad Shallow still."—2 *Henry IV.*, Act iii. 2.

Curious Legend about St. Clement's Lane—Clement's Inn—New Inn—Stanhope Street—Birthplace of Grimaldi—Holywell Street—The "Old Drury" Tavern—Ancient Shop-Signs—"Bookseller's Row"—Wych Street—New Inn—The "White Lion" and Jack Sheppard—The "Angel" Inn and Bishop Hooper—"Saddling the Spit"—Lyon's Inn—The "Spotted Dog"—The Globe Theatre—The Opera Comique—The Olympic Theatre.

TURNING southwards down what used to be a portion of St. Clement's Lane, and which lies between King's College Hospital and New Inn, it occurs to us that the narrow, dark, and irregular alleys in the neighbourhood of Clare Market and Wych Street, encumbered as they were with low projecting eaves, arched doorways, and bulkheads, must have afforded every facility, a century ago, or even less, for the unforeseen attacks of footpads and for the escape of the offenders; and even now it is almost as true as it was a century ago, that in the words of a writer in the *Builder*, "the whole nest of streets and passages behind the south side of Lincoln's Inn Fields requires re-arrangement and improvement. There is a legend hereabout that years ago a young man from the country, bearing a black bag, started one winter night from Portugal Street to get into the Strand, and that he has been wandering round and about ever since, constantly returning with a disconsolate aspect to his original starting-point. On foggy nights his form may be

descried in Clare Market. Anyhow, no one has yet heard that he ever reached the Strand."

Fortescue, a celebrated man of letters in the fifteenth century, was of the fanciful opinion that the name Inns of Court arose from these places being the inns or hotels where young noblemen and others belonging to the Court temporarily resided; for many persons of rank sent their sons here to pursue a course of study, without designing them to follow the profession of the law.

Clement's Inn, the west boundary of the New Law Courts, was so named, as we are told by Stow, "Because it standeth near to Clement's Church, but nearer to the fair fountain called Clement's Well." It is stated by Dugdale to have been an Inn of Chancery in the reign of Edward II.; but Pennant speaks of it as dating back only as far as the reign of Edward IV.

The following is quoted from Sir George Buc, an old writer, whose style at least is quaint and amusing:—"Clement's Inne was a messuage belonging to the parish of St. Clement Dane, the deuise whereof is an anchor without a stocke, with a capital C couchant upon it; and this is grauen in stone over the gate of St. Clement's Inne. It seemeth to be a hieroglyphike, or rebus (as some conjecture), figuring herein. St. Clement, who having been Pope, and so reputed head of the Church (and the Church being resembled to a shippe), both his name and office are expressed in this deuise of the 'C' and anchor."

The entrance to Clement's Inn from the thoroughfare on the north side of the church of St. Clement Danes was formerly through a tall archway, supported by lofty columns, which, however, has been demolished to make room for the New Law Courts. Our readers will scarcely need to be reminded that St. Clement's Inn is the one which Shakespeare has made immortal as the home of "Master Shallow" in his Templar days, as may be seen by the motto prefixed to this chapter.

Clement's Inn is said by Seymour in his "Survey" to have descended to the Earls of Clare from Sir William Hollis, Lord Mayor of London in 1539.

In the garden of this inn used to be a celebrated bronze figure of a negro supporting a sundial, said to have been brought from Italy early in the eighteenth century by Lord Clare, by whom it was presented to the Inn. Dickens, however, in the "Uncommercial Traveller," gives quite another version of the origin of this figure, which has recently been removed to the Inner Temple Gardens. The inn has now been rebuilt, and the Hall is no longer to be found.

New Inn, which adjoins Clement's Inn, is said by tradition to have been removed to Wych Street from Seacole Lane, before which time there was here a common hostelry or inn, known by the sign of the "Blessed Virgin."

"To this inn," says Seymour, with his usual accuracy, in his "Survey of London and Westminster" (1735), "are pleasant walks and gardens. The north-easterly part joints to Clement's Inn, from which it is separated by a handsome iron gate, shut up a nights, which was placed here anno 1723."

Pennant, writing in 1805, says of it—"New Inn, where the students of the Strand Inn nestled after they were routed thence by the Duke of Somerset. In New Inn the great Sir Thomas More received the early part of his education before he removed to Lincoln's Inn." The armorial bearings of this Inn are *Vert, a flower-pot argent.* It became an Inn of Chancery in 1485.

Stanhope Street, in this immediate neighbourhood, is worthy of a passing note as having been the birthplace of the famous clown, Grimaldi, who here first saw the light of day, Dec. 18, 1778. He seems to have been born in the purple of the theatre. His father was of Italian extraction; his mother, according to Mr. Diprose, was a Miss Rebecca Brooker, who had been from infancy a dancer at Drury Lane, and subsequently played "old woman" at Sadler's Wells. From "Pink's History of Clerkenwell" we learn that "Joe Grimaldi" made his first appearance at "the Wells" in 1781 in the character of a monkey, became part proprietor of the house in 1818, and finally quitted it in 1832. He died, somewhat suddenly, at his house in Southampton Street, Pentonville Road, at the end of May, 1837, and was buried in the churchyard of St. James's, Pentonville, by the side of his friend Charles Dibdin.

There is but little in the way of antiquarian lore or of recent anecdote to be told concerning Holywell Street, which no doubt received its name—not, we fear, much in keeping with its real character—from the "holy well" already mentioned near St. Clement's Church. Leigh Hunt, in his "London Journal," passes it by with discreet silence. Allen, in his "History of London," dismisses it in a line, styling it a "narrow, inconvenient avenue of old, ill-formed houses;" and Mr. Peter Cunningham "a narrow, dirty lane, chiefly occupied by old clothesmen and the vendors of low publications."

It appears from honest Strype that in his day it was tenanted by "divers salesmen and piece-brokers," and was commonly called "the Back Side of St. Clement's." Mr. Timbs says that the "holy well" which gave to it its name was "under the 'Old Dog' Tavern" (No. 24); but this is clearly a mistake. He adds that the "salesmen and piecebrokers of Strype's day have nearly deserted it, and that it is now the head-quarters of old bookstalls." A few lofty-gabled and deep-bayed fronts still remain upon some of the houses, especially on the southern side. It is only fair to add that during the last few years the character of the street has shown some improvement, owing to the enforcement of Lord Campbell's Act against the sale of bad books and prints, for which formerly this thoroughfare was a notorious market. At the corner of one of the houses on the south side, near the centre of the street, there remained until quite recently a grotesque carving—a lion's head—probably the last of such ornaments in the metropolis.

Holywell Street, we may be pardoned for adding here, was formerly used as the emporium of the mercers, who had their appropriate signs. Of these one still remains, the "Half Moon," a carved projecting sign; another—the "Indian Queen," painted by one of the members of the first association of the Royal Academy, one Catton—might be seen down to a recent period. The "Golden Ball" in this street was a noted house for silk remnants, and continued in repute to the end of the last century. As the mercery trade declined in Holywell Street, the traffic in frippery and old clothes took its place, but this has now practically disappeared.

A few houses in this street are still occupied by booksellers of a certain class—those who deal in a questionable kind of literature; and in the interest of the more respectable inhabitants, it has been proposed more than once to alter the name to "Booksellers' Row," but the street continues to be known as Holywell Street. It is only right to add that in the street at the present time are many highly respectable second-hand book-shops. The removal of all the buildings on the south side, from St. Clement's Church to St. Mary's-le-Strand, so as to widen this part of the street, is now (1897) under consideration.

Wych Street—our pathway as we walk from St. Clement's Church towards Drury Lane—derives its name from the Via de Aldwych, whereof it originally formed a part, a lane leading from the north side of the Strand to Broad Street, St. Giles's. It still contains, especially on the south side, some of those curious old wooden-fronted and gabled houses which are equally picturesque and inconvenient. Like Holywell Street, of late years this thoroughfare gained a notoriety for the sale of books and prints of an immoral class, but of this traffic few signs are now to be seen. In bygone days, however, it was tenanted by a very different class of persons; although in 1734, according to a statement quoted by Mr. Diprose, this street was "much taken up by upholsterers for the sale of bedding and second-hand household goods."

On the north side of Wych Street, nearly about the centre, is the entrance to New Inn, through which in the day-time there is a thoroughfare into the dismal region of Clare Market. In a narrow court of this street the notorious Jack Sheppard served his apprenticeship to Mr. Wood, the carpenter; and in White Lion Passage stood the "hostelrie" of the "White Lion," the scene of many of the events in the career of that prince of "cracksmen," who used nightly to meet in the tap-room his professional friends and acquaintances, and with whose feats and various adventures the pen of Mr. Harrison Ainsworth has made us so familiar. The house was pulled down in 1880.

The site of the old "White Lion" was at the corner of one of the courts on the northern side, and was latterly occupied as a carpenter's shop.

Speaking of Wych Street as it was in the days of Jack Sheppard, we may say of the Via de Aldwych, as the writer of "Haunted London" says of Holborn Hill—

"The street curves quaint,
And cumbrous sign-boards creak on left and right."

From the "Angel" Inn, at the bottom of Wych Street, Bishop Hooper was taken in 1554 to Gloucester to be burnt at the stake. Something more than two centuries later, the "Angel" Inn figured in a curious advertisement which appeared in the *Public Advertiser*, March 28, 1769:—

"To be sold, a Black Girl, 11 years of age; extremely handy; works at her needle tolerably, and speaks English well. Inquire of Mr. Owen, at the 'Angel' Inn, behind St. Clement's Church, in the Strand."

It is said by Allen, in his "History of London," that the "Great Fire" of 1666 was not the first of its kind which laid London waste, for that "in 1136 a great fire happened within the City, which destroyed all the way westward to St. Clement Danes," but he does not mention the precise spot where this fire ended at the west.

We have seen that the parish of St. Clement Danes was not considered remarkable for decency and order in the reign of Queen Elizabeth; but, in spite of the rank, wit, and fashion which distinguished it a century and a half later, we find that even then it bore no better character; and the Clement's Lane of the First and Second Georges was no bad precursor to the Wych Street of our own day. The *London Spy* of that date observes, half in earnest and half in jest, that it "is deemed an excellent air for breeding attorneys in, the chief subject of all conversation turning here upon verdicts, costs, damages, writs of inquiry, &c."

According to the same authority, published in 1725, there was formerly in the parish of St. Clement's the custom of "saddling the spit," which, the writer adds, "is now laid aside, for reasons well known at Westminster Hall." It would seem that whatever this custom may have been—and as far as we have been able to discover, history preserves a discreet silence as to its nature—it was a rough and boisterous one, "more honoured in the breach than in the observance."

Lyon's Inn, now demolished, was an old Inn of Chancery, belonging in former days to the Inner Temple. It faced Newcastle Street, on its eastern side, between Wych Street and Holywell Street; one entrance led to it from the latter, and also another through Horne Court, next door to an inn known as the "Spotted Dog." Mr. Diprose, in his "Account of St. Clement Danes," tells us that this same "Spotted Dog" had been a hostelry for some 230 years at least before its demolition in 1864, for the purpose of carrying out a building speculation of the "Strand Hotel Company," a speculation which ended in failure. It is said—but we know not with what amount of truth—that the once holy well, which gave its name to the street, was under the "Spotted Dog."

Howes, in his "Annals," in continuation of Stow, quaintly tell us that it was "a guest inn or hostelerie held at the sign of the 'Lyon,' and purchased by gentlemen professors and students in the law in the reign of King Henry VIII., and converted to an Inn of Chancery." Sir Edward Coke was a student there in 1578.

This Inn, never of much importance, had fallen utterly into disrepute before the beginning of this century, and become the resort of gamblers and swindlers. Here lived Mr. Weare, who was murdered near Edgware by Thurtell, in 1824. The latter in defence pleaded in extenuation that Weare had cheated him at cards out of £300.

Each of the three Inns alluded to in this chapter was governed by a Principal or Treasurer, and a number of "Ancients," corresponding to Benchers; and Seymour tells us, in his "Survey," that there were "mootings" in each Inn in every term.

The property of "Lyons Inn" was sold about the year 1863, and on its site now stand two theatres, the "Globe," as if in memory of Shakespeare's theatre, and the "Opera Comique."

The Globe Theatre, which covers its western portion, was built and opened in 1868. It has a narrow frontage in Newcastle Street. On this site the Architectural Association had its first home. The theatre was built from the instructions of Mr. Sefton Parry, the proprietor, and will seat 1,500 persons. The auditorium is effectively decorated in relief, and has a domed ceiling, with a sunlight in the centre. The site having been excavated very considerably for the proposed hotel, the floor of the pit has been made many feet below the line of the street, and is approached by a steep flight of steps from Wych Street. In Wych Street also are the entrances to the gallery stairs, and that to the "royal box." The ordinary boxes are entered from Newcastle Street, and are on a level with the street, so that stairs are avoided. Here, too, enter the occupants of the stalls. The seats are all fairly commodious, and conveniently placed, so that all that is passing on the stage can be distinctly seen and heard from any part of the house. The house opened with Mr. H. J. Byron's comedy of "Cyril's Success," which in itself proved a great success from a financial point of view.

The principal front of the "Opera Comique" is in the Strand, and observant passengers who know the narrowness of the area between the Strand and Holywell Street will find it difficult to imagine how, even in London, where now-a-days theatres are edged in among houses anyhow, an "Opera Comique" can have been · formed there. This frontage, however, is, in truth, nothing but the entrance to a passage which leads across Holywell Street to a theatre that has been built between that and Wych Street. The building, which is very small, backs on the "Globe," and is to a considerable extent underground, as will be understood when we mention that a long flight of stairs in Wych Street leads down to the stage level, and that the pit, of course, is lower than that again. The theatre was opened in 1870, and has seen several changes of lessees. It is nicely decorated, and commodiously arranged. Its greatest prosperity has been in the production of those comic operas with which the names of Messrs. Gilbert and Sullivan are popularly associated, notably "H.M.S. Pinafore," and "The Pirates of Penzance."

The Olympic Theatre, at the end of Wych Street, occupies the site of old Craven House, which was taken down in 1803, the ground being purchased by Mr. Philip Astley, of the "Amphitheatre" over Westminster Bridge, who constructed what was called at the time "a house of public exhibition of horsemanship and droll," which he styled "the Olympic Pavilion." It was opened as such in 1806, but the speculation does not appear to have been successful. In 1813 the lease was sold to Robert Elliston, who introduced pieces of sufficient merit to attract the fashionable dwellers in the West-end, and by that means raised the theatre to something like successful popularity. The building was destroyed by fire in 1849, but rebuilt and opened again in the same year. It was pulled down in 1890, and rebuilt in the following year. Madame Vestris had the management of the "Olympic" from 1832 to 1839, and many eminent actors and actresses appeared upon its boards. The pieces brought out at this theatre were principally melodramas of the superior kind. For many years Robson, one of the most gifted modern comedians, attracted thousands here to witness his wonderful delineations of the tears and laughter, the joys and sorrows, of human life in its humbler aspects. Mr. Horace Wigan was for some time manager here; Mr. Benjamin Webster has likewise had the management, and since then Miss Ada Cavendish and others have taken it in hand.

OLD CRAVEN HOUSE, 1800. (*See page* 35.)

CHAPTER VI.

THE STRAND (NORTHERN TRIBUTARIES).—DRURY LANE AND CLARE MARKET.

"O may thy virtue guard thee through the roads
Of Drury's mazy courts and dark abodes!"—*Gay's* "*Trivia.*"

"Paltry and proud as drabs in Drury Lane."—*Pope.*

The Hundred of Drury—Drury House, afterwards called Craven House—The "Queen of Bohemia"—Drury Lane—Eminent Inhabitants—Residence of Nell Gwynne—The "Cock and Magpie"—The "Craven Head" and the Norfolk Giant—Disreputable Character of Drury Lane in the Past Century—Pepys' Visit to the "Cockpit"—Puritan Observances—The Theatre in Vere Street—"Spiriting Away" an Infant—Princes Street—Clare Market—John Henley, the Demagogue—Clare House—Killigrew's Theatre—Mrs. Bracegirdle's Benevolence—The "Bull's Head" and the Artists' Club—The "Spiller's Head" Tavern—Clare Market Chapel—Denzil Street—Holles Street.

"ON the borders of St. Giles-in-the-Fields," says the *London Spy*, "is situated that ancient and venerable spot the Hundred of Drury, which, I hear, is the property of two or three parishes more." The character of this region may be inferred from the words which follow: "There are reckoned to be one hundred and seven 'pleasure-houses' within and about this settlement; and a Roman Catholic priest, who has lodged here many years, assures me that to his knowledge the Societies for the Reformation of Morals have taken as much pains, and expended as large sums to reclaim this new Sodom, as would have fitted out a force sufficient to have conquered the Spanish West Indies."

Pennant remarks it as a singular occurrence that this lane, "of late times so notorious for intrigue,"

should receive its name from a word which, in the language of Chaucer, had an amorous signification:

"Of bataile and of chevalrie,
Of ladies' love and *druerie*,
Anon I wot you tell."

Drury House, from which the lane originally took its name, stood at the west end of Wych Street. It was built by Sir William Drury, who is reported to have been not only the head of a great family, but Knight of the Garter. He held a command in the Irish wars in the reign of Elizabeth, and showed great ability as an officer. He unfortunately fell in a duel with a Sir John Burroughes, about a foolish quarrel for precedency. The house deserves to be remembered as the place where the rash friends of the Queen's favourite, the Earl of Essex devised those wild schemes which led to the ruin of himself and his adherents. The "Account of St. Clement's in 1734," to which we have so often referred, speaks of it as "a very large house, or which may rather be termed several houses. The entrance," adds the writer, "is through a pair of animated at once by love and duty. When on the death of her husband he could aspire to her hand, he is supposed to have succeeded; at all events history says that they were privately married, and that he built for her the fine seat at Hampstead Marshal, in Berkshire, afterwards destroyed by fire."

THE "COCK AND MAGPIE," DRURY LANE. *From an Original Sketch in* 1840. (*See page* 38.)

gates, which leadeth into a large yard for the reception of coaches." At the back of the house was a handsome garden. "In the following century," says Allen, in his "History of London," "it was possessed by the heroic Lord Craven, who rebuilt it. It was lately a large brick pile, concealed by other buildings, and turned into a public-house bearing the sign of the 'Queen of Bohemia,' the earl's admired mistress, whose battles he fought,

The services rendered by Lord Craven to London, his native city, are worthy of being recorded here. He was so indefatigable in preventing the ravages of fire, that it is said "his horse would smell the outbreak of a fire, and neigh to give the alarm." He and Monk, Duke of Albemarle, stayed in London throughout the visitation of the Great Plague in 1665, and at the hazard of their own lives preserved order in the midst of the horrors of the time. Allen adds that there used to be in Craven Buildings a very good fresco portrait of this hero in armour, mounted on a white horse, and with his truncheon in hand, and on each side an earl's and a baron's coronet, with the letters "W. C." (William Craven). This painting, though several times re-coloured in oils, has long since perished; but an engraving of it is preserved in Smith's "Antiquities of London."

It deserves to be recorded of Sir Robert Drury that he for some time entertained, as a welcome and honoured guest, at his mansion in Drury Lane, the amiable and learned Dr. John Donne, after-wards Dean of St. Paul's, when he was young and poor, having contracted marriage with a young lady of high connections, against the will, or at all events without the consent, of her relatives. It is added that he not only gave him and his wife the free use of apartments, but also was "a cherisher of his studies, and such a friend as sympathised with him and his in all their joys and sorrows." Such friends, no doubt, were rare then; as rare, perhaps, as now-a-days; but it is a pleasure to re-cord such an act of genuine friendship.

The exact date of the removal of Lord Craven's family from Drury Lane to their subsequent residence at Bayswater, where now is Craven Hill, is not known; but it must have been just before the close of the seventeenth century. Craven House itself was taken down early in the present century, and the site is now occupied by the Olympic Theatre, as stated in the last chapter.

Drury Lane was once the "Via de Aldwych," a name still preserved in Wych Street, as already mentioned. Then the great family of the Druries built in it a town house, and the Earls of Craven and Clare followed. It became a Belgravia. Here lived Archibald, the famous and ill-fated Marquis of Argyle. Here, too, close to Cradle Alley, Arthur Annesley, Earl of Anglesey, and Lord Privy Seal under Charles II., had his town house. Here, too, in the heyday of her glory, lived Nell Gwynne, the "pretty Nelly" whom Pepys saw "standing at her lodgings' door in her smock sleeves and bodice, a mighty pretty creature." Here also resided John Lacy, the comedian, and Sir William Alexander, the poet, afterwards Earl of Stirling.

At the same period was residing here a relative of the staid Mr. Evelyn, who, after recording in his "Diary" that he attended the marriage of his niece to the eldest son of Mr. Attorney Montagu, at Southampton Chapel, and eulogising the mag-nificence of the entertainment, adds, "the bride was bedded at my sister's lodgings in Drury Lane."

It was in Drury Lane, not very far from the steps of the Olympic Theatre, that Lord Mohun made his unsuccessful attempt to carry off the beautiful and much-wooed actress, Mrs. Bracegirdle, as we shall presently show.

By the time of Steele, Drury Lane had changed its character, and its narrow, close, and filthy courts were rising into existence.

All that is now left of Drury Lane is its memory of past glories. The shades of the persons above mentioned, as well as those of the pretty Mrs. Bracegirdle, the fiery Lord Mohun, and of the quarrelsome Carlo Fantom, the Croatian, who challenged his man and killed him, "because the noise of his spurs pleased him not," haunt it still. On the west side is a small burial-ground, unknown to Stow or Strype, to most of the map-makers, and to Peter Cunningham. It lies between Russell Street and Long Acre. For many years it had exhibited a most desolate and miserable aspect; indeed, it had become a sort of "no man's land." During the year 1874, however, the authorities of St. Martin's-in-the-Fields, to whom the ground belongs, at some considerable expense had the graveyard levelled and converted into a garden with walks and shrubberies. A neat brick wall separates the grounds from the public street, and on one side a brick building has been erected, to be used as a mortuary.

Towards the lower end of Drury Lane, nearly opposite to Drury or Craven House, is a quaint old gabled house, with its pents still remaining. A quarter of a century ago it was known as the "Cock and Magpie," but more recently as "Stock-ley's Cheap Bookshop." It is said that the region to the north, leading up towards St. Giles's, was once known as "Cock and Pie Fields;" but an-tiquaries are divided on the question as to whether they were so called from the house, or the house from them. Whichever may be the case, it is cer-tain that the "Cock and Magpie" as a sign, is but a travesty of a chivalric legend, which Douce thus explains:—"In the days of ancient chivalry it was the practice to make solemn vows or engage-ments for the performance of any considerable enterprise. This was usually performed during some great feast or entertainment, at which a roasted peacock, being served up by ladies in a dish of gold or silver, was presented to the knight, who then made his particular vow with great solem-nity. When this custom had fallen into disuse, the peacock nevertheless continued to be a favourite dish, and was introduced on the table in a pie, the head, with gilded beak, being proudly elevated above the crust, and the splendid tail expanded.

Other birds of smaller value were afterwards introduced in the same manner; and the recollection of the old peacock vows might occasion the less serious, or even the burlesque, imitation of swearing, not only by the bird itself, but also by the pie: hence, probably, came the oath 'By cock and pie,' for the use of which no very great antiquity can be found." From "Cock o' pie" to "Cock and magpie" the transition was easy and obvious.

Opposite to the above is the "Craven Head" Tavern, which, from 1851 to 1855, was kept by Mr. Robert Hales, the "Norfolk Giant." He was born in 1820, near Yarmouth, where his father was a small farmer, and was one of nine children, all far above the ordinary stature. He was exhibited by Barnum, in America, in 1848, and was one of the curiosities of London in the year of the first Great Exhibition. In the April of that year he was presented to the Queen, who gave him a watch and chain, and also to other crowned heads. He stood upwards of eight feet in height. His death occurred in 1863, at the age of forty-eight.

Drury Court is a narrow little street, leading down from Drury Lane to St. Mary's Church in the Strand. Its eastern side is composed of a range of houses which have stood apparently more than two centuries and a half.

It will be remembered that in the *Tatler* (No. 46) Steele gives a picture of the morality of Drury Lane, describing it as a district divided into particular "ladyships," analogous to "lordships" in other parts, "over which matrons of known ability preside." Its character, too, as well in the present as in the past century, is delicately hinted at by Gay, in the lines quoted from "Trivia," at the head of this chapter. The "Dog," a low public-house in this street, was known as the robbers' den; and nothing can confirm more clearly the character of the immediate neighbourhood, to which we have referred, than the fact that Drury Lane was the scene of the "Harlot's Progress," by Hogarth.

In Drury Lane was one of the several "cockpits," or places reserved for cock-fighting, which a century ago or earlier were to be found scattered about London. Mr. John Timbs tells us that one of our oldest theatres was called the "Cock-pit," namely, the "Phœnix" in Drury Lane, and that the site of it was still to be traced in the name of Pit or Pitt Place, an abridgment of "Cock-pit" Place. Samuel Pepys thus describes in his "Diary" a visit to one of these places, not far from Drury Lane :—
"December 21. To Shoe Lane to a cock-fighting at a new pit : but Lord ! to see the strange variety of people, from Parliament men, to the poorest 'prentices, bakers, brewers, butchers, draymen, and what not; and all these fellows, one with another, cursing and betting. Strange that such poor people, that look as if they had not bread to put in their mouths, shall bet three or four pounds at a time, and lose it, and yet bet as much the next battle, so that one of them will lose £10 or £20 at a meeting ! I soon had enough of it."

From Stubs's "Anatomie of Abuses," published in 1585, it is evident that in the good old Tudor times Sunday was the day of all the week especially set apart for this amusement. As early as the reign of Henry II., according to Fitzstephen, cock-fighting was the sport of school-boys in and around London on Shrove Tuesday ; and from that time, though occasionally forbidden by some of our sovereigns, it continued to exist among us, as we shall see hereafter.

At the beginning of the eighteenth century it would seem that Drury Lane had succeeded to a part at least of the reputation of Grub Street, as the residence of poor poets and hack rhymsters, as witness the words of Pope, in his "Dunciad"—

> "Cries he who high in Drury Lane,
> Lulled by soft zephyrs through the broken pane,
> Rhymes ere he wakes, and prints before Term ends,
> Obliged by hunger, and request of friends."

And in like spirit wrote Oliver Goldsmith—

> "Where the 'Red Lion,' staring o'er the way,
> Invites each passing stranger that can pay ;
> Where Calvert's butt and Parson's black champagne
> Regale the drabs and bloods of Drury Lane,
> There, in a lonely room, from bailiffs snug,
> The Muse found Scroggins, stretch'd beneath a rug."

"Their Majesties' servants," as might have been expected, fared but ill during the austere tyranny of the Puritan faction. At the Restoration the survivors of the old actors naturally formed themselves into a company, and Downes tells us that they acted at the Tennis-court, in Vere Street, Clare Market, till a new theatre was built ; and Guest is of opinion that both before and after that event they performed at the Cockpit in Drury Lane. The theatre in Vere Street was opened November 8th, 1660, by Killigrew and Davenant, under a patent which allowed women to act the female parts, a practice till then unknown in England.

It was at this theatre that an unknown young lady was performing the character of Roxana, in the *Siege of Rhodes*, who fell a victim to Aubrey de Vere, the last (and most unworthy) Earl of Oxford of the ancient line. This scion of a noble house, finding that he could secure his prey in no other way, brought to her lodging a sham clergyman and a sham marriage certificate ; and she learnt to her cost, when it was too late, that she had no pretension whatever to style herself Countess of Oxford.

It is clear that although the Puritans disapproved of plays *pur et simple*, they tolerated mixed entertainments of a musical kind. Such an entertainment, we know from Evelyn, was given after the death of Oliver Cromwell, for he writes, in May, 1659 :—"I went to see a new opera after the Italian way in recitative music and scenes. . . . It was prodigious that in a time of such public consternation such a 'vanity' should be kept up or permitted." That this entertainment was something different from a tragedy or comedy is clear from another entry by Evelyn in his "Diary," in January, 1661 :—"After divers years since I had seen any play, I went to see acted *The Scornful Lady*, at a new theatre in Lincoln's Inn Fields."

Mr. Peter Cunningham tells us that Laguerre, whose "sprawling saints" are immortalised by Pope, was a member of a club of *virtuosi* who used to meet at a house in Drury Lane, and that he painted on its walls a Bacchanalian procession, which he presented to its members. But apparently the *habitat* of this club was unknown to him.

It was in a low lodging-house in Lincoln Court, one of the gloomiest purlieus on the eastern side of the upper part of Drury Lane, that in 1861 was discovered the infant son of a Mr. and Mrs. Hill—relatives of the Burdett family—which had been "spirited away" from its mother's charge at Rugby by its father. The story is thus told by a writer in *Cassell's Magazine* of May 24th, 1873 :—

"The boy's own father, after falsifying the register of its birth, took it to London, and handed it over to some women whom he met in the street. The police were soon put upon the track of the culprits, who were shown to have received the missing infant from its unnatural parent. The papers took up the matter, which became a 'nine days' wonder,' and in a little time the child was discovered in Lincoln Court, Drury Lane, a place tenanted by the lowest class of Irish. It was in a sadly dirty state, and such clothing as it had on its back was not the same which it wore on leaving Rugby; but in spite of dirt and rags, there was something about the child which marked it off from the beggars' brats among whom it was playing, and its *distingué* looks led to its recovery. Ultimately the father was acquitted of the charge on which he was arraigned. Both he and Mrs. Hill, however, died shortly afterwards. This court was pulled down in 1880, to make room for model lodging-houses.

The following brief extract from a daily paper in the year of grace 1874 tells its own sad story :—"On Saturday, Mr. Langham held an inquest on the body of Miss Eliza Merrit, aged fifty-six, who it was said, was the daughter of a Church of England rector, and after struggling amid ill health to earn a living as a governess and by needlework, had ultimately, as the evidence showed, died of want, alone, in a small back room in Drury Lane !"

Drury Lane is rapidly losing its look of dingy antiquity. A few years ago some large blocks of dwellings for the working classes were built on the eastern side, and as these pages go to press (1897) a considerable portion of the western side is being rebuilt.

It should be added here that this street—or, at all events, a part of it—at one time was called Prince's Street; "but the old name triumphed," says Mr. Peter Cunningham, "and Prince's Street was confined to a new row of tenements branching off to the east, and still distinguished by that name."

The thoroughfare known as Clare Market, leading eastwards into Lincoln's Inn Fields, was so called in honour of the Earl of Clare, who lived "in a princely mansion" adjacent. His name is inscribed as a parishioner of St. Clement Danes in the rate-books of 1617. In Howell's "Londinopolis" of 1657 we read :—"Then is there, towards Drury Lane, a new market, called Clare Market; then is there a street and palace of the same name, built by the Earl of Clare, who lived there in a princely mansion, having a house, a street, and a market both for flesh and fish, all bearing his name." It is thus mentioned by Strype :—"Clare Market very considerable and well served with provisions, both flesh and fish ; for, besides the butchers in the shambles, it is much resorted unto by the country butchers and higglers. The market-days are Wednesdays and Saturdays. The toll belongs to the Duke of Newcastle (Pelham-Holles) as ground landlord thereof."

"This market," says Nightingale, in the tenth volume of the "Beauties of England and Wales," "stands on what was originally called Clement's Inn Fields. In the year 1657 a Bill was passed for preventing the increase of buildings, in which was a clause permitting the Earl of Clare to erect the market, which bore his title, in these fields, to be held on Tuesdays, Thursdays, and Saturdays. The earl, it seems, also erected a chapel of ease to St. Clement's, which is said to have been converted to dwelling-houses. That these lands were before in the possession of Holles we have already shown under Clement's Inn. Charles I., in 1640, granted his license to Thomas York, his executors, &c., to erect as many buildings as they thought proper upon St. Clement's Inn Fields, the inheritance of the Earl of Clare, 'to be built on each side of the causeway, leading from Gibbon's Bowling Alley, at the coming-out of Lincoln's Inn Fields, to the Rein Deer Yard, that leadeth unto Drury Lane, not to exceed, on either side, the number of 120 feet in length or front, and 60 feet in breadth, to be of stone or brick.'* Charles I. issued another license in 1642, permitting Gervase Holles, Esq., to erect fifteen houses, a chapel, and to make several streets of the width of thirty, thirty-four, and forty feet. These streets still retain the names and titles of their founders, in Clare Street, Denzil Street, Holles Street, &c." Rein Deer Yard was, probably, what is now called Bear Yard, and Gibbon's Bowling Alley was covered by the first theatre erected by Sir William Davenant, whence he afterwards removed to Portugal Street. Here, during the administration of Sir Robert Walpole, in the reign of George II., John Henley, a disappointed demagogue, stood on a tub and vented his factious ebullitions, which he distinguished by the name of oratory. He is alluded to by Pope, in his " Epistle to Arbuthnot," but not in very quotable terms. Possessing some abilities, he was also obnoxious to Government by the publication of the " Hyp Doctor," and other papers on the politics of the times. A contemporary writer speaks of him as—

" Preacher at once and zany of the age."

On Henley's death in 1756, his demise was thus announced in the *Gentleman's Magazine*:—" Rev. Orator Henley, aged 64."

We learn from the " Harleian Miscellany" that the City had a long lawsuit with Lord Clare for this property, but that at last the City yielded. It appears, also, from the same source, that the success of his lordship in obtaining a charter for his market led to one important result, namely, the establishment of other markets round about the metropolis, some of which are now things of the past, such as Hungerford, Brooke, and Bloomsbury Markets, and that in Petty France, in Westminster, and St. James's and Newport Markets, which are still in existence.

Of the house of Holles, Lord Clare, whose family names are so perpetuated in this vicinity, no remains are left, nor is the precise site of it known. It was a large and stately mansion, shut in with a high wall, and its grounds joined on to the eastern side of those of Craven House. Clare Street is mentioned in Strype's edition of Stow as " a good open place fronting the market," while Clare Market bears the reputation of being " a street well inhabited by tradesmen." No engraving of old

Clare House is known to exist, nor is any detailed description of the house to be found. All that we know is that the Earl of Clare, as we are told by Howell, lived in his " palace" here in a " princely manner," to which, we fear, the present aspect of the place presents a very marked contrast.

With the Earl of Clare, and other aristocratic denizens of St. Clement Danes, have passed away " the butchers in the shambles, and country butchers," who used to supply these wealthy households. The merchandise at present exposed for sale in Clare Market consists principally of dried fish, inferior vegetables, and other humble viands, suited to the pockets of the poor inhabitants of the narrow courts and alleys around.

The celebrated actress, Mrs. Bracegirdle, we are told, was in the habit of going often into Clare Market, and of giving money to such poor basket-women as were out of employ, thereby calling down many blessings on her head.

As Clare Market lay between two great theatres, its butchers and hucksters, as remarked by Mr. Timbs, were the arbiters of the galleries, and the leaders of theatrical rows, as well as the musicians at the marriages of actresses, and the chief mourners at players' funerals. In one of the many public-houses which, as was natural, abounded here, Hogarth, in the days of his apprenticeship, was a frequent boon-companion of Joe Miller.

In Gibbon's Court, Clare Market, was a small theatre, in which Killigrew's company performed for a short time. Pepys speaks of it as a hand-some building, " the finest, I believe, that ever was in England." This, however, must have been an exaggeration. It soon passed away, and its remains were long used as slaughter-houses and carpenters' shops. The butchers of Clare Market are now nearly extinct; but Mr. P. Cunningham tells us that so lately as 1850 from 350 to 400 sheep, and from 50 to 200 oxen, were slaughtered there. He adds, " In a yard distinct from the more public portion of the market is the place where the Jews slaughter their cattle, according to a ceremony prescribed by the laws of their religion."

When Cromwell revived the prohibition of his predecessor against the erection of new buildings in and near London, imposing even a fine on its violation, an exception, we are told, was made in favour of the new buildings then scarcely finished, in Clare Market. In consequence of this exemption, unfortunately for the healthiness of the locality, they were not made " of brick or stone," or " upright, and without projecting their upper storeys into the street."

The " Artists' Club," of which Hogarth was a

---

* Malcolm's " London," vol. iii., p. 292.

member, used to meet at the "Bull's Head" Tavern in this market. Here also was the "Spiller's Head" Inn, named after James Spiller, a well-known actor, where was held a club principally consisting of artists, authors, and actors connected with the Lincoln's Inn Fields Theatre. It was founded about the year 1690, under the auspices of Colley Cibber, Tom D'Urfey, and many noted characters. Of Spiller, Mr. Diprose tells us, "he was an immense favourite with the

In 1701 there appeared at a place of entertainment in Islington, called "Miles's Music House," afterwards known as "Sadler's Wells Theatre," "a strange sort of monster that does everything like a monkey, mimics man like a jackanapes, but is not a jackanapes; jumps upon tables and into windows on all fours like a cat, but is not a cat; does all things like a beast, but is not a beast; does nothing like a man, but is a man! He has given such wonderful content to the butchers of

HALL OF THE ROYAL COLLEGE OF SURGEONS. (See page 46.)

butchers of Clare Market, one of whom was so charmed with his performances that he took down the sign of the "Bull and Butcher," and put up "Spiller's Head." The success or failure both of actors and pieces appears in those days to have greatly depended on the verdict of the butchers of Clare Market, whose approval was sometimes recorded by managers in their advertisements!

To the pen of one of these low patrons of the drama is assigned the following graceful elegy upon the death of James Spiller in 1729 :—

"Down with your marrow-bones and cleavers all,
  And on your marrow-bones ye butchers fall ;
  For prayers from you who never prayed before
  Perhaps poor Jemmy may to life restore."

Clare Market," says a contemporary writer, "that the house is every day as full as the Bear Gardens, and draws the City wives and 'prentices out of London much more than a man hanged in chains."

Something has of late years been done to improve Clare Market, and at present (1897) the "house-breaker" and the builder are hard at work. Gilbert Street has nearly disappeared, and recently a clearance scheme was adopted which is estimated to cost three-quarters of a million.

Adjoining Clare Market are Holles and Denzil Streets, the latter "so called," as we are told by a mural tablet on one of its houses, "by Gilbert, Earl of Clare, in memory of his uncle Denzil, Lord Holles, who died in 1679, a great honour to his

IN LINCOLN'S INN FIELDS.

NEWCASTLE HOUSE.   SIR JOHN SOANE'S HOUSE.

DUKE OF ANCASTER'S HOUSE.

name, and the exact paturne of his father's great meritt, John, Earl of Clare." This Lord Holles, it will be remembered, was one of the five members of the House of Commons whose person Charles I. made an ineffectual effort to seize.

Holles Street, which runs into Stanhope Street, was built in 1647, and was called, like its neighbour Denzil Street, after Holles, Earl of Clare.

Of Vere Street, which runs northwards parallel to Stanhope Street, we know little except what Mr. Peter Cunningham has told us, namely, that in 1688 it numbered among its inhabitants Sir Thomas Lyttelton and also the poet Ogilby, who here disposed of his books by a lottery; and that in it stood Gibbon's Tennis Court, subsequently converted into a theatre by Killigrew. Of these two places, however, nothing now remains, and the street is dull and dreary.

CHAPTER VII.

LINCOLN'S INN FIELDS.

"Laudaturque domus longos quæ prospicit agros."—*Horace.*

Formation of Lincoln's Inn Fields—Dimensions of the Square—Inigo Jones's Plan—Noble Families resident here—The Poet Gay's Estimate of the Place—"Mumpers" and "Rufflers"—Used as Training-grounds for Horses—Bad Reputation of the Fields in Former Times—Execution of Lord William Russell—The Tennis Court—The Royal College of Surgeons—Sardinian Chapel—The Sardinian Ambassador's Residence—The "Devil's Gap"—Institution for the Remedy of Organic Defects, &c.—Society for Promoting Christian Knowledge—Newcastle House—The Soane Museum—Inns of Court Hotel—Whetstone Park—Milto 's Residence—Great and Little Turnstiles—Proposal to erect the Courts of Law in Lincoln's Inn Fields.

THIS open space, which happily still serves to supply fresh air to the residents of the crowded courts of Drury Lane and Clare Market, affords in its central enclosure one of the largest and finest public gardens in London, and in point of antiquity is perhaps the oldest. In 1659, we find from Charles Knight's "History of London," James Cooper, Robert Henley, and Francis Finch, Esquires, and other owners of "certain parcels of ground in the fields, commonly called Lincoln's Inn Fields, were exempted from all forfeitures and penalties which they might incur in regard to any new buildings they might erect on three sides of the same fields, previously to the 1st of October in that year, provided that they paid for the public service one year's full value for every such house within one month of its erection; and provided that they should convey the 'residue of the said fields' to the Society of Lincoln's Inn, for laying the same into walks for common use and benefit, whereby the annoyances which formerly have been in the same fields will be taken away, and passengers there for the future better secured."

It has often been stated, and repeated until generally accepted as true, that the square of Lincoln's Inn Fields was designedly laid out so as to be exactly of the size of the base of the Great Pyramid. "This," remarks Horace Walpole, "would have been much admired in an age when the keep of Kenilworth Castle was erected in the form of a horse-fetter and the Escurial in the shape of St. Lawrence's gridiron;" but a reference to Colonel Howard-Vyse's work "On the Pyramids" will show that the fanciful idea is untrue,

the Fields measuring 821 feet by 625, while the Great Pyramid covers a space of 764 feet square.

The "square" was formed in the seventeenth century by no less a person than Inigo Jones, to whom, along with other gentlemen and one or two members of the Court, a special commission was issued by James I., for the purpose of having the ground laid out and improved under his direction. Several of the houses on the west and south sides are of his design. "The expense of laying out the grounds," as we learn from Northouck, "was levied on the surrounding parishes and Inns of Court." The west side was originally known as Arch Row, the south as Portugal Row, and the north as Newman's Row; but the names dropped out of use at the close of the last century.

The original plan for "laying out and planting" these fields, drawn by the hand of Inigo Jones, is still to be seen in Lord Pembroke's collection at Wilton House. The chief feature in it is Lindsey (afterwards Ancaster) House, in the centre of the west side, now divided into two houses and cut up into chambers for lawyers. It is unchanged in all its external features, except that the balustrade along the front of the roof has lost the handsome vases by which it was formerly surmounted.

Among the noble families who lived in this spot was that of the Berties, Earls of Lindsey and afterwards Dukes of Ancaster; but they seem to have migrated to Chelsea in the reign of Charles II. In this square at various dates lived also the great Lord Somers; Digby, Earl of Bristol; Montague. Earl of Sandwich; the Countess of Middlesex, and the Duke of Newcastle; and in the present century Lords Kenyon and Erskine, Sir John Soane, and Mr. Spencer Perceval. A century ago Lord Northington, Lord Chancellor, lived in a house on the south side of the square, on the site of the Royal College of Surgeons. At the birth of her first son, Charles Beauclerk, afterwards the first Duke of St. Albans, Nell Gwynne was living in lodgings in Lincoln's Inn Fields, being up to that time regularly engaged at the theatre close by.

It is to be feared that although Lincoln's Inn Fields is said to be the largest and handsomest square, not only in London, but in Europe, it has not borne a very good character in olden times. At all events Gay speaks of the Fields in his "Trivia" as the head-quarters of beggars by day and of robbers at night :—

"Where Lincoln's Inn's wide space is railed around,
Cross not with venturous step ; there oft is found
The lurking thief, who, while the daylight shone,
Made the walls echo with his begging tone.
That crutch, which late compassion mov'd, shall wound
Thy bleeding head, and fell thee to the ground.
Though thou art tempted by the linkman's call,
Yet trust him not along the lonely wall ;
In the midway he'll quench the flaming brand,
And share the booty with the pilfering band."

Blount tells us, in his "Law Dictionary," that he used to see idle fellows here playing at "the Wheel of Fortune ;" and it is clear, from more than one contemporary allusion in comedies, that the square was the regular haunt of cripples, with crutches, who lived by mendicancy, which they carried on in the most barefaced, if not intimidating, manner. Here, too, according to Peter Cunningham, "the astrologer Lilly, when a servant at Mr. Wright's, at the corner house, over against Strand Bridge, spent his idle hours in 'bowling,' along with Wat the cobbler, Dick the blacksmith, and such like."

We occasionally find in the literature of the seventeenth century allusions to the "Mumpers" and "Rufflers" of Lincoln's Inn Fields. These were, according to Mr. John Timbs, names given to the troops of idle vagrants by whom the "Fields" were infested ; and readers of the *Spectator* will hardly need to be reminded of "Scarecrow," the beggar of that place, who, having disabled himself in his right leg, asks alms all day, in order to get a warm supper at night. The "Rufflers," if we may accept the statement of the same authority, were "wretches who assumed the characters of maimed soldiers," who had suffered in the battles of the Great Rebellion, and found a ready prey in the people of fashion and quality as they drove by.

The "railing" to which Gay alludes in his poem, it should be here remarked, was only a series of wooden posts and rails, the iron rails not having been put up until the year 1735, when the money for so enclosing and adorning the Fields was raised by a rate on the inhabitants. The plan of the railing, its gates, and its ornaments, was submitted to and approved by the Duke of Newcastle, the minister of George II., who was one of the residents of the square. We are told that before Lincoln's Inn Fields were so railed in they were used as a training-ground by horse-breakers, and that many robberies were committed in its neighbourhood. And Ireland, in his "Inns of Court," tells us a story which shows us that they were surrounded by a rough and lawless set of people : "Sir John Jekyll having been very active in bringing into Parliament a Bill to raise the price of gin, became very obnoxious to the poor, and, when walking one day in the Fields at the time of breaking the horses, the populace threw him down and trampled on him, from which his life was in great danger."

Peter Cunningham, in his "Handbook of London," tells another story which shows that the bad reputation of these Fields at the time of their enclosure was of more than half a century in standing : "Through these fields," he writes, "in the reign of Charles II., Thomas Sadler, a well-known thief, attended by his confederates, made his mock procession at night with the mace and purse of Lord Chancellor Finch, which they had stolen from the Lord Chancellor's closet in Great Queen Street, and were carrying off to their lodging in Knightrider Street. One of the confederates walked before Sadler, with the mace of the Lord Chancellor exposed on his shoulder ; while another, equally prominent, followed after him carrying the Chancellor's purse. For this theft Sadler was executed at Tyburn." And to go back a little further still. "Here," he adds, "even in the place where they had used to meet and confer on their traitorous practices, were Ballard, Babington, and their accomplices beheaded, to the number of fourteen." Here, too, in 1683, a far worthier man, whom it is almost a sin to mention in such company, Lord William Russell, laid his noble head on the block, Dr. Tillotson standing by his side. The reader of Burnet's "History of his Own Time," will not forget his description of the scene of Lord William Russell's execution in this square. He writes, "Tillotson and I went with him in the coach to the place of execution. Some of the crowd that filled the streets wept, while others insulted. He was singing psalms a great part of the way, and said he hoped to sing better ones soon. As he observed the great crowd of people all the way, he said to us, 'I hope I shall quickly see a much better assembly.' When he came to the scaffold, he walked about it four or five times; then he turned to the sheriffs and delivered his papers. . . . He prayed by himself, then Tillotson prayed with him. After that he prayed again by himself, then undressed himself, and laid his head on the block without the least change of countenance; and it was cut off at two strokes." The death of this patriotic nobleman must for ever remain as a blot of deep dye on the memories of those who commanded his execution.

We learn incidentally that early in the last century Betterton and his company were playing at the "Tennis Court,"* in Lincoln's Inn Fields, when it was first proposed to him by Vanbrugh and Congreve, as builder and writer, to join in starting a new theatre in the Haymarket.

On the south side of the square, the Hall of the Royal College of Surgeons is the principal ornament. The building was erected, or rather rebuilt, in 1835-6, under the superintendence of the late Sir Charles Barry. The College of Surgeons was chartered in the year 1800, since which time many valuable advantages have been conferred upon the society by the Legislature. The front of the hall consists of a noble portico, with fluted columns, whilst along the top of the edifice is a bold entablature, with enriched cornice. To the left of the entrance-hall are two or three spacious rooms for the use of the secretary and other officials, and on the right a doorway gives access to the museum, which forms perhaps the chief feature of the building. This occupies three large and lofty rooms, lighted from the top, and each surrounded by two galleries, in which are displayed, as well as in cases on the ground-floor, the valuable collection of objects of which the museum consists. The basis of this collection was originally formed by John Hunter, whose museum was situated in Leicester Square. It was purchased from his widow at his death, by the Government, for the sum of £15,000, and presented to the College of Surgeons. "The main object which he had in view in forming it," says the writer of an admirable account of Hunter and his museum in the *Penny Cyclopædia*, was to illustrate, as far as possible, the whole subject of life by preparations of the bodies in which the phenomena are presented. The principal and most valuable part of the collection, forming the physiological series, consisted of dissections of the

organs of plants and animals, classed according to their different vital functions, and in each arranged so as to present every variety of form, beginning from the most simple, and passing upwards to the most complex. They were disposed in two main divisions: the first, illustrative of the functions which minister to the necessities of the individual; the second, of those which provide for the continuance of the species. . . . The pathological part of the museum contained about 2,500 specimens, arranged in three principal departments: the first illustrating the processes of common diseases, and the actions of restoration; the second, the effects of specific diseases; and the third, the effects of various diseases, arranged according to their locality in the body. Appended to these was a collection of about 700 calculi and other inorganic concretions." This, it may be added, has been considerably augmented by subsequent purchases, and also by gifts to the college; so that it may now be fairly said to form the richest collection of the kind in existence.

Among the objects of curiosity preserved here are the skeletons of several human beings and animals, which during the time of their existence had obtained some celebrity. Among them may be mentioned Jonathan Wild, the notorious thief-catcher; Mlle. Crachani, a Sicilian dwarf, who at the age of ten years was just twenty inches high; Charles Byrne, or O'Brien, the Irish giant, who at his death measured eight feet four inches; and also the gigantic elephant "Chunee," which was formerly exhibited on the stage at Covent Garden Theatre, and afterwards in the menagerie at Exeter Change, where, in 1824, "in consequence of the return of an annual paroxysm producing such ungovernable violence as to endanger the breaking down of the den," its destruction caused so much sympathy at the time. Its death was effected by shooting, but not until the animal had received upwards of 100 musket and rifle shots. The skeleton of this animal is twelve feet four inches high.

In the first room of the museum is a very life-like marble statue of John Hunter, the founder of the collection, by H. Weekes, Esq., R.A., erected by public subscription in 1864. The library of the institution is a noble room extending over the entrance-hall and adjoining offices, and contains a few portraits of eminent surgeons. The council room has a few portraits hanging upon its walls, and also a cartoon of Holbein's great picture of the "Grant of the Charter to the Barber-Surgeons," of which the original is in the council room of the Barbers' Company in Monkwell Street. The lectures to students, of which there are three courses

---

* Pepys writes, Nov. 20, 1660, "Mr. Shepley and I, to the new play-house near Lincoln's Inn Fields, which was formerly Gibbon's Tennis Court. . . . Here I saw for the first time one Moone (Mohun), who is said to be the best actor in the world, lately come over with the king; and, indeed, it is the finest play house, I believe, that ever was in England."

during the year, take place in the theatre, a lofty but somewhat contracted-looking place, with wainscoted walls, crimson seats, and a square-panelled ceiling, in the centre of which is a lantern or skylight. The museum, it should be added, is not intended as a place of exhibition, but a place of study. Members of both Houses of Parliament, the dignitaries of the church and law, members of learned and scientific bodies, physicians, surgeons, &c., have not only the privilege of visiting it personally, but of introducing visitors.

On the western side of Lincoln's Inn Fields, a little south of Lindsey House, is a heavy and gloomy archway (said, however, to be the work of Inigo Jones), which leads into Duke Street. On the south side of this, close to the archway, stands the Sardinian Chapel, the oldest Roman Catholic chapel in London. It was originally attached to the residence of the Sardinian Ambassador, and dates as a building from the year 1648. It is well known that during the reigns of the later Tudors and the Stuarts, the Roman Catholics in England were forbidden to hear mass, or have chapels of their own for the performance of their worship. They therefore resorted in large numbers to the chapels of the foreign ambassadors, where their attendance was at first connived at, and afterwards gradually tolerated and allowed. The ambassador's residence stood in Lincoln's Inn Fields, and originally the only way into it lay through the house. In the Gordon Riots, in 1780, this house and the chapel were attacked and partially destroyed, as being the chief resort of the Roman Catholic nobility and gentry, and of the Bishop or Vicar Apostolic of the London district, who lived in a small house in seclusion in Castle Street, Holborn. After the suppression of the riots, the chapel was rebuilt and enlarged westwards, by adding to it the ground formerly occupied by the ambassador's stables. During the first twenty years of the present century this chapel formed the centre of the Roman Catholic worship and of the charities of that Church ; but it was superseded by the erection of St. Mary's, Moorfields, in 1820, and subsequently by the erection of other Roman Catholic Churches in Islington, Clerkenwell, Soho, &c. It formerly had a fine choir, and still shows in its fine ecclesiastical plate and pictures some remains of its former importance. It has now gradually come to be a chapel for the Catholics of its immediate neighbourhood, many of whom are foreigners. A body of Franciscans, we are told, was established in connection with the Sardinian Chapel, near Lincoln's Inn Fields, in the reign of James II

As late as the reign of George II. there was on this side of the square an archway with a tenement attached to it, known in common parlance as " the Devil's Gap." It was taken down in 1756, in consequence of the dilapidated state into which it had fallen. Its last permanent tenant, some century before, as we learn from the *London Gazette* of that year, was an attorney or money-lender, Jonathan Crouch, a man who, in the days of Civil War, squeezed the life-blood out of his victims, regardless whether they were Puritans or Royalists. He over-reached himself in an effort to secure a rich and youthful heiress as a wife for his son ; and his melancholy end in a death-struggle with the rival for the young lady's hand forms one of the most sensational tales in Waters' " Traditions of London." The affair caused an intense excitement at the time, and it is said that the house, or rather den, of Crouch in the Devil's Gap could not find a tenant for many a year afterwards.

On the same side of the square was, early in the present century, the " Institution for the Remedy of Organic Defects and Impediments of Speech," established by Mr. Thelwall, who, having been in early life a somewhat revolutionary reformer, later turned his attention to philanthropy, and taught elocution with success. All remembrance, however, of the institution and its founder, has long since passed away.

At the northern end of the west side, at the corner of Great Queen Street, over the pathway of which one end of it is carried on arches, the visitor will be sure to note a large and handsome mansion which for the last half-century formed the headquarters of the Society for Promoting Christian Knowledge. It was originally built by the Marquis of Powis* in 1686, no doubt on account of its nearness to the Sardinian Chapel, as the family were at that time Roman Catholics. It afterwards became the residence of the Duke of Newcastle, the Prime Minister of George II.'s reign, after whom it was called Newcastle House till 1879.

Nearly in the centre of the north side of the square stands the museum founded in 1837, by a bequest of Sir John Soane, and called after his name. The son of a common bricklayer in a Berkshire village, he rose into celebrity as an architect, and designed, among other buildings, the Bank of England, and most of the terraces in the Regent's Park. He was also clerk of the works

---

* The marquis was outlawed by William and Mary for his fidelity to James II., whose exile he shared, and by whom after his abdication, he was created Duke of Powis. He was the father of the foundress of the Convent of Augustinian nuns at Bruges, and also of the Countess of Nithsdale, who so nobly effected the escape of her husband from the Tower of London while under sentence of death.

at St. James's Palace, and architect generally to the Houses of Parliament, and other public buildings. He was subsequently elected Professor of Architecture to the Royal Academy. All his life long he had been a collector of books, statues, pictures, coins, medals, and other curiosities mostly

Tuesday, Wednesday, Thursday, and Friday in March, April, May, June, July, and August; at other times the curator must be specially applied to for tickets. Students can obtain from the curator, or from any of the trustees, permission to copy any of the pictures and other works of art.

LINCOLN'S INN GATE, CHANCERY LANE.   (*See page* 52.)

antique, with which he stored the house where he lived and died. The museum, filled from top to bottom with a beautifully arranged collection of models of art in every phase and form, small as it is, may be said to be almost as useful to the art student as is the Louvre at Paris. And yet, standing in the centre of London, it is but little known, though open to the public gratuitously. It is open always to students in painting, sculpture, and architecture; and to the general public every

In 1833 Sir John Soane obtained an Act of Parliament for settling and preserving his museum, library, and works of art "for the benefit of the public, and for establishing a sufficient endowment for the due maintenance of the same." The building may be distinguished from the others in the row in which it stands from the peculiar semi-Gothic style in which it is erected. Between the windows of the ground and of the first floor are fragments of Gothic corbels from ancient buildings, erected, probably, about the close of the twelfth century. Upon each side of the gallery of the second floor are copies in terra-cotta from the Caryatides in front of the Temple of Poseidon at Athens.

The walls of the entrance-hall are coloured to imitate porphyry, and decorated with casts in plaster after the antique, medallion reliefs, and other sculptures. The dining-room and library, which may be considered as one room, being separated only by

Pantheon, and the Tower of the Winds; and there is also a large model in cork of part of the ancient city of Pompeii.

The next room contains a considerable collection of marble fragments of Greek and Roman sculpture, of antique bronzes, and some curious natural productions. In what is called the Monument Court, the walls of which are enriched with various fragments of ancient buildings and pieces of sculpture, is an architectural group about thirty

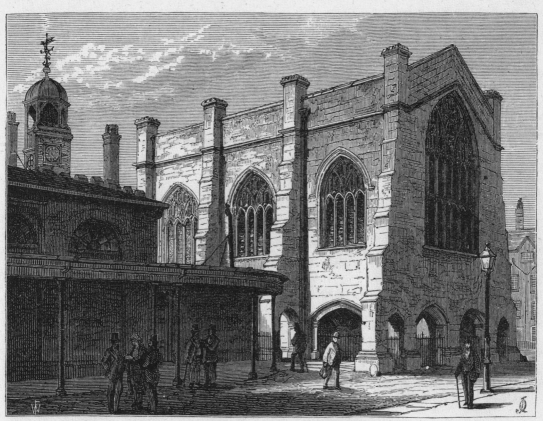

LINCOLN'S INN CHAPEL. (*See page* 54.)

two projecting piers formed into book-cases, is the first apartment entered. The ceiling is formed into compartments, enriched by paintings by the late Henry Howard, R.A. Over the chimney-piece is a portrait of Sir John Soane, painted by Sir Thomas Lawrence, in 1829, almost the last picture painted by that distinguished artist; and beneath this is a highly-finished model in plaster of the Board of Trade and Privy Council Offices, &c., at Whitehall, being a design for completing the buildings north and south of Downing Street, made by Sir John Soane in 1826. This room contains a large number of plaster models of ancient Greek and Roman buildings, such as the Parthenon, the

feet high, comprising works of various forms and nations.

One of the principal apartments in the basement of the building is called the Sepulchral Chamber; and in the centre of it is the splendid ancient Egyptian sarcophagus discovered by the traveller Belzoni in 1817, in a royal tomb in a valley near Thebes. It was purchased by Sir John Soane for the sum of £2,000. The pictures are chiefly in the rooms on the first and second floors, and among them will be seen several by Hogarth, Turner, and Sir Charles Eastlake, and a large number of architectural designs by Sir John Soane himself.

Near the above building stands a palatial

edifice, known as the Inns of Court Hotel. It remained for many years in an unfinished state. In 1874 its appearance was thus graphically described by a writer in one of the illustrated newspapers :—"It is windowless, doorless, and the sky can be seen through the skeleton bones of its untiled roof. It is blackening from exposure to our grimy, smoke-laden atmosphere ; and, for all its bigness of form and solidity of structure, already declining and decaying like a phthisical youth without ever having reached maturity or consummation. It is the monument—after the manner of the broken columns emblematic of mortality, so frequently to be found in cemeteries—of a rage that once existed for monster hotels. The rage is gone—here are its ruins." It was, however, at length taken in hand again, and has been since 1876 one of the busiest and most elegant hotels in London.

Parallel to the northern side of the "Fields," and lying between them and Holborn, is a row of buildings, formerly occupied as houses, and dignified by the name of "Whetstone Park," but afterwards converted into stables. Two hundred years or more ago it was a place of very bad reputation, and was attacked by the London apprentices in 1602. The loose character of Whetstone Park and its inhabitants is a frequent subject of allusion in the plays of Dryden and Shadwell, and occasionally in Butler's "Hudibras" and Ned Ward's *London Spy*. But Whetstone Park is not without at least one distinguished inmate. At all events we read in Philips's "Life of Milton" that the author of " Paradise Lost" " left his great house in Barbican, and betook himself to a smaller (in Holborn) among them that open backward into Lincoln's Inn Fields. Here he lived a private life, still prosecuting his studies and curious search into knowledge."

At each end of this park are narrow foot-entrances leading into Holborn, called the Great and Little Turnstiles, names which testify to the rurality of Lincoln's Inn Fields, when turnstiles were put up to let pedestrians pass through, whilst they checked the straying of the cattle that fed there. Mr. John Timbs says that Turnstile Alley, when first built, was " designed as a change for the sale of Welsh flannels ; " but afterwards both

of these narrow thoroughfares became the homes and haunts of booksellers and publishers. One of these booksellers, Cartwright, was also known in his day as a player, and he left his plays and his pictures to Alleyn's College of "God's Gift" at Dulwich.

The new law buildings belonging to the Society of Lincoln's Inn harmonise finely with the associations of the neighbourhood ; and these, with the low wall of Lincoln's Inn Gardens, occupy the eastern side of the square. Before speaking of these buildings, we may add that this fine open space was very nearly being lost to the public a few years since, for in 1843 the late Sir Charles Barry designed a magnificent structure for the New Courts of Law—which even then were in contemplation—to occupy the centre of Lincoln's Inn Fields. Nearly two hundred years before, a question had been mooted whether it would not be possible to establish an Academy of Painting, the head-quarters of which should have covered the self-same spot. Happily Providence preserved the square on each occasion of danger, and in 1895 the gardens in the centre were acquired by the London County Council and dedicated to the public. At the south-east corner is a handsome four-sided granite fountain, reared in 1889 to commemorate Mr. Philip Twells, a member of Lincoln's Inn, who sat in Parliament for the City of London.

It has always been a matter of complaint that the access to so noble a square on all sides should have been so wretched as it is. It has no direct street leading into it from either Holborn or the Strand, though at the north-east and north-west corners there are the narrow footways known as the Great and Little Turnstiles. From Long Acre it is approached by way of Great Queen Street. At the south-east corner, Serle Street serves as an outlet to Carey Street, and this, with Portsmouth Street at the south-west corner, leads into Chancery Lane, and so on to Fleet Street. Northouck, as far back as 1785, suggested that the " situation " of Covent Garden Market furnished a hint for continuing Great Russell Street in a straight line uniformly to the south-west corner, instead of through Prince's (now Kemble) Street, and Duke Street. But little has yet been done in the way of forming adequate approaches to this fine square.

CHAPTER VIII.

LINCOLN'S INN.

" The walks of Lincoln's Inn
Under the elms."—*Ben Jonson.*

Fortescue's definition of " Inns of Court "—The " Revels"—Regulation of the Growth of Beards—" Mootings"—Lincoln's Inn a mansion of Henry
de Lacy, Earl of Lincoln—Description of the Buildings—The Thurloe Papers—Ben Jonson as a Bricklayer—Humorous Translation of
Inscription on " Foundation stone "—Sir Matthew Hale—The Gardens—History of Lincoln's Inn—Sir Thomas More—Illustrious Members
of Lincoln's Inn.

As distinguished from the Inns of Chancery, such as Barnard's and Staple Inns, Lincoln's Inn is an " Inn of Court ;" in other words, as defined by Waterhouse, the learned commentator on Fortescue, " one of the Hospitia Majora, such as receive not gudgeons and smelts, but the polypuses and leviathans, the behemoths and the giants of the law." How far this remark may be true, and how far an exaggeration, we must leave it to the lawyers of this and other Courts to determine. Fortescue speaks in glowing terms of the Inns of Court in his own time; and, as a member of Lincoln's Inn, he may be presumed to draw his expressions from what he had seen on this spot. He says: "Of the Inns of Court there are four in number. In the least frequented there are about 200 students. In these greater Inns a student cannot well be maintained under £28 a year [equivalent to at least £500 now]. For this reason the students are sons of persons of quality, those of an inferior rank not being able to bear the expenses. There is both in the Inns of Court and the Inns of Chancery a sort of academy or gymnasium, where they learn singing and all kinds of music, and such other accomplishments and diversions (which are called revels) as are suitable to their quality and usually practised at court. Out of term the greater part apply themselves to the study of the law. All vice is discouraged and banished. The greatest nobility of the kingdom often place their children in those Inns of Court, not so much to make the law their study, but to form their manners and to preserve them from the contagion of vice."

Possibly, however, the garrulous old writer has taken rather too *couleur de rose* a view of the domestic virtue taught and practised in his favourite Inns of Court. One subject, however, the celebration of " Revels" at certain seasons of the year within their walls, comes too frequently under the notice of the student of English history to be passed by unnoticed here. The idea of the actual existence of such " Revels" is so much out of keeping with our practical and prosaic age of stuff and silk gowns, and barristers' wigs and the gravity of a judge, that it cannot fail to prove attractive alike to writers and readers. It is to be feared that the popular notion concerning them is drawn by far too exclusively from the lines of Gray, which are not true to fact :—

" The grave Lord Keeper led the brawls,
The seals and maces danced before him."

It would have been far more true to have spoken of the " Revels" as plays performed by the youthful students of each Inn of Court, in the presence of the grave and reverend seigniors of the same.

These " Revels," together with almost every other harmless diversion of the kind, with much that was characteristic of our national manners and habits, would seem to have passed out of use during the time of the Puritan tyranny, which is usually styled the Commonwealth. The plays of Æschylus and Sophocles and of William Shakespeare were alike profane and unholy things in the eyes of these sour-visaged " Saints of the Lord," who tore down the Maypoles in our streets and broke the painted windows that adorned our churches, and which the Reformers had spared. It may, however, be said in their excuse that these " Revels," while they lasted, were got up with great extravagance, and that many a parent suffered for his son's outlay on such " private theatricals." But then, though distasteful to the pockets of paterfamilias, it may be said that they must have been " good for trade."

" Lincoln's Inn," says Charles Knight, in his *Cyclopædia of London*, was never behind the Temple in its masques and Christmas revels ; nor were the exercises of dancing and singing merely permitted, but even insisted on, at this Inn ; for by an order made on February 6th, in the 7th of James I., it appears that " the under-barristers were by decimation *put out of commons* for example's sake, because the whole Bar were offended by their not dancing on the Candlemas Day preceding, according to the ancient order of the Society, when the Judges were present ; and a threat was added, that if the like fault were repeated they should be fined or disbarred."

Very careful provision would seem to have been made by the council or benchers of the

Inn with regard to such minute matters as the apparel of its members, who were bound to dress soberly and to avoid gay colours. On the matter of beards, too, it would seem that they exercised a degree of control which savoured of austerity. For instance, it is on record that the student who wore a beard should pay double for his daily commons and dinner in hall. In the first year of Queen Elizabeth it was ordered "that no fellow of the house should wear a beard of above a fortnight's growth under penalty of loss of commons, and, in case of obstinacy, of final expulsion." Such, however, was the love of long beards, that it triumphed over these sumptuary restrictions, and in November, 1562, all previous orders on the subject were repealed or withdrawn. The long rapier, an appendage of fashion of a still more obnoxious character than the long beard, did not fare equally well. When Elizabeth, whose orders were paramount, ordered watches to be set at each gate of the City to take the measure of every gentleman's sword, and to see that it did not exceed three feet, members of the Inns of Court were obliged to conform, like other citizens, to this standard ; and they were further obliged to lay aside their rapiers on entering their several dining-halls, and to content themselves with the daggers which they wore behind.

The life of a law student at the time of which we speak, when, as at Oxford and Cambridge, the students really lived in their "chambers" instead of in lodgings at a distance, and kept up a real bond of fellowship and social intercourse by the common use of a hall and a chapel, must have presented an immense contrast to the usage of our own day. Even down to so late a period as the close of Elizabeth's reign, we are told, the members of Lincoln's Inn resorted once every year in the summer to Kentish Town, where they dined together and indulged in sports, just as now-a-days the employés of some printing establishment drive off to Richmond or the Crystal Palace to celebrate their "wayz-goose." The, only remnant of the old social customs which once prevailed is to be found in the fact that there is a dinner served daily in the hall during term-time for those who care to partake of it. But this must have been a reality, and only a part of the daily routine of existence at the time when the collegiate system was not as yet wholly banished from the Inns of Court, when men really lived in their chambers and spent their lives in their Inn, at all events until they took on themselves the responsibility of a wife and a domestic establishment. Nor was their legal education neglected even at the dinner-table ; for

at each mess it was a rule that there was to be a "moot" daily. We all of us speak of a "moot-point," but few, perhaps, understand its meaning. The junior member of each mess had to propound to the rest at his table some knotty question of law, which was discussed by each in turn during the dinner. This excellent custom, however, still kept up as it is by members of many religious orders in the Roman Catholic Church, has long since disappeared from the Hall of Lincoln's Inn, although there is extant and probably unrepealed a standing order of the reign of Edward VI., to the effect that every junior at each mess during dinner should "put to the rest a short case of one point which was to be argued thoroughly."

It is obvious that while the lawyer must have an especial, he cannot feel that he has an exclusive, interest in the early history of the Inns of Court, which form so considerable a part of the antiquities of the metropolis. The buildings of Lincoln's Inn for instance, though consecrated to the legal profession for the past five or six hundred years, if they could speak of their earlier years, would tell us of Knights Templars, and of the proud house of De Lacy, Earls of Lincoln, and of more than one bishop who held the Great Seal in the days of the Plantagenets.

If our imagination could carry us back to the thirteenth century, we should notice, as we walked up what now is Chancery Lane, but then was known as New Street, leading from the Temple Bar up to "Old Bourne," the palace of the Bishops of Chichester, the mansion of Henry de Lacy, Earl of Lincoln, and the beautiful church of the Knights Templars, resplendent with the solemn services which were daily celebrated within it. It is from this Earl of Lincoln that what is now "Lincoln's Inn" derives its name ; and it is the opinion of the learned antiquary, Francis Thynne, that it was constituted a regular Inn of Court not long after that nobleman's death in 1312. Those of the buildings which still remain, however, are not older than the Tudor times, the old gateway and the hall having been both erected in the reign of Henry VII. The frontage of these old buildings facing Chancery Lane is about 500 feet in length. The gatehouse is a fine specimen of late red brickwork of a Gothic type, and is now almost the only example of that sort of work to be found in London. The principal gateway, and the two flanking towers on either side, still stand in the same condition as when they were first erected, except that their red colour has been dulled by three centuries and a half of dust and smoke ; but the windows for the most part have been modernised, much to the loss oi picturesque effect. Over the gateway are still to be seen three shields of arms in as many square compartments. The first are those of Lacy, Earl of Lincoln; those in the centre are the royal arms of England; and the third and last are the bearings of the actual builder of the gate, Sir Thomas Lovel, Knight. Beneath these is the date A.D. 1518. These heraldic sculptures were repaired and redecorated in 1815.

It was rumoured some years ago that this gateway was to be removed at no distant date, in accordance with a plan for rebuilding the suites of chambers on one uniform plan; but happily little has been heard more recently of this "improvement." We should be sorry to lose the venerable but somewhat gloomy edifice, on account of the many illustrious personages with whom its memory is associated, and who must have passed beneath its portals on their way to "chambers"—Sir Thomas More, Lord Keeper Egerton, Dr. Donne, Sir Henry Spelman, Sir Matthew Hale, Sir John Durham, Attorney-General Noy, Rushworth, Lord Thurlow, Lord Shaftesbury, Lord Mansfield, Lord Eldon, and Lord Erskine.

Some of the brick buildings adjoining the gateway in Chancery Lane are of a later date than the entrance itself; and it is in all probability to this portion of the structure that quaint old Fuller alludes when he writes of Ben Jonson, that "he helped in the building of the new structure in Lincoln's Inn, and having a trowel in one hand, he had a book in his pocket."

Mr. Peter Cunningham tells us that in the south angle of the great court leading out of Chancery Lane, formerly called the Gatehouse Court, but now Old Buildings, in No. 24, in the apartments on the ground-floor on the left-hand side, Thurloe, the secretary to Oliver Cromwell, had chambers from 1645 to 1659. Cromwell himself must often have darkened by his presence this doorway; and here, by the merest accident, long after Thurloe's death, his papers and correspondence with the Lord Protector and other members of the Roundhead party were discovered, having lain for years concealed behind a false ceiling. Mr. John Timbs, in his "Romance of London," relates a curious anecdote concerning these chambers, to the effect that one evening Oliver Cromwell came thither to talk over with Thurloe a plot for seizing the person of Prince Charles, then at Bruges, and his brothers the Dukes of York and Gloucester, when, finding Thurloe's clerk asleep at his desk, he drew his dagger to kill him, thinking (as was really the case) that he had been overheard, and was with difficulty stopped by his secretary from carrying out

his design. The young clerk found means to warn the royal party of their danger, and the plot fell through. If this story be really true, it may safely be asserted that in this very set of chambers English royalty has been saved.

The "Thurloe Papers," it may be added on the self-same authority, were disposed of by the discoverer to Lord Chancellor Somers, who caused them to be bound up in sixty-seven volumes in folio, and they form the principal part of the collections afterwards published by Dr. Birch, and known by the name of the "Thurloe State Papers."

The old hall, as seen through the archway leading into the court from Chancery Lane, with its high-pitched roof externally, has all the appearance of a monastic building, from its buttresses and pointed windows. It is situated in the first court opposite the entrance gate; it was erected in the twenty-second year of King Henry VII., so that it is nearly of the same date with the gateway; its appearance, however, is very different from the dull red brick of the entrance, being covered with an exterior coating of white plaster or stucco. It has undergone alterations at various dates, and in 1819 it was lengthened by ten or twelve feet, and the present unsightly modern ceiling was substituted for the fine open roof of oak, which was removed or concealed. The hall is about 70 feet by 30, and 32 feet high. "It was divided," says Mr. Spilsbury, the Librarian of Lincoln's Inn, "in 1853, by permission of the benchers, in order to form two courts, the one for the Lord Chancellor, and the other for the Lords Justices of Appeal, until suitable accommodation can be provided by the country for the administration of justice." In 1874 the partition was removed. At the upper end used to be a picture of Paul before Felix, painted for the society by Hogarth, who was paid £200 for the work, as may be seen from his framed autograph letter acknowledging the receipt of the money. This picture, together with a statue of Lord Eldon by Westmacott, has been removed to the new hall. The heraldic achievements in stained glass with which the windows were formerly enriched, as well as those of the panels of the walls, have also been removed to the new hall, where, too, are several other fine-art treasures.

Here were held all the "Revels" of the society, in which the benchers themselves indulged. Dancing was especially enjoined, and was thought to conduce to the end of making gentlemen more fit for their books at other times. One of the latest "Revels," at which King Charles II. was present, is noticed both by Evelyn and Pepys in their respective diaries. On a second visit of that monarch to Lincoln's Inn, on the 27th of February, 1671, he was accompanied by his brother, the Duke of York, Prince Rupert, the Duke of Monmouth, and others of the nobility. These illustrious and distinguished personages were admitted members of the Honourable Society, and entered their names

edifice; but there is evidence which proves conclusively that the present building was erected in the reign of James I., and that the old chapel was standing at the time of the consecration of the new one. It was built from the designs of Inigo Jones, and consecrated in 1623. Ben Jonson is said to

ESSEX WATER GATE, ESSEX STREET, STRAND. (*See page* 68.)

in the Admittance Book, where their signatures are preserved." Hogarth's picture, mentioned above, it may be interesting here to remark, was painted at the instigation of Lord Mansfield, as the best way of expending a legacy of £200 left to the benchers.

The chapel possesses features of peculiar interest. It has been the opinion of some antiquaries that it is a restoration or reconstruction of a much earlier

have assisted with his trowel in the building of this chapel, as well as of the outer wall already mentioned. Its size is 60 by 40 feet, and it is about 44 feet high. The windows are filled with stained glass of very brilliant colours, and the carved work of the oaken seats is of very chaste design, and superior execution, as specimens of the style prevailing in the reign of James I. The crypt under the chapel, now dwarfed by the gradual raising of

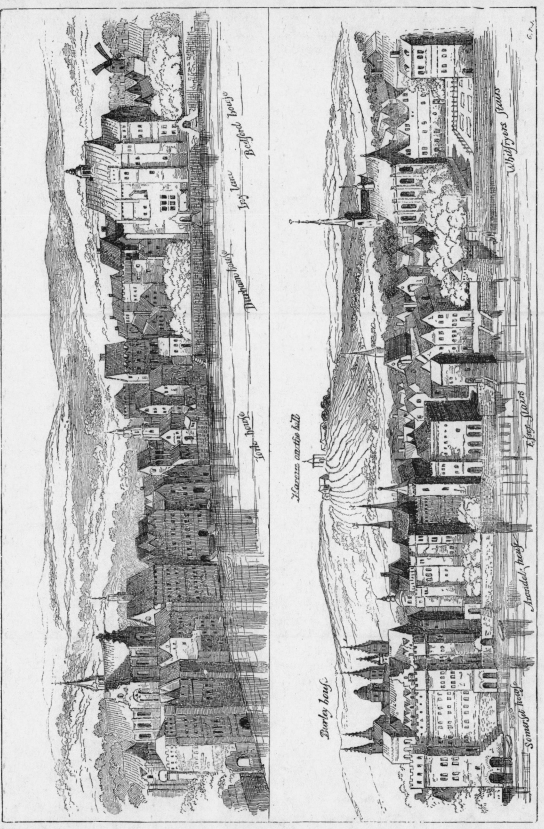

Bedford hou.^{se}

Ivy Lane

Durham house

York house

Houses on the hill

Burley hous.^e

Somerset house

Arundel house

Essex Stairs

Whitefryers Stairs

THE STRAND FROM THE THAMES, SIXTEENTH CENTURY.

the ground, was built, like the cloisters in the Temple, as a place for the students and lawyers " to walk in and talk and confer their learnings." Mr. Peter Cunningham reminds us that the round nave of the Temple Church was formerly used for a like purpose, and Butler and Pepys both allude to the custom. This crypt was long reserved as a burial-place for the benchers of the Inn. In it sleeps Secretary Thurloe, and near him repose Alexander Brome, the Cavalier song-writer, and William Prynne, already mentioned, who wrote against the unloveliness of love-locks, and the inscription on whose grave was already blotted out when Wood wrote his "Athenæ Oxonienses." The chapel was enlarged in 1882–83.

The present noble hall and library, built of red brick, with stone dressings, by the late Mr. Philip Hardwick, R.A., was commenced in 1843. The first stone of the hall was laid on the 20th of April in that year by Sir James Lewis Knight-Bruce, the treasurer of the society. It bears the following inscription :—

> " Stet lapis, arboribus nudo defixus in horto,
> Fundamen pulchræ tempus in omne domûs.
> Aula vetus lites et legum ænigmata servet,
> Ipsa novo exorior nobilitanda coquo.
> XXIJ. CAL. MAIJ, MDCCCXLIIJ."

The inscription was humorously translated by the late Sir George Rose as follows :—

> " The trees of yore
> Are seen no more :
> Unshaded now the garden lies.
> May the red bricks,
> Which here we fix,
> Be lasting as our equities.
> The olden dome
> With musty tome
> Of law and litigation suits :
> In this we look
> For a better ' cook ' *
> Than he who wrote the ' Institutes.' "

The library was originally 80 feet long, but in 1873 it received an addition of 50 feet to its length. The present dimensions are 130 feet by 40 feet, and 44 feet high. The original foundation of this library is of earlier date than any now existing in the metropolis, namely, 1497. At the time of the removal of the books to the present building, in 1845, the number of volumes was about 18,000. It has since gone on increasing, so that the library now contains about 40,000 volumes, on law, jurisprudence, history, and other cognate and collateral studies. In addition to the collection of law books, admitted to be the most complete in this country, the shelves of the library are well furnished with books in historical and various other classes of literature. The Reports of Cases in England are extant in a regular series from the reign of Edward II., from whose time to that of Henry VIII. they were taken by the prothonotaries, or chief scribes of the court, at the expense of the Crown, and published annually, whence they are known under the denomination of the " Year Book." Here also is an unique copy of the fourth volume of " Prynne's Records," purchased in 1849 at the sale at Stowe for £335. Here likewise is preserved the collection of legal MSS. and books bequeathed to the Inn by Sir Matthew Hale, " a treasure," he says in his will, " that is not fit for every man's view." The formation of this library was commenced as early as the reign of Henry VII., and the acquisition of books received a great impulse by an order issued in the early part of the reign of James I., to the effect that every person called to the Bar should contribute to it 13s. 4d., and every bencher on his election 20s. In the Council Room of the society is the portrait of Sir Matthew Hale, by Wright.

Stone Buildings—so called from the material of which they are built—lie at the north-eastern extremity of Lincoln's Inn. The range of buildings forms part of a design made in 1780 for rebuilding the whole Inn. The structure is commodious and imposing when viewed from the gardens, or even from Lincoln's Inn Fields. Part of the eastern side of Lincoln's Inn, abutting upon Chancery Lane, was rebuilt in 1880–81. The new buildings are of red brick, with stone dressings.

The houses in New Square were built in the reign of Charles II. In the open space in the centre of the square there was formerly a Corinthian column, bearing a vertical sun-dial. The houses, which form three sides of the square—as stated, indeed, in a previous chapter—were formerly called Serle's Court, having been erected in 1682 by Henry Serle, one of the benchers of Lincoln's Inn. They are of brick, and are wholly occupied as chambers, many of the most eminent members of the Bar and legal profession holding them. It may be worth while to record here the fact that Sir Samuel Romilly had chambers at Nos. 2 and 6, Sir William Grant at No. 3, and at No. 11 Lord Selborne, whilst as yet only Sir Roundell Palmer. The site upon which New Square is built was originally called Fickett's Field, or Little Lincoln's Inn Field. The garden in the centre was railed and planted in 1845 ; and in 1867 was erected, within the enclosure, the temporary building for the exhibition of the designs for the New Law Courts.

The gardens of Lincoln's Inn, though not

---

* Alluding to Coke's "Institutes," a legal work of high reputation.

washed like those of the Temple, by the "silver" Thames, and though not possessing equal historical associations with the spot where the White and Red Rose were chosen as the badges of two rival and royal houses, were not and indeed are not without a beauty of their own; and the fine elms which they contain are an ornament to the neighbourhood. They were famous of old, however, but have been much curtailed by the erection of the new hall and library at the south-western angle. There is a fine and broad terrace walk; but "the walk under the elms," celebrated by Ben Jonson, has disappeared. In these gardens, as we learn from the *Tatler* (No. 100), old Isaac Bickerstaffe delighted to walk, being privileged to do so by his friends amongst the benchers, who had grown old along there with himself. In the time of the old Earls of Lincoln the gardens are said to have been most fruitful, supplying apples, nuts, and cherries in great abundance, as well as flowers and "kitchen herbs," the produce of which, over and above what was needed for his lordship's household, brought in to the steward of the estate a large sum annually.

The readers of Pepys' "Diary" will scarcely need to be reminded here of the following entry, as it has been so often quoted before:—" 27 June, 1663. To Lincoln's Inn, and there walked up and down to see the new garden which they are making, and will be very pretty, and so to walk under the chapel by agreement."

As to the past history of Lincoln's Inn, a part of its site was occupied in ancient times by the church and house of a body of "preaching friars," who came to England in 1221, and received much encouragement and great support in London. Hubert de Burgh, the powerful Earl of Kent, who died in 1252, and was buried in their church, left to them his house in Westminster, which was nothing less than the ancient White Hall, afterwards York House, of which we shall have to speak presently. The friars sold it to the Archbishop of York, who left it an heirloom to his successors in the see.

In 1250 the friars of this order held a grand convocation at their house, when no less than 500 churchmen were present. On the first day of their meeting, Henry III. attended their chapter, and sat with them at their table to a dinner which his royal self had provided. Afterwards the queen did the same, and her example was followed by the Bishop of London, the Abbots of Westminster, St. Albans, Waltham, and others. Here the friars continued until 1276, when the Mayor and other influential citizens of London gave

them a piece of ground near Baynard's Castle, between Ludgate and the Thames, to build a new monastery and church, which was afterwards known as the "Black Friars." The old house appears to have been the property of William de Haverill, the King's Treasurer, and on his attainder for treason, to have been given by the Crown to Ralph de Nevill, Bishop of Chichester, and Lord Chancellor, who built there a large house which he occupied till his death in 1244. The memory of the bishop is retained in the name of a small court between the Inn and Chancery Lane, still called "Chichester Rents." Having passed through one intermediate owner, it became the residence of Henry de Lacy, Earl of Lincoln, to whom Edward I. made a present also of the old friars' house. The two thus joined together formed a residence for the earl; and hence the place was styled his "Inn," meaning his lodging or house. It is said that the earl introduced law students into his "Inn" as early as the year 1310; but this is at best doubtful. Nor is it clear, nor do historians or antiquaries tell us, how the Bishops of Chichester again became the owners of the "Inn." Such, however, apparently was the case, for they held it until the beginning of the sixteenth century, when Robert Sherborne, bishop of that see, conveyed it to an Essex gentlemen named Sulyard, whose family conveyed it, in 1579, to William Kingsmith and the rest of the benchers for the modest sum of £520.

As the title-deeds of Lincoln's Inn do not go further back than December, 1535, its early history is naturally involved in no little obscurity. The tradition of its establishment in the reign of Edward III., is highly probable, although no evidence of a documentary nature can be adduced to prove it. The first mention of the four Inns of Court — of which Lincoln's Inn beyond a doubt was one—occurs in the writings of Fortescue, who wrote in the latter half of the fifteenth century. According to the received opinion, Lincoln's Inn had flourished for a century and a half before Fortescue wrote; but certainly we meet with no record of any distinguished student within its walls at that date. From a record of the same age with Fortescue, namely, the "Black Book" of the Inn itself, we find that, whether it was the oldest of the four Inns of Court or not, at all events it was the first which instituted a settled order of government, and made provision for the needs of legal education. This Black Book commences in 1423, and gives the name of Fortescue himself as one of its governors or benchers. In 1440 the governors began to be formally sworn on taking office, and the students on admission were also required to take an oath of obedience to that body. In 1464 the Society of Lincoln's Inn made an important step of progress in their organisation of legal education, by appointing a "reader" to give readings in the law to the students during the vacation of the courts. The first reader whose name is recorded is William Huddersfield. The persons chosen as readers were the most eminent lawyers of the day under the degree of serjeant. A reader in 1475, and again in 1481, was Sir Thomas Lovel, who built the gatehouse of the Inn. The name of John More, the autumn reader for 1489, introduces us to an episode in the history of the Inn. In 1464 John More was raised from the office of butler to that of steward. In 1470 his long and faithful services in those two capacities were rewarded by his admission to be a member of the society, and in 1489, and again in 1495, he held the high and honourable office of reader. His son John succeeded the father in the office of butler, and enjoyed the like promotion. The son of this latter John More was the illustrious Sir Thomas More, the chancellor and martyr. On Sir Thomas More's conduct upon the woolsack it was said, in the punning style of the day :—

> "When More some years had Chancellor been,
>   No *more* suits did remain ;
>   The same shall never *more* be seen,
>   Till More be there again."

Allen, in his "History of London," remarks of this Inn that "it ranks next to the Temple, which it equals in the number of eminent lawyers that it has produced." Of these it may be sufficient to mention Sir John Fortescue, one of the "fathers of the English law," who held the Great Seal under Henry VI. ; that virtuous chancellor, Sir Thomas More ; the learned antiquary, Sir Henry Spelman ; the great Sir Matthew Hale, and Lord Chancellor Egerton. Prynne, the well-known victim of Star Chamber tyranny, was also a member of this society. For an alleged libel in the "Histrio-Mastix" he was condemned by that court to pay a fine of £5,000, to lose his ears, to stand in the pillory, and to be imprisoned for life. Nor did the odious sentence end there, for the Chamber, "assuming an authority co-extensive with its vindictiveness," ordered Prynne to be expelled from the University of Oxford and also from the Society of Lincoln's Inn.

The Inns of Court have deservedly been styled "the noblest nurseries of humanity and liberty in the kingdom." They are four in number, viz., the Inner Temple, the Middle Temple, Lincoln's Inn, and Gray's Inn. They are called Inns of *Court*,

because they were anciently held in the Aula Regia, or Court of the King's Palace. They are governed by a self-elected body of benchers, consisting of the most distinguished and successful members of the Bar. The distinction between barristers and solicitors is still maintained ; but it is provided that a student who, at any time before his admission to an Inn of Court, had been in practice as a solicitor for not less than five consecutive years, but who had ceased to be a solicitor prior to his admission as a student, may be examined for Call to the Bar without keeping any Terms, and upon passing the examination may be at once called.

At what time students were first admitted into Lincoln's Inn seems to be a doubtful point. Malcolm, on the authority of an old heraldic MS. which styles the Inn "an ancient ally unto the Middle Temple," observes that "there is no mention of any flourishing estate of the students and professors of the common law resident in this college till the reign of Henry VI., when it appears by the rolls and remembrance of that house the same then began to be famous."

Since the year 1581, when the first appointment of preacher to the society appears to have been made, many of the most eloquent and distinguished divines of the Church of England have filled the office, amongst whom have been Archbishop Tillotson, Dr. Donne, Thomas Gataker, and Dr. Hurd ; Bishops Warburton, Heber, and Maltby ; and Archbishop Thomson. In fact, the Preachership of Lincoln's Inn has often been regarded as a "stepping-stone to a bishopric."

Among the most illustrious students, benchers, treasurers, and members of this Inn have been Sir Robert Atkins, Lord Chief Baron of the Exchequer, *temp*. William III. ; Sir John Fortescue ; Anthony, first Earl of Shaftesbury ; Lord Southampton ; Archbishop Tillotson ; Sir Arthur Plantagenet, natural son of Edward IV. ; Sir Joseph Jekyll ; Sir Thomas Egerton, Lord Keeper of the Great Seal, *temp*. Elizabeth ; Sir Thomas More, Chancellor of England, already mentioned ; the Earl of Hardwicke ; Lord Talbot ; Sir Robert Walpole ; Sir Matthew Hale, whose gift to the library is noticed above ; Lord Mansfield ; Lord Walsingham ; Dr. Warburton, Bishop of Gloucester ; Lord Camden ; Lord Henley ; William Pitt ; Addington, afterwards Lord Sidmouth ; Lord Ellenborough, the Chief Justice ; the Right Hon. Spencer Perceval ; Lord Dunfermline ; and at least seven Lord Chancellors of our own day, Brougham, Cottenham, Campbell, Selborne, Hatherley, Cranworth, and Herschell.

CHAPTER IX.

THE STRAND—INTRODUCTORY AND HISTORICAL.

"Come, Fortescue, sincere, experienced friend,
Thy briefs, thy deeds, and e'en thy fees suspend ;
Come, let us leave the Temple's silent walls ;

My business to my distant lodging calls ;
Through the long Strand together let us stray,
With thee conversing, I forget the way."—*Gay.*

Condition of the Strand in the Days of the Plantagenets and Tudors—Rules for Hackney Coaches—Taylor, the "Water Poet"—Origin of the Name of the Strand—Graphic Sketch of the Strand Five Centuries ago—New Paving Act—State Pageants—Temple Bar in Danger.

DURING the reign of Henry VIII. an active stir had commenced for the reparation of streets and highways in and about the metropolis, and the necessity for such improvement is fully shown by the words of the royal statute which was then enacted for the purpose. In granting permission to lay out a new road in the Weald of Kent, which formed an important thoroughfare to London, we are told that "many other common ways in the said Weald be so deep and so noyous, by wearing and course of water and other occasions, that people cannot have their carriages or passages by horses, upon or by the same, but to their great pains, peril, or jeopardy." Nor in approaching London was the case improved, in several instances at least; for the suburban districts, as yet only villages separated from the City by fields, gardens, and a sprinkling of cottages, were connected with the City by a highway, often left in grievous disrepair through the negligence of the inhabitants. Such was the case even with that great artery of the metropolis—the Strand—of which we are about to treat.

Frequented though it was, and necessary for the comfort of the City, yet this highway, in the thirty-fourth and thirty-fifth years of Henry VIII., is described as a road "full of pits and sloughs, very perilous and noisome." There is extant somewhere or other in the Rolls of Parliament, a complaint of the high-road between the Temple "and the village of Charing" being so deep in mire as to be almost impassable. In fact it had earned a thoroughly bad character. It was described in the statute above quoted as "very noyous and foul, and in many places thereof very jeopardous to all people passing and repassing, as well on horseback as on foot, both in winter and in summer, by night and by day." By this route, however, Cardinal Wolsey, when residing in Chancery Lane, used to ride down to Westminster Hall, in all the magnificence which befitted a "Prince of the Church," as already described in the first volume of this work (page 81).

In speaking, however, of the disgraceful condition of the high-road between London and Westminster in the days of the Plantagenets, we are in danger, perhaps, of forgetting the fact that at that time the traffic along it consisted mainly of foot passengers, or riders on horseback, carriages being then almost as unknown as hansom cabs or omnibuses. Elizabeth, as we know, rode usually on a pillion, even on state occasions; and fifty years after her, we are told, there were only thirty vehicles on wheels in the whole of London. No wonder, therefore, that many of our old thoroughfares are still narrow in the extreme.

In the present admirably-paved state of the streets of the metropolis, the following statement relative to the Strand, Charing Cross, and Parliament Street, must appear strange :—" In 1353, the road from London to Westminster had become so dangerous for the transit of passengers or carriage of goods, as to demand the interference of Government. A mandate was therefore directed, in the name of the king and council, dated Westminster, Nov. 20, to John de Bedeforde, of London, appointing him the commissioner for the paving of the road in question. This instrument recites, that the highway leading from the gate called Temple Bar, London, to the door of Westminster Abbey, by the frequent passage of carts, horses, merchandise, and provisions, to the Staple at Westminster, ever since its establishment, had become so deep and muddy, and the pavement so much injured and broken, that unless soon repaired, great perils must be incurred by the passage both of men and of carriages. In order to remedy this evil, therefore, it was ordained that the foot-pavement adjoining to the houses on the line of the road should be newly laid, at the expense of the owners of the nearest houses; and that money should be levied by tolls on goods sold at the Staple, to defray the charge of paving the road between the kennels on each side."

In 1625 there were *twenty* hackney coaches in London ; but they multiplied so rapidly, that in ten years afterwards Government took the alarm at their general use, and endeavoured to limit it, upon the plea that these carriages " disturbed the ears of king, queen, and nobles, jostled horse and foot passengers, tore up the streets and pavements, and increased the price of hay and horse provender." It was therefore ordered "that no hackney or hired coaches be used or suffered in London, Westminster, or the suburbs thereof, except they be to travel at least three miles out of the same; and also, that no person shall go in a coach in the said streets, except the owner of the coach shall constantly keep up four able horses for our (the king's) service when required." But the time had gone by when such despotic edicts were in force; and Cromwell himself, we are told, was destined soon after to drive four-in-hand, in Jehu fashion, through this forbidden territory, and be capsized for his pains.

Scarcely had this innovation been commenced in London, when Taylor, the "Water Poet," who plied a scull upon the Thames, exclaimed, "They have undone my poor trade!" Speaking of the coaches, he adds, "This infernal swarm of trade spillers have so overrun the land, that we can get no living on the water; for I dare truly affirm, that every day in any term, especially if the court be at Whitehall, they do rob us of our livings, and carry five hundred and sixty fares daily from us." Alluding also to the confusion produced by this startling civic revolution, he adds, "I pray you look into the streets, and the chambers or lodgings in Fleet Street or the Strand, how they are pestered with them (coaches), especially after a mask or a play at the court, where even the very earth quakes and trembles, the casements shatter, tatter, and clatter, and such a confused noise is made, so that a man can neither sleep, speak, hear, write, nor eat his dinner or supper quiet for them."

The scene occasionally presented by the Strand through its entire length, if we may believe such an eyewitness as John Evelyn, was very gay and brilliant. He writes in his Diary, "May 29, 1660. This day his majestie, Charles II., came to London, after a sad and long exile and calamitous suffering both of the king and church, being seventeen years. This was also his birthday, and with a triumph above 20,000 horse and foot, brandishing their swords and shouting with inexpressible joy; the ways strew'd with flowers, the bells ringing, the streets hung with tapestry, fountains running with wine; the mayor, aldermen, and all the companies in their liveries, chains of gold, and banners; lords and nobles clad in cloth of silver, gold, and velvet; the windowes and balconies well set with ladies; trumpets, music, and myriads of people flocking even so far as from Rochester, so as they were seven hours in passing the City, even from two till ten at night. I stood in the Strand and beheld it, and bless'd God. And all this was done without one drop of

bloodshed, and by that very army which rebelled against him; but it was the Lord's doings, for such a restoration was never mentioned in any history, ancient or modern, since the return of the Jews from the Babylonish captivity; nor so joyful a day and so bright ever seen in this nation, this happening when to expect or effect it was past all human policy."

To pass on to a somewhat later date, we are told by Malcolm that when, in 1689, the number of hackney carriages in London was limited by Act of Parliament to 400, the inhabitants of the Strand and Fleet Street petitioned against any increase in their numbers, on the ground that "they prevented the quality from getting to their shops!"

During the time of Queen Elizabeth, considerable improvement had been effected by the filling up of the gaps or blanks left between the dwellings that had already been built along the Strand; and by the end of her long reign, both sides of this line of route had been nearly covered with the mansions of the nobility, so that Westminster may be said at that time to have been joined on to London. The still rural character, however, of the districts abutting on the north side, at the time when the Strand was only an unpaved road, may be gathered from the existence to our own day of such names as the Convent (Covent) Garden, Long Acre, St. Martin's-in-the-Fields, and Lincoln's Inn Fields, most of which were open country at the date of the earliest existing map of the metropolis.

The name of the Strand is clearly of Saxon and not of Norman origin; and, if we may trust a writer in the *Penny Cyclopædia*, it is mentioned by name in the Saxon Chronicle. And as a proof of the statement it is recorded that upon the Strand Earl Godwin and his son Harold drew up their land forces in the insurrection which they headed against Edward the Confessor, in A.D. 1052.

We find this thoroughfare sometimes spoken of as "the High Street of Westminster, commonly called the Strand," as, for instance, in the lease by which Sir Wm. Cecil agrees to take his property in this neighbourhood for a term of years from the Earl of Bedford. The lease is printed *in extenso* in the thirtieth volume of the "Archæologia."

The following graphic sketch, which we take from *All the Year Round*, carries us back to the Strand of five hundred years ago:—

"Beyond the Bars is the river-side road, called 'Strand Street.' It was sorely in need of paving until lately, when a tax for its repair was levied on all goods carried along it to the Staple at Westminster. Here, many lords, spiritual and temporal, have goodly Inns, of which you can see but two or three : the Bishop of Exeter's close on the left ; the Bishop of Bath's beyond it ; and the Bishop of Chester's, with the old stone cross before it. At that cross the Judges have sometimes sat to try pleas. The palace which you can just see to the left is the Savoy, so called from Peter, Count of Savoy, who built it in the reign of our Henry III.,

The church among the fields in the distance is St. Martin's."

Between the Strand and the river-side there are four or five great and noble families whose names and histories are interwoven with the vicinity. Nearest to Temple Bar, the Devereuxes, Earls of Essex ; next the Howards, of the ducal family of

MILFORD LANE IN 1820. (*See page* 70.)

whose Queen was the Count's niece. Now the Duke of Lancaster is the owner thereof, and John, the captive King of France, lodged there not long since. The bridge over the lane in the centre of the road is called 'Strand Bridge.' On the right of St. Clement Danes Church you see the wells of St. Clement and Holy Well ; and, beyond them, the vineyard and convent garden of the Abbey of Westminster, skirted by the woods of Long Acre.

Norfolk ; then the Protector Somerset ; the Cecils, Earls of Salisbury and Exeter ; and Villiers, Duke of Buckingham ; to say nothing of the proud line of Percy, Dukes of Northumberland, who up to 1874 kept up their town residence at Charing Cross. About one and all of these in succession we shall have plenty to say in the next few pages.

Mr. A. Wood, in his "Ecclesiastical Antiquities of London," tells us that "the Abbot of Westminster had a garden on the banks of the Thames, where Westminster and London join, near St. Clement Danes. It was called the 'Frère Pye Garden,' and stood opposite to the palaces of the Bishops of Durham and Carlisle." The site is fixed by its garden, which is now Covent Garden.

The town house of the Duke of Beaufort in the reign of Charles II. stood here, on the site of what now are known as Beaufort Buildings; but the family removed thence to Beaufort House at Chelsea in 1682. Then there was Essex House, and the Inn of the Bishops of Norwich (afterwards York House), which as far back as the reign of Edward III. spread out their embattled fronts towards the Strand, while their extensive gardens, terraces, and water-stairs sloped down to the river. Spelman says that in the troublous times of the Tudors most of the houses of the prelates in the Strand were taken from them by courtiers "without any recompense."

Among the characteristic features of the Strand at this period were the bridges that spanned the various water-courses flowing from the meadows and open fields on the north, and crossing this thoroughfare in their way to the Thames. One or two of these bridges were kept in remembrance down to comparatively recent times in the names of Ivy Bridge Lane and Strand Bridge Lane, of the latter of which—now simply Strand Lane— we shall have to speak presently, in connection with the old Roman bath which is situated there. Then there was the stone cross, of which old Stow speaks as being situated in front of the spot now occupied by St. Mary's Church, and which in its turn gave place to the famous Maypole, thus alluded to in the "Dunciad," and of which we shall speak hereafter :—

"Amidst the area wide they took their stand,
Where the tall Maypole once o'erlook'd the Strand ;
But now, as Anne and Piety ordain,
A church collects the saints of Drury Lane."

Stow states that the Liberty of the Duchy of Lancaster extended from Temple Bar to the east side of Cecil Street, near what is now the Adelphi, and from the stocks just outside Temple Bar to "a stone cross, now headless," over against the Maypole in the Strand, and along by Exeter Change and Burleigh Street.

The foot-pavement of this quarter of the town, as well as of other parts of Westminster, would seem to have been in a deplorable state as recently as the year 1762, when a new paving Act was passed. Until that time, it appears, every inhabitant did before his own house just what was right in his own eyes, without rule or plan. The

consequence was that some parts of the footway were paved admirably, some indifferently, and some were left unpaved—mere pools of mud and water—according to the wealth or caprice of each resident. A proof of the general filth of this part of the Strand may be found in the *London Chronicle* of the time, where we read, *apropos* of the new measure of reform, "All sorts of dirt and ashes, oyster-shells, the offals of fish, poultry, and other kinds of meat, will now no longer be suffered to be thrown loose into the streets, but must be kept until the dustman comes round ; nor will the annoyances erected by coachmakers be permitted ; and when a house is pulled down the rubbish must be carried to the proper place, and not left on the footway."

In the description of the Strand given by him in 1807, Pennant complains of the street as being in some places too narrow for the incredible number of persons and carriages passing through it.

The Strand has witnessed in its day some strange and curious sights. For instance, we read that Queen Elizabeth, when she rode into the City, sat on a pillion behind her Lord Chancellor, wagons and the newly-invented "carriages" being in disfavour with her Majesty. Among the numerous pageants which the thoroughfare of the Strand has witnessed may be mentioned the procession of Queen Elizabeth in state to St. Paul's, to return thanks for the victories over the Spanish Armada. Queen Anne passed this way in state to St. Paul's on several occasions, to commemorate victories over France and Spain. In 1704 there was a state visit to the City to celebrate the victory of Blenheim ; and in like manner have been commemorated the victories of Ramillies and other important triumphs. Then there was the religious ceremonial when George III. and his consort went in state to St. Paul's to offer a nation's thanks for its king's recovery; the solemn conveyance of captured banners and the great naval procession to St. Paul's, headed by the King, in 1797 ; the funeral procession of Lord Nelson in 1806, and that of the Duke of Wellington in 1852 ; and the visits of Queen Victoria, when she went in state to dine at Guildhall, and to open the new Exchange, in 1872 to return thanks for the recovery of the Prince of Wales, and in 1887 on the occasion of her Jubilee.

But probably none of these pageants ever presented a scene so striking as when the gates of Temple Bar were opened at the approach of the second Charles on his restoration, and the King, brought back to his own again, rode gallantly through the City to Whitehall. The houses of the Strand were adorned with the richest tapestry, and window, balcony, and scaffold were crowded with all that was beautiful and loyal. The streets were lined with members of the City companies in their liveries, and the loud music of the trained-bands, and the din of the bells from a hundred steeples, were drowned in the cheers of the enthusiastic populace. This event appears all the more impressive when contrasted with the rueful spectacle presented by Temple Bar just eighty years later, when the heads of the most devoted followers of the house of Stuart were exposed over its gates, as if in bitter derision of the monarchs of the exiled Stuart line whose effigies adorned its niches.

Temple Bar—almost the last relic of the geographical sovereignty of London—had for many years previous to its removal, as already recorded by us (see page 20 *ante*), been in an utterly hopeless and forlorn condition; in fact, it was latterly propped up and supported by wooden beams,

otherwise it would probably have fallen. Its demolition was first suggested rather more than a century ago, as is clear from the following lines which were written on the report of its proposed removal as far back as 1788 :—

"THE METROPOLITAN PROPHECY.

" If that gate is pulled down, 'twixt the Court and the City,
　You'll blend in one mass prudent, worthless, and witty;
　If you league cit and lordling, as brother and brother,
　You'll break Order's chain, and they'll war with each other.
　Like the great wall of China, it keeps out the Tartars
　From making irruptions where industry barters.
　Like Samson's wild foxes they'll fire your houses,
　And madden your spinsters, and cozen your spouses ;
　They'll destroy in one sweep both the mart and the forum,
　Which your fathers held dear and their fathers before 'em."

But it is time to pass from these general remarks to a more detailed account of the thoroughfare of which we treat.

CHAPTER X.

THE STRAND :—SOUTHERN TRIBUTARIES.

" Westward the tide of Empire makes its way."

Thanet Place—The old " Rose " Tavern—Palsgrave Place—The " Palsgrave's Head "—Andrew Marvell—The London and Westminster Joint-Stock Bank—Messrs. Strahan, Paul, and Bates—Messrs. Twining and Co.'s Bank and Tea-warehouse—" George's Hotel "—Devereux Court—" Tom's Coffee House "—The " Grecian "—Eldon Chambers.

EXTENDING from Fleet Street as far as the present Essex Street was formerly an Outer Temple, which, with the Inner and Middle Temples, constituted the residences of the Knights Templars. This space is now for the most part occupied by a large block of offices which perpetuates the name, at the back of the fine new Law Courts branch of Lloyds Bank, and by Thanet Place and Devereux Court.

Thanet Place stands as nearly as possible on the site of the old " Rose Tavern," a place of rendezvous for lawyers and wits in the last century. It was named after the Earls of Thanet, to whom it belonged, and from whom the property passed, in 1780, by purchase to one John Cooke, a bookseller in Paternoster Row. The " Rose Tavern " is described by Strype as being in his day a " well-customed house, with good convenience of rooms and a good garden ;" and T. Fairchild, in his " City Gardener," in 1722, tells us that in this garden was " a vine that covers an arbour where the sun very rarely comes, and has had ripe grapes upon it." It makes our mouths water as we pass along the street on a hot summer afternoon, with the thermometer at 83° in the shade, to hear of grapes growing in the open air close to our left hand even a century and a

half ago. The " painted room " at this tavern is mentioned in Horace Walpole's " Letters," but it has long since passed out of memory.

Palsgrave Place was a narrow paved court, about half-way between Temple Bar and Essex Street, named after the Palsgrave Frederick, King of Bohemia, who in 1612 married the Princess Elizabeth, daughter of James I. Close by was the tavern known as the " Palsgrave's Head," where Prior and Montague make the " country mouse and city mouse " bilk the hackney coachman :—

" But now at Piccadilly they arrive,
　And taking coach towards Temple Bar they drive ;
　But at St. Clement's Church cut out the back,
　And slipping through the ' Palsgrave ' bilk't poor hack."

Some of the taverns of the seventeenth century appear to have been established over the shops in this locality ; for in 1679, according to Mr. Diprose's " Account of St. Clement Danes," " a goldsmith named Crutch carried on business under this tavern, and most of the shops were marked by signs. William Faithorne, an engraver of merit, lived ' at the sign of the Ship, next to the Drake, opposite to the Palsgrave's Head Tavern, without Temple Bar.' " Another house of entertainment or tavern in this neighbourhood, much frequented by members of Parliament and City gallants of the seventeenth century, was "Heycock's Ordinary." Here usually dined Andrew Marvell, some time member for Hull, and famous in his day as a wit and satirist; and here, according to the above authority, he administered a severe castigation to certain members of the House, known to be in the pay of the Crown, which ensured the subserviency of their votes. "Having ate heartily of boiled beef, with some roasted pigeons and asparagus, he drank his pint of port, and on the coming in of the reckoning took a piece of money out of his pocket, held it between his finger and thumb, and addressing his venal associates, said, 'Gentlemen, who would lett himself out for hire while he can have such a dinner for half-a-crown?'"

Another "scene," in which Andrew Marvell appears as the principal character, may possibly have taken place here. The anecdote has been often related, but will bear repetition:—"The borough of Hull, in the reign of Charles II., chose Andrew Marvell, a young gentleman of little or no fortune, and maintained him in London for the service of the public. His understanding, integrity, and spirit were dreadful to the then infamous administration. Persuaded that he would be theirs for properly asking, they sent his old schoolfellow, the Lord Treasurer Danby, to renew acquaintance with him in his garret. At parting, the Lord Treasurer, out of pure affection, slipped into his hand an order upon the Treasury for £1,000, and then went to his chariot. Marvell, looking at the paper, called out after the Treasurer, 'My lord, I request another moment.' They went up again to the garret, and Jack, the servant-boy, was called. 'Jack, child, what had I for dinner yesterday?' 'Don't you remember, sir? You had the little shoulder of mutton that you ordered me to bring from a woman in the market.' 'Very right, child. What have I for dinner to-day?' 'Don't you know, sir, that you bid me lay the bladebone to broil?' ''Tis so; very right, child; go away.' 'My lord, do you hear that? Andrew Marvell's dinner is provided. There's your piece of paper; I want it not. I know the sort of kindness you intended. I live here to serve my constituents. The ministry may seek men for their purpose; I am not one.'"

The house No. 217, Strand, now a branch of the London and Westminster Joint-Stock Bank, but which till lately was occupied as a bank by Messrs. Strahan (originally Snow), Paul, and Bates, has a history approaching in venerable antiquity to that of its neighbour (now rebuilt), Child's Bank. The name of the firm was originally Snow and Walton, who carried on business here as pawnbrokers during the Commonwealth, their house bearing the sign of the "Golden Anchor." Their ledgers went back as far as the year 1672. There was a book in the possession of the late members of the firm, showing that they were established as bankers in the reign of Charles II., when their accounts were kept in decimals. The firm came to a disgraceful and disastrous end in 1855, the leading partners of it being tried criminally and convicted of misappropriating the moneys of their customers, for which they were sentenced to various terms of imprisonment, a climax which offers a striking contrast to the reputation enjoyed by the original owner and founder of the house, a wealthy goldsmith named Snow, whose memory is thus immortalised by Gay:—

" Disdain not, Snow, my humble verse to hear ;
Stick thy black pen awhile behind thy ear.
O thou whose penetrative wisdom found
The South Sea rocks and shelves when thousands drown'd,
When Credit sank and Commerce gasping lay,
Thou stood'st, nor sent one bill unpaid away ;
When not a guinea clinked on Martin's boards,
And Atwel's self was drained of all his hoards,
Thou stood'st—an Indian king in size and hue—
Thy unexhausted store was our Peru."

Adjoining the above house, and opposite to the spot where formerly stood Butcher's Row, are the banking-house and tea-warehouse of Messrs. Twining and Co. The latter was founded about the year 1710 by the great-great-grandfather of the present partners, Mr. Thomas Twining, whose portrait, painted by Hogarth, "Kit-cat size," hangs in the back parlour of the establishment. The house, or houses—for they really are two, though made one practically by internal communication—stand between the Strand and the east side of Devereux Court. The original depôt for the sale of the then scarce and fashionable beverage, tea, stood at the south-west angle of the present premises, on the site of what had been "Tom's Coffee House," directly opposite the "Grecian." A peep into the old books of the firm shows that in the reign of Queen Anne tea was sold by the few houses then in the trade at various prices between twenty and thirty shillings per pound, and that ladies of fashion used to flock to Messrs. Twining's house in Devereux Court, in order to sip the enlivening beverage in very small china cups, for which they paid their shillings, much as now-a-days they sit in their carriages eating ices at the door of Gunter's in Berkeley Square on hot days in June. The bank was gradually engrafted by Messrs. Twining on the old business, after it had been carried on for more than a century from sire to son, and may be said, as a separate institution, to date from the commercial panic of 1825. It is, perhaps, worthy of note that a member of this family, which has been so long and so honourably connected with commerce, was that elegant and accomplished scholar, the Rev. Thomas Twining, the translator of Aristotle's "Poetics" in the days of our grandfathers.

Separated from the above-mentioned establishment by the entrance to Devereux Court is "George's Hotel," which stands on the site of what was once "George's Coffee House"—one which, though not equal in reputation to "Tom's" or the "Grecian," had associations of its own. It is mentioned by Foote in his "Life of Murray," as a place where the wits of the town in 1751 would assemble in the evening; and among its frequenters was the poet Shenstone—he of the "Leasowes"—who tells us that for a subscription of a shilling he could read all the lesser pamphlets of the day. It ceased to be known as a coffee-house about the year 1842, and has since been used as an hotel.

When the new sewers were being constructed in the Strand, a little to the east of St. Clement's Church, in 1802, the workmen found a stone bridge of a single arch, strongly built, and covered to some depth with rubbish and soil. A doubt arises as to whether this could have been an arch turned over a gully or ditch at a time when the fields along the north side of the Strand were furrowed with water-courses, or whether it was actually the *Pons Novi Templi* passed by the lords and others who went from London to attend the Parliament at Westminster in the reign of Edward III., and the repair of which that monarch called upon the Templars to effect. In the absence of architectural details, or at least a sketch of the bridge, we shall not attempt to decide so knotty a point.

Devereux Court, into which we now pass, is famous as having been the *locale* of two of the most celebrated coffee-houses—"Tom's" and the "Grecian." It takes its name from Robert Devereux, Earl of Essex, the Parliamentary general, who was born in Essex House (part of which stood upon this spot), and of whom we shall have more to say presently.

Of "Tom's" coffee-house we know that Akenside was a frequenter in the winter evenings, and that Pope here addresses a letter to Fortescue, the "counsel learned in the law." Another of its frequenters was Dr. Birch, the antiquary.

The "Grecian," again, was much frequented by a goodly company of wits and poets, including Addison, Steele, and Goldsmith, and derived its name from having been kept originally by a Greek

from the Levant. As far back as 1664-5, says Mr. Diprose, "he advertised his Turkey coffee-berry, chocolate, sherbet, and tea, good and cheap; and announced his readiness to give gratuitous instruction in the art of preparing the said liquors." And Steele, in the first number of the *Tatler*, supplies us with an idea of the character of this house, when he tells the public that he "shall date all gallantry from 'White's,' all poetry from 'Wills's,' all foreign and domestic news from 'St. James's,' and all learned articles from the 'Grecian.'" The existence of the rival coffee-houses gave a high literary character to Devereux Court in the seventeenth and eighteenth centuries. The face of the "Spectator" himself was very well known at the "Grecian," "adjacent to the law," and the house was frequented by the Irish and Lancashire Templars, and also by Fellows of the Royal Society. It was Foote's morning lounge, and in a snug and cozy corner here Goldsmith occasionally "wound up his shoemaker's holiday with supper."

In the *Spectator* (No. 49) Addison describes his feelings at seeing the young Templars lounge at the "Grecian" early in the morning, either dressed for Westminster, and with the assumed air of men with heavy business engagements, or else in gay caps and slippers, as though wishing to display their indolence.

Dr. King relates how two hot-blooded young gentlemen quarrelled one evening at the "Grecian" upon the appropriate subject of the accent of a certain Greek word, and not being able to adjust the matter amicably, stepped out into the court and settled it with their swords, the one falling by the other's hand. The topographer of Leeds, Ralph Thoresby, describes how on one occasion, after a meeting of the Royal Society, he came back to the "Grecian," and spent the rest of the evening there in the company of Sir Isaac Newton.

At the "Grecian" Akenside spent such of his winter evenings as he could spare from "Tom's," as we learn from Sir John Hawkins's "Life of Johnson," "entangled in disputes and altercations, chiefly on subjects of literature and politics, that fixed on his character the stamp of haughtiness and self-conceit, and drew him into disagreeable situations." The "Grecian" ceased to be a coffee-house or tavern about the year 1842, and shortly afterwards it was converted into "chambers." A part of the building, however, now known as "Eldon Chambers," is used as a refreshment-bar. High up, on the front of this house, is a bust of Lord Essex, and beneath it the inscription, "This is Devereux Court, 1676."

LONDON, FROM THE TOP OF ARUNDEL HOUSE. *From an Etching by Hollar.* (*See page* 71.)

CHAPTER XI.

THE STRAND:—SOUTHERN TRIBUTARIES (*continued*).

"The glories of our birth and state
Are shadows, not substantial things."—*Shirley.*

Exeter House—Attacked by the Populace—Seized by Lord Paget, and Bequeathed to Robert, Earl of Essex—Paterson, the Auctioneer—Essex Street—"Sam's" Club at the "Essex Head"—Anecdote of the Young Pretender—The Robin Hood Society—Charles Dibdin—The Unitarian Chapel—Earliest Inhabitants of Essex Street.

THE site now covered by Essex Street and Devereux Court was, as stated above, originally a portion of the Outer Temple, and, as Dugdale supposes, belonged at one time to the "Prior and Canons of the Holy Sepulchre." In the reign of Edward III. it passed into the hands of the Bishops of Exeter, whose town residence was built here. It was called Exeter House, and they occupied it till the time of Henry VI. In 1326, as readers of English history are aware, Queen Isabella, "the she-wolf of France," consort of Edward II., landed from France to chase the Spensers from the side of her husband, and advanced upon London. The king and his evil counsellors fled to the frontiers of Wales; but Walter Stapleton, then Bishop of Exeter, Lord Treasurer of England, held out stoutly for his sovereign in his house, and as custos of London, demanded from the Lord Mayor the keys of the City to prevent any uprising in the disaffected City. And then a scene occurred which would require the pen of a Macaulay to paint in adequate colours. "The watchful populace," says Mr. Diprose, "fearing the Mayor's submission, and roused by Isabella's proclamation, which had been hung on the new cross in Cheapside, rose in arms and took the keys. They ran to Exeter House, then newly erected, fired the gates, and plundered or burnt all the plate, money, jewels, and goods that it contained. The bishop rode to the north door of St. Paul's to take sanctuary; but there the mob tore him from off his horse, stripped him of his armour, and dragging him to Cheapside, proclaimed him a traitor and an enemy of their liberties, and lopping off his head set it on a pole." Bishop Stapleton's remains were buried under a heap of rubbish or sand hard by his own gateway.

At the Reformation the house was seized on by Lord Paget, who called it after his name. The great Earl of Leicester was its next occupant. He changed it to "Leicester House," and bequeathed it to his son-in-law, the unfortunate favourite of Queen Elizabeth, Robert, Earl of Essex, from whom it derived the name under which it was known

ARUNDEL HOUSE (TO THE SOUTH). (From an Etching by Hollar.)

ARUNDEL HOUSE (TO THE NORTH). From an Etching by Hollar. (See page 71.)

for many years, and the memory of which is still retained in Essex Street. It will be remembered that it was from this house that he made, towards the end of Elizabeth's reign, his frantic and imprudent sally, in the vain hope of exciting the citizens of London to take up arms against their sovereign. Finding that his star at court was sensibly waning after the death of Lord Burleigh, and the estrangement of his sovereign, he listened to the advice of those who would have had Raleigh, Cecil, and Cobham banished from the Queen's councils. To strengthen his interest in antagonism to the Queen and the Court, he threw open the gates of Essex House to all discontented persons, and especially to those of the Puritan party. In February, 1601, he took part in an overt act of rebellion, assembling his friends, to whom he stated that his life was threatened by Raleigh and Cobham. " In consequence of this news, Lords Sandys and Monteagle, the Earls of Rutland and Southampton, with nearly 300 other gentlemen, assembled at Essex House, where it was divulged that Essex had resolved at once to rid himself of his enemies by forcing his way to the Queen, and informing her of his danger from those who had so long abused their influence with her Majesty. Having shut up within his gates the Lord Keeper, the Lord Chief Justice, and others whom the Queen, aware of what was passing, had sent to inquire into the cause of the tumult, Essex proceeded with his friends to the City, where, crying aloud, ' For the Queen! for the Queen! a plot is laid against my life!' he tried to enlist the citizens in his favour. But notwithstanding his popularity no one took up arms : the cause of the tumult was either unknown or mistaken. At length the Earl endeavoured to return home, but he was met by a party of soldiers near Ludgate, where a tumult ensued, in which he was twice shot through the hat. At last he reached Essex House; but after a short defence he was compelled to surrender, and along with Lord Southampton was committed to the Tower. . . . . He was tried for high treason in Westminster Hall on the 15th of the same month, and executed on the 25th on Tower Hill." His son, the next Earl, the celebrated Parliamentary general, was born here; and in the Cavalier songs of the day the house is often alluded to as " Cuckold's Hall." It was here, according to Whitelocke, that the Earl, after the battle of Newbury, received a deputation from the House of Commons and the citizens of London with the Speaker and the Lord Mayor at their head.

Spenser thus speaks of Essex House in his " Prothalamium : "—

" Next whereunto there stands a stately place,
     Where oft I gaynèd gifts and goodly grace
Of that great Lord which therein wont to dwell,
     Whose want too well now feeds my friendless case."

It is said that Sir N. Throgmorton was poisoned here; and within its walls was lodged, in 1613, the Count Palatine of the Rhine, when he came to London as the accepted suitor of " the Lady Elizabeth," daughter of James I.

It appears that in or about 1640 the great mansion of Essex House was divided, the one half being let by Lord Essex on a long lease to William Seymour, Earl of Hertford, whose name is so well known to history in connection with that of Lady Arabella Stuart. Twenty years later we find Lord Southampton, the Lord Treasurer of Charles II., living here; and the house was tenanted by Sir Orlando Bridgman, the Lord Keeper in 1669, when it is described by Pepys as " large but ugly." Strype tells us that after this it was purchased by a builder, who appears to have converted the site into a good speculation, the houses which he erected in its place being soon occupied by " the quality." Old Essex House was partly demolished about the year 1682, and Essex Street rose on the site of its ruins about two years later.

The other half of the original edifice long retained its name of Essex House, and it is worthy of note that it served as a receptacle for the Cottonian Library in the reigns of Anne and George I. It appears that this part of the house was afterwards inhabited by an auctioneer. It was at Essex House, according to Horace Walpole, that this auctioneer, named Paterson, in 1761, first offered for public sale subjects in painted glass—the art of producing which appears to have been lost—imported by him from Flanders.

It must be owned that the architecture of Essex Street, with its unsightly square-headed archway at the lower end, leading by a flight of stone steps to the Embankment, is by no means attractive or tasteful; but in this respect it resembles its precursor, Essex House, which is described by Pepys as a " large but ugly " mansion. The property was divided and let, as stated above, and ultimately the house was pulled down and the materials sold, towards the middle of the reign of George III., from which the present houses date. The arch and the steps at the end of the street are said by John Timbs to have formed the water-gate of old Essex House; if so, we can only say that it presented a sorry contrast to the work of Inigo Jones half a mile further west. In a view of the " Frost Fair " on the Thames in the reign of Charles II., where the royal party are walking on to the ice at the Temple stairs, to witness the sport, this heavy archway is seen in the background, and through it can be descried the gardens and terraces and the eaves of Essex House.

At the "Essex Head" in this street, rebuilt the year before he died (1783), Dr. Johnson established a club called "Sam's," for the benefit of the landlord, one Samuel Greaves, who had been an old servant of his friends, the Thrales. It was not so select as the Literary Club, but cheaper. Johnson, in writing to Sir Joshua Reynolds, and asking him to join it, says, "The terms are lax and the expenses light; we meet thrice a week, and he who misses forfeits twopence." The rules of this club, as drawn up by Dr. Johnson himself, will be found at length in Boswell's "Life;" and our readers may be amused to learn that the "forfeit" for non-attendance being found too low, was raised to three-pence!

It was in Essex Street that Dr. King, as we learn from his "Anecdotes of His Own Time," was privately presented by Lady Primrose, "in her dressing-room," to Prince Charles Edward Stuart, "the Young Pretender," during his short, secret, and stolen visit to London, between the 5th and the 11th of September, 1750. The house of this same lady, in this street, some three years before, curiously enough, had afforded a temporary home to Flora Macdonald, after her release from the mild imprisonment to which she had been subjected by the Government.

In the year 1613 the Robin Hood Society was established at the house of Sir Hugh Middleton in this street. It was removed to the "Robin Hood" Tavern in Butcher Row, when it was presided over by a baker. "Here," Mr. Diprose tells us, "Burke displayed those oratorical powers which afterwards became so transcendent. When, becoming reconciled to the Pitt administration, he went over to the Tory benches, exclaiming, 'I quit the camp,' Sheridan instantly rose and observed, 'As the honourable gentleman had quitted them as a deserter, he hoped he would not return as a spy;' and when the king settled a pension on Burke, Sheridan remarked that 'it was no wonder that Mr. Burke should come to the House of Commons for his bread, when he formerly went to a baker for his eloquence'—meaning the Robin Hood Club." Poor Oliver Goldsmith was a member of this club. The meetings were held on Monday nights, when questions were proposed on which any one present might speak if he did not exceed seven minutes. When these were finished, the "baker," who presided with a hammer in his hand, summed up the arguments.

In 1788 Charles Dibdin, being "tired of dramatic uncertainties," made a start on his own account by turning some rooms in this street into a theatre of his own, from which, however, he soon afterwards moved to a more fashionable neighbourhood further west.

On the west side of Essex Street is a building formerly a Unitarian chapel, in which during the last hundred years have ministered in succession Theophilus Lindsey, Dr. Disney, Thomas Belsham, and Thomas Madge; it is now the head-quarters of the denomination.

Of the founder of this Unitarian chapel it may be well here to add a few particulars. His name was Theophilus Lindsey, and he was a godson of the Earl of Huntingdon, in whose family his mother had resided. He took his degree at St. John's College, Cambridge, and was presented by a connection of the Huntingdon family, whilst quite a young man, with the chapel in Spital Square. He afterwards became chaplain to Algernon, Duke of Somerset, and after the duke's death was continued in the same post by the Duchess, who sent him abroad with her grandson, the Duke of Northumberland, as tutor. Having held for a few years a living in Dorsetshire, he exchanged it, by the interest of his old friend Lord Huntingdon, for that of Catterick in Yorkshire, where he was promised a bishopric in Ireland on the appointment of Viscount Townshend as Lord Lieutenant. In 1773, on account of scruples which he had long cherished, he resigned his Yorkshire living and became a convert to Unitarianism. He preached his first sermon at Essex House in 1774, and the new chapel was opened shortly after, Franklin, with many other eminent men, being present. He acted as pastor of it for twenty years, during the latter part being assisted by Dr. Disney, who had also seceded from the Church of England. He died in 1808. Whether we agree or disagree with the creed he adopted, we must admire the man who in a selfish and thoughtless age could sacrifice his worldly prospects to his conscience. The chapel was built on part of the site of the property of Essex House. In the forecourt, facing Essex Street, a monument was erected in 1880 in honour of the first twelve originators of Sunday Schools, from the time of Cardinal Borromeo in 1580 to that of Theophilus Lindsey and Robert Raikes in 1780.

Among the earliest inhabitants of Essex Street were Chamberlain (the author of several works on banks of credit, on land, security, &c.) and Arthur Maynwaring. Here also lived Dr. George Fordyce, a noted epicurean of the eighteenth century. In Jeaffreson's "Book about Doctors," we are told that "during twenty years he dined daily at 'Dolly's' chop-house, and at his meat he always took a jug of strong ale, a quarter of a pint of brandy, and a bottle of port. Having imbibed these refreshing stimulants, he walked back to his house, and gave a lecture to his pupils."

The late Lord Cholmondeley, who died in 1770, and who was not unknown as an antiquary, used to say that one day, when visiting a house in this street, he found, scratched to all appearance with a diamond, on a weather-stained piece of glass in a top room, the following letters, "I . C . U . S . X . & E . R ," which he interpreted, "I see you, Essex, and Elizabeth Regina." If he was right in his interpretation, it would seem probable that some inquisitive occupant of this room, overlooking Essex House, had seen the Queen flirting with the Earl, and, like Captain Cuttle, had on the spot "made a note" of it.

CHAPTER XII.

THE STRAND :—SOUTHERN TRIBUTARIES (continued).

"All the blood of the Howards."—Pope.

Milford Lane—The Chapel of the Holy Ghost—The *Illustrated London News*—Messrs. Woodfall and Kinder's—Arundel House—The Arundel Collection—Lord Seymour's Dalliance with the Princess Elizabeth—The Duc de Sully at Arundel House—"Old Parr"—Distinguished Inhabitants of Arundel Street—The "Crown and Anchor" Tavern—The Whittington Club—The Temple Club—Messrs. W. H. Smith and Son's News Agency—An Early News Mart—Strand Lane—The Old Roman Bath—Jacob Tonson.

It may reasonably be supposed that just on the west of Temple Bar the ground five or six centuries ago was marshy and low, and that a brook ran thence into the Thames. This, too, is rendered probable by the name of Milford Lane, which leads down from St. Clement's Church to the river-side ; and the supposition is confirmed by the fact that in 1802 the remains of a bridge of stone, eleven feet in length, and covered by rubbish, was found on digging between Temple Bar and the east end of St. Clement's Church, as stated already in a previous chapter. It is suggested by Mr. T. C. Noble, in his "Memorials of Temple Bar," that this was probably the very bridge mentioned in the reign of Edward III. as built by the Templars of that day by command of the king. Towards its lower end the lane winds round to the east, meeting the steps at the bottom of Essex Street. This part of the parish appears to have been always inhabited by the poorer and less "respectable" classes ; and it suffered accordingly most severely from the Plague in 1665.

Stow remarks that he could not account for the origin of the name of Milford Lane ; but no doubt it comes from a *ford*—not over the Thames, as Mr. Timbs suggests, but across the little stream which ran there across and under the Strand into the Thames, near which was a *mill*. Mr. Timbs tells us that the former is shown in a print of the reign of James I., and that he has seen a "token" of the Windmill, near Temple Bar ; but this may possibly have been an inn. It is a narrow, crooked, and ill-built thoroughfare, and now contains more stables and warehouses than private dwellings.

Yet it was once well tenanted. In it lived Sir Richard Baker, the author of the "Chronicles," which, as most readers of the *Spectator* will remember, was the favourite work of Sir Roger de Coverley. The rectors of St. Clement Danes for many generations dwelt about half-way down the lane. It would not now be regarded as a desirable situation.

An unwelcome notoriety has been given to this lane in a poem by Henry Saville, commonly attributed to the witty Earl of Dorset, and beginning—

"In Milford Lane, near to St. Clement's steeple ;"

and Gay also mentions it in his "Trivia," in the following terms :—

"Behold that narrow street which steep descends,
Whose building to the slimy shore extends.
Here Arundel's famed structure rear'd its frame,
The street alone retains an empty name ;
There Essex' stately pile adorn'd the shore,
There Cecil, Bedford, Villiers—now no more."

The lane, it should be mentioned here, when it really was a lane, acted as a boundary between the property of Lord Essex on the east, and that of the Earl of Arundel on the west.

Tradition assures us that in the Strand, between Essex Street and Milford Lane, was formerly a chapel dedicated to the Holy Ghost ; but no prints of it have been preserved, nor is it known when or by whom it was founded, or when it passed away. Mr. Newton, in his "London in the Olden Time," conjectures that it was originally a chapel belonging to the Knights Templars, and that in after time it became the chapel of the Bishop of Exeter's Inn.

He identifies its site, as nearly as possible, with the Unitarian chapel in Essex Street already mentioned.

At the top of the lane, on the eastern side, there stood down to about the year 1850 some picturesque wooden houses, with gables and ornamental fronts; but these were pulled down to make room for the erection of Milford House, in which since that date the *Illustrated London News* has been printed. It is published at the corner of Milford Lane and the Strand, on the other side of the way. This paper—the first of our "illustrated" journals—was started by the late Mr. Herbert Ingram, a native of Boston, in 1841, and by his energy and ability soon grew into a splendid property; but it needs no description here. We should, however, record in this place his melancholy death by drowning in 1860, on one of the American inland lakes. At the opposite corner house was published in 1858 its short-lived rival, the *Illustrated News of the World*.

At the bottom of this lane stood till 1888 the printing-office of Woodfall and Kinder. It was Mr. Woodfall's grandfather who printed the famous "Letters of Junius." "The business," says Mr. John Timbs, "was first established about the year 1720, in Grocers' Hall Court, and in Angel Court, Skinner Street, George Woodfall printed his edition of 'Junius'—the first book printed there."

Between Milford Lane and Strand Lane—a narrow and rather winding thoroughfare leading to the Embankment a few yards to the east of Somerset House—the entire space, about three hundred yards in length and the same in breadth, formed the site of the town residence of the Howards, Earls of Arundel and Dukes of Norfolk. It was a dull, heavy structure, as may be seen from Hollar's prints; but its gardens and terraces were as extensive as befitted the dignity of so noble a house and family. The outlines and extent of the estate, as it was in the days of the Stuarts, may be easily gathered from the names subsequently given to the streets which were laid out upon its site, perpetuating the names of Norfolk, Arundel, Howard, and Surrey—names so familiar to the readers of English history under the Tudors, and also to the students of art and antiquity. Hollar's prints, however, do not give a very attractive view of it, for though it covered a considerable space, the buildings themselves were low and mean.

But it did not belong to the Howards in very ancient days, having been before the Reformation the "Inn" or house of the Bishops of Bath and Wells, and known also as Hampton House. In the reign of Henry VIII., or of his successor

Edward VI., it was seized and appropriated by royalty, and from royal hands it passed by an easy transition into the hands of Lord Thomas Seymour of Sudley, High Admiral of England, brother of the Protector Somerset, who called it Seymour Place. On the execution of Lord Seymour for treason, the dead lord's house was bought, together with its gardens and lands adjoining, by Henry Fitzalan, Earl of Arundel; and, Strype tells us, for the incredibly small sum of little more than forty pounds. This Lord Arundel, at his death in 1579, was succeeded in his title by his grandson, Philip Howard, son of the Duke of Norfolk who had been beheaded for taking part with Mary, Queen of Scots; and, though Philip Howard died in exile and attainted, his son Thomas contrived to obtain from James I. a reversal of the attainder and a restoration of his coronet.

Under this Earl of Arundel, the house which stood here became not merely a depôt, but the very home and centre of art and art treasures, as the repository of that collection long known as the "Arundelian Marbles," and "of which," to use the words of Mr. Peter Cunningham, "the very ruins are now ornaments to several private cabinets." We learn that the collection, when in its entire state, comprised no less than 37 statues, 128 busts, and 250 inscribed marbles, besides sarcophagi, altars, gems, and fragments of ancient art, all antique, and obtained with great care and discriminating skill in Italy. Besides these, "there really belonged to the collection a variety of other art-treasures which the Earl had purchased in Italy, but which he never could obtain leave to transport to England." However faulty he may be represented by Lord Clarendon, his judgment as a connoisseur in the fine arts will always remain undisputed. Views of the galleries in Arundel House are to be seen in the backgrounds of Van Somer's portraits of the Earl and Countess.

During the Cromwellian wars, Arundel House and its contents, of which, especially at that time, any nobleman might well have been proud, were given back to the Earl of Arundel's grandson, Henry Howard, sixth Duke of Norfolk, who, at the recommendation of John Evelyn and John Selden, the author of "Marmora Arundeliana," gave the marbles to the University of Oxford, which they still adorn, and the library to the Royal Society, which held its meetings for some time at Arundel House.

The Compleat Gentleman, a publication of the seventeenth century, informs the world, and with some truth, that to the Earl's "liberal charges and magnificence this angle of the world oweth the first

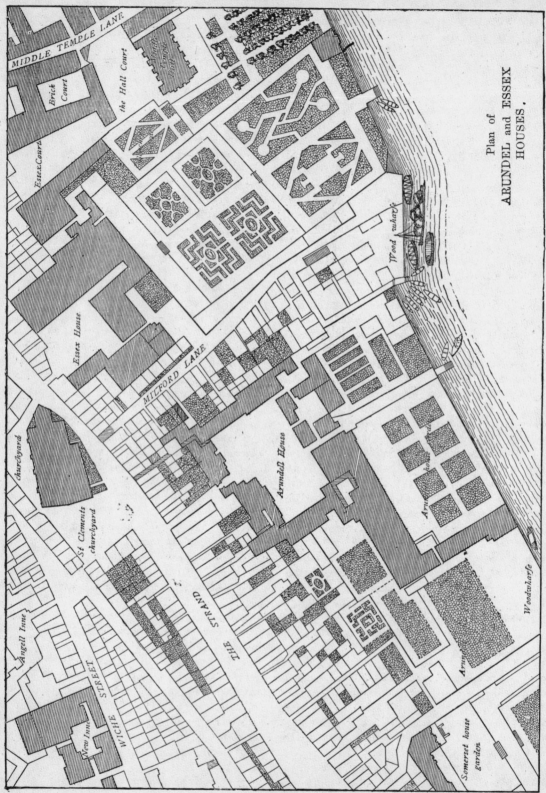

PLAN OF ARUNDEL AND ESSEX HOUSES. (*From an original Etching by Hollar, published in Ogilby and Morgan's Twenty-Sheet Plan of London.*)

sight of Greek and Roman statues, with whose admired presence he began to honour the gardens and galleries of Arundel House, and hath ever since continued to transplant old Greece to England." It may be mentioned here that the remainder of the Earl of Arundel's collection was kept for many

design was one Thomas Parry, cofferer to the princess, to whom he offered for her Grace's accommodation the use of his house and all its furniture during her stay in London. The queen's death, and her own suspicions on her death-bed, gave just cause for the worst surmises. Seymour's

JACOB TONSON.   (*See page* 79.)

years at Tart House, the residence of Howard, the unfortunate Lord Stafford, in Pimlico, and was ultimately sold in 1720.

"This place," says Pennant, "was one of the scenes of Lord Seymour's indecent dalliance with the Princess Elizabeth, afterwards queen. At first he certainly was not ill received, notwithstanding he had just espoused the unhappy Catherine Parr. Ambition, not lust, actuated this wretched man ; his designs on Elizabeth, and consequently on the crown, spurred him on. The instrument of his

execution, which soon followed, put an end to his projects, and saved Elizabeth and the nation from a tyrant possibly worse than him from whom they had but a few years before been released." The whole of Seymour's infamous conduct respecting the unhappy Queen Dowager is fully detailed in Lord Burleigh's State papers.

Arundel House came to the Duke of Norfolk from the Earl of Arundel by the marriage which united in one line the Fitzalans and the Howards. While tenanted by the Howards, the mansion is described as "a large and old-built house, with a spacious yard for stabling towards the Strand, and with a gate to enclose it, where there was the porter's lodge, and as large a garden towards the Thames."

The house was at one time occupied by the Duc de Sully, who in spite of its humble appearance on the outside, tells us that it was one of the finest and most convenient in London, on account of the number of rooms and apartments on the ground-floor. At Arundel House, too, in its best and palmy days, John Evelyn and his family were frequent visitors. He tells us in his "Diary," under date July, 1662, that he was forced to take home his son John, "who had been much brought up amongst Mr. Howard's children here, for feare of their perverting him to the Catholic religion."

Arundel House, too, is in other ways connected with history. To it the Earl invited Hollar, the artist, who engraved some of his finest plates while enjoying its princely hospitality—among others his (now very scarce) "View of London from the Roof of Arundel House." There also lived for a short time Lord William Howard, the "Belted Will" of border fame. And there also, in November, 1635, died Thomas Parr, known to the world as "Old Parr," having been invited to come thither from his home in Shropshire, in order to become domesticated in the Earl's household, and to be introduced to Charles I., when upwards of a century and a half old. He did not, however, long survive the change; high feeding and the close air of London in a few months brought him to his grave, at the age of 152 years and nine months. His body, as we learn from the *Philosophical Transactions*, was dissected at the king's command by Harvey, who attributed the old man's death to peripneumonia, brought on by the impurity of a London atmosphere and sudden change in his diet.

Taylor, the water poet, gives us the following description of Old Parr, when he saw him in London :—

> " His limbs their strength have left,
> His teeth all gone but one, his sight bereft,
> His sinews shrunk, his blood most chill and cold—
> Small solace !—imperfections manifold.
> Yet still his spirits possess his mortal trunk,
> Nor are his senses in his ruins shrunk ;
> But that his hearing's quick, his stomach good,
> He'll feed well, sleep well, well digest his food.
> He will speak merrily, laugh, and be merry,
> Drink ale, and now and then a cup of sherry ;
> Loves company and understanding talk,
> And (on both sides held up) will often walk.
> And though old age his face with wrinkles fill,
> He hath been handsome, and is comely still ;

> Well fac'd ; and though his beard not oft corrected,
> Yet neat it grows, not like a beard neglected.
> From head to heel his body hath all over
> A quick-set, thick-set, natural, hairy cover."

Thomas Parr, according to the inscription on his tomb in Westminster Abbey, was born in Shropshire in 1483; and it is added, " he lived in the reign of ten princes, viz., Edward IV., Edward V., Richard III., Henry VII., Henry VIII., Edward VI., Mary, Elizabeth, James I., and Charles I. ; aged 152 years, and was buried here Nov. 15, 1635. He lived at Alberbury, in Shropshire ; had an illegitimate child born to him when over 100 years old ; and married his second wife, Catherine Milton, at the age of 120. By her he had one child, and after his second marriage he was employed in threshing, and other husbandry work. King Charles, on seeing him, said, ' You have lived longer than other men ; now what have you done more than other men ?' ' Sir,' he replied, ' I did penance when I was a hundred years old.' " There is a portrait of Old Parr, said to be by Rubens.

"When Arundel House was pulled down," in the seventeenth century, we are told by Allen, "there was a design to build a mansion-house for the family out of the accumulated rents on that part of the gardens which faced the river, and an Act of Parliament was obtained for the purpose ; but the design was never carried out." He adds that it was to Arundel House that the Royal Society removed from Gresham College, after the Fire of London, being invited thither by Henry, Duke of Norfolk. They returned to their old home in 1674, soon after which the house was sentenced to be taken down. The Duke, as we are informed by Pennant, had presented his valuable library to the society.

It would seem, from Gay's "Trivia," that for a long time after the demolition of Arundel House the eastern part of the Strand lay forsaken and neglected, though perhaps there may be some little amount of poetic exaggeration in the following lines :—

> " Where Arundel's famed structure reared its frame,
> The street alone retains an empty name ;
> Where Titian's glowing paint the canvas warm'd,
> And Raphael's fair design in canvas charm'd,
> Now hangs the bellman's song, and pasted there
> The coloured prints of Overton appear.
> Where statues breathed the work of Phidias' hands,
> A wooden pump or lonely watch-house stands."

Arundel Street, however, built in 1678 on part of the site of Arundel House, has had in its time some distinguished inhabitants. Amongst others were Simon Harecourt, afterwards Lord Chancellor ; Rymer, the antiquary, and author of the celebrated "Fœdera;" John Anstis, Garter King-at-Arms; and the well-known actress, Mrs. Porter.

At the upper end of this street, on the site of the Temple Club, formerly stood the noted "Crown and Anchor" Tavern—so named, no doubt, from the anchor of St. Clement already alluded to—the head-quarters of the Westminster Reformers in the days of Fox and "Old Glory," Sir Francis Burdett. Here, too, were held many of the meetings of the Catholic Association before the passing of the Roman Catholic Relief Act in 1829. The tavern stood as nearly as possible on the site of the buildings in which the Academy of Ancient Music was first instituted in the reign of Queen Anne. The premises extended a considerable way down the street, and at the back of them was a large and spacious room, upwards of eighty feet long, which was used as a banqueting apartment. Upon the occasion of Fox's birthday, in 1798, a great banquet was given here, at which 2,000 Reformers sat down to drink the toast of "The People the Source of Power."

Here the portly form of Dr. Johnson, in company with his friend Boswell, might often be seen; and during the Westminster elections in the last century it became one of the principal houses where the candidates of both sides were wont to address the constituents. It was at the "Crown and Anchor" that Daniel O'Connell first assailed that "venerable champion of civil and religious liberty," Henry Brougham; and it was here, too, that Cobbett fell foul of Sir Francis Burdett, who, we are told, "at once angrily responded by stating that Cobbett owed him a thousand pounds. Cobbett acknowledged receiving the money, but stated that it was a gift, and consequently not a debt." The "King of Clubs" was instituted here early in the present century; its members met every Saturday. One of the chief members was Richard Sharpe, a West India merchant and a well-known Parliamentary speaker during Addington's and Percival's administrations.

The coffee-room of the "Crown and Anchor" had for many years hanging upon its walls a picture which caused some stir among the parishioners of St. Clement Danes early in the last century. It appears that in 1725 the parish was thrown into a state of commotion by an order from Dr. Gibson, then Bishop of London, for the removal of an altarpiece lately painted by Kent, which had cost no small sum, and was supposed to be really a satire on the reigning house of Hanover, by containing scarcely disguised portraits of the wife and children of "The Pretender." The painting, of course, at once became famous, and Hogarth engraved an exact fac-simile of it, as may be seen in Nichol's "Biographical Anecdotes" of that painter. The original, after being removed from the church, was hung up in the coffee-room of this tavern, from which it was subsequently removed into the parish vestry-room.

In 1846 the Whittington Club was instituted at the "Crown and Anchor," under the auspices of Douglas Jerrold and several other gentlemen connected with literature and art. The "Whittington Club and Metropolitan Athenæum," for such was its ambitious name, was founded as a cheap club for men and women of the middle or upper-middle classes, and "with a view to throw open to them those increased physical comforts and facilities for moral and intellectual education, which are the most attractive characteristics of modern London life, but which, in the absence of individual wealth, associated members can alone command." Accordingly, in addition to the usual conveniences in the way of dining, &c., courses of lectures, and classes in chemistry, music, modern languages, and literature, &c., were established, together with weekly re-unions, in which dancing had a place. The subscription was low, £1 1s. or £2 2s. yearly, according to the residence of the member in country or in town; and 10s. 6d. for ladies.

The Whittington Club was named after Richard Whittington, the former "Lord Mayor of great London," and in one of its large rooms hung a picture of "Dick Whittington listening to the sound of Bow Bells," by Newenham, which was given to the club by its founder. The original premises of the "Crown and Anchor" were burnt down in 1854, but they were subsequently rebuilt on the former plan. The Whittington Club, however, languished, and at last came to an end in 1873. The building then underwent considerable alteration, and at the end of the same year was re-opened as the Temple Club. The house, which was erected at a cost of more than £20,000, contained above thirty rooms; what was formerly the hall, a magnificent apartment, capable of seating 1,000 persons, became the dining-room. One of the principal objects which the founders had in view was to "create the nucleus of a community whose members, uninfluenced by any political bias and unconfined to any literary or scientific pursuit, might enjoy a neutral ground whereon to reciprocate their ideas with regard to art, literature, and science." The Temple Club in 1881, when it was broken up, numbered about 2,000 members.

At the opposite corner of Arundel Street, with its principal entrance in the Strand, is that great emporium of modern intelligence, the news-agency of Messrs. Smith and Son, which is, perhaps, the most extraordinary house of business in London, not alone from the rapidity and dexterity of its operations, but the facility and certainty with which business is transacted to such an enormous extent in so short a time. The building is lofty, and covers a large space of ground, and is complete in every department. On the ground-floor is a noble and spacious hall, forming almost the extent of the entire premises, and is surrounded by two galleries. The bustle is at its height at an early hour in the morning, when vehicles are bringing in the morning papers from the different printing-offices : these are at once folded into oblong packages, wrapped in brown paper covers already addressed, and dispatched in light red carts to the various railway stations for transmission to different parts of the world. Thousands of newspapers are transmitted to their destination in the course of the week from this establishment, and a large staff of clerks are engaged, besides men and boys employed in the packing departments. In addition to this extensive wholesale newspaper business, Messrs. W. H. Smith and Son have established a circulating library upon a most extensive scale ; and they also have in their railway bookstalls an exceedingly valuable monopoly. Printing, advertising, and bookbinding likewise form important items in this vast commercial establishment, and so admirable are the arrangements that each department is complete in itself, and conducted as a separate business ; the whole giving employment to many hundreds of hands.

From the *Bookseller* we learn that Mr. W. H. Smith, grandfather of the present proprietor, and founder of this gigantic establishment, was born in the year 1792, and "at a very early age undertook the management of a newspaper business at the West-end of the town, removing in a few years to the site of the present premises. At the early part of this century newspapers required two days to go to Manchester, Liverpool, and other great towns far distant from London, for they were only conveyed by the night coaches, which took from twenty to thirty hours to reach their various destinations, so that Monday's newspapers could not be received before Wednesday morning. To obviate this inconvenient delay Mr. Smith started express carts and saddle-horses, so as to overtake the early morning coaches, and thus the day's paper was delivered by the morrow, making a saving of twenty-four hours in the transmission. For some time this admirable project scarcely paid its way, and it seemed almost a failure ; but the per-severance of its projector was such that he boldly pursued his course under all its difficulties, and eventually won his way, acquiring the largest newspaper agency trade in London, to which he then devoted himself wholly and solely, giving up entirely the stationery business with which he had previously incorporated it. As time changes all things, so coach travelling was superseded by railway locomotion, and Mr. Smith was not slow in adapting the conduct of his business to suit this wonderful alteration. In 1852 Mr. Smith retired into private life, and for above six years he resided at Bournemouth, doing all the good he could in his new neighbourhood, for his activity was such that he could not be idle. He died in 1865." The son of this gentleman, and his successor as head of the establishment, was Mr. William Henry Smith. He was Financial Secretary of the Treasury from 1874 to 1877, and First Lord of the Admiralty from 1877 to 1880. In 1880 he became First Lord of the Treasury, and Leader of the House of Commons in 1886, dying in 1891, when a peerage was conferred upon his widow.

A rough idea may be formed of the extent of the agency at work in the circulation of newspapers and other publications of a serial kind, one-third of which it is calculated pass through the hands of Messrs. Smith, when we give our readers the following statement, courteously furnished by Mr. Wellsman, the editor of "The Newspaper Press Directory" :—There are now (1897) published in the United Kingdom 2,396 newspapers distributed as follows :—England—London, 494 ; provinces, 1,377—1871 ; Wales, 102 ; Scotland, 232 ; Ireland, 171 ; British Isles, 20. Of these there are—172 daily papers published in England ; 7 ditto in Wales ; 19 ditto in Scotland ; 18 ditto in Ireland ; 2 ditto in the British Isles. On reference to the first edition of this useful Directory for 1846, we find the following interesting facts—viz., that in that year there were published in the United Kingdom 551 journals ; of these 14 were issued daily, viz., 12 in England and 2 in Ireland ; but in 1897 there are now established and circulated 2,396 papers, of which no less than 218 are issued daily, showing that the press of the country has more than quadrupled during the last fifty-one years. The increase in daily papers has been still more remarkable ; the daily issues standing at 218 against 14 in 1846. The magazines now in course of publication, including the quarterly reviews, number 2,184, of which 537 are of a decidedly religious character, representing the Church of England, Wesleyans, Methodists, Baptists, Independents, Roman Catholics, and other Christian communities.

It is not a little singular that a century and a half ago the chief news-mart stood not far from this very place. In proof of this assertion we would quote the following passage from the *London Spy* published in 1725 :—" Now I am in this neighbourhood I know it will be expected that some notice should be taken of Mr. William, the faithful messenger of the Muses, who is constantly administering to the public the advices foreign and domestick, and is early every morning ranging his papers in order, . . . according to their seniority and credit respectively, upon the counter." The list of these, with which the writer favours us, is strange and well worth a passing note :—The *Daily Courant* he posts first, as superior in credit to any other, excepting the *Gazette*, for the affairs abroad. After him the *Daily Journal* and *Daily Post*, as the two intelligencers at home. The *Post Boy* takes the right hand of the *Flying Post* and *Postman*, and the weekly journals and pamphlets are piled in the window on one side. Those paying no stamp duties are not permitted to herd among the friends of the Revenue. But this is not all. The Strand, if second, has been for a century second only to Fleet Street in literary interest of this particular kind. At No. 132 an enterprising citizen named Wright established, in 1740, the first of those circulating libraries which, for about a century and a half, have afforded so large a market for our novelists. Mr. John Timbs tells us that he was so far successful that he shortly had four rivals in Holborn, Fleet Street, and in his own more immediate neighbourhood ; but some of these must have failed, if it be true, as stated by him, that in 1770 there were only four circulating libraries in the entire metropolis. Another literary celebrity, connected with the Strand, was the friend of Pope, old Jacob Tonson, of whom we give a portrait on page 73, and of whom we shall have more to say at the close of the chapter.

A narrow and rather winding lane a few yards to the east of Somerset House, and just opposite to St. Mary's Church, led in former times to the water-side. It was called Strand Lane, and the pier or small landing-place at the bottom of it was known as "Strand Bridge." In it was a row of old tenements formerly known as Golden Buildings, but the name has disappeared. On its western side stood the "Strand Inn." The "landing-place on the bank of the Thames" at this spot is mentioned by Stow, and no doubt was constantly used by the inmates of the Inn. Occasionally, however, it afforded accommodation to other persons ; and in the *Spectator*, No. 454, we read how Addison "landed with ten sail of apricot boats at Strand Bridge, after having put in at Nine Elms and taken in melons, consigned by Mr. Cuffe of that place to Sarah Sewell and Company, at their stall in Covent Garden."

Mr. Newton, in his "London in the Olden Time," says that the bottom of Strand Lane appears to have been an ancient landing-place, communicating directly with Lambeth, and with the Via de Aldewych, which led toward the north-west country.

It is just worth noting here that the term "Strand Bridge" was applied by Stow and others to a bridge *in* the Strand, by which the roadway just to the west of the Maypole was carried over a brook. In the present century, too, it was the name originally designed for Sir John Rennie's noble structure subsequently known as Waterloo Bridge.

It is thought by antiquaries that Strand Lane, which is somewhat tortuous, follows pretty nearly the line of a little brook or rivulet which carried off the water from the higher grounds about Catherine Street and Drury Lane, passing under the thoroughfare of the Strand, which, as Stow observes, was carried over it by a bridge. On the left-hand side of this lane, in passing from the Strand, may be noticed a somewhat rural-looking cottage, on which hangs a notice that within is "The old Roman Bath." It will thus be seen that passengers along the Strand in the present day are within some fifty or sixty feet of one of the oldest structures in London, one of its few real and genuine remains which date from the era of the Roman occupation of England, and possibly even as far back as the reigns of Titus or Vespasian, if not of Julius Cæsar himself.

The piece of land in which the bath is situated formed part of the property of a very ancient family, the Danvers (or D'Anvers), of Swithland, in Leicestershire ; and although the existence of the bath was evidently unknown to Stow, Maitland, Pennant, and Malcolm, from the absence of any mention of it in their pages, yet, from time immemorial, in the neighbourhood, the fact of its being a Roman bath has been received with implicit credence.

There is apparently a dim tradition existing, to the effect that the bath had been closed up for a long period, and then re-discovered. Of this old bath Mr. Newton observes in his "London in the Olden Time," that it is "without doubt a veritable Roman structure, as an inspection of the old walls will prove." A descent of four or five steps leads to a lofty vaulted passage, on the left of which is a doorway leading into a vaulted chamber, about sixteen feet in length, the same in height, and about nine feet in width, in the floor of which is the bath itself. This is about thirteen feet long, six broad, and four feet six inches deep. Mr. Charles Knight, in his "London," tells us that "the spring is said to be connected with the neighbouring holy well, which gives name to Holywell Street, and their by thin layers of stucco; whilst the pavement consists of a layer of similar brick covered with stucco, and rests upon a mass of stucco and rubble. The bricks are nine inches and a half long, four inches and a half broad, and an inch and three-quarters thick. At the farther end of the bath is a

OLD ROMAN BATH, STRAND LANE. (*See page* 77.)

respective position makes the statement probable.* Through the beautiful clear water . . . . appear the sides and bottom of the bath."

The walls of this extremely interesting building are formed of layers of brick, of that peculiar flat and neat-looking aspect which certainly seems to imply the impress of Roman hands, divided only

small projecting strip or ledge of white marble, and beneath it a hollow in the wall slanting down to one corner. These are beyond doubt the remains of a flight of steps which once led down into the water. Mr. Charles Knight adds :—" Immediately opposite the steps was a door connected with a vaulted passage, still existing below ; and towards the back of three houses in Surrey Street, and continuing from thence upwards in the direction of

* See, however, *ante*, p. 21.

the Strand. These vaults have some remarkable features ; among others, there is a low arch of a very peculiar form, the rounded top projecting gradually forward beyond the line of its sides, in the house immediately behind the bath." The bath is perpetually supplied from the spring, and discharges at the rate of ten tons per day. The water in this

through the sandy bottom, and its flow is pretty even, both winter and summer. There are no pipes which supply it ; and as it has in no way been affected by the excavations for the Law Courts, nor for the Underground Railway, which runs along the Embankment, it is plainly natural, and not artificial, and sparkles as clear as crystal.

GOLDEN BUILDINGS. (*See page* 77.)

old Roman bath, which is beautifully clear and extremely cold, is now used solely for drinking ; there is, however, another bath-room on the right of the passage by which we entered, which is used as a plunging bath, and is open all the year round. This new bath, the proprietor tells us, "was built by the Earl of Essex, in the reign of Queen Elizabeth, 1588." The source of the water which supplies this bath is unknown. It bubbles up

It may as well be mentioned here, though we have not travelled quite as far westward yet, that at No. 141 in the Strand, between St. Mary's Church and the corner of Wellington Street, on a site now covered by part of Somerset House, was the book-shop of Jacob Tonson, the friend and publisher of Pope, &c. Hither he removed from Gray's Inn Gateway in 1712, and the shop was known by the sign of the "Shakespeare's Head."

It is described as being "over against Catherine Street."

The subsequent history of the house occupied by Tonson is thus told by Mr. Peter Cunningham:—"The house (No. 141), since rebuilt, was afterwards occupied by Andrew Millar, the publisher, and friend of Thomson, Fielding, Hume, and Robertson ; and, after Millar's death, by Thomas Cadell, his apprentice, the friend and publisher of Gibbon. Thomson's 'Seasons,' Fielding's 'Tom Jones,' and the 'Histories' of Hume, Robertson, and Gibbon, were first published at this house. Millar was a Scotchman, and, true to his country and countrymen, distinguished his house by substituting Buchanan's head for that of Shakspeare as its sign. Could any one save a Scotchman have been guilty of such a deed of Vandalism?"

The name of Jacob Tonson is familiar to every reader, not only of Pope, but of Horace Walpole, as the secretary of the "Kit-Cat" Club. The son of a barber-surgeon in Holborn, he was born about the year 1656. At fourteen years of age he was bound apprentice to a bookseller, and on reaching manhood joined with his brother Richard in partnership. He published extensively for Addison, Dryden, and Pope ; and his edition of Clarke's "Cæsar," which issued from his shop in 1712, is said to have been the largest and most expensive work which up to that time had been published in England. It was this Jacob Tonson who had the portraits of the members of the "Kit-Cat" Club painted for him in a uniform size, which still retains the name. On retiring from business he lived chiefly at Barn Elms, in the village of Barnes, where his house was for many years a centre of literary society. He died in 1736, but his memory survives, having been kept alive on the title-pages of many great works in the eighteenth century, and by the pen of Mr. Charles Knight, in his "Shadows of the London Booksellers." In a dialogue between Tonson and Congreve, published in 1714, in a volume of poems by Rowe, there is a pleasant description of Tonson before he was spoiled by grand associates :—

> "While, in your early days of reputation,
> You for blue garters had not such a passion ;
> While yet you did not live, as now your trade is,
> To drink with noble lords, and toast their ladies,
> Thou, Jacob Tonson, were, to my conceiving,
> The cheerfullest, best, honest fellow living."

CHAPTER XIII.

THE STRAND:—SOUTHERN TRIBUTARIES (continued).

"Interdum rapere occupat."—Horace.

Sir Thomas Lyttelton and Bishop Burnet—Norfolk Street—Royal Farmers' and General Insurance Company—St. John's House—Conservative Land Society—Eminent Residents in Norfolk Street—Office for Licensing Hackney Coaches—Voltaire and Will Congreve—Howard Street—Attempted Abduction of Mrs. Bracegirdle, the Actress—Murder of Mr. Mountfort.

BETWEEN Arundel and Norfolk Streets were two houses which were only demolished in 1896, to provide a site for Horrex's Hotel. Sir Thomas Lyttelton, Speaker of the House of Commons in 1698, lived in one, and next door to him the father of Bishop Burnet. "Here Burnet and Sir Thomas spent much of their time together ; and it was the custom of the latter, when he had any great business to transact in Parliament, to talk it over previously with Burnet, who was to act the part of 'devil's advocate,' by bringing forward against it every conceivable argument, true or false." Burnet's house continued to be in the family until the end of the last or early in the present century, when it was possessed by a bookseller named Burnet, a collateral descendant of the bishop.

Norfolk Street, the next street westward from Arundel Street, was built in 1682, on a part of the site of Arundel House and grounds. Most of the houses in this street have of late been used as private hotels ; but there are one or two which call for special mention. At No. 3 are the offices of the Royal Farmers' and General Insurance Company.

About half way down on the western side is St. John's House, the home of a sisterhood of ladies belonging to the English Church, who devote their lives to the work of nursing the sick poor, and of training up a body of nurses really fitted for that work. It was founded in 1848, under the modest title of "The Training Institution for Nurses in Hospitals, Families, and the Poor," beginning its work in St. John's, a poor district of St. Pancras. In 1852 the sisterhood removed to Queen Square, Westminster, in order that the sisters might have the double advantage of the religious services of the Abbey and of a more special training in the wards of the Westminster Hospital.

In 1854 the sisterhood supplied some of the nurses who accompanied Miss Nightingale to the Crimea, whither twenty more of their number were dispatched in the following year. In 1856 the sisters removed to Norfolk Street, having entered on the work of nursing the patients in King's College Hospital. The sisters wear a distinctive dress, with a small cross and medal. Besides King's College Hospital, the sisters of St. John's House nurse the patients in Charing Cross Hospital, and those of the Galignani English Hospital at Paris. They also dispense annually about 4,000 diets, which are supplied for the use of convalescent patients by the members of the Order of St. John. In this invaluable institution everything is carried out on the voluntary principle, and although it is styled a "sisterhood," under a superioress, the members are not tied down by any "vows of poverty, monastic obedience, or celibacy;" there is "no cloistered seclusion, but a full, free, and willing devotion to the great cause of Christian charity."

Among the notabilities who have resided in Norfolk Street may be named Dr. Birch, the historian of the Royal Society, and John Hamilton Mortimer, the painter, styled "the English Salvator Rosa." A "Supper at Mortimer's" forms the subject of a chapter in those chatty volumes entitled "Wine and Walnuts," published in 1823. Sir Roger de Coverley is stated by Addison to have put up in this street, before he went to live in Soho Square. Mr. Dowling, a gentleman well known in sporting circles, and some time editor of *Bell's Life*, lived for many years in this street; as also did Sam Ireland, the father of the author of the Shakespearian forgeries; Albany Wallis, the friend and executor of Garrick; Mountfort, the actor; Mr. William Shippen, the incorruptible M.P.—the only man, according to Sir Robert Walpole, who was proof against a bribe; Penn, the founder of Pennsylvania; Peter the Great; and Samuel Taylor Coleridge, who from 1814 to 1816 lived at No. 42, on the east side, in a house which was removed in 1896 to make way for Horrex's Hotel, a large building of white stone with Aberdeen granite pilasters, fronting both the Strand and Norfolk Street. The street has been largely rebuilt during the last few years, and now contains several handsome blocks of offices, such as Hastings House, Amberley House, and Mowbray House.

We learn from Sir John Hawkins's "Life of Doctor Johnson" that the house occupied by Penn was at the south-western angle of the street, close to the river-side, and he chose the house as one out of which he could slip by water in case of any emergency. It would appear that this house was actually that occupied by Peter the Great, if the following notice in the *Postman* of January 13, 1698, be correct:—"On Monday night the Czar of Muscovy arrived from Holland, and went directly to the house prepared for him in Norfolk Street, near the water-side." While staying here he was visited by King William III. and by very many other members of the Court and aristocracy.

Surrey Street, built about the same time, is described by Strype as "replenished with good buildings." He draws especial attention to the two houses at the bottom, which "front the Thames," with pleasant, though small, gardens "towards the river," that on the east side belonging to "the Hon. Charles Howard, Esq., brother to Henry, Duke of Norfolk." Towards the Strand, he also tells us that there was a fine large and curious house built by a Mr. Nevinson Fox. In this street, during the last century, was the head office for the licensing of hackney coaches, but this building being burnt down, the office was transferred to Great Queen Street, Lincoln's Inn Fields.

Voltaire, as we learn from his life, when in London, paid a visit to Will Congreve, who was living in this street, and who also died in it. "On this and on other occasions," says Peter Cunningham, "Congreve affected to be thought a man of fashion rather than of wit, on which Voltaire remarked, with his usual cynicism, that 'if he had been only a gentleman, he should not have come thither to visit him.'" Another celebrated literary character, who lived in Surrey Street, was George Sale, the translator of the Koran; his death took place here in 1736.

Howard Street, which runs at right angles across the centre of Norfolk Street, from Arundel Street to Surrey Street, and like neighbouring streets, has been largely rebuilt of late years, has never been remarkable for distinguished residents. It was, however, before it had been built twenty years, the scene of a terrible tragedy, the remembrance of which still survives. In it Will Mountfort, one of "his Majesty's servants"—in other words, a player—was murdered on the night of December 9th, 1692. The story is one of interest, and involves some celebrated characters. We tell the tale as told to us by Mr. Peter Cunningham in his "Handbook of London:"—

"A gallant of the town, a Captain Richard Hill, had conceived what Cibber calls a 'tendre,' or passion for Mrs. Bracegirdle, the beautiful actress. He is said to have offered her his hand, and to have been refused. His passion at last became ungovernable, and he at once determined on carrying her off by force. For this purpose he borrowed a suit of night linen of Mrs. Radd, the landlady in whose house in Buckingham Court he lodged, induced his friend Lord Mohun to assist him in his attempt, dodged the fair actress for a whole day at the theatre, stationed a coach near the 'Horseshoe' Tavern, in Drury Lane, to carry her off in, and hired six soldiers to force her into it as she returned from supping with Mr. Page, in Princes Street (off Drury Lane), to her own lodging in the house of a Mrs. Dorothy Brown, in this street. As the beautiful actress came down Drury Lane, about ten at night, accompanied by her mother and brother, and escorted by her friend, Mr. Page, one of the soldiers seized her in his arms, and endeavoured to force her into the coach. Page resisting the attempt, Hill drew his sword, and struck a blow at Page's head, which fell, however, only on his hand. The lady's screams drew a rabble about her, and Hill, finding his endeavours ineffectual, bid the soldiers let her go. Lord Mohun, who was in the coach all this time, now stepped out of it, and with his friend Hill, insisted on seeing the lady home, Mr. Page accompanying them, and remaining with Mrs. Bracegirdle for some time after for her better security.

"Disappointed in their object, Lord Mohun and Captain Hill remained in the street, Hill with his sword drawn, and vowing revenge, as he had done before, to Mrs. Bracegirdle on her way home. Here they sent to the 'Horseshoe' Tavern in Drury Lane, for a bottle of canary, of which they drank in the middle of the street. In the meantime Mrs. Bracegirdle sent her servant to her friend Mr. Mountfort's house in Norfolk Street adjoining, to know if he was at home. The servant returned with an answer that he was not, and was sent again by her mistress to desire Mrs. Mountfort to send to her husband to take care of himself : ' in regard my Lord Mohun and Captain Hill, who (she feared) had no good intention toward him, did wait in the street.

"Mountfort was sought for in several places without success, but Mohun and Hill had not waited long before he turned the corner of Norfolk Street, with, it is said by one witness (Captain Hill's servant), his sword over his arm. It appears in the evidence before the coroner, that he had heard while in Norfolk Street (if not before) of the attempt to carry off Mrs. Bracegirdle, and was also aware that Lord Mohun and Hill were in the street ; for Mrs. Brown, the landlady of the house in which Mrs. Bracegirdle lodged, solicited him to keep away. Every precaution was, however,

ineffectual. He addressed Lord Mohun (who embraced him, it would appear, very tenderly), and said how sorry he was to find that he (Lord Mohun) would justify the rudeness of Captain Hill, or keep company with such a pitiful fellow, or words to the like effect. ' And then,' says Thomas Leak, the Captain's servant, ' the Captain came forward and said he would justify himself, and went toward the middle of the street, and Mr. Mountfort followed him and drew.' Ann Jones, a servant (it would appear, in Mrs. Bracegirdle's house), declared in evidence that Hill came behind Mountfort and gave him a box on the ear, and bade him draw. It is said they fought. Mountfort certainly fell, with a desperate wound on the right side of the belly, near the short rib, of which he died the next day, assuring Mr. Page, while lying on the floor in his own parlour, as Page declares in evidence, that Hill ran him through the body before he could draw the sword. Lord Mohun affirmed they fought, and that he saw a piece of Mountfort's sword lying on the ground. As Mountfort fell, Hill ran off, and the Duchy watch coming up, Lord Mohun surrendered himself, with his sword still in the scabbard.

"The scene of this sad tragedy was that part of Howard Street lying between Norfolk Street and Surrey Street. Mountfort's house was two doors from the south-west corner. Mountfort was a handsome man, and Hill is said to have attributed his rejection by Mrs. Bracegirdle to her love for Mountfort, an unlikely passion it is thought, as Mountfort was a married man, with a good-looking wife of his own, afterwards Mrs. Verbruggen, and a celebrated actress withal. Mountfort (only thirty-three when he died) lies buried in the adjoining church of St. Clement Danes."

Mrs. Bracegirdle continued to inhabit her old quarters for very many years. "Above forty years since," says Davies, "I saw at Mrs. Bracegirdle's house in Howard Street a picture of Mrs. Barry, by Sir G. Kneller, in the same apartments with the portraits of Betterton and Congreve." The seconder of Captain Hill in this discreditable affair was the Lord Mohun, whose name we shall have occasion to mention again hereafter, when we come to speak of Hyde Park, as having fallen in a duel with the Duke of Hamilton.

Mrs. Bracegirdle, born in 1663, was known as one of the most attractive and fascinating of our earliest actresses, and it is said that every one of her male audience became her lover, or at all events her admirer. Her virtue was remarkable, being "as impregnable as the rock of Gibraltar." She is called by Dr. Doran "that Diana of the stage before whom Congreve and Lord Lovelace, at the head of a troop of bodkined fops, worshipped in vain."

This troop of fops, it may be added, would sometimes include the Dukes of Devonshire and Dorset and the Earl of Halifax ; amongst whom it is said that the latter remarked at a coffee-house one day, "Come, you are always praising the lady's virtue : why then do you not reward the lady who will not sell it ?" then and there offering to head a subscription list with £200, *pour encourager les autres*. "Four times that amount was raised," says Dr. Doran, "and with it the nobles, with their swords in their hands, waited on Mrs. Bracegirdle" —no doubt in Howard Street—"who accepted the testimonial."

Mrs. Bracegirdle was very kind to the poor, and especially to the poorer members of her profession. She is described by Aston as "of a lovely height, with dark brown hair and eyebrows, black sparkling eyes, and a fresh blushing complexion ; and when-ever she exerted herself, had an involuntary flushing in her breast, neck, and face, having continually a cheerful aspect and a fine set of even white teeth, and never making an exit without leaving the audience in imitation of her pleasant countenance." Colley Cibber tells us that "she inspired the best authors to write for her ; and two of them (Rowe and Congreve), when they gave her a lover in a play, seemed palpably to plead their own passions, and make their private court to her in fictitious characters."

But there is a reverse to this exquisite medal. In Spence's "Anecdotes," and in Bellchambers' edition of "Colley Cibber," it is asserted or assumed that this chaste lady was really Congreve's mistress ; and Dr. Young seems to hint the same thing, when he says that "Congreve was very intimate with Mrs. Bracegirdle, and lived in the same street with her, his house being very near hers, until his acquaintance with the young Duchess of Marl-borough."

This scandal would seem to have been confirmed by the voice of contemporary testimony. Lord Macaulay calls her, however, a "cold, vain, in-terested coquette, who perfectly understood how much the influence of her own charms was increased by the fame of a severity which cost her nothing, and who could venture to flirt with a succession of admirers in the just confidence that the flame which

she might kindle in them would not thaw her own ice." It was probably in a good-natured banter at the lady's real proclivities that Nicholas Rowe, in one of his short poems, exhorts Lord Scarsdale to

> "All publicly espouse the dame,
> And say, Confound the town."

Thackeray confirms the above account of the attempted seizure of Mrs. Bracegirdle, which, he says, occurred "opposite to my Lord Craven's house in Drury Lane, by the door of which she was to pass on her way from the theatre." He adds, "Mr. Page called for help ; the population of Drury Lane rose ; it was impossible to effect the capture ; and so, bidding the soldiers to go about their busi-ness, and the coach to drive off, Hill let go of his prey sulkily, and he waited for other opportunities of revenge." As to her acting, if we may credit C. Dibdin, "she equally delighted in melting tender-ness and playful coquetry ; . . . . . and even at an advanced age, when she played Angelica in *Love for Love*, for Betterton's benefit, she retained all her powers of pleasing." She died in 1748.

At one time, as our readers will remember, when it had been resolved to erect the long-expected buildings for the New Law Courts of the future, even after the site between St. Clement's Church and Carey Street had been cleared, it was in con-templation to build them on the ground which lies between Howard Street and the Thames Embankment ; and Mr. G. E. Street, the archi-tect to whom this work had been entrusted, put forth in print his reasons, both æsthetic and practical, for preferring the site between the Strand and the river. But into these it is not necessary that we should now enter, as the sub-ject has long since passed out of the range of discussion.

It may, however, be said that in the long run the proposal of the Embankment site was nega-tived by the Art Commissioners, and that the Legislature in 1873 fixed definitely and con-clusively that the Law Courts of the future were to stand, as indeed they do now, between the Strand and Carey Street. In fact, the building and opening of them settled the question for ever. Howard Street, Norfolk Street, Surrey Street, Arundel Street, and Essex Street will therefore, so far as they are concerned, be allowed to remain *in statu quo*.

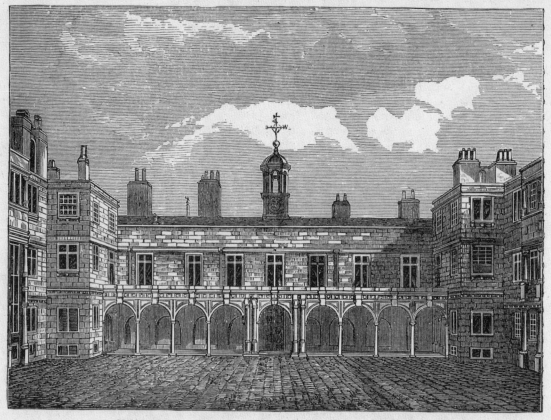

COURT OF OLD SOMERSET HOUSE, FROM THE NORTH. (*See page* 92.)

CHAPTER XIV.

ST. MARY-LE-STRAND, THE MAYPOLE, &c.

" Fairly we marched on, till our approach
    Within the spacious passage of the Strand
    Objected to our sight a summer broach
    Yclep'd a Maypole, which, in all our land,

No city, town, nor street can parallel ;
    Nor can the lofty spire of Clerkenwell—
    Although we have the advantage of a rock—
    Perch up more high his turning weather-cock."

Building of St. Mary-le-Strand Church—Singular Accident—The Young Pretender here renounces the Roman Catholic Faith—Strand Bridge—
Strand Theatre—The Original Church of St. Mary-le-Strand—Setting up the Maypole—Anne Clarges, Wife of the First Duke of Albemarle
—Maypole Alley—Sir Isaac Newton purchases the Maypole—An Ancient Cross—Chester, or Strand Inn.

IT is said by all the antiquaries who have written on the subject of London topography, that the present church of St. Mary-le-Strand covers the site of the spot on which in the olden time was set up the Maypole which the sour-visaged Puritans pulled down as dangerous to the morals of youth. It was called "St. Mary's as a matter of course, because its predecessor, which stood on the south side of the Strand, and was demolished by the Protector Somerset, was dedicated to St. Mary the Virgin." It is said that the Protector was at the time so all-powerful in matters of state, that he was never forced to make to the parishioners any compensation for the robbery of which he was guilty, though from his time down to the year 1723

they were churchless, and in order to be decently baptised, married, or buried, they were forced to have recourse to the ministers of neighbouring parishes.

In accordance with an Act passed in the reign of Queen Anne, for building fifty new churches in and around the metropolis, this site was fixed on for the first of these sacred edifices, which must have been much needed, on account of the growth of the population westward of St. Clement Danes. The first stone of it was laid in 1714, but it was not till nine years later, as we have said, that it was actually consecrated. Gibbs was the architect, and in his own account of St. Mary's Church says it was the first building he was employed upon after his

SOMERSET HOUSE IN 1755. (See page 93.)

arrival from Italy; and few structures, perhaps, have been more severely criticised. The building is fine of its kind, but not extensive, and stands, as it were, in the centre of the roadway of the Strand, in a line with the houses which form the southern side of Holywell Street, and from which it is separated by the entrance to Newcastle Street. The entrance, at the west end, is by a circular flight of steps which lead to a portico of Ionic columns, covered with a dome, which is crowned with an elegant vase. The columns are continued along the body of the church, with pilasters of the same order at the corners; and between the columns are niches, handsomely ornamented. Over the dome is a pediment, supported by Corinthian columns, which are also continued round the body of the church, over those of the Ionic order beneath, between which are the windows placed over the niches. A handsome balustrade is carried round the top, and its summit is adorned with vases. The steeple at the west end is ornamented with composite columns and capitals. There was at first no steeple designed for the church; only a small campanile, or turret, for a bell, was to have been over the west end of it; but at the distance of eighty feet from the west front it was intended to have erected a column, 250 feet high, in honour of Queen Anne, on the top of which her statue was to be placed. The design for the column was approved by the commissioners, and a great quantity of stone was brought to the place for laying the foundation of it; but the idea of erecting that monument was abandoned upon the Queen's death, and the present steeple was erected instead of the campanile, as at first proposed. Internally the church has a sumptuous appearance. The side walls display two ranges of pilasters, one above the other; the ceiling is slightly arched, and is divided into compartments, covered with decorations in stucco, and richly coloured; and the altar at the east end, which is placed within a very large and striking-looking recess, has above it three large windows filled with stained glass, with subjects of the Annunciation, the Passion, &c. The church underwent restoration in 1862, but in 1888 it was closed as unsafe, though reopened in 1889.

A sad accident happened at this spot during the procession of royalty to St. Paul's on the proclamation of peace in 1802. Just as the heralds came abreast of the building, a man who was standing on the roof of the church happened to lay his hand on one of the stone arms upon the parapet, knocked it down upon the crowd below, and so killed three persons.

If we may believe the statement of David Hume, it was in this church that Charles Edward Stuart, "the Young Pretender," as he is more generally styled, formally renounced the Roman Catholic faith, and professed the religion of the Church of England, doubtless for political rather than religious motives.

The author of "Walks through London" says that "at the digging the foundation for the St. Mary-le-Strand Church, the virgin earth was discovered at the depth of nineteen feet; a proof that the ground in this neighbourhood originally was not much higher than the Thames. This village was, therefore, truly denominated the Strand, from its situation on the bank of the river. Where Catherine Street now stands a stream of water ran into the Thames. Over this, in the Strand, was a bridge called Strand Bridge."

Nearly opposite to St. Mary's Church is the Strand Theatre. The house is small, and at one time was commonly known as the "Bandbox." It was originally built for the exhibition of a panorama, but was altered to a theatre in 1831. We will reserve a detailed description of this house for a future chapter.

The original Church of St. Mary-le-Strand was built under the dedication of "The Nativity of our Lady and the Innocents," and in consequence of a religious sisterhood attached to it. It was sometimes styled also "St. Ursula of the Strand." It was formerly in the patronage of the Bishops of Worcester, possibly because built or endowed by one of those prelates, whose town-house adjoined it, while the Inns of the Bishops of Lichfield and Coventry, Llandaff, and Chester were not far off. The old Church of St. Mary occupied the site of the eastern part of the present Somerset House. In the reign of James I. a windmill, and also a watch-house stood on the site of the present church; and Stow observes that on this spot there was "a stone building or conduit over a spring."

The Maypole, to which we have already referred as formerly standing on the site of the church of St. Mary-le-Strand, was called by the Puritans one of the "last remnants of vile heathenism, round which people in holiday times used to dance, quite ignorant of its original intent and meaning." Each May morning, as our readers are doubtless aware, it was customary to deck these poles with wreaths of flowers, round which the people danced pretty nearly the whole day. A severe blow was given to these merry-makings by the Puritans, and in 1644 a Parliamentary ordinance swept them all away, including this very famous one, which, according to old Stow, stood 100 feet high. On the

Restoration, however, a new and loftier one was set up amid much ceremony and rejoicing. From a tract printed at the time, entitled "The Citie's Loyaltie Displayed," we learn that this Maypole was 134 feet high, and was erected upon the cost of the parishioners there adjacent, and the gracious consent of his sacred Majesty, with the illustrious Prince the Duke of York. "This tree was a most choice and remarkable piece; 'twas made below bridge and brought in two parts up to Scotland Yard, near the king's palace, and from thence it was conveyed, April 14, 1661, to the Strand, to be erected. It was brought with a streamer flourishing before it, drums beating all the way, and other sorts of musick. It was supposed to be so long that landsmen could not possibly raise it. Prince James, Duke of York, Lord High Admiral of England, commanded twelve seamen off aboard ship to come and officiate the business; whereupon they came, and brought their cables, pullies, and other tackling, and six great anchors. After these were brought three crowns, borne by three men bareheaded, and a streamer displaying all the way before them, drums beating and other musick playing, numerous multitudes of people thronging the streets, with great shouts and acclamations, all day long. The Maypole then being joined together and looped about with bands of iron, the crown and cane, with the king's arms richly gilded, was placed on the head of it; a large hoop, like a balcony, was about the middle of it. Then, amid sounds of trumpets and drums, and loud cheerings, and the shouts of the people, the Maypole, 'far more glorious, bigger, and higher than ever any one that stood before it,' was raised upright, which highly did please the Merrie Monarch and the illustrious Prince, Duke of York; and the little children did much rejoice, and ancient people did clap their hands, saying golden days began to appear." A party of morris-dancers now came forward, "finely decked with purple scarfs, in their half-shirts, with a tabor and a pipe, the ancient music, and danced round about the Maypole."

The setting up of this Maypole is said to have been the deed of a blacksmith, John Clarges, who lived hard by, and whose daughter Anne had been so fortunate in her matrimonial career as to secure for her husband no less a celebrated person than General Monk, Duke of Albemarle, at a time when courtiers and noble lords and princes did not always look to the highest rank for their wives. With her is connected a story which may best be told, perhaps, by a brief outline of a certain *cause célèbre* in which her name figures prominently :—

"During the trial of an action for trespass between William Sherwin, plaintiff, and Sir Walter Clarges, Baronet, defendant, at the bar of King's Bench, in November, 1700, the following circumstance occurred :—The plaintiff, as heir and representative of Thomas Monk, Esq., elder brother of George, Duke of Albemarle, claimed the manor of Sutton, in Yorkshire, and other lands in Newton, Eaton Bridge, and Shipton, as heir-at-law to the said duke, against the defendant, to whom they had been left by his only son and successor, Christopher, the second duke, who died without issue in 1688."

In the course of the trial some very curious particulars were disclosed with respect to the family of Anne Clarges, the wife of George, the first Duke of Albemarle. "It appeared that she was daughter of John Clarges, a farrier in the Savoy, who was farrier to the duke, then Colonel Monk. She was married in 1632, in the church of St. Lawrence Pountney, to Thomas Ratford, son of another man of the same name, who had been a farrier and a servant in the employment of Prince Charles, and resident in the Mews (no doubt the King's Mews at Charing Cross). She had a daughter who was born in 1634, and who died at four years old. She lived with her husband at the 'Three Spanish Gipsies,' in the New Exchange, in the Strand, and sold such things as washballs, powder, and gloves, and also taught girls plain work. About 1647 she was acting as sempstress to Colonel Monk, and used to carry him his linen. In 1648 her father and mother died, and in the following year she and her husband 'fell out and parted,' but no certificate from any parish register could be produced to prove his burial. However, in 1652, she was married at the church of St. George, Southwark, to General George Monk, and was delivered in the following year of a son, Christopher, who, as stated above, became, or at all events was called, the second duke, and who died in 1688. Several witnesses were brought forward to swear that they had seen Thomas Ratford, her Grace's first husband, alive as lately as January, 1669–70, many years after her marriage with the first duke and the birth of the second. In opposition to this evidence, it was alleged that all along, during the lives of Dukes George and Christopher, this matter was never questioned; that the latter was universally received as the son of the former; and further, that the matter had been thrice already tried at the bar of the King's Bench, and the defendant had gained three verdicts. A witness swore that he owed Ratford five or six pounds, which he had never demanded; and a man who had married a cousin of the Duke of

Albemarle had been told by his wife that Ratford died five or six years before the duke married. In summing up, Lord Chief Justice Holt told the jury, 'If you are certain that Duke Christopher was born while Thomas Ratford was living, you must find for the plaintiff. If you believe that he was born after Ratford was dead, or that nothing appears what became of him after Duke George married his wife, you must find for the defendant.' In the end a verdict was given for the defendant, who was only son to Sir Thomas Clarges, Knight, brother of the duchess, and who was created a baronet in 1674."

Newcastle Street, at the north-east corner of the church of St. Mary-le-Strand, was formerly called Maypole Alley, but early in the last century was changed to its present name, after John Holles, Duke of Newcastle, the then owner of the property, and the name has been transferred to another place not far off. At the junction of Drury Lane and Wych Street, on the north side, close to the Olympic Theatre, is a narrow court, which is still known as Maypole Alley, near which stood the forge of John Clarges, the blacksmith, alluded to above as having set up the Maypole at the time of the Restoration.

As all earthly glories are doomed in time to fade, so this gaily-bedecked Maypole, after standing for upwards of fifty years, had become so decayed in the ground, that it was deemed necessary to replace it by a new one. Accordingly, it was removed in 1713, and a new one erected in its place a little further to the west, nearly opposite to Somerset House, where now stands a drinking fountain. It was set up on the 4th of July in that year, with great joy and festivity, but it was destined to be short-lived. When this latter Maypole was taken down in its turn, Sir Isaac Newton, who lived near Leicester Fields, bought it from the parishioners, and sent it as a present to his friend, the Rev. Mr. Pound, at Wanstead in Essex, who obtained leave from his squire, Lord Castlemaine, to erect it in Wanstead Park, for the support of what then was the largest telescope in Europe, being 125 feet in length. It was constructed by Huygens, and presented by him to the Royal society, of which he was a member. It had not long stood in the park, when one morning some amusing verses were found affixed to the Maypole, alluding to its change of position and employment. They are given by Pennant as follows :—

" Once I adorned the Strand,
    But now have found
    My way to Pound
On Baron Newton's land ;

Where my aspiring head aloft is reared,
T' observe the motions of th' ethereal Lord.
Here sometimes raised a machine by my side,
Through which is seen the sparkling milky tide ;
Here oft I'm scented with a balmy dew,
A pleasant blessing which the Strand ne'er knew.
There stood I only to receive abuse,
But here converted to a nobler use ;
So that with me all passengers will say,
' I'm better far than when the Pole of May.'"

Of the old cross in the Strand, Mr. Newton tells us, in his " London in the Olden Time," that it was mutilated at the time of the Reformation, and that it stood for some years headless, and was eventually taken down in the reign of Charles II. He identifies its site with that of the Maypole, already mentioned.

Allen, in his " History of London," says that " opposite to Chester Inn " (which, by the way, appears to have been the same building that was afterwards called " Strand Inn," and which stood where now is the east end of Somerset House) " stood an ancient cross, at which the judges occasionally used to sit to administer justice outside the City walls."

The origin of the judges administering justice in public is of very remote antiquity, as is evident from the frequent allusion to the custom made in Holy Scripture, where judges are spoken of as sitting " in the gate ;" and the reason of so public a situation being chosen, says Herbert, in his " Inns of Court," was on two accounts : " that their proceedings might be generally seen, and that none might go out of the common way to seek for justice."

" Strand Inn " was one of those Inns of Court belonging to the Middle Temple so ruthlessly pulled down in the reign of Edward VI., by the Protector Somerset, for the building of Somerset House, when the students settled at New Inn, in Wych Street, another of the Inns of Chancery. Pennant records the tradition that it was in this place that Occleve, the poet of the reign of Henry V., studied law.

Mr. Newton tells us, in his " London in the Olden Time," that " Strand Inn " having ceased to be occupied as an episcopal residence, " a part of it became separated, and let off to students of the law, in whose occupation it was known both as ' Chester Inn ' and ' Strand Inn.' " He adds that when seized on by the Protector Somerset, he " for some time kept his court there." On its west side was another large house, called the " Bishop of Worcester's Inn," of which we know nothing except it was a long time the residence of the Bishops of that see, and no print or view of it has come down to our times.

CHAPTER XV.

SOMERSET HOUSE AND KING'S COLLEGE.

" Before my gate a street's broad channel goes,
Which still with waves of crowding people flows ;
And every day there passes by my side,

Up to its western reach, the London tide,
The spring-time of the term. My front looks down
On all the pride and business of the town."—Cowley.

Old Somerset House—Rapacity of the Protector Somerset—John of Padua, Architect of the Original Building—Downfall and Execution of the Protector—Somerset House assigned to the Princess Elizabeth—Afterwards the Residence of the Queens of England—Its Name changed to Denmark House—Additions made by Inigo Jones—Banishment of the Capuchin Fathers, and Desecration of the Chapel—The Services in the Chapel restored, and Pepys' Account of them—Catherine of Braganza—Attempt to implicate the Royal Household with the Murder of Sir Edmundbury Godfrey—The Cemetery—Description of the Old Buildings—Their Demolition—Building of New Somerset House—Amusing Tradition relative to Somerset House—King's College.

THE building so familiar to Londoners, old and young, by the name of Somerset House, occupies the space formerly covered by four or five buildings of note in their day, of some of which we have already spoken. It appears from Stow that in order to make a level space of ground to hold the fair new palace which he purposed to erect—" that large and goodly house now called Somerset House"—the Protector Somerset pulled down, and " without any recompense," the Inns, as they were called, of the Bishops of Chester, Llandaff, Lichfield and Coventry, and Worcester, with all the tenements adjoining, and also the old parish church of St. Mary's.

The original Somerset House, it is almost needless to remark, took its name from the Duke of Somerset, the Lord Protector of the reign of the boy-king, Edward VI. ; but the present building is of much more recent date. By the attainder of Somerset it reverted to the Crown, and it was frequently tenanted by Queen Elizabeth. Anne of Denmark, the wife of James I., and Catherine of Braganza, the neglected queen of Charles II., both in succession held their courts within its walls. At length it came to be appropriated by usage as a residence to the queens-dowager, and was frequently appointed as a temporary residence for such of the ambassadors of foreign princes as the later Stuarts and the earlier Brunswick sovereigns cared especially to honour.

Mr. A. Wood, in his " Ecclesiastical Antiquities of London and its Suburbs," is of opinion that the Protector Somerset already possessed some property on the site of Somerset House when he began the great work of pulling down his neighbours' houses around their ears and his own. But be this true or not, he seems to have known, or at all events to have made, little distinction between *meum* and *tuum*, and when he had once resolved on his end—namely, to build a palace on this central site, at a bend commanding the view of the river from London Bridge to the Abbey at Westminster—he was not likely to be at much loss as to the means to be employed. Wide space and materials were all that he needed, and these he soon obtained in a manner such as we should now probably distinguish by the term " by hook or by crook." And further, in order to complete the undertaking in a thoroughly substantial and, as it would now be called, " first-class" style, he pulled down also the charnel-house of Old St. Paul's and the chapel over it, together with a structure in " Pardon Churchyard, near the Charterhouse, throwing the dead into Finsbury Fields," and the steeple, tower, and part of the church of the Priory of St. John of Jerusalem at Clerkenwell. With these materials he commenced his work, unblessed by either the Church, or the people, or the poor.

Bishop Burnet, alluding to the Protector's rapacity, admits that " many bishops and cathedrals had resigned many manors to him for obtaining his favour," though he adds, " this was not done without leave obtained from the king." He also accuses the Protector of selling chantry lands to his friends at easy rates, for which it was concluded he had great presents. The rise of Somerset House exposed its owner to the reflection that " when the king was engaged in such wars, and when London was much disordered by the plague that had been in it for some months, he was then bringing architects from Italy, and designing such a palace as had not been seen in England."

Pennant tells us that the architect employed by the Protector Somerset in the erection of Somerset House was the celebrated John of Padua, the architect of Longleat, in Wiltshire, who is said, in Walpole's " Anecdotes of Painting," to have held, under Henry VIII., the post of " Devizer of His Majesty's Buildings."

Whether the Protector Somerset ever resided in the palace he had thus been at so much trouble in building, there is some room to doubt. The building itself was commenced in 1546-7, and as soon after as the month of October, 1548, at which time the works were still going on, he was deprived of the Protectorship and committed to the Tower.

He was, however, pardoned after two years' imprisonment, and restored to the Council; but in the following year he was again committed to the Tower on charges of high treason, and was beheaded on Tower Hill in January, 1552. One of the grounds of dissatisfaction at first exhibited against him appears to have been "his ambition and seeking of his own glory, as appeared by his building of most sumptuous and costly buildings,

most probably, however, at the expense of her kinsman, Lord Hunsdon, to whom she had given the use of it. Such, at all events, was the opinion of Pennant.

Stow tells us that the queen of James I. made this house her palace, and that she entertained the king with a feast within its walls on Shrove Tuesday, 1616, when the latter was so delighted at her reception of him that he ordered it to be

SOMERSET HOUSE AND STAIRS.
As they appeared before they were pulled down in 1776. (*See page* 93.)

and specially in the time of the king's wars, and the king's soldiers unpaid." On the attainder of the Duke of Somerset his palace was, of course, forfeited to the Crown, and his nephew, King Edward, appears to have assigned it to his sister, the Princess Elizabeth, for her use whenever she visited her sister's court. But when she came to the throne, she preferred the regions of Whitehall and St. James's, and fashion followed in the wake of royalty westwards. At this period the building is spoken of as "Somerset Place, beyond Strand Bridge." On Elizabeth's succession to the throne some partial restoration of Somerset's property was probably made, for Somerset Place became the residence of the Dowager Duchess.

Elizabeth seems to have lived here occasionally,

called Denmark House in her honour. The palace was greatly improved and beautified by the queen, who added much to it in the way of new buildings, Inigo Jones being called in to furnish the designs. She also brought a supply of water to it by pipes laid on from Hyde Park. In 1626 it was settled for life on Henrietta Maria, the queen of Charles I., for whom it had been stipulated on her marriage that she should be allowed the free practice of her religion, having been born and brought up a pious Catholic. Accordingly it was fitted up for the reception of herself and her household, including, of course, a body of priests to say mass daily, and to celebrate the offices of the Church. The priests in attendance on the queen were Capuchins. They had succeeded to the

Oratorians, who had been expelled by the influence of Buckingham (Steenie) with his royal master. The foundation-stone of the chapel was laid by the queen, the work being carried out under the direction of Inigo Jones. The first stone was laid with great ceremony. From six in the morning

chapel seems to have been also turned to account constantly in other ways. There were frequent "conferences" for the edification of Catholics and the instruction of Protestants, and on three days in each week the Catholic doctrine was taught catechetically in English and in French. The con-

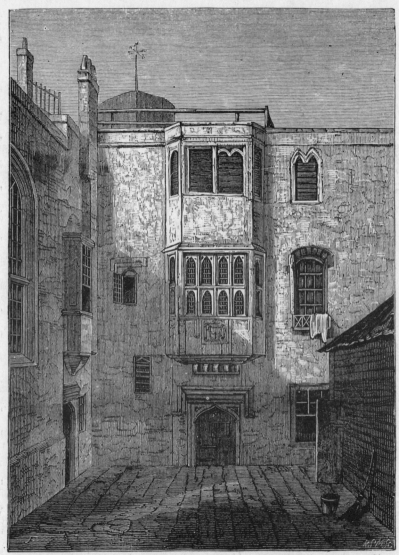

THE SAVOY. *From a Drawing by J. P. Neale, published in* 1815. (*See page* 96.)

there was a succession of masses daily till nearly noon, and as it was difficult to approach the sacraments elsewhere, except clandestinely, the confessionals were thronged constantly. On Sundays and festivals there was a controversial lecture at noon, and soon after followed vespers, sung by the Capuchins and musicians in the galleries. When vespers were over, there was a sermon on the gospel of the day, and lastly, compline. The

sequence was that there were frequent conversions to the ancient faith, and the name of the chapel began to offend the ruling powers. Accordingly, when the queen was absent in Holland, it was resolved by the authorities to make an assault upon the place. The Capuchin fathers were silenced and driven out, then imprisoned, and at length banished; their dwelling itself was pulled down, and the chapel desecrated, in spite of its being the property of the queen. The Capuchins were brought back, and the chapel was repaired, when Henrietta Maria returned to England, a widowed queen, after her son's restoration.

Here, in September, 1660, died the Duke of Gloucester, from the small-pox; and hence his body was taken by water "down Somerset Stairs," as Pepys tells us, to Westminster, to be buried in the Abbey.

Pepys, in his "Diary," gives an account of a service held in the chapel of Somerset House in 1663–4. "On the 24th, being Ash Wednesday, to the Queen's chapel, where I staid and saw mass, till a man came and bade me go out or kneel down; so I did go out; and thence to Somerset House, and there into the chapel, where Mons. D'Espagne, a Frenchman, used to preach." In October he again visits Somerset House, and saw the queen's new rooms, "which are most stately and nobly furnished!" In January, 1664–5, he went there again, and was shown the queen's mother's chamber and closet, "most beautiful places for furniture and pictures." In consequence, however, of the plague in the June following, the Court prepared to leave Whitehall and Somerset House. The Queen went to France, and there died in 1669. On the death of Charles II. in 1685, Somerset House became the residence of Catherine of Braganza, who lived here until her return to Portugal in 1692. It had previously belonged to her as Queen Consort, and during the ultra-Protestant *furore*, which exhibited itself for some years prior to the Revolution, attempts were made to implicate her household in the pretended Popish Plot of the time, and to connect the mysterious murder of Sir Edmundbury Godfrey in 1678 with persons in her service.

There is so much doubt and uncertainty mixed up with the story of the murder of Sir Edmundbury Godfrey, that it is almost impossible to winnow the truth from the falsehood, owing to the perjuries of Titus Oates and his confederate, Bedloe, the discharged servant of the Lord Belasyse. But it appears clear that the worthy justice of the peace was inveigled to a spot close to "the Watergate at Somerset House," under the pretence of his presence being wanted to allay a quarrel, and that he was strangled on the spot with a twisted handkerchief. His dead body, it would seem, was afterwards carried to Primrose Hill, at that time a retired and lonely spot, where a sword was run through it. For their presumed share in this murder three persons were hung at Tyburn in 1679. An attempt was made by Oates and Bedloe to implicate the Jesuits in the plot, and even the Queen, who then resided at Somerset House; but

Charles, with his usual wit, refused to listen to the charge, telling Burnet that though "she was a weak woman, and had some disagreeable humours, she was not capable of a wicked thing."

We have already said that, under the Stuarts, Somerset House was frequently appointed for the reception of ambassadors whom the sovereign and the court delighted to honour. The last foreigner of importance who lodged there was the Venetian ambassador, who made a public entry into it in 1763, shortly before the building was pulled down.

From the time of the departure of Catherine of Braganza, Somerset House ceases to possess any interest in its strictly palatial character. It continued as an appurtenance of successive queens down to the year 1775, when Parliament was recommended, in a message from the Crown, to settle upon Queen Charlotte the house in which she then resided, "formerly called Buckingham House, but then known by the name of the Queen's House," in which case Somerset House, already settled upon her, should be given up and appropriated "to such uses as shall be found most useful to the public."

Mr. Wood, in his "Ecclesiastical Antiquities," tells us that in the reign of James II., Dr. Smith, one of the four vicars-apostolic who acted as Catholic bishops in England, was consecrated at Somerset House. There was also in the grounds of Somerset House a small cemetery, in which the Catholic members of the Queen's household were buried. In 1638 Father Richard Blount, who had "reconciled" Anne of Denmark, the consort of James I., to the Roman Church, was buried here by the Queen's permission. The value of such a permission at that time may be inferred from the fact that, owing to the severity of the penal laws, Catholics were for the most part obliged to be buried in Protestant cemeteries, with rites distasteful to themselves; and they were only too glad when the priest who attended them in their last illness could bless a little mould which was put into their coffin, and perform the usual ceremonies in secret, and even at a distance from their bodies.

A map and ground-plan of old Somerset, or Denmark House in 1706, shows that it consisted of one large and principal quadrangle, called "the Upper Court," facing the Strand. Its out-buildings were very extensive, and still more so its terraced gardens, facing the Thames, with stairs at either end. In the southern front of the quadrangle named above were the Guard Chamber, with a waiting-room, the Privy Chamber, the Presence Chamber, from the west end of which a flight of stone steps led down into the garden. On the western side, from the Strand nearly to the river-side, there ran along Duchy Lane (now absorbed in Wellington Street South) a row of coach-houses, stables, and store-yards. To the south-east angle of the chief quadrangle there was a passage down the " Back Stairs " to a second, or lower court, two storeys lower than the upper court. Here were the more private apartments of the queen—the " Coffee Room," " Back Stair Room," " Oratory," dressing-room, bed-chamber, and " Withdrawing Room," the two last-named facing the gardens and commanding a fine view of the reach of the river. Still further to the east, extending across what now is part of King's College, as far as Strand Passage, or Lane, were a variety of other buildings, occupied by the members of the Court, called the French Buildings, connected with the Yellow Room, the Cross Gallery, the Long Gallery, and leading to a " pleasance " which opened into the garden. A print in the *Gentleman's Magazine*, showing some of these last-named buildings before they were pulled down, together with the new building of Sir William Chambers on the north, leads us to suppose that, though interesting as a specimen of the style of Edward VI., their removal was no great loss from an architectural point of view.

The gardens were laid out in the square and monotonous style of the period, so well described by Pope—

" Grove nods to grove, each alley has its brother,
　And half the garden just reflects the other."

This was literally true here, for in front of both the greater and the lesser quadrangle there were square gardens, with straight gravel walks on each side, and three avenues of trees ; a handsome flight of stone steps, with iron gates ; and on either side some handsome statues of Tritons and Nereids. Along the river ran a raised terrace, with a heavy dwarf wall. In a print of the river front of Somerset House, dated 1706, there appears moored a little way off the stairs a sort of house-barge, under which is written " The Folly," and a queer-shaped wherry, approaching the form of a gondola.

" I am extremely pleased," observes Stow, " with the front of the first court of Somerset House, next the Strand, as it affords us a view of the first dawning of taste in England, this being the only fabric that I know which deviates from the Gothic, or imitates the manner of the ancients." How amused would Pugin or Sir Gilbert Scott be to read this statement ! and also the sentiment which follows :—" Here are columns, arches, and cornices that appear to have some meaning ; if proportions are neglected, if beauty is not under-stood, if there is in it a strange mixture of bar-

barism and splendour, the mistakes admit of great alleviations." In all probability the architect was an Englishman, and this his first attempt to refine on the work of his predecessors.

It is currently believed that James Stuart, the elder " Pretender," was at one time secreted in old Somerset House ; and there is an allusion to this belief in the *Town Spy*, published in 1725 :— " The Pretender's residing at Somerset House in the year of Peace was blabbed out by one of the Duke d'Aum—nt's postilions."

The demolition of the old building was commenced as soon as an Act could be passed, and Sir William Chambers was appointed architect of the new buildings. They were commenced in 1776, and in 1779 one of the fronts was completed. The site occupies an area of upwards of 800 feet by 500. The front towards the Strand consists of a rustic basement of nine arches, supporting Corinthian columns, and an attic in the centre, and a balustrade at each extremity. Emblematic figures of Ocean and of the eight principal rivers of England in alto-relievo adorn the keystones of the arches. Medallions of George III., Queen Charlotte, and the Prince of Wales were formerly placed over the three central windows of the first floor. The attic is divided into separate portions by statues of Justice, Truth, Valour, and Modera-tion ; and the summit is crowned with the British arms, supported by emblematical figures of Fame and the genius of England. The chief feature of the river front of Somerset House is its broad terrace, about 600 feet in length, raised on rustic arches, and ornamented with emblematic figures of the Thames. The centre of the large quadrangle opposite the chief entrance from the Strand is occupied by a gigantic piece of bronze work, executed by Bacon. The principal figure is a fanciful and almost allegorical representation of Father Thames.

The building affords at present accommodation during the working hours of the day to upwards of 900 Government officials, belonging to the Audit Office, the Inland Revenue Office, the Office of the Registrar-General, and the offices connected with Doctors' Commons. In the north front the annual exhibition of the Royal Academy was held from 1780 down to about the year 1837, when it was transferred to the National Gallery in Trafalgar Square. The use of apartments in Somerset House for the meetings of the society was also granted in 1780. The Royal Society removed from Somerset House to Burling-ton House, Piccadilly, in 1856. The Society of Antiquaries, and also the Royal Astronomical and the Geological Societies, have also at various times occupied apartments in Somerset House.

"The royal patronage of the arts," writes Malcolm, in 1806, "is most conspicuous in this grand building, which contains the apartments of the Royal Society, the Society of Antiquaries, and the Royal Academy of Painting. The two former assemble on the east side of the vestibule or entrance, and the latter on the west."

The Society of Antiquaries dates its origin from the year 1751. Malcolm tells us that previous to that time several unsuccessful, or at least interrupted, attempts had been made, in the reigns of Elizabeth, James, and Charles I., to establish such a society, but nothing effective was done until the reign of George II., who granted a charter, styling himself the founder and patron of the Society of Antiquaries, appointing Martin Folkes, Esq., as its president, and limiting the society's permanent income to £1,000 a year. The president must be assisted by a council of twenty members, half of whom are elected annually, along with himself, and the officers and members of the society are required to possess an accurate knowledge of the history and antiquities of their own and foreign nations, and to be "loyal and virtuous members of the community." The Archbishop of Canterbury, the Lord Chancellor, the Lord Privy Seal, and the Secretaries of State for the time being, are visitors of the society. The number of fellows is not limited by their charter. At their meetings descriptions and dissertations are read, and illustrative drawings are exhibited. Their transactions as a body are under the control of an elective director in the arrangement of communications to be published. Their official publication, in a handsome quarto form, is known as the "Archæologia."

Pennant writes, in 1806: "The Royal Society and the Society of Antiquaries both hold their meetings here; and here also are annually exhibited the works of the British painters and sculptors."

Mr. John Timbs, in his "Romance of London," tells us an amusing traditionary story relative to this place:—"A little above the entrance-door to the Office of Stamps and Taxes is let into the wall a white watch-face. Of this it is told that when the wall was being built a workman fell from the scaffolding, and was saved from being killed only by the ribbon of his watch, which caught upon a piece of projecting ornament. In thankful remembrance of his wonderful preservation, he is said, and is believed to this day, to have inserted his watch in the face of the wall." A very

pretty story, indeed, if it was only true. But, unfortunately for the age of poetry, Mr. Timbs lets us into the real secret of the watch, which is essentially prosaic. "It was placed," he says, "in its present position, many years ago, by the Royal Society, as a meridian mark for a portable transit instrument in one of the windows of the anteroom;" and the late Admiral W. H. Smyth, the eminent hydrographer to the Admiralty, would often tell his friends that, having assisted in mounting the instrument, he well remembered the watch being inserted in the wall. We fear, therefore, that the poetic view must be dismissed.

Running parallel with the buildings forming the west side of the quadrangle, and having its frontage towards Lancaster Place, a new wing was built in 1857, from the designs of Mr. Pennethorne, in a style of architecture corresponding with the rest of the building. Here are the offices of the Inland Revenue Department, and in the basement several rooms are set apart for the printing of postage and other stamps, postal wrappers, envelopes, &c.

The vaults were once used for keeping some of the public records, now collected into one repository in Fetter Lane. Most of the wills formerly kept in Doctors' Commons are now housed here.

The whole of the east wing was left incomplete by Sir William Chambers, but in 1829 this part of the edifice was finished from the designs of Sir Robert Smirke, R.A., and it now forms King's College, which was founded by royal charter in the previous year. The entrance is a neat, though confined semi-circular archway from the Strand, over which stand the Royal Arms, supported by figures symbolical of Wisdom and Holiness, with the motto, "Sancte et Sapienter." The building extends from the Strand to the Thames, and occupies a considerable area of ground. The interior, which is very capacious, is well calculated for its intended objects. The centre of the principal floor is occupied by the chapel, under which is the hall for examinations, &c., and a new triangular wing, one storey high, built in a line with Somerset House, and fronting the Thames Embankment, adjoining the residence of the Principal, has been erected for the purposes of the college.

The government of King's College is vested in a Council, which reports annually to the Court of Governors and Proprietors, as the official title of the corporation runs. Forty-two members compose this council, nine of whom are the official governors; one is the treasurer, eight are life governors, and the other twenty-four, of whom six go out every year, are elected by the Court of Proprietors, from a list prepared by the Governors.

There are certain endowments, which are specially appropriated to certain prizes, scholarships, and professorships, classical and scientific ; but the College possesses no endowment applicable to general purposes, and the whole of the expenditure required for the ordinary every-day work of the College, with the exception of a small parliamentary grant, has to be defrayed out of the fees paid by the students.   The general education of the College is carried on in eight distinct departments—viz., the theological department ; the department of general literature ; the department of engineering ; the medical department ; the evening classes ; the Civil Service department ; the department for ladies, carried on in Kensington Square ; and finally, the school.   This last is in the hands of a head master, subject to consultation with the Principal, who has the general supervision of the whole College.   There are five Divinity professors, namely, the Revs. R. J.

Knowling (who is also Vice-Principal and Chaplain), Dr. Stanley Leathes, A. I. M'Caul, C. Hole, H. C. Shuttleworth, W. E. Collins, and Harold Smith. It should be added that the education given here is strictly in accordance with the principles of the Church of England.   The grant was withdrawn by the last Liberal Government, but restored by the present Ministry.

The students of King's College are divided into two classes—the " matriculated " and the " occasional."   The former are those who are admitted to the full prescribed course of study, while the latter, through inability to attend the whole course, devote themselves to the pursuit of one particular subject, as at the two great universities of England.   The Principals of King's College in the forty years which have passed since its foundation have been distinguished theologians, Bishops Otter, Lonsdale, and Barry, Canon Jelf, and Dr. Wace.

CHAPTER XVI.

THE SAVOY.

" There is a power
And magic in the ruined battlement,

To which the palace of the present hour
Must yield its pomp, and wait till ages are its dower."

Early History of the Savoy Palace—John, the French King, lodged here—The Savoy attacked by the Citizens of London, and by Wat Tyler—Converted into a Hospital by Henry VII.—Assembly of the Commissioners for the Revision of the Liturgy—A Colony of Jesuits established in the Savoy—The Chapel of St. Mary—Distinguished Persons buried here—Funeral of the Earl of Bedford—The " Worshipful Company of Upholders."

A LITTLE to the west of Somerset House, on ground sloping rather steeply down to the riverside, stood what was originally the Palace, and afterwards the Hospital, of the Savoy.   It was built by that all-powerful noble, Simon de Montfort, Earl of Leicester, in 1245 ; but in the thirtieth year of Henry III. it was granted by the king to Peter of Savoy (from whom it took its name), uncle of his queen, Eleanor of Provence, according to Pennant, " on condition of yielding yearly at the Exchequer three barbed arrows for all services." This Peter of Savoy, Earl of Savoy and of Richmond, was son of Thomas, Earl of Savoy, brother of Boniface, Archbishop of Canterbury.

From the Earl of Savoy the place passed, probably by gift, to the Brethren de Monte Jovis, that is, of the Great St. Bernard in Savoy, who had a priory at Hornchurch, in Essex ; and, according to Stow, Queen Eleanor purchased the site from this fraternity and gave it to her second son, Edmund, Earl of Lancaster.   This gift was confirmed by letters patent by the earl's elder brother, King Edward I., in his twenty-first year, and " from that time the Savoy was reputed and taken as parcel of the earldom and honour of Lancaster."

John, the French king, was lodged here in 1357, when brought to England as a captive by the Black Prince, after the battle of Poictiers, and here he was often visited by Edward III. and his queen.   At this time it bore the reputation of being " the fairest manor in England."   Six years later he returned of his own accord, and again took up his final residence at the Savoy.   In Stow's " Chronicles," under the date of 1364, we find the following passage :—" The 9th day of April, died John, King of France, at the Savoy ; his corpse was honourably conveyed to St. Denis, in France."

In 1377 the Savoy stood a narrow chance of being demolished by the citizens of London, who had flocked thither, " evidently bent on mischief," after the support which John of Gaunt gave to Wickliffe at a synod held in St. Paul's Cathedral. The Bishop of London, on hearing of the riot, hurried to the Savoy, and averted the danger that threatened it.   But this quelling of the tumult appears to have been only temporary, for the palace of the Savoy was fired, pillaged, and almost demolished with gunpowder by a lawless mob of rebels, led by Wat Tyler, in 1381, " for the malice

which they bore to John of Gaunt and his principles." And there is no doubt that they did their
work thoroughly, for not only was the hall blown
up and the houses destroyed, but the rebels had a
narrow escape from perishing in their ruins. The
leaders of the party, it appears, were so con-
scientious in their anger, that they gave orders that
none of their men should turn anything found to
their own use, but that gold, silver, and all other
spoil, should be burnt. Finding, therefore, certain
boxes, which they thought might contain such loot,
they threw them into the flames, with the result
above stated. Others of these hypocritical ruffians

later, its revenues being seized upon by royalty.
The hospital was re-founded and re-endowed by
Queen Mary soon after her accession, when "the
ladies of the court and maids of honour . . . .
stored it anew with beds, bedding, and other
furniture in a very ample manner."

The hospital, however, fared but badly under
Elizabeth. It escaped, indeed, the royal claws,
but it was most unfortunate in its master, who
"embezzled its revenues exceedingly, and sold
away divers chantries belonging to it." Happily,
he was deprived.

For a number of years the Savoy Chapel served

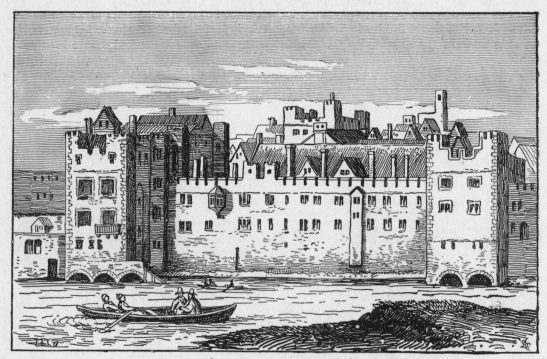

THE SAVOY IN 1650. (*From a very scarce Etching by Hollar.*)

perished at the same time. "To the number of
thirty-two," we are told, "the rebels entered a
cellar of the Savoy, where they drank so much of
sweet wines, that they were not able to come out
in time, but were shut in with wood and stones,
that walled up the doors, where they were heard
crying and calling seven days after, but none came
to help them out until they were dead."

Reverting to the king's hands after this, we next
find it beautifully restored and rebuilt by Henry
VII., who dedicated it to St. John, in 1509, as a
hospital for the reception of a hundred poor people.
In spite of a report made by the Royal Commissioners in the fifth year of Edward VI., to the effect
that there was "no default and no disorder" to be
found in its inmates, it was dissolved two years

for both the neighbouring parishioners of St. Mary-
le-Strand as well as for inmates of the "precinct
of the Savoy."

In the time of the plague appearing, the liberty
of the Duchy of Lancaster was looked upon as
"some security to the Court," to keep the unwelcome visitor from making its way thither from
the City; and it was accordingly entrusted to the
care of bailiffs, who were charged to ward it off.
And thus Stow tells us that in the year 1577, when
the plague was in the City, and the Court was removed in consequence to Windsor, the Earl of
Leicester appointed a bailiff to take charge of the
district, and to see that it was kept closed against
infection, threatening to pluck his coat from off
his back in case of his neglect. We read that the

Recorder Fleetwood, an active and a good man, lent his help to the bailiff in surveying the duchy, "passing constantly with all the constables between the Bars and the Tilt Yard, in both the liberties, to see the houses shut in." It is to be hoped that this primitive quarantine arrangement was successful in its results.

the Revision of the Liturgy to be held. Twelve of the chief bishops of the time, with nine assisting clergymen, took part in its proceedings on behalf of the Established Church, while the Nonconformist party were represented by Baxter, Calamy, Reynolds, and other leaders of the Dissenters. The meeting is known to history as the Savoy

THE "FOX-UNDER-THE-HILL," 1860. (*See page* 101.)

The place, too, is not without its literary associations, for Chaucer wrote some of his poems in the Savoy.

It was here that the "Confession of Faith" by the Independents was drawn up, in the time of Cromwell and his Directory.

The Savoy is also famous in connection with the history of the Church of England, having been the place in which Charles II., after the Restoration, ordered the assemblies of the Commissioners for

Conference, and its results were to confirm the High Church party in the Catholic or sacramental view of the Prayer Book (which was enforced by the Act of Uniformity), and to disallow the Presbyterian scruples.

Mr. Peter Cunningham reminds us that " at this time Fuller, author of the ' Worthies,' was Lecturer at the Savoy, and that the poet Cowley was a candidate at court for the office of Master."

The Savoy has not been exempt from sundry

vicissitudes in respect to the religion of its tenants, and at one time has given shelter to exiled Roman Catholics, and at another to Protestants driven from France by the revocation of the Edict of Nantes.

It is recorded by Roman Catholic historians that in the reign of James II. a colony of Jesuits was established in the Savoy under one F. Palmer, as rector. He opened schools which numbered some four hundred pupils, half Catholics and half Protestants; and adjoining the schools was a printing-press. Rules were provided for these schools and published in print. It was declared therein that the intention of them was to teach youth virtue and learning; that those that came thither should be taught gratis, and to be at no further charge than of buying of their own pens, ink, paper, and books; that these schools should be common to all, of what condition soever, and none to be excluded when they should be thought fit to begin to learn Latin and wrote sufficiently well. "In these schools to be taught Greek and Latin, poetry and rhetoric. And whether Catholics or Protestants came to these schools, yet in teaching no distinction to be made, yet all to be taught with equal diligence and care; and neither by masters or scholars any tampering or meddling to persuade any one from the profession of his own religion. But few there were but did believe —nay, could not believe otherwise than that this pretended charitable project was for the advantages hereby to be compassed for the promoting the Roman religion. These schools were soon dissolved upon the ceasing of the Government of King James; and the clock that was made for the use of the Savoy School was afterwards bought and set up upon a gentleman's house in Low Layton, as was said. In this Savoy were placed by William III. many families of poor French Protestants, and where they that had skill in trade and manufacture wrought to get something for their livelihood; however, they were opposed and complained of by many of the tradesmen of London as hindering and prejudicing them. Here also was, and is, a church for them. The late Bishop of London came hither himself sometimes, and passionately desired their good, and maintained many of their proselytes. The poor French here inhabiting with their families had many of them three shillings allowance weekly, and some four. To countenance them more, to this church came many of the said king's privy councillors, secretaries of state, and other great officers of the kingdom; and through them and their contributions, the church was chiefly able to subsist.

They use the Liturgy of the Church of England turned into French, and their ministers are episcopally ordained."

Strype, writing in 1755, thus describes the then existing state of the Savoy :—

"This Savoy House is very great, and at this present a very ruinous building. In the midst of its buildings is a very spacious hall, the walls three feet broad at least, of stone without and brick and stone inward. The ceiling is very curiously built with wood, and having knobs in due places hanging down, and images of angels holding before their breasts coats of arms, but hardly discoverable; for one is a cross gules between four stars, or else mullets. It is covered with lead, but in divers places perished, where it lies open to the weather. This large hall is now divided into several large apartments. A cooper hath a part of it for the stowing of his hoops and for his work; other parts of it serve as two marshalseas for keeping prisoners—as deserters, men pressed for military service, Dutch recruits, &c. Towards the east end of this hall is a fair cupola with glass windows, but all broken, which makes it probable the hall was as long again, since cupolas are wont to be built about the middle of great halls.

"In the Savoy, of how ruinous soever is, are divers good houses. First, the king's printing-press, for proclamations, Acts of Parliament, gazettes, and such-like public papers; next, a prison; thirdly, a parish church and three or four other churches and places for religious assemblies, viz., for Dutch, for High Germans, and Lutherans, and lastly, for Protestant Dissenters and Quakers. Here are also harbours for many refugees and poor people."

The old hall, as stated above, had the usual louvre in the centre of the roof; this roof was of fine timber, with pendants supposed to have resembled those in Crosby Hall. Images of angels at the corbels bore on their breasts shields with coats of arms, as in the roof at Westminster Hall.

According to a map or ground-plan of the Savoy in 1736, the part between the present chapel and the river was a prison, between which and the Lutheran Church were "barracks" and some "gardens," since used as a Lutheran burying-ground. Nearer still to the river, with which it was connected by a "water-gate," was the chapel of the German Calvinists, so that two different sets of doctrines were being taught by German preachers almost within earshot of each other. To the east stood the ancient hospital of St. John, then used as "barracks," divided from the Lutheran

Church by some "officers' houses" and "the Friery." Between this and the Strand again were gardens, and two houses, the one occupied by "Nutt, the printer," and the other marked "Vaillant, bookseller, his warehouse."

Nearly where now are Wellington Street South and Lancaster Buildings, were a "French Church," a small close known as "Green Tree Court," and sundry dwellings, some of them marked as "Dutchy Houses."

Prints of the remains of the Savoy in 1793 and 1798 show a few of the walls of the Hospital of St. John the Baptist still standing. They were, apparently, of the Tudor, or latest Gothic style, as was also the "prison," which has a fine Perpendicular entrance, and oriel window above it. At the foot of the print is a statement to the effect that "this part of the Savoy is now occupied by the army as a place of confinement for their deserters and transports."

Henry VII. helped to rebuild the Savoy, as a hospital for a hundred distressed people. This building was in the form of a cross, and Pennant adds that its walls were entire down to his time (1806). The Records of the Duchy of Lancaster were formerly kept in a building close by, in Lancaster Place.

A considerable part of the old Savoy was standing at the beginning of the present century; but it was demolished to form the approach to Waterloo Bridge.

The present "Chapel of St. Mary in the Hospital, or of St. John the Baptist in the Savoy"—for it rejoices in the double name—is of early sixteenth century date. Its interior was burnt in 1864, but subsequently restored in the ancient style, at the cost of Her Majesty the Queen, under the superintendence of Mr. Sydney Smirke. It is small, but well-proportioned, consisting of a nave without aisles or chancel.

It has a rich reredos over the altar, which faces the north, having niches with domed canopies at either extremity. The window over the altar is of five lights, with vertical mullions of the Perpendicular or Tudor style. There are two sedilia, with a piscina between them and the east, or rather, north wall; the oak roof is coved at the sides, and divided with quatrefoil panels, showing the emblems of the Passion, the sacred monogram, the Lamb and Flag, the pelican in her piety, the types of St. John the Baptist, and sundry heraldic ornaments. It is richly painted throughout, and the prevailing colour is blue. Among the "memorial" windows that have been inserted is one to the Prince Consort, placed here by the Queen, in her capacity as Duchess of Lancaster and patroness of the living.

In the Savoy Chapel were buried many famous personages; among others, Gavin Douglas, the poet-Bishop of Dunkeld, son of Archibald "Bell the Cat," Earl of Angus. The reader of Scott's "Marmion" will remember how, at the wedding of De Wilton and Clare—

"A bishop at the altar stood—
A noble lord of Douglas blood;"

and he will be glad to learn that in the Savoy he "sleeps the sleep that knows not waking." Here, too, was buried, at his own request, Christopher Davenport, better known as Franciscus à Sanctâ Clarâ, who translated from the Portuguese the "Chronicles of the Franciscan Order," and who "reconciled Anne, Duchess of York, to the church which her husband had joined."

Among the persons who have either been buried or had monuments erected to them here are Mrs. Killigrew, the actress, daughter of Dr. Killigrew, one of the Masters of the Savoy; George, third Earl of Cumberland, of the old line of Clifford; Richard Lander, the African traveller; George Wither, the poet and satirist; and the Earl of Feversham, who commanded King James's troops at Sedgemoor. In the burial-ground attached to the church is the tomb of William Hilton, many years Keeper of the Royal Academy.

The precinct of the Savoy was made into a parish by Bishop Grindal, in the reign of Elizabeth, when the Protector Somerset demolished the old Church of St. Mary, to make room for his new palace, and it is probably the smallest parish in the metropolis or its suburbs west of Temple Bar.

A very distinguished man became the Master of the Savoy in the reign of James I. We refer to Antonio de Dominis, ex-Archbishop of Spalatro, who, adopting strong anti-papal tenets, came to England, where he published a learned treatise, "De Republicâ Ecclesiasticâ," and was ultimately made Dean of Windsor. He was a Master also of Natural Philosophy. He does not, however, lie buried here, as late in life he went to Rome, in order to make his peace with the Church which he had left.

Machyn, in his "Diary," records the burial, in 1554, of the Earl of Bedford, Lord Privy Seal, who died "at his house beside the Savoy," and was carried thence to his home at Chenies for interment. His funeral procession, as it started hence, must have been a splendid sight. He was carried with three crosses before him, and many clerks and priests in attendance, "till they came to the hill above St. James's, when some turned back.

All were mounted on horseback. First, there rode one in black bearing a silver cross; then came priests in surplices; then came the standard; then the gentlemen and chief officers; then the heralds, with the helmet, mantle, and crest, the armour and insignia; then came the funeral car with painted banners; then the saddle-horse; then the mourners, chief of them Lord Russell's son; then the Lord Treasurer, the Master of the Horse, and various members of the nobility, all clad in black. Everywhere on the course of the procession the clergy came forth to meet it, and alms were distributed among the poor."

In speaking of the parish of St. Mary-in-the-Savoy, the *London Spy*, published in 1725, says that it was the head-quarters of "the Worshipful Company of Upholders," meaning the undertakers;

and the writer adds a graduated scale of fees paid by those black-coated and keen-eyed gentry to coachmen, footmen, and other persons in positions where news travels quickly, for ready information as to the deaths, actual or approaching, of titled and wealthy personages.

A number of dingy coal-wharves was all that, during the first half of the present century, and, indeed, until the formation of the Thames Embankment, stood by the river-side to mark the site of a palace which had been the residence of John of Gaunt, Duke of Lancaster, and of the poet Chaucer. Some lofty buildings, including an hotel and the Medical Examination Hall, have been erected on their site, and between the Savoy and the Embankment now is a garden, where shrubs and flowers delight the eye of the weary Londoner.

CHAPTER XVII.

THE STRAND:— SOUTHERN TRIBUTARIES (*continued*).

"Here Essex' stately pile adorned the shore;
There Cecil's, Bedford's, Villiers'—now no more."—*Gay*.

Beaufort Buildings—Fielding, the Novelist—Worcester House—Carey House—The "Fox-under-the-Hill"—Beaufort House—Salisbury House—The Middle Exchange—Cecil Street—The Arundel Club—Ivy Bridge Lane—Durham House—The New Exchange—The Duchess of Tyrconnel, the "White Milliner"—A Singular Tragedy and Curious *Dénouement*—Coutts's Bank—The Adelphi—Garrick's House—The "Shades"—The Society of Arts—Buckingham Street—York Stairs—Buckingham Water Gate—Villiers Street.

PROCEEDING still westward on our pilgrimage along the Strand, we next arrive at Beaufort Buildings, where in the last century resided Fielding, the novelist, of whom an interesting anecdote is told in the *Gentleman's Magazine* for 1786:—"Some parochial taxes for his house in Beaufort Buildings being unpaid, and for which he had been demanded again and again, or, in the vulgar phrase, dunned *de die in diem*, he was at last given to understand by the collector, who had an esteem for him, that he could delay the payment no longer. In this dilemma the author of 'Tom Jones' called a council of his thoughts to whom he should apply for a temporary accommodation, on the pledge of the embryos of his own brain. Jacob Tonson was his usual resource on these occasions. To him, therefore, he addressed himself, and mortgaged the coming sheets of some work then in hand. He received the cash—some ten or twelve guineas. Full freighted with this sum, he was returning home, when lo! fate, in the guise of friendship, had determined to intercept him in his passage, and to prevent him reaching his destination with his pecuniary cargo. When within a few doors of his own house he met an old college chum, whom he

had not seen for many years, and finding he had been unfortunate in life, gave him all the money he had just received. On reaching home he was informed that the collector had called twice for the taxes. Fielding's reply was laconic, but memorable:—'Friendship has called for the money and had it; let the collector call again!" The reader will be glad to hear that a second application to Jacob Tonson enabled him to satisfy the parish demands." At the corner house, No. 96, Strand, now occupied by Eugene Rimmel, the perfumer, formerly lived another of the same profession, Charles Lillie, whom Steele has commemorated in the pages of the *Tatler*, and whose name is also embalmed in the *Spectator*.

On the site of Beaufort Buildings, between the Savoy and Durham Place, stood Worcester House, the town mansion of the Earls of Worcester, and previously the residence of the Bishops of Carlisle. Its gardens extended to the river-side. The great Earl of Clarendon occupied this house before his own mansion was built, paying for it the annual rent of £500.

In the Strand, near the Savoy, was a house known as Carey and afterwards as Stafford House.

It is casually mentioned by Pepys as "a house now of entertainment, next my Lady Ashly's, where I have heretofore heard Common Prayer read." Dryden, too, in his "Wild Gallant," speaks with evident delight of "the sack at Cary House with the apricot flavour." We must also mention another house of some repute which stood close by this spot down to a recent date, namely, the tavern known as the "Fox-under-the-Hill," the entrance to which was at No. 75 in the Strand. This inn was shut up after the erection of the Victoria Embankment, and, along with the rest of the dilapidated tenements between the Savoy, the Adelphi, and the Embankment Garden, has since been swept away. We have preserved a representation of the old inn on page 97.

Concerning the old house of the Earls of Worcester, afterwards called Beaufort House, honest John Stow tells a story to the effect that "there being a very large walnut-tree growing in the garden, which much obstructed the eastern prospect of Salisbury House, near adjoining, it was proposed to the Earl of Worcester's gardener, by the Earl of Salisbury or his agent, that if he could prevail with his lord to cut down the said tree, he should have £100. The offer was told to the Earl of Worcester, who ordered him to do it and to take the £100; both which were performed to the great satisfaction of the Earl of Salisbury, as he thought; but, there being no great kindness between the two earls, the Earl of Worcester soon caused to be built in the place of the walnut-tree a large house of brick, which took away all his prospect." The house was burnt down in 1695.

The building adjoining, Salisbury House, gave place to Cecil Street and Salisbury Street, the latter of which, before the construction of the Thames Embankment, led to Salisbury Stairs. Salisbury House—or, as it was sometimes called, Cecil House—was built by Robert Cecil, first Earl of Salisbury, a son of the great Lord Burghley, and was a "large and stately" mansion. In 1678 a great part of it was pulled down, and Cecil and Salisbury Streets were built on its site. A portion of Cecil House, consisting of one large room, was subsequently fitted up with shops on both sides, and opened as "the Middle Exchange." This building extended to the river, where there was a flight of steps for the use of passengers by water. The place seems to have borne anything but a good reputation—being called the "Whore's nest"—and in the end going to ruin it was pulled down, with the remains of great Salisbury House, about the year 1696. Upon the site was built Cecil Street, of which Strype speaks as a "fair street with very good houses, fit for persons of repute," so that it is to be hoped that the former tenants of the "nest" were put to flight.

Of Cecil Street we have little or nothing to remark, as its annals appear to be a blank of late years, except that in the last century it was inhabited by the Lord Grey, the Archbishop of York, and Dr. Wollaston, and both it and Salisbury Street are now nothing but approaches to the Hôtel Cecil.

At the bottom of Salisbury Street, on the left hand, in a house swept away to make way for the hotel, had been established, since 1865, the Arundel Club, so called from its original abode in Arundel Street, and now housed in Adelphi Terrace. It consists mainly of literary men and artists. One of its possessions is a fine portrait of Marinarni, many years scene-painter at Drury Lane, painted by the late Mr. Clarkson Stanfield, R.A., and presented to the club by his son, Mr. G. C. Stanfield.

The next turning westwards of Salisbury Street, down to what once was the river-side, was called Ivy Lane, leading to Ivy Bridge, or Pier—the same which in our own memories was used as the landing-stage of the halfpenny steamboats that used to ply between the Strand and London Bridge, but was discontinued shortly after the disastrous explosion of the *Cricket* at the "Fox" pier (so called after the "Fox-under-the-Hill" tavern), in August, 1847. The place is mentioned by both Stow and Strype. The former says that the lane "parted the Liberty of the Duchy (of Lancaster) and the city of Westminster on the south side," and that the "bridge" had been lately taken down. Strype adds that the road was very bad and almost impassable.

Near this spot, Pennant tells us, the former Earls of Rutland had "a house at which several of that noble family breathed their last." He does not, however, say anything which can enable us to identify its situation.

Adjoining Ivy Bridge Lane on the west was Durham House, the "Inn" of the Bishops of Durham, one of the most interesting of the old Strand palaces. According to Pennant, its original founder was Anthony de Beck, Patriarch of Jerusalem and Bishop of Durham in the reign of Edward I. It was rebuilt by Thomas Hatfield, soon after his nomination to that see, in 1345; he was Secretary of State to Edward III., and lived here till he was old. Even from the rough sketch of it in Aggas's map, Durham House would seem to have been an "Inn" of some importance; but from Hollar we gather a more correct idea of its appearance, when viewed from the river. It is described by Norden as "high and stately, supported with lofty marble pillars;" but it would appear to have been dull and heavy, as well as

It had been proclaimed in France, Flanders, Scotland, and Spain, for all comers that would undertake the challenge of England, which were Sir John Dudley, Sir Thomas Seymour, Sir Thomas Poynings,

IVY BRIDGE LANE, 1860. (*See page* 101.)

grand, like many of its neighbours on the banks of the river. Henry VIII. obtained this house by way of exchange from Cuthbert Tonstall, the bishop whose name is so well known in English history. It is to be hoped that in this case the "exchange" was not really a "robbery." Durham House, after it passed out of the hands of the Church into those of royalty, became celebrated as a gay scene of chivalric entertainment on many occasions. In the year 1540, for example, as Stow informs us, a magnificent tournament was held at Westminster.

and Sir George Carew, Knights, and Anthony Kingston and Richard Cromwell, Esquires. The old chronicler then gives a vivid picture of the tournament in detail, and adds, "That day, after the jousts performed, the challengers rode into Durham House, where they kept open household, and feasted the king and queen, with their ladies and all the court." On one day the Lord Mayor of London and the aldermen, with their wives, were entertained with a display of jousting, and there was a merry dance in the evening.

YORK STAIRS AND THE WATER TOWER. *From a Print dated* 1780. (*See page* 108.)

Young Edward, on reaching the throne, gave Durham House to his sister, the Princess Elizabeth, and she in her turn, when she became queen, bestowed it on Sir Walter Raleigh. On his attainder, however, the property was restored to the Bishops of Durham, but soon after sold to the Earl of Pembroke. In Edward's reign a royal mint was established at Durham House, under the direction of the Lord High Admiral Seymour. It was at Durham House that, in May, 1553, the Duke of Northumberland, who then inhabited it, beheld the accomplishment of the first act of his plan for placing his niece, Lady Jane Grey, upon the throne—namely, her marriage with his son, Lord Guildford Dudley. Two months later, and within four days of the death of the king, the Lady Jane was conducted from Durham House to the Tower with great pomp and ceremony, and openly proclaimed queen. The result is but too well known to every reader of English history.

In the reign of James I. the thatched stables of the mansion, fronting the Strand, were pulled down, and a large building, called the " New Exchange," erected in their place. It was opened in 1609 in the presence of the king, the queen, and Prince Henry, when his Majesty bestowed upon it the name of " Britain's Burse." A rich banquet was served on the occasion, at the expense of Lord Salisbury.

The New Exchange consisted of a basement, in which were cellars; the ground-floor, level with the street, a public walk; and an upper storey, in which were stalls or shops occupied by milliners and sempstresses, and other trades that supply dresses. The building did not attain any great success till after the Restoration, when it became quite a fashionable resort, and so popular that there is scarcely a dramatist of the time of Charles II. who is without a reference to this gay place. The shops, or stalls, had their respective signs, one of which, the " Three Spanish Gipsies," was kept by Thomas Radford and his wife, the daughter of John Clarges, a farrier in the Savoy. The farrier's daughter, as we have stated in a previous chapter, ultimately became Duchess of Albemarle. She died within a few days of the duke, and was buried by his side in Henry VII.'s Chapel, at Westminster Abbey.

But she was by no means the only duchess associated with the New Exchange. The Duchess of Tyrconnel, wife of Richard Talbot, Lord Deputy of Ireland under James II., after the abdication of the one and the death of the other, is said to have supported herself for a short time in one of the trades of the place; and she is commemorated by Horace Walpole with his usual piquancy. Pennant speaks of her as " a female suspected to have been his duchess," adding that she " supported herself here for a few days, till she was known and, otherwise provided for, by the trade of the place, for she had delicacy enough to wish not to be detected." She sat in a white mask and a white dress, and was known as the " White Milliner." This anecdote was dramatised by Douglas Jerrold, and produced at Covent Garden Theatre in 1840, as " The White Milliner." She died in 1730 in the Convent of the Poor Clares in Dublin.

It was here, too, that a certain Mr. Gerard was walking one day, meditating how he should best carry into execution a certain plot in which he was engaged—the assassination of no less a person than Oliver Cromwell—when he was insulted by Don Pantaleon, brother of the Portuguese ambassador, and resented it so warmly that the latter, in revenge, the next day sent a set of ruffians to murder him. His murderers mistook their victim, and killed another man. The *dénouement* is curious, as well as tragical. Don Pantaleon was tried, found guilty, and condemned. On the scaffold he met the very man whom he had intended to destroy, Mr. Gerard, whose plot in the interim had been discovered, and the two suffered in company.

The New Exchange was a long building running parallel with the Strand, and its site is now occupied by the houses Nos. 54 to 64, the bank of Messrs. Coutts being the centre. It stands on the court garden front of Durham House, and, next to Drummond's, is the oldest of the West-end banks. It was founded by one George Middleton, and originally stood in St. Martin's Lane, not far from St. Martin's Church, but was removed to its present site by Mr. Thomas Coutts, an enterprising Scotchman, the story of whose rise is thus narrated :— His father was a merchant at Edinburgh, who had four sons, the two youngest of whom, James and Thomas, were brought up in the paternal counting-house. James, at the age of twenty-five, came to London, and first settled in St. Mary Axe, as a Scotch merchant, but from that business, however, he subsequently retired to become a banker. He took a house in the Strand, the same in which the firm still exists; and he was joined here, some years after, by his brother Thomas, as a partner. On the death of James soon afterwards, Thomas continued to carry on the banking business, and with such an energetic spirit, that he soon gained many friends, and found himself on the sure road to success. Mr. Lawson, in his " History of Banking," tells a story concerning Mr. Coutts' shrewd-

ness and enterprise which will bear repeating :—
" In the early part of his career Mr. Coutts, anxious
to secure the cordial co-operation of the heads of
the various banking-houses in London, was in the
habit of frequently inviting them to dinner.   On
one of these occasions, the manager of a City bank,
in retailing the news of the day, accidentally remarked that a certain nobleman had applied to his
firm for the loan of £30,000, and had been refused.
Mr. Coutts listened, and said nothing ; but the
moment his guests had retired, about ten o'clock
in the evening, he started off to the house of the
nobleman mentioned, and requested the honour of
an interview with his lordship the next day.   On
the following morning the nobleman called at the
bank.   Mr. Coutts received him with the greatest
politeness, and taking thirty one-thousand pound
notes from a drawer presented them to his lordship.
The latter, very agreeably surprised, exclaimed,
' But what security am I to give you ?' ' I shall be
satisfied with your lordship's note of hand,' was the
reply.   The ' I.O.U.' was instantly given, with
the remark, ' I find I shall only require for the
present £10,000 ; I therefore return you £20,000,
with which you will be pleased to open an account
in my name.'   This generous—or, as it may more
truly be called, exceedingly well-calculated—act
of Mr. Coutts was not lost upon the nobleman,
who, in addition to paying in within a few months
£200,000 to his account, the produce of the sale
of an estate, recommended several high personages
to patronise the bank in the Strand.   Among new
clients who opened accounts there was King
George III."   Most members of the king's family,
the late Duke of Wellington, &c., banked here,
and so did Dr. Johnson and Sir Walter Scott.

Mr. Coutts had not only many friends, but even
real admirers, among the nobility, and he is said to
have been an object of attraction to not a few designing matrons, who had marriageable daughters.
But all these aristocratic matrimonial speculations
were somewhat rudely dispelled and frustrated, and
Mr. Coutts in the end "took unto himself a wife,"
in the person of one Elizabeth Starkey, a domestic
in his brother's service.   The union, it is affirmed,
was productive of great happiness to the banker,
and he was blessed with three daughters, each of
whom became married to men of title—namely, the
Marquis of Bute, the Earl of Guildford, and Sir
Francis Burdett, Bart.   After the death of his first
wife, Mr. Coutts gave his hand to Miss Harriet
Mellon, the celebrated actress.   On this second
marriage, both Mr. and Mrs. Coutts were made the
constant subjects of unworthy ridicule, which, however, had no other effect than that of strengthening

the confidence of the husband in his wife, a confidence which was displayed in a remarkable manner
in the will made by Mr. Coutts shortly before his
death, which happened in 1821.   By this will he
left the whole of his fortune, amounting to some
£900,000, to his widow, " for her sole use and
benefit, and at her absolute disposal, without the
deduction of a single legacy to any other person."
Mrs. Coutts subsequently (1827) married the Duke
of St. Albans ; but under the marriage settlement
wisely reserved to herself the whole control of the
immense fortune left to her by her first husband.
On her death, in 1837, she bequeathed her vast property to the favourite granddaughter of Mr. Coutts,
Miss Angela Burdett, the youngest daughter of
Sir Francis Burdett, the estimable and beneficent
lady, founder of so many churches, schools, and
other buildings for ameliorating the condition of
the working classes, on whom the Queen has been
pleased to confer the title of Baroness, and who is
now well known as Lady Burdett Coutts.

The partners in "Coutts and Co." (1897) are
Messrs. William M. Coulthurst, G. J. Marjoribanks,
Hugh L. Antrobus, W. Rolle Malcolm, the Hon. H.
Dudley Ryder, J. H. Dudley Ryder, F. J. W. Farquhar, Lord Archibald Campbell, the Hon. W. F. D.
Smith, and the Baroness Burdett Coutts.   It is supposed that Messrs. Coutts' is the largest private bank,
and has the most extensive connection among the
nobility and landed gentry of any existing firm.

We learn from Mr. Peter Cunningham's " Hand-
Book of London," that the interior of the house
occupied by Messrs. Coutts is very handsome and
well decorated, containing, *inter alia*, some "good
marble chimney-pieces of the Bacon and Cipriani
school."   He adds : " The dining-room is hung
with Chinese subjects on paper, sent to Mr. Coutts
by Lord Macartney, whilst on his embassy to China,
in 1792–5.   In another room is a collection of portraits of the early friends of the wealthy banker,
including the portrait of Armstrong, the early poet,
by Sir Joshua Reynolds.   The strong rooms and
vaults of the house will repay an endeavour to
obtain a sight of them.   Here, in a succession
of cloister-like avenues, are stored, in boxes of
all shapes, sizes, and colours, the patents, title-
deeds, plate, &c., of many of the nobility and
gentry ; and the order in which the place is kept
is perfectly wondrous."

The estate of Durham Yard, having become an
unprofitable heap of ruin, was purchased by Messrs.
Adam, four brothers, architects by profession, who
built upon it, in 1768, parallel with the river, the
noble terrace known as the Adelphi, and also two
or three streets running at right angles with it,

and communicating with the Strand, in which they have preserved their respective Christian names, as well as family name—as Adam Street, John Street, Robert Street, &c.

The following account of the brothers Adam we take from "Pilgrimages in London :"—

"Robert Adam was the eldest brother ; he had travelled much, had visited Palmyra and Baalbec, and in all his architectural works there is a peculiar style, which displays itself in the ornamental portions of the Adelphi buildings—the introduction of an exuberance of delicate ornament. Scotchmen are proverbially fond of their country, and the immense building speculations into which the Messrs. Adam had entered afforded them an opportunity of giving employment to their countrymen, as well as of obtaining their services, when engaged in Scotland, at a lower rate of wages than was demanded by English bricklayers and labourers. Some hundreds were, therefore, imported from Scotland, and came attended by half-a-dozen bagpipes, for the purpose, as was asserted, of keeping up the national feeling. These pipers played daily while the embankments were formed and the foundations laid ; and as the sweet chords of the classic lyre of Orpheus are said to have moved inanimate objects, so arose the Adelphi to the squeak of the Scotch bagpipes. But the charms of music to soothe the savage breast were, in this instance, vainly tried, as the workmen soon discovered that they were paid less than the London market price of their labour, and they consequently very speedily relinquished what they called "the curse of Adam," for more pay and less work, as an extra hour had been stipulated for. What was to be done ? The undertaking could not be allowed to stand still, but it was impossible to comply with the advance of wages and the diminution of time demanded. In this state of things Ireland was thought of, and a similar bargain to that which had been made in Scotland was made there, with the exception of the bagpipers whose national melodies had produced so little harmony. It was this importation from Ireland, I believe, that first opened the channel for the export of labourers and hodmen to England, and which stream of emigration has flowed regularly from the same source down to the present hour. But as nothing of importance long remains secret, the Irishmen, although satisfied to abide by their bargain of hard work and small pay, felt displeased that they had been deprived of the music enjoyed by their predecessors, and vented their humour in a coarse joke, upon which I have remarked that Scotchmen of all ranks are, even to the present

moment, peculiarly sensitive ; for Pat, with a knowing wink of his eye, asserted that if his employers had deprived him of the drone of the bagpipes by day, their honours had given him instead, both day and night, the lively amusement of the fiddle."

We ought not, and indeed we cannot forget to record here the fact that in the centre house of Adelphi Terrace died, in 1779, no less a man of note than David Garrick, within a few hundred yards from the scene of his professional triumphs. He had been an inmate of it for the last seven years of his life. The house, marked by one of the tablets of the Society of Arts, is now occupied by the Institute of Naval Architects. In the same street lived Topham Beauclerk, the wit, politician, and friend of Johnson.

The author of "Haunted London" tells us an interesting story connected with this part of the Strand. "When the Adelphi was building, Garrick applied for the western corner house of Adam Street on behalf of his friend, Andrew Beckett, the bookseller, and obtained it, promising the brothers, if the request were granted, to make the shop, as old Jacob Tonson's shop once was, the rendezvous of the first people in London." At Osborne's Hotel in the Adelphi, the King and Queen of the Sandwich Islands resided during their visit to this country in 1824. They both died during their sojourn in London in July of that year, and were buried in the vaults under St. Martin's Church.

Garrick died in the back room of the first floor of his house in the Adelphi. The ceiling of the drawing-room, if we may believe Mr. J. T. Smith, the author of "A Book for a Rainy Day," was painted by Zocchi, the subject being "Venus attired by the Graces ;" and the chimney-piece of the same room is said to have cost £800.

Mr. Timbs remarks that "the Adelphi arches, many of which are used for cellars and coal-wharves, remind us, in their grim vastness, of the Etruscan cloaca of ancient Rome. Beneath the ' dark arches,' as they were (and are) called, the most abandoned characters used to lurk ; outcasts and vagrants came there to sleep ; and many a street-thief escaped from his pursuers in those subterranean haunts, before the introduction of gas-lights and a vigilant police. Even now tramps prowl in a ghastly manner down the dim-lit passages." The piers on which the Adelphi arches rest having shown symptoms of insecurity, the whole of the structure was gradually underpinned, and otherwise strengthened, in the years 1872–4.

The ' Shades "—or, as the place was called in slang terms, the " Darkies "—was in former days one of the places of bad reputation with which the neighbourhood abounded ; but the name and the reality have both passed away.

In John Street, at No. 18, is the building designed and erected for the Society of Arts. This society has a history of its own, and has not been without its influence on the world of art and science in England. It originated, in 1753, through the public spirit of William Shipley, a drawing-master, and brother to the then Bishop of St. Asaph. Mr. Shipley first obtained the approval and concurrence of Lord Folkestone, Lord Romney, the Bishop of Worcester, Dr. Isaac Maddox, and a few other friends, and in 1754 the first meeting was held at Rawthmell's Coffee House. Its meetings were afterwards held in Crane Court, Fleet Street ; next in Craig's Court, Charing Cross ; and subsequently in a house in the Strand, opposite Beaufort Buildings. In 1774 the Society took up its quarters in the building it now occupies. The object of the society was the encouragement of art in connection with manufacture, &c. In 1755 the society met at Peel's Coffee House. The Royal Academy is said to have sprung from the Society of Arts, and in 1776 the latter proposed to the Academy — which had been instituted in 1768—that they should paint the great council-room at the Adelphi, and be remunerated by the public exhibition of their works therein. The Academy, with Sir Joshua Reynolds at its head, refused this proposal ; but in the following year James Barry, who had signed the refusal with the rest, volunteered to decorate the room without any remuneration at all. His offer was accepted, and the result was the production of six great pictures, which occupied him seven years in painting. The subjects are so connected as to illustrate this great maxim of moral truth : " That the attainment of happiness, individual as well as public, depends on the cultivation of the human faculties."

There are here a few other pictures and minor works of art and ingenuity, and they are open to the inspection of the public, free of charge, from ten till four, every week-day except Wednesday and Saturday. It is worthy of note that in 1844 Sir William Fothergill Cooke, who was at that time a member of the Council, and Vice-President of the Society of Arts, originated at a council-meeting his scheme for an International Exhibition of Industry, which was eventually carried out in 1851. In the same street, No. 14, are the headquarters of the Royal National Lifeboat Institution, founded in 1824.

Buckingham Street, our next turning in passing westward along the Strand, and Villiers Street, a thoroughfare running parallel with it, mark the site of York House, a building so named from having been the town residence of the Archbishop of that see, after the fall of Wolsey and the loss of their former and more magnificent palace at Whitehall, which has passed irrevocably into the hands of the Crown. It had been in ancient times the house or "inn," as it was termed, of the Bishops of Norwich, who, however, exchanged it for an abbey in Norfolk in the early part of the reign of Henry VIII. The next owner, Charles Brandon, Duke of Suffolk, obtained it in exchange for his own residence, Southwark House, across the river. In the reign of Queen Mary it was purchased by Heath, Archbishop of York, who called it York House ; but the name did not long continue, as his successor, Archbishop Matthew, under James I., exchanged it with the Crown for certain manors in the far North. It was afterwards inhabited by Lord Chancellor Egerton, also by Sir Nicholas Bacon, the philosopher's father, as Keeper of the Great Seal ; and subsequently by Bacon himself, on his attaining the dignity of Lord Chancellor, and it was here that he was deprived of the " Great Seal," on his degradation. York House then passed, as we have said, into the hands of the Crown, and was granted a few years later to George Villiers, Duke of Buckingham, who rebuilt it in a style of great magnificence. In the year after the execution of Charles I. the Parliament bestowed it on General Fairfax, whose daughter and heiress marrying Villiers, the second Duke of Buckingham of that line, it reverted to its rightful owner, who resided here for several years after the Restoration. He was, however, a man whose taste and extravagances led him into pecuniary difficulties, and to pay his debts he sold it for building purposes, bargaining, however, that his name and titles should be kept in memory by the streets built upon it, and which were called, respectively, George, Villiers, Duke, and Buckingham Streets. These are all that now remain to tell the antiquary of the nineteenth century the story of George Villiers, Duke of Buckingham, his rise at Court, and his fall.

His mansion never lost its name of York House, and the water-gate at the foot of Buckingham Street continued to be known as "York Stairs." The water-gate is the only vestige now remaining of this once splendid mansion.

On the side next the river appear the arms of the House of Villiers, and on the north side is their family motto, " Fidei Coticula Crux " (the Cross is the Touchstone of Faith).

At York House, within a few yards of the spot

where he first saw the light, Bacon kept his sixtieth birthday. How much he loved the place may be gathered from his answer to the Duke of Lennox, who had urged him to sell his mansion. "In this you will pardon me : York House is the house where my father died, and where I drew my first breath ; and there I will yield my last breath, if it so please God and the King." He did not, however, return to the house after his imprisonment in the Tower.

The old mansion was pulled down, as we have

de Bologna's "Cain and Abel." The "superstitious" pictures were sold by order of the Parliament in 1645, and the house was given by Cromwell to General Fairfax, by the marriage of whose daughter and heiress with George, second Duke of Buckingham, as we have already said, it was re-conveyed to the Villiers family. The duke resided here for a time, but in 1672 he sold the estate for £30,000.

Not far from the gate stood formerly a high and not very shapely tower of wood, erected in 1690-5,

BUCKINGHAM GATE IN 1830.

already noticed, by the Duke of Buckingham, who erected in its place a modern fashionable residence, the state apartments of which were fitted up with large mirrors, and other costly pieces of luxury. Between the house and the river he carried a long terrace with an embattled wall, in the middle of which was the water-gate above mentioned. After the duke's death, in the year 1628, York House was let on lease to the Earl of Northumberland. "Here was," says Mr. Timbs, "a fine collection of paintings, among which is supposed to have been the lost portrait of Prince Charles, by Velasquez." Here also was the collection of sculptures which belonged to Rubens, and in the garden was John

for supplying the Strand and its neighbourhood with the water of the then silvery Thames. Happily both the tower and the water-works, and also the water so supplied, have long been things of the past. In a print published in 1780, representing York Stairs and the Water-gate, the wooden tower of the water-works close by is shown. It was an octangular structure about seventy feet high, with small round loopholes as windows, to light the interior.

The two houses at the bottom of Buckingham Street, facing the river, have each an association of its own with the past. That on the west side was the residence of Samuel Pepys, from whose amusing

"Diary" we have drawn so largely; but it has been entirely remodelled, if not rebuilt, since his time. At the last house, on the opposite side of the street, lived Peter the Great during part of his stay in this country. And among the other celebrated persons who have made Buckingham Street their home, for a time at least, are the witty Earl of Dorset, Robert Harley, Earl of Oxford, John Henderson, the actor, and William Etty, the painter. The latter lived at No. 14, occupying chambers

Sir Richard Steele for the first two or three years after the loss of his wife in 1721.

Mr. Timbs identifies the site of the house in which Bacon was born with that of No. 31, in the Strand, at the west corner of Villiers Street. It was for many years the shop of Messrs. Roake and Varty, and contained a portion of the old ceiling of the house once inhabited by Bacon. The house was pulled down in 1863 to form the approach to the railway station.

EXETER CHANGE IN 1826. (*See page* 116.)

and a studio at the top of the house, from 1826 down to a few months before his death in 1849. In the lower rooms of the same house Mr. Clarkson Stanfield had chambers, when commencing his career as a scene-painter, and before he became known by his noble sea-pieces. At Hampton Court there is a very good view of Buckingham Street, taken from the river, about the year 1756, which shows the houses of Peter the Great and Pepys.

In Villiers Street John Evelyn was living in 1683-4, as he tells us in his "Diary." "I took a house in Villiers Street, York Buildings, for the winter, having many important causes to dispatch, and for the education of my daughters." Here, too, as Mr. Peter Cunningham reminds us, lived

"In former times," writes Allen, in his "History of London," "the banks of the Thames, from Whitehall to Somerset House, were ornamented with numerous palaces of the nobility, many consisting of two and three courts, and fitted up in the most sumptuous manner. Even as late as the time of Edward VI. elegant gardens, protected by lofty walls, embellished the margin of our great river, from Privy Bridge to Baynard's Hall. The gardens appended to the sumptuous buildings of the Savoy, and York, Paget, and Arundel Palaces." Each intervening spot was still guarded by a wall, and frequently laid out in decorative walks, a most pleasing contrast to the present state of the same district. On the Strand side of the original

Somerset Place the lapse of two centuries has worked wonders in improvement. There was no continued street here till about the year 1553. The side next the Thames then consisted of distinct mansions, screened from the vulgar eye by cheerless extensions of massive brick wall. The north side was formed by a thin row of detached houses, each of which possessed a garden, and all beyond was country. St. Giles's was a distant country hamlet.

It was on account of these numerous palatial residences, no doubt, and not on account of the magnificence of its shops, that Middleton, the dramatist, styles the Strand "luxurious." These, it would seem, were, for the most part, far from being "luxurious," consisting mainly of fishmongers' stalls and sheds, against the erection of which the authorities were often forced to protest, and sometimes to take even stronger measures. For instance, Howes writes: "For divers years of late certain fishmongers have erected and set up fish-stalls in the middle of the street in the Strand, almost over against Denmark House; all which were broken down by special commission this month of May, 1630, lest in a short space they might grow from stalls into sheds, and then to dwelling-houses."

It has been often remarked that out of the mansions which lay crowded between the Strand and the Thames, a very large number appear to have belonged to prelates of the Church in proportion to those of the titled aristocracy—the Howards and the Cecils. And if a reason is asked, it may be found in the "Table Talk" of John Selden, who observes that "anciently the noblemen lay within the City for safety and security, but the bishops' houses were by the water-side, because they were held to be sacred persons whom nobody would hurt." In consequence, we are told by Mr. Peter Cunningham as many as nine bishops possessed inns or hostelries in this district previous to the Reformation.

As an instance of the insecurity of life—for the laity, at least—in the neighbourhood of the Strand, in the reign of George I., we take the following from a newspaper of the year 1720:—"Last night a gentlewoman returning late from the Court at St. James's, was stopped a little before she came to her lodgings, in Cecil Street, in the Strand, by one Captain Fitzgerald, who would have taken her out of her chair by force; but upon her making an outcry, the chairmen were about to pull out the poles, in order to secure her from his violence; which seeing, the captain drew his sword, and sheathed it in the body of an unfortunate watchman, just come to their assistance, who instantly dropped down dead. The captain was secured for that night in St. Martin's Roundhouse, and the next day committed to the Gatehouse."

CHAPTER XVIII.

THE STRAND:—NORTHERN TRIBUTARIES.

"Where Catherine Street descends into the Strand."—*Gay.*

Catherine Street—Derivation of its Name—The *Morning Chronicle* and Mr. John Black—Wimbledon House—D'Oyley's Warehouse—Exeter Street—Exeter Arcade—The Strand Music Hall—The Gaiety—The *Morning Post*—Exeter House, and Visit of Queen Elizabeth to Lord Burleigh—Exeter Change—The Menagerie—The Elephant "Chunee"—The Lyceum Theatre—The Beef-steak Club—Exeter Hall—The Adelphi Theatre—Maiden Lane and its Noted Residents—Southampton Street—The "Bedford Head"—The Corps of Commissionaires—Bedford House—The *Lancet* and Mr. T. Wakley—General Monk and the Duchess of Albemarle—Newspapers published in the Strand.

THAT the Strand, especially that part of it which lay nearest to the two royal theatres, bore no good reputation in the days of our great-grandfathers, may be gathered from Gay's "Trivia." The poet, who speaks of the dangers of the "mazy" purlieus of Drury Lane, gives an equally bad character to the inhabitants of Catherine Street, in spite of the derivation of its name from the Greek word denoting "purity." The street, it may be added, is now chiefly devoted to second-class coffee-rooms and eating-houses, and the offices of various newspapers. About half-way down the street, on the eastern side, at No. 22, is the office of the *Echo*, a newspaper which is worthy of record here, since the publication of its first number, in 1868, marked an era in the history of the cheap press, as being the first halfpenny daily paper started in London.

In Catherine Street were published the *Court Gazette* and *Court Journal*, the *Naval and Military Gazette*, the *Racing Times*, the *London Herald*, the *Illustrated Times*, and also the *Literary Gazette* in the last days of its existence. The *Era* also was published here for many years. The upper part of the thoroughfare was formerly called Brydges Street, but the two were made into one and called Catherine Street by the authority of the Board of Works in 1872.

Before going further westward we may notice

that at No. 332, Strand, opposite Somerset House, now the office of the *Weekly Times*, was published for many years prior to its decease in 1861, at the age of more than a century, the *Morning Chronicle*. This was the organ of the Whig party in the days of Fox, and afterwards in those of Lord Grey, Lord Melbourne, and Lord John Russell; and under the successive editorships of Mr. J. Perry and Mr. John Black it obtained a leading position such as that now held by the *Times*. Among the contributors of literary and political articles who, during the hundred years of its existence, were frequent visitors to the editor's inner room, were Richard Brinsley Sheridan, Professor Porson, Jekyll, the wit and M.P., David Ricardo, James Mill, the historian, Lords Erskine and Durham, Albany Fonblanque, Horace Smith, Mr. Poulett Thomson (afterwards Lord Sydenham), Harry Brougham, Lord (then "plain John") Campbell, Joseph Hume, Mr. J. R. M'Culloch, Sir John Bowring, Mr. Charles Buller, and Mr. N. W. Senior. The supposed ghost of Sir Philip Francis also haunted the editorial sanctum, and it will not be forgotten that it was as a reporter on the staff of the *Morning Chronicle* that Charles Dickens earned some of the first five-pound notes which afterwards flowed into his pocket so freely.

The following story will serve to illustrate at once the character of Mr. Black (who died in 1855) and the position of the *Chronicle* in its palmy days:—Mr. Black was a great favourite with Lord Melbourne when the latter was Prime Minister. His lordship esteemed him not only for his great learning, his wonderful memory, his apt illustration of every topic of discourse by an apparently inexhaustible fund of anecdote derived from the most recondite sources, but for his simplicity and *bonhomie*. John Black was a modern Diogenes in everything but his ill-nature. On one occasion Lord Melbourne said to him, "Mr. Black, you are the only person who comes to see me who forgets who I am." The editor opened his eyes with astonishment. "You forget that I am Prime Minister." Mr. Black was about to apologise, but the Premier continued, "Everybody else takes especial care to remember it, but I wish they would forget it; they only remember it to ask me for places and favours. Now, Mr. Black," added his lordship, "you never ask me for anything, and I wish you would; for, seriously, I should be most happy to do anything in my power to serve you." "I am truly obliged," said Mr. Black, "but I don't want anything; I am editor of the *Morning Chronicle*. I like my business, and I live happily on my income." "Then, by Heaven,"

said the peer, "I envy you; and you're the only man I ever did."

On the west side of Catherine Street, and covering the ground now occupied by the Gaiety Theatre and Restaurant and the adjacent buildings, formerly stood Wimbledon House, a noble mansion built at the close of the sixteenth or early in the seventeenth century by Sir Edward Cecil, third son of Thomas, Earl of Exeter. He was an eminent military character in the reigns of James I. and Charles I., by the latter of whom he was created Viscount Wimbledon; but, as he died without issue, the title ceased at his death. This mansion was burnt down, as we learn from John Stow, in 1628, the next day after its noble owner's country seat at Wimbledon had been accidentally destroyed by an explosion of gunpowder. Strange to say, the name of Wimbledon House is entirely forgotten in this neighbourhood, its memory not being perpetuated even by a court or an alley. *Sic transit gloria!*

Part of the site of Wimbledon House was afterwards occupied by "D'Oyley's warehouse," a shop which has never been outdone in name and fame even in these days of monster establishments. The following account of it we take from the *European Magazine*:—"There have been few shops in the metropolis that have acquired more celebrity than D'Oyley's warehouse. . . . We have been told that the original founder of the house was a French refugee, who sought an asylum in this country after the revocation of the Edict of Nantes, and formed a connection in the weaving branch of business with some persons in Spitalfields, whose manufactures, most judiciously fostered by the Government and patriotically encouraged by the nobility, were just then reaching that eminence which they afterwards attained. D'Oyley himself was a man of great ingenuity, and having the best assistance he invented, fabricated, and introduced a variety of stuffs, some of which were new, and all of them such as had never been seen in England. He combined the different articles silken and woollen, and spread them into such an infinite number of forms and patterns, that his shop quickly became the mart of taste, and his goods, when first issued, came to be the height of fashion." To this gentleman it is that the *Spectator* alludes in one of its papers, when it says that "if D'Oyley had not by his ingenious inventions enabled us to dress our wives and daughters in cheap stuffs, we should not have had the means to have carried on the war." In another paper (No. 319) the gentleman who was so fond of striking bold strokes in dress characteristically observes: "A few months after I brought up the *modish* jacket, or the coat with close sleeves, I struck the first in a plain doiley; but that failing, I struck it a second time in blue camlet, which was also one of Doiley's stuffs." In Vanbrugh's *Provoked Wife*, in the scene in Spring Gardens, Lady Fanciful says to Mademoiselle, pointing to Lady Brute and Belinda, "I fear those doiley stuffs are not worn for want of better clothes." "The warehouse was almost equally famous, even in very early times, not only for articles to suit the ladies, but also as the grand emporium for gentlemen's night-gowns and night-caps. . . . In the former part of the eighteenth century, all the beaux who used to stick to the custom of breakfasting at coffee-houses appendant to the Inns of Court, made their morning strolls in their elegant *déshabille*, which was carelessly confined around the waist by a band or sash of yellow, red, green, or blue, according to the taste of the wearer; these were also exclusively of D'Oyley's manufacture. This idle fashion of lounging during the morning in such a dress was not quite extinct in 1760-70, for we remember about that period to have seen some of those early birds in their night-gowns, caps, &c., at Wills's Coffee House near Lincoln's Inn Gate, in Searle Street, about that period." D'Oyley's warehouse, however, was celebrated not for this article alone, but in general for its woollen manufactures. Steele, it may be remembered, speaks in the *Guardian* (No. 102) of his "Doily suit," and Dryden in one place mentions "Doyly petticoats;" but if we may believe Gay's "Trivia," these articles were more elegant than useful in winter, and but a sorry protection against the cold.

It was only at some date between 1848 and 1852 that the name of "D'Oyley's Warehouse (A. Walker & Co., 346, the Strand)" disappeared from the annual issues of Messrs. Kelly's *Post Office Directory*. The site of this famous warehouse is now the printing and publishing offices of the *Morning Post* newspaper.

Exeter Street has witnessed some of those early struggles which either make or mar the lives of literary men. It is well known to every reader of Boswell that it was in this street that Dr. Johnson, on his first arrival in London, lodged and dined at a staymaker's, paying for his keep the large sum of fourpence-halfpenny per day; and that he was living here when he and his friend Garrick "were compelled to borrow five pounds on their joint note from Mr. Wilcox, the bookseller."

Running obliquely from the bottom of Catherine Street to Wellington Street was formerly a small arcade, built by the late Marquis of Exeter—a lineal descendant of the great Lord Burleigh, whose family still own the property—with the view of resuscitating the glories of old Exeter 'Change. He entrusted the work to Mr. Sydney Smirke, the well-known architect, who designed a polygonal compartment at each end of the arcade, which comprised ten neat shops with dwellings over them. There were "polychromic arabesque decorations, imitation bronze gates, and other ornamentations; and the street fronts, of fine red brick, with stone dressings, were in good Jacobean style." But the place, as a business speculation, was a total failure; the public gave the arcade "the cold shoulder;" the shops were mostly tenantless, and an air of solitariness and desertion seemed to take possession of it. The site was in the end considered eligible as part of the design for a large music hall, fronting the Strand; and within the year 1863, after a short and struggling career, the arcade disappeared. The Strand Music Hall, which rose upon its site, does not appear to have been much more successful than its predecessor, for in a very short time the company, under whose auspices the music hall was erected, collapsed, and the building underwent another transformation. An elegant and fashionable theatre—the "Gaiety"—with a commodious and well-appointed restaurant adjoining, has taken its place.

The "Gaiety," which was opened in 1868, will seat 2,000 persons. It was built from the designs of Mr. C. J. Phillips, and in the Gothic style of architecture. The entrance in the Strand leads by a few steps to the level of the stalls, and by a spacious staircase to the balcony or grand tier, and the upper boxes. Another entrance in Exeter Street, designed as a private entrance for the Royal Family, is available as an exit way in case of a sudden panic, there being a stone staircase from the doorway to the highest part of the theatre, with communications on every level. The entrances to the pit and gallery are in Catherine Street, and the stage entrance is in Wellington Street. The columns supporting the various tiers of boxes, &c., are carried up to a sufficient height above the gallery, and from the cap springs a series of pointed arches, supporting cornice and coved ceiling, in the centre of which is a sun-light burner. There is a depth of some twenty feet below the stage, for sinking large scenes, and a height of fifty feet above. The original decoration of the interior was striking and effective, a very noticeable feature being the frieze over the proscenium, which was designed and painted by Mr. H. S. Marks. It represents a king and queen of mediæval times, with surrounding courtiers, watching a "mask" which is being performed before them. The "Gaiety" deserves the credit, be it great or small, of having been the first to acclimatize in London what is known as the *Opera Bouffe* of Paris. The pieces played on the night of the opening were the operetta of *The Two Harlequins* and a comedy drama, entitled *On the Cards*, in the last of which pieces the veteran Mr. Alfred Wigan displayed some admirable acting. The opening night closed with the extravaganza of *Robert the Devil*. The entertainment given at the "Gaiety" consists of burlesque, farce, operetta, &c., and among the names associated with the house are those of Miss Nellie Farren, Mr. Edward Terry, and the late Fred Leslie. A sumptuous restaurant was attached to the theatre at first starting; but it was afterwards separated, owing to the stringency of a clause in the Licensing Act.

In Wellington Street has been printed and published, for more than half a century, the *Morning Post*, the first number of which appeared on the 2nd of November, 1772, thirteen years before the establishment of the *Times*. The paper was originally published at No. 14, Fleet Street; but it was removed to the Strand, and subsequently to Wellington Street, where it is now housed in handsome new offices. Its earliest editor was the Rev. Henry Bate Dudley, at once a man about the town of fashion, an Essex rector, a Cambridgeshire magistrate, and a political and dramatic writer. At one time he held a deanery in Ireland. Whilst editor of the *Morning Post* he inserted an article which happened to give offence to a Captain Stoney, and, on refusing to give up the writer's name, he received a challenge, which he accepted. The parties adjourned to the "Adelphi" Tavern, in the Strand, hard by, and called for a private room and a brace of pistols. These having failed, the combatants resorted to swords, and, both being wounded, they were separated with some difficulty. Dudley (who, having made the acquaintance of the Prince Regent, in after life was created a baronet) soon after this quarrelled with the proprietors of the *Post*, and established the *Morning Herald* as its rival. In 1776 a pirated edition of the *Post* was brought out, but soon suppressed by an affidavit sworn at Bow Street that the paper established in 1772 was "the original *Morning Post*."

Among the contributors to the *Post* during the first half century of its existence were Charles Lamb, Robert Southey, Sir J. Mackintosh, William Wordsworth, Arthur Young, and S. T. Coleridge. Lord Byron alludes to this latter fact in the third canto of "Don Juan:"—

> "Or Coleridge, long before his flighty pen
> Lent to the *Morning Post* its aristocracy."

The connection of Coleridge with the paper dated from 1797, when he began to supply "political pieces," and three years later, as he tells us himself, he was "solicited to undertake the literary and political departments" of the paper. He ceased to write for the *Post* regularly in 1802. More recently the paper numbered among its contributors William Jerdan, Thomas Moore, W. Mackworth Praed, and Mr. James Stephen, afterwards M.P., the father of Sir James Stephen. On account of the firm adherence of its managers to the side of George IV., in the trial of Queen Caroline, the office was more than once attacked by the Radical party; and its windows were broken with brickbats by the mob because the editor refused to illuminate his windows to celebrate the release of Sir Francis Burdett from the Tower. Lord Byron, in more than one passage of his poems, mentions the *Morning Post* by name, and on one occasion he records the fact that the literature of the Prince Regent at his breakfast table at Carlton House consisted of "Death warrants and the *Morning Post*." Elsewhere he couples it with the then brilliant and high-standing papers, the *Courier* and the *Chronicle*, and it is worth noting that one editor of Byron commences his list of "testimonies in favour of Don Juan" with an extract from "the most courtly, decorous, and high-spirited of papers, the *Morning Post*." In June, 1881, the *Morning Post* followed the example of most of its daily contemporaries, and reduced its price to a penny!

On the site of Exeter House, and of its successor, the "Exeter 'Change" of the age of our grandfathers, antiquaries tell us that there once stood the rectory-house belonging to St. Clement Danes' parish, "with a garden and a close for the parson's horse." Such, at all events, was the case until a certain Sir Thomas Palmer, during the reign of Edward VI., came into possession of the living, which he lost by forfeiture for treason. Sir Thomas pulled down the house, and "rebuilt the same of brick and timber very large and spacious." Sir. T. Palmer is called "a creature of the Duke of Somerset," his mansion "a magnificent house of brick and timber." In the first year of Mary it reverted to the Crown, in which it remained vested until it was granted by Elizabeth to Sir William Cecil, her Lord Treasurer, who enlarged and partly rebuilt it, and called it Burleigh or Cecil House. According to Pennant, Burleigh House was "a noble pile, built with brick, and adorned with four square turrets." As appears from ancient plans, it faced the Strand, its gardens extending "from the west side of the garden walk of Wimbledon House (nearly where now runs Wellington Street) to the green lane westwards, which now is Southampton Street."

Cecil, when he became Lord Burleigh, was honoured in this house by a visit from Queen Elizabeth, who, knowing him to be a martyr to the gout, would allow him to sit in her presence.

of wire, lace, ribbons, and jewels, which shot up to so great a height, and made part of the fashion of the day ; for, when the principal esquire in attendance ushered her into the house, he suggested to her Majesty to stoop. 'For your master's sake, I will stoop,' she replied haughtily, 'but

THE OLD ADELPHI THEATRE, 1860.   (*See page* 119.)

This was, of course, a great concession from such an imperious queen, even to such a favourite ; and when he would apologise for the weak state of his legs, her Majesty would playfully remark, "My lord, we make use of you not for the badness of your legs, but for the goodness of your head." Allen remarks, in his "History of London," that "in all probability when she came to Burleigh House, the queen wore that pyramidical head-dress, built

not for the King of Spain.'" Lord Burleigh spent most of his days between this house and his country residence at Theobalds, in Hertfordshire. "At his house in London," we learn from the "Desiderata Curiosa," "he kept ordinarily in household fourscore persons besides . . . . such as attended him at court. The charge of his housekeeping in London amounted to thirty pounds a week," a very large sum indeed in those days, "and the whole sum yearly £1,560, and this in his absence; and in term time, or when his lordship lay at London, his charges increased ten or twelve pounds more. Besides keeping these houses he bought great quantities of corn in times of dearth, to furnish markets about his house at Savoy, twenty suits of apparel: so as his certain alms, besides extraordinaries, was cast up to be £500 yearly, one year with another."

Lord Burleigh died here in 1598. The house afterwards passed into the hands of his son Thomas, who, being created Earl of Exeter, gave it that

TURNER'S HOUSE IN MAIDEN LANE. *From an Original Sketch.* (See *page* 119.)

under prices, to pull down the price so as to relieve the poor. He also gave, for the releasing of prisoners in many of his latter years, thirty and even forty pounds in a term. And for twenty years together he gave yearly in beef, bread, and money at Christmas to the poor of Westminster, St. Martin's, St. Clement's, and Theobalds, thirty-five, and sometimes forty pounds per annum. He also gave yearly to twenty poor men lodging at the name, which it retained almost to our own days. After the Fire of London it was occupied for some few years by the members of Doctors' Commons, and the various courts of the Arches, the Admiralty, &c., were carried on here. At last, being deserted by the family, it was divided, the lower part being turned into shops of various descriptions, while the upper part, containing a menagerie of wild beasts and reptiles, became known as "Exeter 'Change."

Exeter 'Change, when it arose on the ruins of Exeter House, was in no sense externally beautiful, being designed wholly and solely for business purposes. It consisted of three spacious floors, which contained apartments on each side fitted up as shops for milliners, sempstresses, hosiers, &c., and has been from time to time the home of many interesting exhibitions. It appears to have passed through several phases of existence during the last two centuries. It is said by Malcolm to have been built, as it stood till lately, about the time of William and Mary, by a Dr. Barbon, "a speculator in houses," who mortgaged it to the Duke of Devonshire and Sir Francis Child. In 1708 the lower storey comprised forty-eight shops, mostly occupied by milliners, while the upper storey was tenanted by the "Company of Upholsterers." In 1714, one John Gumley, of whom little is known beyond his name, rented the upper part of the building as a warehouse for pier-glasses, &c.; and it is worthy of note that Sir Richard Steele devotes part of one of his papers in the *Tatler* to what looks much like what Mr. Sneer, in *The Critic*, would have called a "puff direct" in his favour. In 1721 it was used by a Mr. Cany as an exhibition room for the display of a wonderful bed, eighteen feet in height, for the sight of which—still more wonderful—visitors paid half-a-crown! In 1732 the body of the poet Gay lay in state here before its interment in Westminster Abbey. In 1764, Malcolm tells us "the great room was opened as an improvement on modern statute halls," and in 1772 the eccentric Lord Baltimore's body here lay in state before its removal in a hearse to Epsom. For some years after this it appears to have been used as a warehouse for storing the printed volumes of the Rolls and Journals of the House of Lords. After this it became "Pidcock's Exhibition of Wild Beasts," and as such it long continued a most popular place of resort, being constantly visited by "country cousins." The beasts were in cages and dens upstairs, the lower part being made a thoroughfare lined with shops on either side, like the Lowther and Burlington Arcades of our own day.

Thornton, in his "Survey of London and Westminster," in 1786, describes it as "erected for the purposes of trade, and consisting of two floors, the lower being laid out in small shops ranged on each side of a long gallery, and the upper one used for auctions and other temporary purposes."

In the early part of the present century the front of Exeter 'Change, projecting as it did over the pavement of the Strand, and daubed all over with pictures of monsters and wild beasts between its Corinthian pillars, must have presented a grotesque appearance not easily to be forgotten by the "country cousins" who came in shoals to see it; and its attractions were heightened in the eyes of the children by Mr. Pidcock's sham Yeoman of the Guard, stationed outside (like the Beef-eaters at the Tower), to invite the passers-by to step in and see the lions, tigers, elephants, and monkeys.

It appears that the wild beasts, which formed such an attraction to the Londoners and their "country cousins" at the commencement of the present century, had not become domesticated in Exeter 'Change so early as 1773. At all events, Northouck, in his "History of London," published in that year, is silent on the subject, and speaks of it only as an old-fashioned building erected for the purposes of trade, and consisting of a long room with a row of shops on each side, and a large room above, "now used for auctions." The 'Change itself projected into the street so as greatly to narrow it; and Northouck remarks that in his opinion it ought to be taken down, the street being greatly contracted by its projection, and by "the sheds stuck round it on the outside;" and his opinion will be confirmed on referring to our engraving of its frontage (see page 109).

The menagerie was successively occupied by Pidcock, Polito, and Cross; and some half a century ago the sight-lover had to pay half-a-crown to see a few animals confined in small dens and cages in rooms of various size, the walls painted with exotic scenery, in order to favour the illusion; whereas now the finest collection of living animals in Europe may be seen in a beautiful garden for a shilling, and on Mondays for sixpence! The roar of the lions and tigers of Exeter 'Change could be distinctly heard in the street, and often frightened horses in the roadway. During Cross's tenancy, in 1826, the elephant "Chunee," which had been shown here since 1809, became ungovernable, as it is said, through the return of an annual paroxysm, and so greatly endangered the safety of the menagerie that it was deemed advisable to put the animal to death. For this purpose a file of soldiers was engaged, and 152 bullets were fired before it fell. The elephant weighed nearly five tons, stood eleven feet in height, and was valued at £1,000. The skin, which weighed 17 cwt., was sold to a tanner for £50; the bones weighed 876 lbs.; and the entire skeleton, sold for £100, is now in the museum of the Royal College of Surgeons in Lincoln's Inn Fields. "Chunee" had achieved some theatrical distinction: he had performed in the spectacle of *Blue Beard*, at Covent Garden; and he had kept up an intimate acquaintance with Edmund Kean, whom he would fondle with his trunk, in return for a few loaves of bread.

Mr. J. T. Smith, in his "Book for a Rainy Day," tells us how he went late at night to the menagerie, accompanied by his friend, Sir J. Winter Lake, when they had the gratification of taking a pot of "Barclay's Entire," in company with Chunee, whom they had met shortly before, being led by its keeper between ropes along the narrow part of the Strand.

The greatness of the Exeter 'Change departed with Chunee; the animals were removed to the King's Mews, in 1828, and two years afterwards Exeter 'Change was entirely taken down. Previous to the opening of the Zoological Gardens in the Regent's Park, Exeter 'Change and the Tower were the only two places in the metropolis where wild beasts could be seen alive, except in travelling menageries; and it was to those two places that "country cousins" were taken on their first arrival in London, so that to "see the lions" passed into a proverb.

The Lyceum Theatre, on the western side of what is now known as Wellington Street, stands on part of the site of old Exeter House, according to Newton's "London in the Olden Time." The ground whereon the theatre stands was purchased about the year 1765, when the Society of Artists was incorporated, by James Payne, the architect of Salisbury House, and on it he built an academy or exhibition room, to anticipate the royal establishment then in contemplation; and here several exhibitions took place. The apartments consisted of a large saloon, with a sky-light, and lesser rooms adjoining. Upon the insolvency of the society this place was deserted, and sold by auction to proprietors, who converted the back part of it into a theatre, and here Mr. Dibdin and Dr. Arnold exhibited their musical talents for some time. It was afterwards taken by a Mr. Porter for the exhibition of his "Grand National Paintings of the 'Siege of Seringapatam,' 'The Siege of Acre,' 'The Battle of Lodi,' 'The Battle of Agincourt,' &c." The place was subsequently used for a variety of miscellaneous entertainments. Here, in 1802, was first shown Madame Tussaud's exhibition of wax-work figures, on her arrival in England from France. The theatre was rebuilt in 1816, but destroyed by fire in 1830. It was again rebuilt, and opened with English Opera in 1834; but although success at first appeared certain, the losses of the lessee subsequently became so great that the theatre was closed in the following year. In 1841 the theatre was taken by the English Opera Company, under the management of Mr. Balfe; equestrian performances were introduced in 1844; and in the same year it was re-opened with a dramatic company, under the management of Mrs. Keeley. The Lyceum has since been under the management of, or had among its members, several theatrical celebrities, by none of whom has more been done to elevate its reputation than by Sir Henry Irving, whose Shaksperian revivals must ever be memorable in theatrical annals.

Behind the scenes of this theatre are some rooms in which a society of roysterers known as "The Sublime Society of Beef-steaks," used to meet on Saturdays, from November to the end of June, to partake of a dinner of beef-steaks. "They abhor," writes Mr. Peter Cunningham in 1851, "the notion of being thought a club; they dedicate their hours to 'Beef and Liberty,' and enjoy a hearty English dinner with hearty English appetites. The room in which they dine, a little Escurial in itself, is most appropriately fitted up—the doors, wainscoting, and roof of good old English oak, being ornamented with gridirons, as thickly as Henry VII.'s chapel with the portcullis of its founder. Everything here assumes the shape, or is distinguished by the representation of their favourite implement—the gridiron. The cook is seen at his office, through the bars of a spacious gridiron, and the original gridiron of the society (the survivor of two terrific fires), holds a conspicuous position in the centre of the ceiling. Every member has the right of inviting a friend, and pickles are not allowed till after the third helping. The 'Steaks' had their origin in a convivial gathering, founded in 1735 by John Rich, the patentee of Covent Garden Theatre, and George Lambert, the scene-painter."

Among the members of this defunct association were George, Prince of Wales, and his brothers, the Dukes of York and Sussex, Richard Brinsley Sheridan, Lord Sandwich, Paul Whitehead, David Garrick, Sir F. Burdett, Harry Brougham, John Wilkes, the Duke of Argyle, Alderman Wood, the Duke of Leinster, and Lord Saltoun. The club had its president and vice-president, its "bishop," or chaplain, who said grace, and its "boots," as the steward or burser was called; and our readers may be amused at learning that the Dukes of Sussex and Leinster in their turn discharged the duties of "boots." Its evening for meeting was Saturday, and its festivals were of a somewhat bacchanalian character; the standing dish of "beef-steaks," from which it derived its name, being washed down by the best of ale and wine, to say nothing of stronger liquors. The wine, as it passed round the table, was always accompanied by songs; and the

"Laureate of the Steaks" was the celebrated wit, Charles Morris, who in early life had been in the Life Guards, and who lived to be ninety before he resigned his office and his life. One of his effusions, composed for this club, has the following stanza :—

> " Like Briton's island lies our steak,
>   A sea of gravy bounds it ;
> Shalots, confus'dly scattered, make
>   The rockwork that surrounds it.
> Your isle's best emblem these behold,
>   Remember ancient story :
> Be, like your grandsires, first and bold,
>   And live and die with glory."

This song rendered Morris so great a favourite with the Prince that he adopted him into the circle of his intimate friends, and made him his constant guest both at Carlton House and at the Pavilion at Brighton. He was succeeded in his "Laureate-ship of the Steaks" by Mr. C. Hallett.

When the club was broken up in 1869, the pictures of former members, which adorned the walls of the room where they assembled for dinner (mostly copies, however, not originals), were sold for only about £70. The plate, however, brought very high prices ; the forks and table-spoons, all bearing the emblem of the club—viz., a gridiron—fetched about a sovereign apiece ; but the grand competition was for a punch-ladle, with a handle in the shape of a gridiron, and inlaid with a Queen Anne guinea, which realised £14 5s., and for the ribbon and badge of the president, a gridiron of silver, made in 1735, and knocked down at £23. Other articles fetched equally fancy prices, as souvenirs of a bygone institution. Thus a cheese-toaster brought £12 6s., a *couteau de chasse*, the reputed work of B. Cellini, the gift of Dr. Askew, £84 ; a brown jug of stone ware, silver mounted, £7 ; a pair of halberts, £3 10s. ; an Oriental punch-bowl, presented by Lord Saltoun, £17 15s. Some wine-glasses, engraved with the gridiron, realised from 27 to 34 shillings a pair ; while the pewter dishes, plates, and quart pots fetched nearly the price of silver. The chairs, which had been occupied by so many distinguished members, in-cluding that of the president, were knocked down at various prices between £7 and £14 apiece. The actual gridiron, which had for years been the centre of so much veneration and homage, plain as it was, fetched five guineas and a half. Almost all the articles, in addition to being stamped with the gridiron, were labelled " Beef and Liberty." The marble bust of Wilkes, which formerly had adorned the dining-room, fell under the auctioneer's hammer for twenty-two guineas. For the above particulars

we are indebted to "The Life and Death of the Sublime Society," by " Brother " W. Arnold, pub-lished by Messrs. Bradbury, Evans, and Co.

At a short distance westward of the Lyceum Theatre stands the building known to the religious and musical world as Exeter Hall. It was erected in the years 1830–31, by Mr. G. Deering, in the Græco-Corinthian style of architecture, but has since been much improved. In 1880 the Hall became the property of the Young Men's Christian Association ; and in March, 1881, it was re-opened, after having undergone extensive alterations and enlargement, the cost of which, together with the purchase-money for the building, amounted to nearly £50,000. The edifice is intended as a place for holding public meetings, the most noted of which are those annual religious gatherings known as " May Meetings." Besides these, the Hall is occasionally used for the meetings of charit-able and other institutions ; and also for choral assemblies. Here for many years took place the concerts of the Sacred Harmonic Society, which consisted principally of oratorios, by some well-known composer, and occasionally of purely church music, such as the anthems sung in divine worship.

Oratorios, like the sacred plays, are of ancient date, and, according to a writer in *Chambers's Cyclopædia*, were so called from the chapel or *oratory*, the place where these compositions were first performed. St. Filippo Neri, born in 1515, has been considered as the founder of the oratorio. He engaged poets and composers to produce dialogues, on subjects from Scriptural and legendary history, in verse, and set to music, which were per-formed in his chapel or oratory on Sundays and Church festivals. The subjects were " Job and his Friends," " The Prodigal Son," " The Angel Gabriel with the Virgin," and " The Mystery of the Incarnation." By far the greatest master of oratorio was Handel, who perfected that species of music, and was the first to introduce it into England. On the occasion of the first public per-formance of an oratorio in London, in the year 1732, it was so complete a novelty that it was deemed necessary to give the following explanation in advertising it :—" By His Majesty's command, at the King's Theatre in the Haymarket, on Tuesday, the 2nd of May, will be performed the sacred story of ' Esther,' an oratorio in English, composed by Handel, and to be performed by a great number of voices and instruments.—N.B. There will be no acting on the stage, but the house will be fitted up in a decent manner for the audience." The oratorio of " Esther " had been privately given, some years previously, in the chapel at Canons, the seat of the "princely" Duke of Chandos. The two crowning works of Handel were "Israel in Egypt" and "The Messiah." The former is considered to rank highest of all compositions of the oratorio class; but the latter has attained an even more universal popularity, and from the time when it was first brought out down to the present day, it has been performed for the benefit of nearly every charitable institution in the kingdom. In Handel's time the orchestra was but very imperfectly developed; and since that period it was customary in London to have oratorios performed twice a week during Lent in the various theatres, but these performances were given up on the institution of the oratorios at Exeter Hall. At various halls in London, and at musical festivals elsewhere, oratorios are now performed on a large scale, and with a power and a perfection previously unknown. The greatest oratorio performances, however, are now those of the Handel Triennial Festivals at the Crystal Palace. At the first of these festivals, in 1862, the chorus amounted to 3,120 voices, and there was an orchestra of 505 performers; at the present time even these numbers are exceeded.

About half-way between Exeter Hall and Charing Cross are the Vaudeville and the Adelphi Theatres. The former, which was erected in the year 1870, from the designs of Mr. C. J. Phillips, is a neat building internally, but has very little pretension to architectural display in its exterior. It will seat about 1,000 persons, and was built for the performance of comedy, burlesque, and farce. The pieces produced on the opening night were *Love or Money*, a comedy by Mr. A. Halliday, and a burlesque, entitled *Don Carlos, or the Infant in Arms*.

The Adelphi Theatre stands opposite Adam Street, and is the second building of the kind that has stood here. Mr. John Scott, colour-maker, of the Strand, was the original architect, and it was built in 1806 under his superintendence. The old theatre was pulled down in the summer of 1858, and the first stone of the present edifice was laid by Mr. Benjamin Webster, in his Masonic capacity. The Adelphi has been principally celebrated for melodramas. Terry's Theatre, also in the Strand, was built for Mr. Edward Terry; the Tivoli Music-hall, at the Charing Cross end, dates from 1890.

Parallel with the Strand at this part, and to the south of Covent Garden Market, is Maiden Lane, sometimes, though erroneously, supposed to have been so called from a sisterhood of nuns, attached to the abbey, whose sheltered "Convent Garden" it bounded on the southern side. In early rate-books of St. Paul's, Covent Garden, it is spoken of as Maiden Lane, behind the "Bull" Inn. Bull Inn Court, no doubt, marks the site of the inn here mentioned. In Maiden Lane Voltaire lodged during his visit to London in 1726, and in it lived Andrew Marvell, of whom we have already made mention as an honest member of Parliament, and whose name we shall again have occasion to record as a satirist, when we come to Charing Cross. Here, too, at one time, lived Archbishop Sancroft, the nonjuror, before he had taken his seat on the episcopal bench. No. 20 (now removed) was a tavern called the "Cyder Cellars," a house which gained some notoriety in its day. It was a favourite haunt of Professor Porson, and afterwards became a "School of Arms." "Proctor, the sculptor," says Mr. Peter Cunningham, "died in reduced circumstances, in a house in Maiden Lane, opposite the 'Cyder Cellars.'" Here also, at No. 26, on the north side, was born, in May, 1775, no less an artist than Joseph Mallord William Turner, his father being at that time a hair-dresser and a householder. Here the great painter early began to draw from Nature, and a front room in the old house in Maiden Lane is said to have been his first studio. The house has been lately rebuilt. The Roman Catholic church of Corpus Christi occupies the south-east corner of Maiden Lane.

Southampton Street was so called in compliment to Lady Rachel Russell, daughter of Thomas Wriothesley, Earl of Southampton, and wife of William, Lord Russell, the patriot. At No. 27 in this street Garrick resided before his removal to the Adelphi. Mrs. Oldfield, the actress, also lived in Southampton Street. Tavistock Street was the stable-yard to Bedford House; and where Tavistock and York Streets meet was "the horse-pond."

In Southampton Street was a celebrated eating-house, known as "The Bedford Head," which is several times mentioned by Pope and Walpole. Its exact site is not known, but it is recorded that the steps of its back door were on the south side of Denmark Court. Pope writes in his "Satires:"—

"Let me extol a cat on oysters fed,
I'll have a party at the 'Bedford Head.'"

And again, in his "Sober Advice," he expresses himself in terms which would seem to imply that the house was well known for its good fare:—

"When sharp with hunger, scorn you to be fed,
Except on pea-chicks at the 'Bedford Head?'"

And this is confirmed by the fact that Paul Whitehead ordered for himself and a party of gay roisterers a "great supper" at the "Bedford Head," as Horace Walpole tells his correspondent, Sir Horace Mann, under date November, 1741. There is now a "Bedford Head" in Maiden Lane, but it is a new tavern, and does not inherit the traditions of the former house.

In Exchange Court, on the north side, between Nos. 419 and 420, Strand, near Bedford Street, are band. They were first organised in the year 1859; and at the present time their strength is about 2,000 men, of whom the great majority are employed in various parts of London.

On what is now Southampton Street stood the

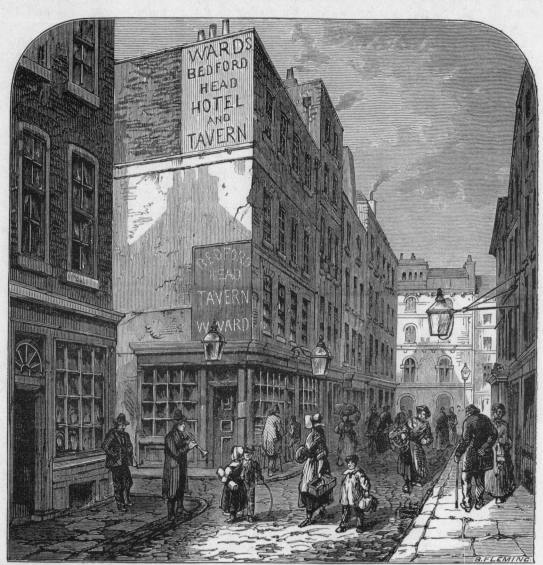

THE OLD "BEDFORD HEAD."

the head-quarters of the Corps of Commissionaires, a set of men who, having served in the army, the navy, or the police, and having good characters and being in the receipt of pensions, are willing to earn a livelihood by going on messages, delivering circulars, or being detailed off on private business. Some are permanently and others temporarily employed. They are all amenable to the authority of an adjutant, and wear a uniform. They have a mess-room, reading-room, &c., and also a military ancient mansion of the Earls and Dukes of Bedford. It is described by Strype as having been "a large but old-built house, with a great yard before it for the reception of carriages; with a spacious garden, having a terrace-walk adjoining to the brick wall next the garden, behind which were coach-houses and stables, with a conveyance into Charles Street, through a large gate." This house and garden being demolished in 1704, the site was covered by Tavistock, Southampton, and some other streets.

Before the Russell family built the town-house in the Strand they occupied, for a time, the Bishop of Carlisle's "inn," over against their newly-erected mansion, the site of which was afterwards built upon and called "Carlisle Rents." Stow speaks of it in 1598 as "Russell or Bedford House." In 1704 they removed to Bedford House, Bloomsbury, of which we shall speak hereafter.

At the corner of Bedford Street is now the publishing office of the *Lancet*. This journal was established in 1823 by Mr. Thomas Wakley, who, as we learn from the "Autobiographical Recol-

that name—assisted him in the first seven or eight numbers of his new journal. After a time the *Lancet* was printed at the office of Mills, Jowett, and Mills, in Bolt Court, Fleet Street. *Cobbett's Register* was printed at the same establishment, and Wakley, to some extent, made the style of Cobbett his model. At this time it was no uncommon occurrence for four persons to meet in a little room in Mills's office. Three of them made themselves famous—William Cobbett, William Lawrence, and Thomas Wakley; the fourth was a barrister of the name of Keen, who used to join

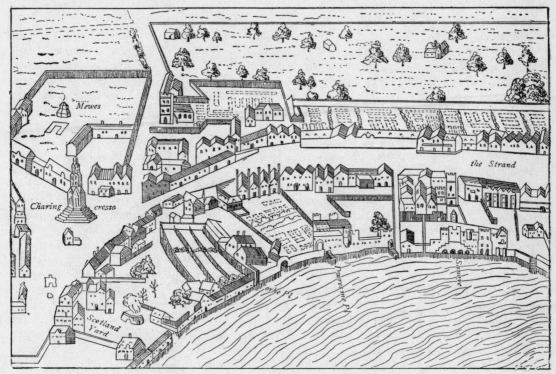

THE STRAND IN 1560. (*From the Map of Ralph Aggas.*)

lections of J. F. Clarke, M.R.C.S.," for many years on the staff of the *Lancet*, was the son of a village farmer in Devonshire. As a boy he was of a restless disposition, and anxious to go to sea. He was apprenticed to an apothecary at Taunton, but finished his indentures with two other gentlemen, one at Henley-on-Thames, and the other at Beaminster. He became a student at the united hospitals of Guy's and St. Thomas's, where Sir Astley Cooper was then the popular lecturer on surgery. He passed the College of Surgeons in 1817, and from thence till 1823 he kept a shop in the Strand, at the east corner of Norfolk Street. His old schoolfellow, Mr. Collard—the venerable head of the firm of pianoforte manufacturers of

the party on printing nights, probably with a view of determining whether the productions which were about to appear were libellous. The sanctum was seldom violated. The printer's boy was the only person admitted, and he in after life described the room as the scene of the utmost merriment. He could hear as he ascended the stairs the boisterous laugh of Cobbett above the rest; the loud, cheerful, good-humoured ring of Wakley; and on entering the room, could see the quiet, sneering smile of Lawrence; and hear the suppressed giggle of the lawyer. Lawrence left the *Lancet* when he achieved power, and his place was supplied by Wardrop—witty, and able, and unscrupulous. The *Lancet* soon got into hot water, and the insertion of an account of a defective operation for the stone, by Mr. Bransby Cooper, the nephew of Sir Astley, led to the latter bringing against it an action for libel, which created a great sensation at the time. In addition to the report, leading articles of an exciting kind, and squibs and epigrams—some in the worst taste—were inserted. The following is given as a specimen :—

> " When Cooper's ' nevvy ' cut for stone,
>   His toils were long and heavy ;
>   The patient quicker parts has shown,
>   He soon cut Cooper's nevvy."

Mr. Wakley defended himself on his trial, and the verdict for the plaintiff, £100 damages, was considered to be in his favour. Outside Westminster Hall there was a large crowd who cheered him vociferously, and the *Sun* newspaper kept up its type till twelve o'clock at night in order to record the verdict. The reporter of the case, the late Mr. Lambert, was expelled the hospitals, and a board was placed in the hall of Guy's, cautioning all students against reporting for the *Lancet*. This restriction, however, is no longer in force, and the bitterness of the contest is almost forgotten.

Among the many scenes enacted in the Strand, we may be pardoned for mentioning one in which some of the personages whom we have already mentioned were concerned, including General Monk and the Duchess of Albemarle. On the news of Monk being called upon to concert the first measures towards the restoration of royalty, in February, 1659, Pepys tells us, in his " Diary," that the Strand was one blaze of bonfires, and that he himself counted no less than " fourteen between St. Dunstan's Church, Fleet Street, and the Strand Bridge," near Somerset House. A day or two afterwards he records a very different sight—" Two soldiers hanged in the Strand for their late mutiny at Somerset House."

Pepys has the following entry in his " Diary," under date 4th November, 1666 :—" The Duke of Albemarle is grown a drunken sot, and drinks with nobody but Troutbecke, whom nobody else will keep company with. Of whom he " (Mr. Cooling) " told me this story : That once the Duke of Albemarle in his drink taking notice, as of a wonder, that Nan Hyde should ever come to be Duchess of York. ' Nay,' says Troutbecke, ' never wonder at that, for if you will give me another bottle of wine, I will tell you as great, if not greater, miracle. And what was that but that our dirty Besse' (meaning his duchess) ' should come to be Duchess of Albemarle.' "

Aubrey says that the mother of this low-born and low-bred duchess was one of " five women

barbers " belonging to the locality, thus celebrated in a ballad of the day :—

> " Did ever you hear the like,
>   Or ever hear the fame,
>   Of five women barbers
>   That lived in Drury Lane ?"

As Aubrey published his " Lives " as early as 1679, he is probably to be trusted on a fact which would be within his own knowledge. And he identifies the site of the blacksmith's forge with " the corner shop, the first turning on yᵉ right, as you come out of the Strand into Drury Lane ;" and Mr. John Timbs adds, that " it is believed to be that at the right-hand corner of Drury Court, now (1850) a butcher's."

In spite of her low birth and vulgar habits, however, the Duchess of Albemarle is credited with having had a considerable hand in bringing about the Restoration. She was a great loyalist, and Monk, though not afraid of an enemy in the field, was terribly afraid of her and of her tongue ; so that it is not improbable that in his case " the grey mare was the better horse," and that it was at her suggestion that he put himself at the head of the movement for bringing King Charles " to his own again." And yet this was the woman of whom Pepys could write in his " Diary :"—" 4th April, 1667. I find the Duke of Albemarle at dinner with sorry company—some of his officers of the army—dirty dishes and a nasty wife at table, and bad meat, of which I made but an ill dinner."

The Duchess of Albemarle seems to have been anything rather than attractive personally, but Pepys seems to have regarded her with positive aversion. He never has a good word to say for her, and calls her a " plain and homely dowdy," and a very " ill-looked woman." Could ill-nature well go further ?

Next to Fleet Street, the thoroughfare of the Strand has been during the present century the chief home of that Muse who presides over the newspaper press. Here, or else in the streets leading out of it, have been published not only the *Morning Chronicle*, the *Post*, and the *Daily Telegraph*, and the *Illustrated London News*, as mentioned already, but the *Sun*, the *Globe*, *Bell's Life in London*, the *Observer*, the *Leader*, the *Press*, the *Economist*, the *Court Journal*, the *Spectator*, the *Examiner*, the *Field*, the *Queen*, and the *Graphic*, besides a host of other inferior journals, the list of which " were long to tell," and whose obituaries are well-nigh forgotten. It may be worth recording that in 1835, the year prior to the reduction of the Newspaper Duty, the gross amount of duty on newspapers in the United Kingdom was £553,197.

The reduction of the Newspaper Duty took effect on the 15th of September, 1836. In the half-year ending April 5, 1836, the number of newspapers stamped in Great Britain was 14,874,652, and the net amount of duty received was £196,909. In the half-year ending April 5, 1837, the number of newspapers stamped in Great Britain was 21,362,148, and the net amount of duty received was £88,502; showing an increase in the number in the last half-year, as compared with the corresponding half-year before the reduction, of 6,487,496, and a loss of revenue of £108,317. Of the above number of stamps taken out in the half-year ending April 5,

1837, 11,547,241 stamps were issued since 1st of January, 1837, when the distinctive die came into use; whereas only 14,784,652 were issued in the six months ending April, 1836.

Before quitting the literary associations of the Strand, we may note that the first publisher of Samuel Rogers was Mr. Cadell, in the Strand. It was in 1786 that the former first appeared in print with his "Ode to Superstition." The author called and left his MS. in Cadell's shop with a short note containing a bank-note to cover any possible loss that might arise from publication. Mr. Rogers lived down to the end of 1855.

CHAPTER XIX.

CHARING CROSS, THE RAILWAY STATIONS, AND OLD HUNGERFORD MARKET.

> "Erect a rich and stately carved cross,
> Whereon her statue shall with glory shine;
> And henceforth see you call it Charing Cross."—*Peele*, "*King Edward I.*"

Derivation of the Name of Charing—Description of the Original Cross—Lines on its Downfall—Sir Thomas Wyatt's Encounter with Queen Mary's Troops—A Cunning Royalist—The Statue of Charles I.—Andrew Marvell's Satire—The Story of the Sword—Execution of the Regicides—Curious Exhibitions at Charing Cross—The Royal Mews—The Charing Cross Hosp'tal—Westminster Ophthalmic Hospital—Toole's Theatre—The "Golden Cross"—Charing Cross Railway Station and Hotel—The New Eleanor Cross—The Railway Bridge—Old Hungerford Market—Hungerford Bridge—The Lowther Arcade—Adelaide Gallery—Craven Street—Northumberland Street.

CHARING CROSS, as every Londoner knows, is the name given to the open space at the western end of the Strand, from which Whitehall, Cockspur Street, and St. Martin's Lane branch off in different directions; but of late years a considerable portion of it has been absorbed in what is now called Trafalgar Square. The name is most probably derived from the old village of Charing, which stood here, a sort of halting-place in bygone times for travellers between the cities of London and Westminster; though some fanciful writers have sought its derivation in the words *chère reine*, alluding to the cross which was here set up by Edward I. in memory of his "dear Queen" Eleanor. The latter, as every reader of a child's History of England knows, accompanied Edward I. to the Holy Land, where, on his "being wounded by a certain Moor with a poisoned dagger, and rather growing worse than better by the applications of his physicians, she administered a new and unheard-of remedy. Full of affection and duty, she daily licked the wound which the force of the poison prevented from closing, and sucked out the deadly matter. By dint of this, or, to speak more truly, by the power of conjugal affection, she so drew out the noxious matter, that the wound healing, the king perfectly recovered, and she received not the least harm." It is

well known that wherever her bier rested, as at Waltham, Tottenham, and other places, her sorrowful husband erected a cross, or, as Tom Hood whimsically said, in his usual punning vein, *apropos* of the cross at Tottenham:—

> "A royal game of fox and goose,
>   To play for such a loss;
> Wherever she put down her *orts*,
>   There he—set up a *cross!*"

The original cross was of wood, wholly or to a great extent; but it was built in stone by Richard, and, after his death, by a son or brother, Roger de Crundale. The material used was Caen stone, and the steps were of fine smooth marble. It appears to have been of an octagonal form, and, in an upper stage, ornamented with eight figures. On Aggas' map is shown a small house occupying the spot where the equestrian statue of Charles I. now stands. This may possibly have been an erection known as the Hermitage, described otherwise as "a small chapel dedicated to St. Catharine, which stood over against the cross."

"This cross," says Stow, "builded of stone, was of old time a fair piece of work, there made by command of Edward I." Mr. Newton, in his "London in the Olden Time," tells us that it "appears to have been more elegant than any of the other eight crosses erected to Queen Eleanor's

memory. It was of Caen stone, beautifully wrought
with many figures, and raised upon steps of marble."
He also subsequently styles it a "superb piece of
architecture." The cross itself was sentenced by
the Parliament to be taken down in 1643, but its
actual demolition was not carried out till some
four years later, namely, in the summer of 1647.
Lilly, in his "Observations on the Life of King
Charles I.," published in 1715, says that part of
the stones of which it was composed were em-

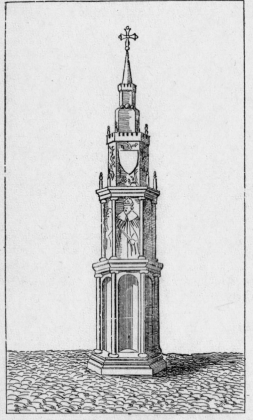

OLD CHARING CROSS.
From a Copy of a very old Print published by N. Smith in 1792.

ployed in paving the front of Whitehall, whilst
other stones were made into knife-hafts and other
articles, which, when polished, looked like marble.

The following lines on the downfall of the cross
itself, which are quoted from "Percy's Reliques,"
are interesting and amusing :—

"Undone, undone the lawyers are ;
    They wander about the towne ;
Nor can find the way to Westminster,
    Now Charing Cross is downe :
At the end of the Strand they made a stand,
    Swearing they are at a loss,
And, chaffing, say, that's not the way—
    They must go by Charing Cross.

"The Parliament to vote it down
    Conceived it very fitting,
For fear it should fall and kill them all,
    In the house as they were sitting.
They were told, God wot, it had a plot,
    Which made them so hard-hearted,
To give command it should not stand,
    But be taken down and carted.

"Men talk of plots ; this might have been worse.
    For anything I know,
Than that Tomkins and Chaloner
    Were hanged for long agoe.
Our Parliament did that prevent,
    And wisely them defended ;
For plots they will discover still
    Before they were intended.

"But neither man, woman, nor child
    Will say, I'm confident,
They ever heard it speak one word
    Against the Parliament.
An informer swore it letters bore,
    Or else it had been free ;
I'll take, in troth, my Bible oath,
    It could neither write nor read.

"The committee said, that verily
    To Popery it was bent ;
For aught I know it might be so,
    For to church it never went.*
What with excise, and such device,
    The kingdom doth begin
To think you'll leave ne'er a cross
    Without doors nor within.

"Methinks the Common Council should
    Of it have taken pity,
'Cause, good old cross, it always stood
    So firmly to the City.
Since crosses you so much disdain,
    Faith, if I were as you,
For fear the king should rule again,
    I'd pull down Tyburn too."

Mr. Wood, in his "Ecclesiastical Antiquities of
London," gives the site of the ancient Hospital of
St. Mary of Rounceval (de Roscidâ valle), at the
angle of Whitehall and the Strand, so that no
doubt it formed a part of Northumberland House.
Dugdale, in his "Monasticon," tells us that the
original hospital at Charing Cross was founded for
the benefit of "lunatic and distracted people," but
that the date of its foundation is not known.

In the year 1554, Charing Cross became the
scene of an encounter between the troops of Queen
Mary and a band of rebels headed by Sir Thomas
Wyatt, who, having taken up arms against the
Queen, was advancing against the City. The
episode is thus described by the honest chronicler,
John Stow :—

"The same night (February 6th), about five of

* An allusion to the absence of Catholics from the Protestant worship.

the clock, a trumpeter went about, and warned all horsemen and men-at-arms to be at St. James's Field ; and all footmen also to be there by six of the clock next morning. The Queen's scout, on his return to the court, declared Wyatt's being at Brentford, which sudden news made all in the court wonderfully afraid. Drums went through London at four of the clock in the morning, commanding all soldiers to armour, and so to Charing Cross. Wyatt, hearing that the Earl of Pembroke was come into the field, stayed at Knightsbridge until day, when his men rested, being very weary with the travel of the night and day before, and also partly feebled and faint, having received small sustenance since their coming out of Southwark. There was no small ado in London, and likewise the Tower made great preparation of defence. By ten of the clock, the Earl of Pembroke had set his troop of horsemen on the hill in the highway above St. James's, his footmen were set in two battles somewhat lower, and nearer Charing Cross, at the lane turning down by the brick wall from Islington-ward (St. Martin's Lane), where he had also certain other horsemen, and he had planted his ordnance upon a hill-side in the meantime. Wyatt and his company planted his ordnance upon a hill beyond St. James's, almost over against the Park Corner ; and himself, after a few words spoken, to his soldiers, came down the old lane on foot, hard by the court gate at St. James's, with four or five ancients, his men marching in good array. The Earl of Pembroke's horsemen hovered all the while without moving, until all was passed by saving the tail; upon which they did set, and cut off ; the other marched forward in array, and never stayed or returned to the aid of their tail. The great ordnance shot off freshly on both sides. Wyatt's ordnance overshot the troop of horsemen. The Queen's whole battle of footmen standing still, Wyatt passed along by the wall towards Charing Cross, where the said horsemen that were there set upon part of them, but were soon forced back. At Charing Cross there stood Sir John Gage, Lord Chamberlain, with the guard and a number of others, almost a thousand ; the which, upon Wyatt's coming, shot at his company, but at the last fled to the court gates, while certain pursued, and forced with shot to shut the court gate against them. In this repulse, the Lord Chamberlain and others were so amazed that they many cryed treason in the court, and had thought that the Earl of Pembroke, who was assaulting the tail of his enemies, had gone (over) to Wyatt, taking his part against the Queen." The upshot of the affair, however, was that Wyatt surrendered.

Of late years the working classes of London have claimed a right to hold large meetings in Trafalgar Square, but a riot having on one occasion taken place in connection with a Socialistic demonstration, all meetings were for a time prohibited.

The bronze equestrian statue of Charles I. at Charing Cross is generally reckoned one of the best of our public statues, and certainly is admirably placed. It was modelled by Hubert Le Sueur, a Frenchman who came to England about the year 1630, and the statue was cast by a commission from the Earl of Arundel, in 1639, "on a spot of ground hard by Covent Garden Church." It was erected just before the beginning of the serious troubles between Charles and the Parliament. A writer in *Chambers's Journal* thus sums up its history :— " When the hapless monarch was consigned to the block, his statue became as unpopular as himself ; accordingly, it was taken down by order of the revolutionary Parliament, and was sold to one Rivers, a brazier, who lived at the Dial near Holborn Conduit, with strict injunctions that it should be broken up. But Rivers was either a royalist or a sly-boots ; he kept the statue intact, buried it underground, and drove a brisk trade in knives and forks, with bronze handles, which he pretended were made out of the obnoxious statue. He clearly must have made a good thing out of the knives and forks which he manufactured in bronze for sale, since ' the Royalists no doubt eagerly bought them as relics of their unfortunate and lamented sovereign, whilst the Puritans and Roundheads would be equally glad to secure them as trophies of the downfall of a despot.' Long after the season of turmoil, when Charles II. and the Royalists were in power and in fashion, the bronze statue came again forth into light, and was set up in 1674 on its present position. The stone pedestal, sculptured with the royal arms, trophies, &c., was long regarded as the work of Grinling Gibbons ; but, if we may believe Mr. John Timbs, a written account is extant, proving it to be by Joshua Marshall, master-mason to the Crown. On the 29th of May— the anniversary of the restoration of Charles II.— the statue was formerly decorated with boughs of oak. The poet Waller praised the king and the statue with most courtly panegyric, but Andrew Marvell contrived to make a good deal of fun out of both, and in the following way :—Sir Robert Vyner, Lord Mayor of London, about that time had put up an equestrian statue of Charles II. at the Stocks Market, on the spot where the Mansion House now stands ; and as Marvell had not much more love for the one than for the other monarch, he wrote a clever satiric dialogue purporting to be held between the two rival horses. Each horse reviled the king who bestrode the other horse—the one attacking the profligacy of Charles II., the other the despotic conduct of Charles I. The Charing Cross steed making an attack on the

had omitted to put girths to the saddle and trappings of the horse, till it was too late to remedy the defect, put an end to his existence. The omission is stated to have been pointed out by a countryman. Horace Walpole observes of it that

THE KING'S MEWS. (*From a View by Wale, about* 1750.)

Stocks Market monarch, said, amongst other bitter things, that it was wondrous

"That he should be styled 'Defender of Faith,'
Who believes not a word that the word of God saith."

And added, in allusion to the current belief that Charles II. had professed himself a Roman Catholic :—

"Though changed his religion, I hope he's so civil
Not to think his own father is gone to the devil."

It has been said, but we know not with how much of truth, that the sculptor, on finding that he

"the commanding grace of the figure and the exquisite form of the horse, are striking even to the most unpractised eye."

The statue of Charles was once furnished with a sword. The story of the base theft of the weapon, which we have taken from Chambers' "Book of Days," is a strange one, as our readers will see for themselves :—In *Notes and Queries* for 1850, Mr. Planché asked, "When did the real sword which, but a few years back, hung at the side of the equestrian statue of King Charles at Charing

CHARING CROSS FROM NORTHUMBERLAND HOUSE IN 1750.

Cross, disappear? That the sword was a real one of that period, I state upon the authority of my learned friend, Sir Samuel Meyrick, who had ascertained the fact, and who pointed out to me its loss." To this query Mr. Street replied, "The sword disappeared about the time of the coronation of her present Majesty, when some scaffolding was erected around the statue, which afforded great facilities for removing the rapier—for such it was; and I always understood that it found its way into the so-called museum of the notorious Captain D——, where, in company with the wand of the Great Wizard of the North, and other well-known articles, it was carefully labelled and numbered, and a little account appended relating the circumstances of its acquisition and removal." The editor of *Notes and Queries* pointedly added to this communication, "The age of chivalry is certainly past, otherwise the idea of disarming a statue would never have entered the head of any man of arms even in his most frolicsome mood." We may conclude then that the present sword of this remarkable statue is a modern substitute. The pedestal upon which this statue stands is very ornamental. The plinth, formerly of Portland stone, was renewed in granite and slightly raised in 1856; the restoration being made under the superintendence of Sir Gilbert Scott.

The cross was also used for other practical purposes; at its foot royal proclamations were read, and in general any matter of public interest was proclaimed. To this fact Swift alludes:—

> "And all that passes *inter nos*
> May be proclaimed at Charing Cross."

Here, also, occasionally culprits stood in the pillory, as being the most public place in the west of the metropolis. Amongst those who so suffered here was the bookseller, Edmund Curll, who lost his ears on the occasion. His memory is embalmed in the "Dunciad" of Pope, as the author of sundry pieces which deserved anything but immortality. He died in 1748.

We may remark here that some of the regicides, including General Harrison, Peters, and Cook, were executed on the very site where the cross had stood; and Wood, in his "Athenæ Oxonienses," adds that Harrison was put to death with his face looking towards the Banqueting House at Whitehall. Pepys, in his "Diary," thus records the event:— "Oct. 30, 1660. I went out to Charing Cross to see Major-General Harrison hanged, drawn, and quartered; which was done there, he looking as cheerful as any man could do in that condition. He was presently cut down, and his head and heart shown to the people, at which there was great

shouts of joy. . . . Thus it was my chance to see the king beheaded at Whitehall, and to see the first blood shed in revenge for the king at Charing Cross." The fanatic Harrison, we may here observe, was the son of a butcher at Newcastle-under-Lyne, appointed by Cromwell to convey Charles I. from Windsor to Whitehall, in order to stand his trial, on which he sat also as one of the judges.

The two regicides Cook and Peters suffered together; and the body of Harrison having hung the due time, was cut down, and the process of quartering commenced, when, at the suggestion of Colonel Turner, Peters was brought forward that he might be witness of the horrible mutilation. The hangman, rubbing his bloody hands, asked him how he liked it. "I am not terrified; do your worst," was the reply; and a few minutes later his strangled body was quivering beneath the knife of the executioner. If the accounts of the last moments of the daring men who suffered at this time be true, it will be seen that, whatever crimes might be laid to their charge, the guilt of cowardice could not be imputed to the regicides.

Charing Cross was one of the places most frequented by shows and exhibitions in the days of Charles II. and James II. In August, 1664, Samuel Pepys writes in his "Diary:" "At Charing Cross, I there saw the great Dutchman that is come over, under whose arm I went with my hat on, and could not reach higher than his eyebrows with the tips of my fingers."

It was at the "Admiral Duncan" tavern, Charing Cross, that, in March, 1824, the men of Cumberland and Westmoreland in the metropolis met together, and resolved to found the Annual North Country Wrestling Matches, which have ever since that time been celebrated year by year on Good Friday, and which we shall mention more fully hereafter.

We are reminded by the author of "Haunted London" that, in 1666–67, an Italian puppet-player set up his booth at Charing Cross, and probably introduced "Punch" into England. He paid a small rent to the overseers of St. Martin's parish, and is called in their book, "Punchinello." "In 1668," adds Mr. Cunningham, "a Mr. Devone erected a small playhouse in the same place." In the Harleian MSS. there is still extant a song in rather rugged verse, written to ridicule the long delay in setting up the king's statue; it is curious as containing an early allusion to "Punch:"—

> "What can the mystery be that Charing Cross
>   These five months continues still blinded with board?
> Dear Wheeler impart: we are all at a loss,
>   Unless Punchinello is to be restored."

Milton, we are told, lodged at one Thomson's,

next door to the " Bull's Head Tavern," at Charing Cross, close to the opening into Spring Gardens, during the time that he was writing his " Angliæ Defensio."

Thornton, in his " Survey of London and Westminster," published in 1785, tells us that on the north side of Charing Cross there is a large square, on one side of which is a handsome building, used as stabling for his Majesty's horses, and generally known as the " Mews," or " Meuse." The word is derived, as every antiquary knows, from the " mew " of the young of the falcon and hawk tribe. It appears that, as early as the year 1377, this place was used for the purposes of the king's hawks and falconers, the sport of falconry being then one of the most favourite pastimes of the aristocracy, and the Chief Falconer being one of the most important members of the Royal Household. This office, which is hereditary, was granted by Charles II. to Charles, Duke of St. Albans, his son by " Mrs. Gwynne," and " the heirs male of his body ; " and it still continues attached to the title. At one time it would seem that the king's stables were at Lomesbury, or, as it is now styled, Bloomsbury ; but these stables being burnt down in 1537, King Harry ordered the hawks to be removed, and the " Mews " altered and enlarged for the reception of his steeds ; so from that day down to the reign of George IV. the royal stables stood here, and the word " mews," in London at least, has become equivalent to a range of stabling.

It would appear, from such books of London topography as we have been able to consult, that the old building of Henry VIII.'s time having become decayed, a new and handsome edifice was begun in 1732, by George II. It was built in the classical style, with central columns and a pediment, and adorned with cupolas and lanterns ; but the effect of this architectural display was spoiled by the narrow space in front, and on either side of it, and by the small and mean buildings with which it was hemmed in. It stood as nearly as possible on the site of the front of the present National Gallery, as is clear from a print in Thornton's " Survey of London and Westminster."

Charing Cross Hospital, which stands a little to the east of St. Martin's Church at the junction of Agar Street and King William Street, was built from the designs of Mr. Decimus Burton. It is one of the twelve general hospitals of the metropolis, and was founded in 1818. The general hospitals, as distinguished from the special hospitals or dispensaries, are " institutions for administering medical and surgical relief to patients within the building (in-patients), or attending at specified times (out-patients), and suffering under any illness cr disease, except such as are incurable and contagious." The present hospital was erected in 1831. By this institution not only are patients treated both as out-patients and in-patients, but such as require it are attended at their homes, particularly midwifery cases, and children suffering under contagious disorders. In-patients with letters are admitted on Mondays at twelve ; cases of accident at all times immediately. The present yearly average number of patients is about 25,000, and the hospital is almost entirely dependent upon voluntary contributions. Close by, in Chandos Street, is the Eye Hospital, or, to give it its full title, " The Royal Westminster Ophthalmic Hospital." This institution is most cosmopolitan in the bounty which it distributes.

Toole's Theatre, in King William Street, once known as the Charing Cross Theatre, was reopened by Mr. J. L. Toole, after enlargement, in 1882, and finally closed in 1896, the noise from it being found detrimental to the patients of the Charing Cross Hospital. It was formerly used as a chapel and residence by the Fathers of the London Oratory of St. Philip Neri (1848—56), before their removal to Brompton. In 1850 Dr. Newman delivered here his celebrated " Lectures on Anglican Difficulties."

The " Golden Cross," previous to the days of railroads, was a busy and important coaching hotel ; in fact, it was called " The Bull and Mouth of the West." Of late years it has degenerated into a railway parcel-office. The author of " Haunted London " tells us that, " till late in the last century, a lofty sign-post, and a long water-trough, such as still adorn country towns, stood before the gate of this inn." It may be well to note here that the old " Golden Cross " Inn, at the door of which Charles Dickens represents Mr. Pickwick to have had the memorable encounter with the philosophic cabman, stood several yards to the west of its present position, and was removed to make way for the laying out of Trafalgar Square.

Re-crossing the Strand at this point, we come to Charing Cross Railway Station and Hotel ; and here we may pause to say a few words about the metropolitan railways. The vast strides that have been made in railway communication in the metropolis within the last few years, have been such as almost to encircle London and its suburbs with three distinct lines. The havoc that has been made during this time by the railways which have entered and intersected the metropolis is far greater than could have been imagined ; and to describe it we cannot do better than quote the words of a writer in one of the principal illustrated newspapers :—

"First," he says, "the hideous hoarding — and once raised, a hoarding seems the most difficult thing in the world to level : London has become a very city of hoardings ; then the task of destroying houses, or of snapping off odd bits of streets, and leaving maimed and melancholy fragments— unsightly, untenantable, forlorn *débris;* then the shapeless scraps of land, unneeded by the railway, and unavailable for other purposes ; wretched enclosures, where rubbish may be shot, broken crockery heaped, with the usual refuse of cabbage-stalks, rusty, battered saucepans, dead animals, oyster-shells, and cast boots and shoes—odd ones, always, pairs never come together in these waste territories. Of the abominable bridges that cross the roads at ugly angles ; of the viaducts that provide dry arches for the congregation and accommodation of street Arabs and gutter children ; of the cucumber frames that supply light and air to the underground traffic ; of the colossal sheds of stations, notably those that mar the river's banks, that soar and project like Brobdingnag poke-bonnets —we have no need to remind the reader. These are only to be classed as ruins, inasmuch as they are productive of and occasion ruins, and are themselves ruinous to all chance of the good-looking of London. But that, perhaps, is past praying for. Still, admitting the plainness of our city, we need not surely take pains to make its disadvantages in point of aspect more and more self-assertive and offensive. By discretion and consideration in the matter of mien and attire, even the ugliest can avoid at any rate advertising lack of comeliness and charm.

" But there are other modern ruins than those wrought by railway enterprise and experiment. In various parts of the town may be traced ' our failures ' in regard to change and improvement : inchoate works that seem to be the grave-stones of abortive speculation and buried capital. Close to Charing Cross Railway Bridge—itself founded, we may observe, on the ruin of a graceful suspension bridge, of quite modern construction — groups of piles may be discerned, denoting where much treasure has been sunken. These and certain devastations in Scotland Yard are the only evidences that remain of a remarkable scheme, abandoned, or very long in abeyance, for connecting Whitehall and the Waterloo Road by means of a pneumatic railway tube passing under the river. The project may be stone dead or only fast asleep for a term : it has produced a modern ruin, however, not in the least picturesque in its aspect."

At Charing Cross we have two railway stations within a stone's-throw of each other : one is the West-end terminus of the South-Eastern Railway, and the other is a station on the Metropolitan District Railway. The former, which was built about the year 1863, occupies the site of what was once Hungerford Market, and, with the vast building forming the booking-offices and hotel, covers a large space of ground. In the centre of the enclosure facing the Strand, and in front of the hotel and entrance to the railway station, there is a very handsome and elaborate cross, in the decorated Gothic style of the thirteenth and fourteenth centuries, erected in 1863. It is built on or near the spot whereon, if tradition be correct, formerly stood the cross erected by Edward I., to which we have already alluded above. It is said to be a reproduction, as near as possible, of the old one; it is from the designs of Mr. E. M. Barry, R.A., based on the scanty guidance of two or three scarce and indistinct prints. The height from the base to the summit is about seventy feet, and it cost between £1,700 and £1,800. It is of Portland and Mansfield stone, and Aberdeen granite, and the sculptor was Mr. Thomas Earp. Unfortunately, it is dwarfed and obscured by the huge hotel under whose shadow it nestles. It is thus described in the " Curiosities of London:"—"In the upper story are eight crowned statues of Queen Eleanor, four representing her as queen, with the royal insignia, and the other four with the attributes of a Christian woman. At the feet of the statues are eight kneeling figures of angels. The shields in the lower stage are copied from those existing on the crosses at Waltham and Northampton, and on the queen's tomb, displaying the royal arms of England with those of Leon, Castile, and Ponthieu. The diaper above the tracery, in the lowest stage of the monument, is composed of octagonal patterns, richly undercut, representing alternately the Castle of Castile and the lion rampant of Leon ; the pillar and couch of the effigy have a similar design. The carving generally of the crockets, capitals, canopies, diapers, gurgoyles, &c., agrees with the best remains of the English art of the thirteenth century."

The bridge by which the lines of railway are carried over the Thames consists of nine spans— six of 154 feet, and three of 100 feet—and is supported by cylinders sunk into the bed of the river, and by the piers and abutments of the old suspension-bridge, the site of which it occupies. The superstructure of each of the 154-feet openings consists of two main-girders, to the outer side of which are suspended cross-girders for carrying the roadway platform. The cross-girders extend beyond the main-girders, and form a series of cantilevers on the outer side, for supporting a foot-path seven feet in width, by which foot-passengers can now pass over toll free. The superstructure of the three 100-feet openings is fan-shaped, and forms the connection of the bridge with the railway station. A beautiful view of the Thames Embankment is obtained from the north end of Charing Cross bridge. Looking eastward, the water-gate, built by Inigo Jones for Villiers, Duke of Buckingham, alluded to in an earlier chapter, appears half hid behind an artificial mound covered with foliage; whilst westward we have a magnificent view of the Houses of Parliament, Westminster Abbey, Lambeth Palace, and other historical buildings.

The Charing Cross station of the Metropolitan District Railway is at the bottom of Villiers Street, and near the stairs leading to the footway over the bridge. The railway, which passes under the roadway of the Embankment, affords a communication between the City and the extreme western suburbs, Richmond, Ealing, &c., by way of Westminster and South Kensington.

The site of Hungerford Market, which existed from the close of the seventeenth century down to 1862, when it was pulled down to make room for the Charing Cross Hotel and Railway Station, was formerly the property of a family of the same name, whose landed estates were at Farley Castle, on the borders of Wiltshire and Somersetshire, not many miles from Bath, and whose tragic fortunes have often been told, but by no one more eloquently than by Sir Bernard Burke, in his "Vicissitudes of Families." Sir Edward Hungerford, who was made a Knight of the Order of the Bath at the coronation of Charles II., had here a magnificent mansion, which, on the break-up of Durham Yard, was cut up and converted into small tenements, which together formed a market, being connected by a covered piazza of not very attractive appearance. Over the market was a large room called "the French Church," from having been used as a place of worship by the Protestant refugees expelled from that country on the revocation of the Edict of Nantes. This building afterwards became a charity-school for the parish of St. Martin's-in-the-Fields, but at the beginning of the present century was in a very dilapidated state. It was subsequently converted into a tavern and music-hall. On the north side of the building stood a very poor bust of Charles II., marking the date of the erection.

The greatness of the Hungerford family ceased with Sir Edward Hungerford, who, by his excessive extravagance, squandered a princely fortune, and died a poor Knight of Windsor in the year 1711, at the advanced age of 115. The town house of the Hungerford family was destroyed by fire during his life, and the circumstance is thus mentioned by Pepys in his "Diary:"—"April 26, 1669.—A great fire happened in Durham Yard last night, burning the house of one Lady Hungerford, who was to come to town to it this night; and so the house is burned, new furnished, by carelessness of the girl, sent to take off a candle from a bunch of candles, which she did by burning it off, and left the rest, as is supposed, on fire. The king and court were here, it seems, and stopped the fire by blowing up the next house." Sir Edward obtained permission to hold a market three days a week on the site of his former mansion, and this was the origin of the Hungerford Market.

The market was rebuilt early in the present century, in a very heavy Italian style of architecture, by Mr. Fowler, the architect of Covent Garden Market. The upper part of the market consisted of three avenues, with shops on each side, the whole roofed into one mass. The business done in the sale of fish was very considerable, and there were also shops or stalls for the sale of fruit, vegetables, and butchers' meat.

The failure of Hungerford Market as a commercial speculation was but the perpetuation of the unhappy fate which seems always to have overhung the fortunes of that name. More than three centuries and a half ago, in 1523, a member of the Hungerford family—Dame Agnes, or Alice, Hungerford—was hung at Tyburn for the murder of her step-son; and some curious details concerning the household stuff remaining at her husband's house at Charing Cross may be found in the thirty-eighth volume of the "Archæologia." The Sir Edward Hungerford of 150 years later, known in history as "the spendthrift," gave 500 guineas for a wig in which to figure at a court ball at St. James's; and to satisfy his fondness for play, he sold no less than twenty-eight manors. It was this Sir Edward who pulled down the town mansion of the Hungerfords. The glory, or shame, of Sir Edward was not forgotten in the market-house which arose on its site, for in a niche on its northern side was placed a bust of that gentleman in a large wig, probably intended to immortalise the extravagant purchase which we have recorded above.

"On my way towards the rotten old Hungerford Stairs," writes Mr. J. T. Smith, in 1829, "my organ of inquisitiveness was arrested by two carvings in stone of a wheatsheaf and sickles, let into the sides of the houses at the north end, leading to the 'Swan.' A waterman said that the southern end of the market was used for the sale of corn; but probably the truer reason is to be found in the fact that that device was the crest of the Hungerfords."

In the row of houses fronting the old market, and forming part of the Strand, at No. 18, where his father was a bookseller, the elder Charles Mathews first saw the light, in 1776. The shop, at that time, was the favourite resort of the leading Nonconformist ministers of the time, including Rowland Hill, Dr. Adam Clarke, &c.

Hungerford Bridge, the approach to which was through the market, was constructed in 1845 upon

bridge, it was transferred to Clifton, near Bristol, where it now spans the waters of the Avon.

Nearly opposite the railway station, and running diagonally towards Adelaide Street, is the Lowther Arcade. It is nearly 250 feet in length, and has shops on either side for the sale of fancy goods. As the admission is free, and the place is considered one of the "sights" of London, it is continually thronged with children and their attendants, buying

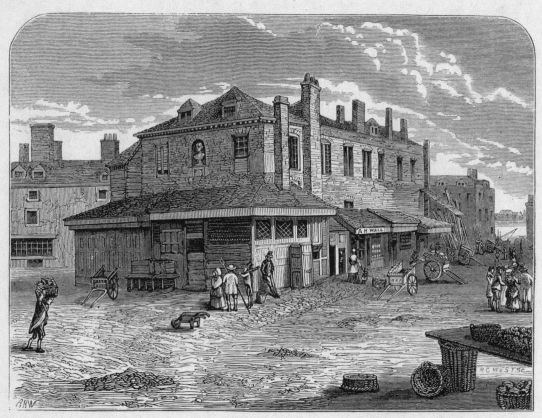

OLD HUNGERFORD MARKET. (*From a View published in* 1805.)

the suspension principle, and was the work of the late Mr. Brunel. The centre span was, perhaps, the largest of any existing work of the kind, being no less than 676 feet, whilst the total length of the bridge was 1,352 feet. The chains to which the suspending-rods were fastened were double on each side of the bridge; the two piers were of ornamental brickwork, whilst the clear height of the bridge above high water in the centre was 32 feet, and at the sides 28 feet, thus giving a rise of four feet. The span of the centre division of the bridge was the only part worthy of any particular notice. The bridge, which is said to have cost £100,000, opened up a communication between Hungerford Market and the worst part of Lambeth. On its removal, to make room for the present railway

toys at the French, German, and Swiss shops. The Lowther Bazaar, which flourished for a time at the period of the Great Exhibition in 1851, was on the other side of the Strand. Besides stalls for the sale of fancy articles, it had many other objects of interest for the amusement of visitors.

Adjoining the Lowther Arcade, with its entrance in Adelaide Street, is the Adelaide Gallery, originally intended as a place of amusement and instruction combined. It was first opened in the year 1830, and named after Queen Adelaide, the consort of William IV. Its varied fortunes, from the day when it was opened as a temple of science, down to its transformation into a casino, are thus cleverly sketched by the late Mr. Albert Smith in his little book on "London Life and Character:"—

"Some time back—dates are dry things, so we need not care about the precise year—there existed in the neighbourhood of the Lowther Arcade an establishment called the Adelaide Gallery. It was at first devoted to the diffusion of knowledge. Clever professors were there, teaching elaborate sciences in lectures of twenty minutes each; fearful engines revolved, and hissed, and quivered, as the fettered steam that formed their entrails grumbled about. The oxy-hydrogen light was slily applied to the comic magic-lantern; and laughing gas was made instead of carbonic acid. By degrees music stole in; then wizards; and lastly, talented vocal foreigners from Ethiopia and the Pyrenees. Science was driven to her wit's end for a livelihood, but she still endeavoured to appear respectable. The names of new attractions were covertly put into the bills, sneaking under the original engines and

HUNGERFORD MARKET, FROM THE BRIDGE, IN 1850. (*See page* 131.)

sullenly in its bondage; mice led gasping subaqueous lives in diving-bells; clock-work steamers ticked round and round a basin perpetually, to prove the efficacy of invisible paddles; and on all sides were clever machines which stray visitors were puzzled to class either as coffee-mills, water-wheels, roasting-jacks, or musical instruments. There were artful snares laid for giving galvanic shocks to the unwary; steam-guns that turned bullets into bad sixpences against the target; and dark microscopic rooms for shaking the principles of teetotalers, by showing the wriggling abominations in a drop of the water which they were supposed daily to gulp down.

"Then came a transition stage in the existence of the Adelaide Gallery, at first stealthily brought machines in smaller type. But, between the two stools of philosophy and fun, Science shared the usual fate attendant upon such a position—she broke down altogether. Her grave votaries were disgusted with the comic songs, and the admirers of the banjo were bored with the lectures. So neither went to see her; poor Science declined into the *Gazette*, and fled to America.

"But during all this time a mania for dancing had been gradually coming on, and at last burst forth. Not even the propensity of St. Vitus, when, in the Middle Ages, a red slipper placed on the highway was sufficient to collect and set going a host of dancing maniacs in his popular *pas*, could have kept pace with the movement. New dances were called for, and new music for them. The supply was equal to the demand; the domestic 'Paine's First Set,' of Quadrille's childhood, was laid aside for Herz; then for Musard; and then for Jullien, Weippert, Coote, and others. Clever people had always defined the earth to be one large ball, and there was every chance of its practically proving the truth of the statement.

"Travellers also began to tell bright legends of Terpsichore's palaces in her own land—of the Chaumière, with its bosquets and Montagnes Russes; of the *guinguettes* beyond the barriers of Paris; of the Chateau Rouge; and lastly, of the glittering Bal Mabille, with its palm-tree lights and trellises of bronze vines—its ruling spirits, whose names became great facts in Paris—*grande brune* Mogador, the graceful Frisette and Rigolette, the inimitable student Brididi — *le moulin perpetuel*, as he was called in Quartier Latin—whom no one could approach in his wonderful gyrations; and, finally, the veteran Chicard. And at last all the steam-engines and water-works were cleared away, and the Adelaide Gallery was devoted entirely to the goddess of the 'twinkling feet,' and called a casino. Imagine a long and very high room—so high that there are two rows of museum-like galleries running round the walls, between the floor and ceiling. At one end is a capital orchestra, and beneath it a refreshment room; the entrance staircases are at the other." It was altered into the Marionette Theatre in 1852, and is now one of the refreshment rooms of Messrs. Gatti.

In Craven Street, the next turning westwards after passing the railway station, No. 7, on the west side, as the passer-by is informed by a tablet affixed to the front, was at one time the abode of Benjamin Franklin. It was afterwards used as the headquarters of the "Society for the Relief of Persons Imprisoned for Small Debts." The abolition, however, of imprisonment for debt in ordinary cases has rendered the work of this society unnecessary. The society was mainly established by the influence of the celebrated Dr. Dodd. It is stated, as a proof of the hardship of the former laws in respect of debtors, that in fifteen months from its commencement, the society was enabled to discharge no less than 986 persons, many of whom were confined only for their fees, and who together had dependent on them as many as 566 wives and 2,389 children. "The objects of this charity," says an old prospectus, "are those, whether men or women, whose debts do not exceed ten pounds; those have the preference who are infirm or have large families."

Craven Street, as we learn from the rate-books of St. Martin's, was known until 1742 as "Spur Alley." It is the property of the Earl of Craven, who gave it his name. According to one account, Grinling Gibbons, whose exquisite wood-carving adorns St. Paul's, was a native of this street, but the fact is disputed. Here, too, lived the Rev. Mr. Hackman, who shot Miss Ray in Covent Garden, as we shall relate hereafter. And here, too, lived and died James Smith, one of the two brothers to whose wit we owe the "Rejected Addresses." In his day, as in our own, the street was largely tenanted by solicitors as offices, a fact which served as the basis of a double epigram; for a friend, noticing the fact, and also the pleasant view of the Thames at the bottom of the street, expressed himself thus—

"Fly, honesty, fly, to some safer retreat,
For there's *craft* in the river, and *craft* in the street."

In answer to which James Smith remarked, offhand, that there was no necessity to make any such rapid exodus, and why?—

"For the lawyers are *just* at the top of the street,
And the barges are *just* at the bottom."

It was in "Green's Lane in the Strand, near to Hungerford Market," that Sir Edmundbury Godfrey was living at the time when he was murdered: he was a wool merchant, and his wharf was at the bottom of Northumberland Street.

Northumberland Street, which runs down from the Strand, a few doors to the west of Charing Cross Railway Station, was formerly known as Hartshorne Lane. Here lived Ben Jonson in his schoolboy days, going first to a private school near St. Martin's Church, and afterwards to Westminster School. In Northumberland Street was published the *Pall Mall Gazette* for many years after its first appearance in 1864. In Northumberland Court, hard by, Nelson lodged when a young lieutenant.

It is worthy of note that the house next door to Northumberland House, eastwards (now absorbed in the Grand Hotel), was for many years the official residence of the Secretary of State. Sir Harry Vane, as we know, lived here, as also did several of his predecessors and successors in that office.

In concluding our notice of the Strand, we may be pardoned for adding that we love to think of it as it appeared years ago, when it was an open highway, with here and there a great man's house with gardens to the water-side. The scene has now indeed changed, both in the appearance of the great thoroughfare, and in the people by whom it is frequented, so that we are tempted to exclaim with Charles Lamb, "I often shed tears in the motley Strand, for fulness of joy at such multitude of life."

CHAPTER XX.

NORTHUMBERLAND HOUSE AND ITS ASSOCIATIONS.

"Descendunt statuæ, restemque sequuntur."—*Juvenal*.

Situation and Early Owners—Passes into the Hands of the Howards—Called Northampton House—Name changed to Suffolk House—Again altered to Northumberland House—The "Proud" Duke of Somerset—Sir Hugh Smithson, afterwards Duke of Northumberland—Description of the Building—Anecdote about the Percy Lion—The Gardens—Sale and Demolition of the House.—Northumberland Avenue.

AFTER having stood for nearly three hundred years, a most conspicuous feature of London, and the most notable house in the most characteristic of streets, the old town mansion of the Percies was levelled with the ground, in the autumn of the year of grace, 1874, in order to form a new thoroughfare from Charing Cross to the Victoria Embankment. Thus one more landmark of old London, one more witness of the life of the past, has been effaced.

Northumberland House, it is true, could not lay claim to much architectural beauty; and it had been so much altered and rebuilt at various times, that it had no very high pretensions to notice on account of its antiquity; yet few places were more familiar to the Londoner and his "country cousins," few fronts gave more character to their neighbourhood. It was a dull, plain building, full of a certain dignity, indeed, but of the unloveliest fashion of a period when men built houses more for living in than being looked at. "The progress of wealth and of luxury," says a writer in the *Standard*, shortly before its demolition, "has long since dimmed the splendours of what was once the proudest of the London houses of the English nobility. The march of fashion westward had left it isolated amidst an uncongenial neighbourhood of small shops. Commerce had overtaken and overwhelmed it, so that it stood out somewhat abruptly in the full stream of London life, making it too violent a contrast with the surrounding houses, and destroying whatever of felicity there might have been in the situation. In the days when the Strand was but a road between London and Westminster, lined with private houses of the great and noble on either side, and with gardens going down to the river, it might have been an abode fit even for the proud Earls of Northumberland, to whom it descended. But with the Thames Embankment on one side, and Trafalgar Square on the other, with omnibuses perpetually passing its front door, Northumberland House was a standing anachronism, if not an impediment, which was destined to succumb to the influence of time and the Metropolitan Board of Works."

The Percies, it is true, did not build the house, nor was it their first abode in London. Stow mentions two others occupied by this family, before they obtained possession of their Strand tenement, as of many other fair property, by marriage. The first was in the parish of St. Anne's, close to Aldersgate, which in Strype's days had become degraded into a tavern. It was inhabited by Henry Percy (Hotspur) before it was forfeited to Henry IV., who bestowed it upon his wife, Queen Jane, as her "wardrobe." Another Northumberland House was in the parish of St. Katherine Colman, on the south side of Fenchurch Street, the memory of which still survives in Northumberland Alley. This belonged to Henry, the third Earl of Northumberland, in the reign of Henry VI.; and after his time it became converted into a gambling-house, and its gardens into bowling-alleys. A third Northumberland House, occupied by Henry, the ninth earl, was in the Blackfriars, in a house abutting on the property of William Shakespeare.

The Northumberland House which forms the subject of this chapter, was, at the time of its removal, at the close of 1874, the very last relic of all the noble mansions and palaces which, in the seventeenth century, adorned the river-front of the Strand. It may therefore be well to enter into a more elaborate description of it.

It stood, if the antiquary, Pennant, was rightly informed, on the site of a certain chapel, or hospital, of St. Mary, which had been founded in the reign of Henry III., by William, Earl of Pembroke, on a piece of ground which he had given to the priory of Rouncivalle, in Navarre. In the reign of Henry V. the hospital was suppressed, as belonging to an alien monastery, with all the other houses of the kind in the kingdom, but was again restored by Edward IV., to be finally dissolved at the Reformation.

By Henry VIII. the house was granted to a private individual, who is styled Sir Thomas Cawerden, but of whom little or nothing is known. It afterwards belonged to Sir Robert Brett, and from his hands it appears to have passed into those of Henry Howard, Earl of Northampton, who, in the time of James I., built here a house, calling it after his own name. He left it to his kinsman, the Earl of Suffolk, known to history as Lord High Treasurer; and by the marriage of Algernon Percy,

Earl of Northumberland, with Elizabeth, daughter and heiress of Thomas, Earl of Suffolk, it passed into the hands of the Percies, Earls, and afterwards Dukes, of Northumberland.

From a paper privately printed by the Duke of Northumberland, in 1866, we learn that the site of this house and garden was purchased, with other property, in the beginning of the seventeenth century, from Sir Robert Brett, by Henry Howard, Earl of Northampton, the second son of Henry, Earl of Surrey, "the poet." On this site, the Earl of Northampton built a "sumptuous palace," having for his architects Benard Jansen, a foreigner of some repute in the time of James I., and also Gerard Christmas. The house, which was of brick, was finished in the year 1605, and was then called "Northampton House." The initials of Gerard Christmas were preserved in the letters C. Æ, (Christmas Ædificavit), which used to be in large capitals over the old stone gateway, which was pulled down and replaced by a new front towards the Strand, in the reign of George II. The house at that time consisted of three sides of a quadrangle, the centre fronting the Strand, and open towards the garden and river. The Earl of Northampton died here in 1614. By his will, dated the 14th of June, 1614, he devised this house and garden, with the river-side property, to his nephew, Thomas Howard, first Earl of Suffolk, the second son of Thomas, fourth Duke of Norfolk. This was the Earl of Suffolk who, as Lord Thomas Howard, "being in that memorable engagement of the Spanish Armada, was, at sea, knighted for his good services therein." He was created Earl of Suffolk, and appointed Lord High Treasurer by James I. He completed the quadrangle by building the front towards the garden and the river.* It was then called "Suffolk House;" and it may be mentioned as a proof of the ease with which names are changed in London, that Howell, in his "Londinopolis," speaks of it as "that most stately palace of Suffolk or Northampton House." To this house Suckling refers in his ballad on the marriage of Roger Boyle, Lord Broghill, with the Lady Margaret Howard, daughter of the Earl of Suffolk. The Earl of Suffolk died here in 1626, when the property passed to his son Theophilus, second Earl of Suffolk, and then to his grandson James, third Earl of Suffolk, whose

sister, the Lady Elizabeth Howard, married, in 1642, Algernon Percy, Earl of Northumberland. On this marriage the property was, by an indenture dated a few days previously, conveyed by the Earl of Suffolk and his trustees to the trustees of the Earl of Northumberland. The principal apartments were then on the Strand side, but the Earl of Northumberland reconstructed the garden or river front, under the direction of Inigo Jones, and that front then comprised the principal apartments; it is mentioned by Evelyn as being "the new front," when he visited the house in 1658. The house was afterwards called "Northumberland House."

This Earl of Northumberland was the earl who was so celebrated in- the times of Charles I. and the Commonwealth, and to whom the care of the royal children was committed by the Parliament. It was in the spring of 1660, after he had taken up his quarters at Whitehall, that "General Monk was invited, with the Earl of Manchester, Hollis, Sir William Waller, Lewis, and other eminent persons, to Northumberland House," by Earl Algernon, and here (says Lord Clarendon), "in secret conference with them, some of those measures were concerted which led to the speedy restoration of the Monarchy."

The *menu* of the noble family at Northumberland House about this time was curious, if we may judge from an entry in the Earl of Northumberland's Household Book, where we find allowed for "my Lord and Ladie's table," "ij. pecys of salt fische, vj. pecys of salt fische, vj. becormed herryng, iiij. white herryng, or a dish of sproots (sprats)." Surely, a deep draught of Canary or Malvoisie would be needed to wash down so dry a repast !

The Earl of Northumberland last-mentioned died in the year 1688. Joceline, his son and successor, was the last of the old male line, and on his death, in 1670, without sons, Northumberland House became the property of his only daughter, the Lady Elizabeth Percy,† the celebrated heiress of that day, who married the "proud" Duke of Somerset, for, it is said, her third husband. Her first husband, whom she married when only fourteen years of age, was Henry Cavendish, Earl

---

* This nobleman also built Audley End, in Essex, now the seat of Lord Braybrooke. Evelyn, in his description of this place ("the goodly palace built by Howard, Earl of Suffolk, once Lord Treasurer"), which he visited in 1654, refers to the pavilions, where, "instead of railes and balusters, there is a bordure of capital letters, as was lately also at Suffolk House, near Charing Cross, built by the said Lord Treasurer."

† Lady Elizabeth Percy was, in her own right, Baroness Percy. On the death of her father, in 1670, the honours created by Queen Mary ceased. Charles II. created, in 1674, his natural son, by the Duchess of Cleveland, George Fitz Roy, Earl, and afterwards Duke of Northumberland; but that nobleman dying in 1716 those dignities expired. In the meantime one James Percy, a trunk-maker, claimed the honours of the Percy family, and so annoyed the House of Lords that their lordships at last sentenced him to wear a paper in Westminster Hall, declaring him "a false and impudent pretender to the earldom of Northumberland."—*Burke's Peerage.*

of Ogle (son and heir of Henry, Duke of Newcastle), who assumed the name of Percy. According to Sir Bernard Burke, her ladyship "appears to have been only contracted to Thomas Thynne, Esq., of Longleate, who was assassinated in February, 1681-2;" but she married, in 1682, Charles Seymour, Duke of Somerset, who also assumed, by preliminary engagement, the surname and arms of Percy, "but from that stipulation he was released when her grace attained majority." At Northumberland House the Duke and Duchess lived "in great state and magnificence."

With reference to this nobleman a story is told, which may bear repetition here, to the effect that he was in the habit of driving up to town from his residence at Petworth, in Sussex, in imitation of royalty, in a coach and six. On one occasion, when sitting in his easy chair, after his second or third marriage, the duchess entered the room, and was about to salute him with a kiss. This so wounded the dignity of his Grace, that he is reported to have severely reprimanded the duchess, telling her that even his first wife, the noble heiress of the Percies, would not have thought of taking such liberties with him.

On the death of his Grace, in 1748, the property passed to his son Algernon, who, on the death of his mother, in 1722, had been summoned to Parliament as Baron Percy. His Grace greatly improved the north, or Strand front, and built the gallery, or great room, forming the western wing to the south front. In the cornice or balustrading on the top of the south front he caused to be inserted the letters and date, "A. S. P. N. (Algernon Seymour Princeps Northumbriæ), A.D. 1749." As there was already a Somerset House, the mansion, during the time it was the residence of the Dukes of Northumberland, was still called "Northumberland House." His Grace was created Baron Warkworth of Warkworth Castle, Northumberland, and Earl of Northumberland, in 1749, with remainder, in default of male issue, to Sir Hugh Smithson, Bart., a country gentleman of Stanwick, in Yorkshire, who had married his only daughter, the Lady Elizabeth Seymour.

It was at Northumberland House, about this time, that Oliver Goldsmith, "our gentle poet," when waiting upon the Earl of Northumberland, mistook the earl's servant for the earl, and only discovered his error after the delivery of a neatly-ordered address, after which the poor author precipitately fled. His Grace died in 1750, when the property passed to his said daughter, whose husband was afterwards created Duke of Northumberland. This nobleman faced the quadrangle with stone, and added to the gallery wing, built by the Duke of Somerset. He also restored the Strand front and other parts which had been damaged by a great fire there in 1780. From Hugh, first Duke of Northumberland, the property passed to his son Hugh, second duke, and then to his grandsons, Hugh, Algernon, and George, the third, fourth, and fifth dukes successively.

"The noble family of Northumberland," says a writer in the *Builder*, "have always been famed for their hospitality and humanity. The name of Smithson has obtained fame and an adjectival form in the United States, where the munificence of an Englishman (who claimed some kind of connection with the noble family of Northumberland) has given that country the opportunity of raising a noble institution for the advancement and popularisation of science."

Besides the principal quadrangle, which was to the north, and which the visitor entered at the porter's lodge from the Strand, the building had two wings running down at right angles from the main body of the house towards the river; that on the eastern side being devoted to the accommodation of the domestics, with stabling beyond; whilst the western wing contained the Grand Ball Room, in which royalty must often have been present, at various dates, from the days of Horace Walpole to our own time.

Along the Strand front, as we learn from Evelyn's memoirs, instead of the customary ornamental railings, there ran "a border of capital letters;" and that this was the case is corroborated by an entry in the burial register of St. Martin's Church, where a young man named Appleyard was buried in May, 1618, "slain by a stone falling from my Lord Treasurer's house."

According to a drawing by Hollar in the Pepysian Library at Cambridge (we give a facsimile of it on page 6), Northumberland, or, as it was then called, Suffolk House, is represented as a square, dull, and heavy-looking building, with lofty towers at the four angles, ending in domes of irregular shape. The house is apparently three storeys high, and has a high pitched roof. Each side is pierced with nine heavy-looking windows. The print represents it as it appeared in the early part of the reign of Charles I. The gardens between the house and the Thames are filled with a grove of trees, and alongside the river is a dull, long wall, with stairs leading down to the water.

Evelyn thus records in his "Diary," under date 1658:—"I went to see the Earl of Northumberland's pictures at Suffolk House, whereof that of the 'Venetian Senators'" (better known by its other name of the "Cornaro Family"), "was one of the best of Titian's; and another of Andrea del Sarto, viz. 'a Madonna, Christ, St. John, and an Old Woman,' &c.; a 'St. Catharina' of Da Vinci, with divers portraits of [by] Vandyke; a 'Nativity' of Georgioni; the 'Last of our Blessed Kings' (Charles I.), and the 'Duke of York,' by Lely; a 'Rosarie' by the famous Jesuits of Bruxelles, and severall more.

The new front towards the gardens is tolerable, were

From 1605, when the house was finished by the Earl of Northampton, almost down to the time of its demolition, so many changes were made in the building at different periods, that, in fact, with the exception of the front, little of the old house remained. Great alterations were made at Northumberland House in the years 1748–1752, which were begun by Algernon, Duke of Somerset, and completed by his son-in-law and daughter, the Earl and Countess of Northumberland. Northumber-

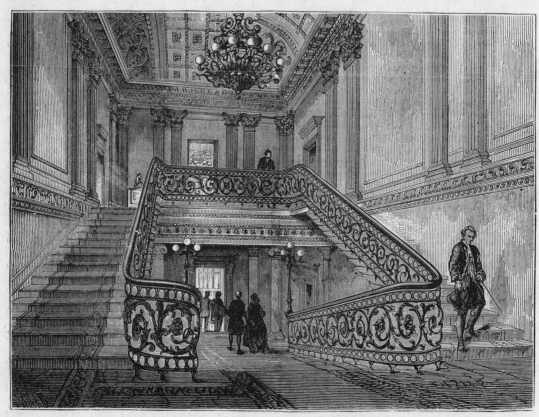

STAIRCASE IN NORTHUMBERLAND HOUSE. *From an Original Sketch.* (*See page* 140.)

it not drown'd by a too massie and clomsie pair of stayres of stone, without any neate invention."

There is a fine picture of Northumberland House by Canaletti, showing the small houses and other tenements opposite to it, and the Strand with the sign-boards in front of the houses. A copy of the picture is given on page 139.

"There is a tradition," says Mr. Nightingale, in the "Beauties of England," "that when the Earl of Northampton erected his mansion at the village of Charing, he was ridiculed for having chosen a situation so far distant from his town residence; and, indeed, if we cast our eye over the maps of London, published about that period, we shall not be surprised at the remark."

land House more than once suffered very severely from fire. The following is an account of one that occurred on Saturday, March 18th, 1780:— "It broke out about five in the morning, and raged till eight, in which time it burnt from the east end, where it began, to the west. Among the apartments consumed are those of Dr. Percy, Dean of Carlisle. We are happy to inform our readers that the greatest part of the doctor's invaluable library is fortunately preserved." It was here that the poetical doctor, whilst residing as chaplain, was visited by his brother poet, Oliver Goldsmith.

In the year 1749 the whole building was repaired and altered, the blue lion (the crest of the Percies) being placed in the position in which he was to be

NORTHUMBERLAND HOUSE. (*From the View by Canaletti.*)

seen for 125 years. There is an apocryphal legend in connection with that noble brute, that he was at first placed with his head towards Carlton House and St. James's Palace, but afterwards, on the occasion of some slight received by one of the Dukes of Northumberland, turned round with its face to the Corporation of London. The quarrel being made up after the accession of the Prince Regent as George IV., the lion returned to his original bearings. It was on this occasion, we believe, that "the first gentleman in Europe" remarked that "the king knows nothing and remembers nothing of the quarrels of the Prince of Wales."

Pennant, writing in 1806, observes, "It is unfortunate that nothing can be more confined than the situation of this great house. The noble front is pent up by a very narrow part of the Strand, and behind by a mean cluster of houses, coalwharves, and other offensive objects, as far as the banks of the Thames." He congratulates himself, however, on the probability of seeing, in a little time, these nuisances removed, and a terrace arising in their stead, rivalling that of Somerset House. What would the zealous old antiquary have said had he lived to our day, and seen the materials of the palace of the proud house of Percy sold as old building materials under the auctioneer's hammer?

As to its interior, it was a grand, but dull and gloomy house, containing a large number of rooms. Everything in it, pictures, furniture, &c., were massive and costly in the extreme; but the want of light caused it to lack that air of cheerfulness which is so characteristic of the modern Italian style.

The central part of the Strand front, which, in a tablet on the top, bore the date when some alterations in that part of the building were made about the year 1752, might be considered as the most valuable remnant of the original pile. The lion, by which it was surmounted, was cast in lead, and was about twelve feet in length. The vestibule of the interior was eighty-two feet long, and more than twelve in breadth, ornamented with Doric columns. Each end communicated with a staircase, leading to the principal apartments facing the garden and the Thames. They consisted of several spacious rooms fitted up in the most elegant manner, embellished with paintings, among which might be found the well-known "Cornaro Family," by Titian, a work well worthy of its reputation, and for which Algernon, Earl of Northumberland, is stated to have given Vandyck 1,000 guineas; and a wonderful vase, which now has a story of its own; "St. Sebastian Bound," by Guercino; "The Adoration of the Shepherds," by Bassano; and others by well-

known masters. The great feature of the house was the ball-room, or grand gallery, upwards of 100 feet in length, in which were placed large and very fine copies by Mengs, after Raphael's "School of Athens," in the Vatican, of the size of the originals; also the "Assembly of the Gods," and the "Marriage of Cupid and Psyche," in the Farnesina; the "Triumph of Bacchus and Ariadne," from Caracci's picture in the Farnese Palace; and "Apollo driving the Chariot of the Sun," from Reni's fresco in the Villa Rospigliosi, at Rome. These celebrated works, and the decoration of the noble apartment, constituted it one of the landmarks of high art in the metropolis. The grand staircase consisted of a centre flight of thirteen moulded vein marble steps, and two flights of sixteen steps, with centre landing twenty-two feet by six feet, two circular plinths, and a handsome and richly-gilt ormolu scroll balustrade, with moulded Spanish mahogany hand-rail. The mansion contained nearly 150 rooms appropriated for the private uses of the family.

Previously to 1851, those few who obtained admission to the fine apartments of this grand old mansion, did so with considerable difficulty, and few therefore had any idea of what was behind the familiar front; but in that year, when multitudes visited London and the Great Exhibition, the house was thrown open to the public, and thousands availed themselves of the privilege to walk across the courtyard and up the handsome marble staircase, into the noble ball-room and picture-gallery, and inspect the rich treasures which the house contained.

The gardens on the river-front occupied a larger space than might have been suspected, but had long been left unkempt and neglected, forming a little wilderness in close proximity to the busiest thoroughfare in London. Their aspect, when at last the light of publicity was thrown upon them, was somewhat sad and ghastly, the old hawthorns and hazels looking like Dryads of old suddenly exposed to the gaze of an irreverent troop of Satyrs. With their departure, under the ruthless decree of the Board of Works, has disappeared one more green spot from the heart of London.

We may add, that in the privately-printed documents referred to above, the last owner of this noble mansion appeared to have given his sanction for its removal with great reluctance, if we may judge from the tenor of the concluding paragraph, which runs thus:—"The Duke of Northumberland is naturally desirous that this great historical house, commenced by a Howard, continued by a Percy, and completed by a Seymour, which has been the residence of his ancestors for more than two centuries and a half, should continue to be the residence of his descendants; but the Metropolitan Board of Works are desirous that this house, which, with its garden, is one of the landmarks of London, and is probably the oldest residential house in the metropolis, should be destroyed." Arrangements for its sale to the Metropolitan Board of Works, in order to open an entrance to the Thames Embankment, were completed in 1873, the purchase-money agreed upon being £500,000. The sale was concluded definitely in June, 1874. In the following month the lion, which had stood for a century and a quarter, keeping watch and ward over the great entrance, was taken down and removed to Sion House at Isleworth; and the work of demolition was soon afterwards commenced.

In September, 1874, the fine old mansion underwent its final phase of degradation, its materials being brought under the hammer of the auctioneer. The lots consisted of 3,000,000 bricks, the grand marble staircase, the elaborate ornamentation of the hall, dining, and reception rooms, the state decorations which adorned the hall and corridors, &c. The aggregate sum realised by the sale amounted to but little more than £6,500, and of this the grand staircase alone fetched £360.

On the site of Northumberland House and its gardens three monster hotels, called the Grand, the Victoria, and the Métropole, have been erected. The fronts of the hotels open upon a broad roadway, connecting Charing Cross with the Embankment, and known as Northumberland Avenue. In this thoroughfare are the Royal Colonial Institute and the offices of the Society for Promoting Christian Knowledge. The former of these institutions, established in 1868, furnishes a point of contact for those connected with the Colonies and India.

CHAPTER XXI.

TRAFALGAR SQUARE, THE NATIONAL GALLERIES, &c.

"England expects that every man
This day will do his duty."—*Old Song.*

Formation of Trafalgar Square—The "King's Mews"—Mr. Cross's Menagerie—A State Coach-house—The Royal Humane Society—The Nelson Monument—Sir E. Landseer's Lions—Statues of George IV., Havelock, Napier, and General Gordon—Proposal for planting Trafalgar Square as a Garden—The Royal College of Physicians—Dr. Harvey's Benefaction—Anecdote of Dr. Baillie—Dr. Radcliffe and Sir Godfrey Kneller—History of the Foundation of the College of Physicians—Cockspur Street—O'Brien, the Irish Giant—Statue of George III.—Society of Painters in Water-colours—The National Gallery—Its Formation and Subsequent Additions—Agitation for an Academy of Painting—Sir Godfrey Kneller's Drawing Academy—Sir James Thornhill's Propositions rejected—Establishment of the Royal Academy—Sir Joshua Reynolds, Benjamin West, Sir Thomas Lawrence, Sir Martin A. Shee, Sir Charles L. Eastlake, Sir Francis Grant, Lord Leighton, Sir John Millais, and Sir E. J. Poynter—The National Portrait Gallery.

THE large and open space known as Trafalgar Square, occupying as it does a commanding position, as it looks down Parliament Street towards the Abbey and the Houses of Parliament, was pronounced by the great Sir Robert Peel, perhaps with a little exaggeration, the finest site in Europe. Its formation was commenced about the year 1830, on a spot of ground that up to that time was covered with a knot of filthy and disreputable abodes. In 1829, it appears, a variety of improvements were made immediately around St. Martin's Church. Amongst others, a whole labyrinth of close courts and small alleys was then cleared away—a district including places known as the Bermudas, the Caribbee or Cribbe Islands, and Porridge Island, notorious for its cook-shops; whilst, nearer Charing Cross, several wretched buildings were swept away, with the same object in view. The savoury delights of "Porridge Island" as a provocation to the appetite more than once formed the subject of banter between Dr. Johnson and Mrs. Thrale, at Streatham.

There had previously been an open space or square on this spot, but of more contracted dimensions. On its north side, where now stands the National Gallery, was the large building called the "King's Mews," to which we have alluded in a previous chapter. It was from this place, during the civil wars of the houses of York and Lancaster, that the Lincolnshire rebels, under Robert Rydsdale, took Lord Rivers and his son John, carried them away, and beheaded them at Northampton. Early in the present century the "Mews" was occupied by Mr. Cross's collection of wild animals, which were removed hither on the breaking-up of Exeter 'Change; here also the first exhibitions of machinery were held, and the public records were for a long time preserved—or, at least, such of them as were not eaten by rats. It may be added that Chaucer was not only Clerk of the King's Works, but also "Clerk of the Mews at Charing."

On the east side of the square was a mean-looking building, with folding doors, used as a state coach-house in the time of George II. Here at the present time are the offices of the Humane Society. This benevolent institution, which was founded by Dr. Hawes in the year 1774, has been instrumental in saving thousands of lives from drowning, more especially in the Thames and in the ornamental waters in the public parks. We shall have to speak of its operations hereafter, when we come to describe the Serpentine.

In the centre of the open space, facing the statue of King Charles, and looking down White-hall to the Abbey and Houses of Parliament, stands the statue of Lord Nelson, upon the summit of a column which the nation raised, it must be owned, with a tardy generosity, in 1840–3, in honour of her greatest naval hero. The fluted column itself, with capital cast in gun-metal, which is 176 feet high, and in the Corinthian style, was designed by Mr. William Railton, architect; whilst the colossal statue of the great naval hero is the work of the late Mr. E. H. Baily, R.A., and is admired for its fine proportions. The square pedestal is thirty-six feet in height, and is of beautiful proportion, the four sides containing, in basso-relievo, representations of Nelson's four great battles, cast in gun-metal taken from the enemy in his various engagements—namely, the Battle of the Nile, by Woodington; the Battle of St. Vincent, by Watson; the Battle of Copenhagen, by Ternouth; and the Death of Nelson, by Carew. These four works are fine examples of English sculpture, and, with the statue, cost above £28,000. The four gigantic lions at the angles of the base were at first assigned to the sculptor, Mr. Lough, but were sub-sequently executed by the late Sir Edwin Landseer. The attempt to add the laurels of a sculptor to those of a painter can hardly be said to have been a successful one. For many years the lions were not forthcoming, and the guardians of the pillar were still in the artist's studio at St. John's Wood Road. They were so constantly promised that at last the public patience was sorely tried, and Sir Edwin's embryo lions began to furnish a standing jest to the newspaper writers. At length, in the year 1868, they were set up; but many a cruel joke was uttered at their expense: amongst others it was said that the old lion on the top of Northumberland House would not acknowledge them as brethren.

On the north side of the enclosure, between the column and the National Gallery, are two fountains, supplied by a well near Charing Cross, upwards of 380 feet deep, sunk by Messrs. Easton and Amos, for the Government, for the purpose of supplying these fountains, Buckingham Palace, and several of the Government offices in Whitehall. The

fountains are of Peterhead granite, but are by no means striking objects. They were an after-thought, being added in 1845, from a design by the late Sir Charles Barry.

In the north-east corner of Trafalgar Square is the bronze equestrian statue of George IV., by Sir F. Chantrey, which was placed in its present position in 1845. It is considered a very fine work of art, and cost 9,000 guineas. At the south-east corner of the Square is the bronze statue erected in 1861, to the memory of Major-General Sir Henry Havelock, from the design of Behnes; and at the south-west corner is another bronze statue, of Sir Charles Napier, by Adams, erected in 1857; while in 1888 a statue of General Gordon, by Thornycroft, was erected in the centre of the Square facing the Nelson column.

Upon the demolition of Northumberland House, mentioned in the preceding chapter, the Duke of Northumberland offered to lay out some of the purchase-money which he received for his late residence in beautifying Trafalgar Square. *Apropos* of this intention, it may be observed that this was not the first time that such a plan had been con-templated, as in the "British Almanack and Com-panion," published in 1838 by Charles Knight, the following notice occurs:—"How the area of Trafalgar Square will be laid out or decorated we cannot yet say. At present a strong opposition is manifesting itself to the plan of its being made an enclosed garden, under the pretence that the people will thereby be deprived of an open promenade. This, however," observes Mr. Knight, "does not exactly follow, for the public might be admitted into the garden under the same regulations as those under which they are now admitted into St. James's Park."

In 1879 the work of "beautifying" Trafalgar Square, by planting it with trees, was carried out; the trees being continued on either side of North-umberland Avenue, to those on the Embankment.

At the north-west corner of the Square, with its frontage in Pall Mall East, is the Royal College of Physicians. This elegant and commodious building was erected in 1825, from the designs of the late Sir Robert Smirke. The principal front of the structure is composed of a hexastyle projecting portico of the Ionic order, which supports a well-proportioned pediment. The front is elongated by two antæ in one each side of the portico, which is repeated, with a break between them, in the eastern front; it has also a distinguishing centre-piece of two slightly-projecting antæ and an elevated attic, with a balustrade in each wing.

The building is divided into two storeys, and the windows are decorated with architraves and sub-cornices. The columns are beautifully wrought, and impart to the edifice at once a pleasing and grand appearance. Within, the apartments are of airy and noble proportions. A door on the left of the entrance-hall leads into the dining-room, which is lighted by six windows overlooking Trafalgar Square. The room is handsomely decorated, and has over the fireplace a fine portrait of Dr. Harvey. During the time of the Civil War, when the property of the College at Amen Corner was condemned as part of the possessions of the Church, and actually put up to auction, Dr. Harvey became the purchaser, and shortly afterwards settled it in perpetuity upon the College. From the entrance-hall a staircase leads towards the gallery or landing, whence are entered the library and Censor's room. This latter apartment has its oak-panelled walls adorned with pictures and busts. Here Candidates for diplomas used to undergo their examinations, at three separate meetings of the Censors' board, the *vivâ voce* part of each such examination being carried on in Latin. These examinations are strict, and afford good security to the public that none but those who have had a liberal and learned education can hope for success, and that the order of English physicians shall always consist of men who will do honour to their profession by their general abilities and high qualifications. Among the busts that adorn the Censor's room, is one of Dr. Baillie, of whom the following anecdote is told in Charles Knight's "London:"—"This learned doctor was occasionally very irritable, and indisposed to attend to the details of an uninteresting story. After listening with torture to a prosing account from a lady who ailed so little that she was going to an opera that evening, he had happily escaped from the room, when he was urgently requested to step up stairs again ; it was to ask him whether on her return from the opera she might eat some oysters. 'Yes, ma'am,' said Baillie, 'shells and all !'"

The library, a splendid room—long, broad, and high—is lighted by three beautiful lanterns in the ceiling, and the walls consist of two storeys, marked at intervals by flat oaken pillars below, and clusters of flat and round imitation-marble pillars above. In the lower storey the shelves round the walls are filled with books, mostly the gift of the Marquis of Dorchester, who left his valuable library to the College. In the gallery which extends round the upper part of the room, the walls are fitted up with bookcases, hidden by crimson curtains, containing preparations, amongst which are some of the nerves and blood-vessels constructed by Hunter. From the gallery a narrow staircase leads up to a small theatre or lecture-room, where are some interesting busts and portraits, and among the latter a fine one of Hunter. Among the portraits in the library is one of Dr. Radcliffe, the founder of the magnificent institution at Oxford which bears his name, and whose executors gave £2,000 towards the erection of this building. It was painted by Sir Godfrey Kneller. An anecdote in which both the painter and the doctor are concerned we give as it is related :—" They lived next to each other in Bow Street, Covent Garden, and the painter having beautiful pleasure-grounds, a door was opened for the accommodation of his friend and neighbour. In consequence of some annoyance, Sir Godfrey threatened to close up the door ; to which Radcliffe replied that he might do anything with it, if he would not paint it. 'Did my very good friend Dr. Radcliffe say so ?' cried Sir Godfrey. 'Go you back to him, and after presenting my service to him, tell him that I can take anything from him but physic.'"

The eminent society of which we are speaking was established in 1523, under a charter from Henry VIII., which authorised its council to forbid any one to practise as a physician within seven miles of London without having been admitted a licentiate or fellow of this College. Nor can any one become a fellow without having taken a degree in the faculty of medicine at Oxford or Cambridge, or be admitted a licentiate without a previous study at an English university, or obtaining a diploma from Edinburgh, Glasgow, or Dublin, and passing an examination before the Censors of the College.

The first building which served as a " college " for the society was a mansion in Knightrider Street, given to them by Dr. Linacre, physician to King Henry VIII. They afterwards removed to a house which they purchased in Amen Corner, Paternoster Row, where Dr. Harvey built a library and a public hall, which he granted for ever to the College, and endowed it with his estate, which he resigned to them in his lifetime. Part of this estate is assigned for an annual oration in commemoration of their munificent benefactor, and to provide a dinner for the members of the College. This building was burned down in the Great Fire of 1666, after which the society purchased a piece of ground on the west side of Warwick Lane, and raised a considerable sum in 1674 for the erection of a new college. Sir John Cutler offering to subscribe a large donation, a committee was appointed to wait upon him to thank him for his liberality ; and in 1668 statues in honour of the king and the liberal donor were ordered to be executed at the expense of the College. In 1689, the buildings being completed, the Fellows borrowed a sum of money of Sir John to defray the expenses ; but, upon his death, to their great surprise, his executors demanded upwards of £7,000 of them ; as in his books he had made them debtors, not only for the sum he had lent them, but also for the sum he had given them, and all the accumulated interest. The executors

Accordingly they removed their establishment to the substantial and elegant structure in Pall Mall East here described.

Cockspur Street, the thoroughfare uniting Charing Cross with Pall Mall East, skirts the south side of the Union Club, which joins on to the Royal College of Physicians, and of which we will say more in our chapter on the Club-land of Pall Mall. In this street died, in 1783, O'Brien, the

GARDEN FRONT OF NORTHUMBERLAND HOUSE. *From an Original Sketch.* (*See page* 140.)

at length accepted £2,000, and the College expunged the inscription of the old miser's liberality from under his statue, that remained in a niche in the western front of the theatre, which was standing in Warwick Lane down to a very recent period.*

The majority of the leading physicians and of their opulent patients now reside more to the westward of the metropolis than they did in the reign of Charles II., when the fellows assembled in that goodly building of brick and stone which Dr. Garth describes in his " Dispensary " as a place—

" Where stands a dome majestic to the sight,
  And sumptuous arches bear its oval height ;
A golden globe, placed high with artful skill,
  Seems to the distant sight a gilded pill."

       * See Vol. I., p. 216, and Vol. II., p. 431.

famous Irish giant, whom we have already mentioned in our account of the College of Surgeons in Lincoln's Inn Fields. At the junction of this street with Pall Mall stands the equestrian statue of George III., by Wyatt, which, though it has been considered, in an equestrian sense, one of the best " seats " for a horseman in London, has been much derided on account of the stiff "pig-tail" so characteristic of that monarch. When it was cast, in 1835 or 1836, permission was obtained for its erection on the triangular spot of waste ground on which it stands—not a bad place to show off a statue to advantage. But some of the tenants of the adjoining houses, finding that in their leases it was covenanted that the open space should not be occupied, raised objections which were held valid by the then Vice-Chancellor. His ruling, however, was set aside on appeal to the Lord Chancellor, and so the statue was set up.

Returning along Pall Mall East we have on our left, next to the United University Club House, the building devoted to the uses of the Royal Society of Painters in Water-Colours, of which Sir John Gilbert, R.A., is president. The exhibition of the works of members of this society takes place twice in the year, in spring and winter, and the public are admitted on payment of a shilling.

the main front is too much cut up in petty detail, and some have even humorously nicknamed it "The National Cruet-stand"—an idea which has evidently been suggested by the pepperbox-shaped cupolas with which it is crowned.

The National Collection of Paintings originated in the year 1824, in the purchase of the Angerstein gallery of thirty-eight pictures, for which a sum of £57,000 was voted by Government. The owner of these pictures, Mr. Julius Angerstein, was an opulent banker, and secured his collection abroad,

SIR JOSHUA REYNOLDS. (*See page* 148.)

We now arrive at the National Gallery, and ascend the steps leading to the portico, where we certainly obtain one of the finest views in London. Looking across Trafalgar Square, its fountains sparkling (occasionally) in the sunlight, the scene embraces the open vista of Whitehall and Parliament Street, which is closed by the towers and pinnacles of the Houses of Parliament and the venerable walls of the Abbey.

From its first conception to the present time no building, perhaps, has been the subject of more lively criticism than that which now serves as the chief depository of the pictures belonging to the nation. The edifice is hardly a fine one in itself, nor is it considered in any sense adequate to its national object. Most persons agree that

chiefly during the war against the Great Napoleon. The nucleus of a National Gallery having been thus formed, several bequests and presentations of valuable paintings were afterwards made to the nation by public-spirited individuals, and extensive purchases have also been at different times effected by the Government, mainly on the recommendation of the President of the Royal Academy. Sir George Beaumont, an amateur artist of great taste and skill, presented to the country, in 1826, fifteen choice pictures, chiefly by the ancient masters. In the same year the Rev. William Holwell Carr, who is stated to have expended a fortune in acquiring it, bequeathed to the nation the whole of his collection, amounting to about thirty in number, and all of a high class. This was followed, in 1838, by a bequest from Lord Farnborough of fifteen paintings, comprising specimens of the Dutch, Flemish, and Italian schools. Eighteen more pictures were presented by Lieut.-Colonel Ollney. George IV., William IV., and the Duke of Northumberland are also to be included amongst the liberal contributors to the national collection. The Governors of the British Institution likewise presented several valuable paintings. To these were added the collections made by Mr. Vernon and Mr. Wynn Ellis; and last, though not least, there is the Turner collection, which was presented to the nation by the greatest of our modern landscape painters.

These pictures—at least, such of them as were national property—were at first shown to the public in a small, dingy, ill-lighted house on the south side of Pall Mall, until 1833, when it was proposed to erect a special building for them. The site chosen was that hitherto occupied by the Royal Mews, and the present building was erected. The new building was completed in 1838, from the designs of Mr. Wilkins, the architect; but it was scarcely occupied before it was discovered to be much too small. In preparing his design, Mr. Wilkins was sorely hampered with conditions. The edifice was not to intercept the view of the portico of St. Martin's Church; it must not infringe on the barrack space in the rear; the public must have one right of way through it, and the Guards another; the old columns of Carlton House were to be used up; and the true faith in architecture insisted on having porticoes, dome, and cupolas; moreover, the building, by no means too large for a National Gallery, was to be shared with the Royal Academy. With such instructions Mr. Wilkins prepared his plans and estimates. The building was to cost £50,000, but, as in most other instances, perhaps, the architect was not to be bound by his estimate. The entire cost reached, we believe, some £25,000 in addition.

Notwithstanding the limited space in the new building, the pictures belonging to the nation were brought thither and deposited in the eastern wing, whilst the other portion of it was handed over to the Royal Academy, of which institution we will here say a few words.

It is stated by several writers that the establishment of an academy for painting was agitated as far back as the time of Charles II.; and when the subject was revived at a subsequent date, its projectors and patrons appear to have intended to erect the necessary buildings for its accommodation in the centre of Lincoln's Inn Fields. Happily, however, the idea was never carried out, and that square was still preserved as an open space.

For long years the sentiment had prevailed in England that art was no affair of the State, had no sort of interest for the governing power of the country, or, indeed, for the general public; and it was, of course, left to those persons to whom an academy of art was in any way a matter of necessity or importance to found such an institution for themselves. For the benefit of his brother artists, therefore, Sir Godfrey Kneller instituted a private drawing-academy in London, in the year 1711; but certain forms and ceremonies having been introduced into the academy which were objectionable to several members, divisions and jealousies arose in the general body; and finally, the president and his followers, finding themselves caricatured and opposed, locked out their opponents, and closed the academy.

Sir James Thornhill, who had headed the most important of the parties into which the institution had become divided, and who held the appointment of historical painter to George I., then submitted to the Government of the day a plan for the foundation of a Royal Academy which should encourage and educate the young artists of England; and the site proposed by him was at the upper end of the King's Mews, Charing Cross. The Government, however, declined to find the means for carrying out the design, and the proposition accordingly fell to the ground.

Not altogether daunted by this ill success, Sir James Thornhill determined to do what he could on his own responsibility, and without the aid of the Treasury. He therefore opened a drawing-academy at his house in James Street, Covent Garden, and gave tickets to all who desired admission. It is to be feared that Sir James's generosity was somewhat abused. At all events, dissensions arose in his academy, as in Kneller's, and a rival school was founded, where, according to Hogarth, a "female figure was introduced, to make it more inviting to subscribers." This, however, did not last long; and, on the death of Sir James, his academy was also closed.

It is mentioned casually in a London newspaper of October 12, 1723, as an article of information, that "the Academy of Painting and Sculpture opened on Monday last, as usual, in St. Martin's Lane." We may, however, search in vain through the diaries of Pepys and Evelyn, and through the letters of Horace Walpole, for information as to the members and the character of this academy. Malcolm, whose industry in hunting up old and curious facts is above praise, tells us, in his "Londinium Redivivum," that an academy for students in painting was held in Queen Street for some years previous to 1724, in which year, a difference arising on some question of art, its members parted company. One part of them seceded with Vanderbank, who opened an academy in what had been a Presbyterian meeting-house, in the same neighbourhood; "but this," adds Malcolm, "soon came to nothing." Sir James Thornhill, the head of the other party, built at the back of his house, near Covent Garden Theatre, a room for this purpose; and this subsisted till his death, in 1734, when his son-in-law, Hogarth, becoming possessed of the models, lent them to a society of artists, who took a house for their accommodation in St. Martin's Lane. The members of this society afterwards met at the "Turk's Head," in Gerrard Street; and in 1760 they were bold enough to make their first exhibition of paintings, at "the great room of the Society for the Encouragement of Arts, Manufactures, and Commerce, opposite Beaufort Buildings." Encouraged by success, they next year again exhibited, under the title of "A Society of Artists associated for the Relief of the Distressed and Decayed of their own Body, their Widows and Children." Their exhibitions were continued afterwards for several years—first in Spring Gardens, and then in Pall Mall, where they were visited, on June 1, 1767, by George III. and his queen, who presented the association with a purse of a hundred pounds. This gift being made known in the journals of the day, set the tide of fashion in the right direction, and ensured the success of "the Exhibition." as it soon became to be called *par excellence.*

The first formal meeting of the Royal Academy was held in Pall Mall, on the 14th of December, 1768. Mr. Chambers, the architect, who had been appointed treasurer, read a report to the artists assembled, relating the steps that had been taken to found the Academy. It set forth that on the previous 28th of November, Messrs. Chambers, Cotes, Moser, and West had had the honour of presenting a memorial to the Crown, signed by twenty-two artists, soliciting the royal assistance and protection in establishing a new society for promoting the arts of design. The objects of the society were stated to be "the establishing a well-regulated school or academy of design, for the use of students in the arts, and an annual exhibition open to all artists of distinguished merit, where they may offer their performances to public inspection, and acquire that degree of reputation and encouragement which they shall be deemed to deserve." Statements of the intentions of the memorialists were afterwards drawn up and submitted to the king, who, on the 10th of December, signified his approbation, ordered

that the plan should be carried into execution, and with his own hand signed Mr. Chambers' plan—"the Instrument," as it was then and has ever since that time been called. Mr. Chambers then read the "Instrument" to the meeting, after which the artists present signed an obligation, or declaration, promising to observe all the laws and regulations contained in that document, and all future laws that might be made for the better government of the society, and to employ their utmost endeavours to promote the honour and interest of the establishment so long as they should continue members of it. The Academy thus obtained its constitution, and assumed such form of legal existence as it has ever since possessed.

The rules declared that the Academy should consist of forty members only, who should be called Academicians; they were to be at the time of their admission, painters, sculptors, or architects of reputation in their professions, of high moral character, not under twenty-five years of age, resident in Great Britain, and not members of any other society of artists established in London.

Of the forty members who were to constitute the Academy, the "Instrument," as signed by the king, named thirty-six only; and of these, while many were artists of fame, there were many others whose names, but for their registry upon the list of original Academicians, would probably never have been known to posterity in any way. Having named the original members, the "Instrument" proceeded to lay down the rules for the further government of the institution; to prescribe the manner of electing future members, a council and president, a secretary and keeper (the treasurer was to be nominated by his Majesty, "as the king is graciously pleased to pay all deficiencies"), the appointment of different professors, the establishment of schools, and a library for the free use of students, and of an annual exhibition of works of art to be "open to all artists of distinguished merit." New laws were to be framed from time to time, but to have no force until "ratified by the consent of the general assembly and the approbation of the king." At the end of the Instrument the king wrote: "I approve of this plan; let it be put in execution"—adding his signature, "George R."

Thus the plan was matured, and the Royal Academy was instituted, under the patronage of King George III. The success of the institution was further secured by the fortunate appointment of Sir Joshua Reynolds, whose grasp of the first principles of art has never been excelled, as its first president.

The members of the Royal Academy used to

give large dinners to the nobility and gentry and the exhibitors, at the "Freemasons' Tavern," on the king's birthday; but subsequently the exhibitors were left out of the list of invited guests. In 1770 they celebrated the king's birthday in the following manner, by the aid of their own pencils, as we learn from the *London Chronicle* of June 5th in that year:—" Yesterday being the anniversary of his Majesty's birthday, the Royal Academicians gave an elegant entertainment at their house in Pall Mall; and in the evening the whole front of the Royal Academy was illuminated with transparent paintings, as usual, executed by the Academicians." The designs were fanciful in the extreme, and the paintings on this occasion, it may interest our readers to learn, were by Cipriani, Dance, Richards, Baker, and Benjamin West (afterwards president).

A few short notices of the distinguished men who have successively occupied the presidential chair of the Royal Academy may not be out of place here.

Sir Joshua Reynolds, the first on the list, was a native of Plympton, near Plymouth, in Devonshire, where he was born in the year 1723. At the age of seventeen he became a pupil of Hudson, but after two years' study he returned to Plymouth. He subsequently paid visits to Italy with Keppel, and afterwards settling in London, founded the Literary Club, in conjunction with Johnson, in the year 1764. He was a man highly cultivated and scholar-like, and had immense power in grasping the principles of art; in fact, he may be put down as the real originator of the English school of painting. Among his principal pictures may be mentioned, "Garrick between Tragedy and Comedy," "Mrs. Siddons as the Tragic Muse," "The Infant Hercules," "Sheridan," &c. Sir Joshua was appointed principal painter to the king in 1784, became partially blind in 1789, and died in 1792.

Benjamin West, his successor, who was born at Springfield, in Pennsylvania, in 1738, was somewhat heavy and formal in his style of painting. He visited Rome in 1760, and three years later arrived in England, where he became the *protégé* of George III. He was appointed historical painter to the king in 1772, and occupied the presidential chair from 1792 down to his death in 1820.

Sir Thomas Lawrence, the next president in succession, was a native of Bristol, where he first saw the light in the year 1769. He became a student at the Royal Academy in 1787. Courtly, graceful, with perhaps more beauty than Sir Joshua Reynolds, but not half his power, Thomas Lawrence soon became a rising man in the art world, and in 1792 was appointed to the post of painter to George III. He was knighted by the Prince Regent in 1815, and succeeded to the presidential chair of the Royal Academy in 1820. For many years Sir Thomas Lawrence derived from his works an income approaching the large sum of £15,000 per annum; but so eagerly did he contest the possession of any rare and valuable art productions when occasion offered, that even this princely income was not enough for him; and true as it is that the value of the collection which he had formed was estimated, after his decease, at £50,000, he nevertheless died in straitened circumstances. His death occurred in the year 1830, and his memory was honoured by a tomb in St. Paul's Cathedral.

Sir Martin Archer Shee, who will be remembered as the author of "Rhymes on Art," and similar works, was born in Dublin, in 1770. He came to London at the age of eighteen, and in the following year exhibited at the Royal Academy. He became a Royal Academician in 1800, and received the honour of knighthood on his appointment to the presidential chair, in 1830. He died at Brighton, in 1850.

Sir Charles Locke Eastlake, the successor of the above, was a native of Plymouth, and was born in 1793. He became a student of the Royal Academy in 1808, and in early life paid visits to Italy in company with Sir C. Barry and Brockendon. He was appointed Secretary to the Commission of Fine Arts in 1841, and Librarian to the Royal Academy in the following year. He was afterwards chosen Keeper of the National Gallery, and subsequently became Director. Sir Charles Eastlake died at Pisa, in 1865.

Sir Francis Grant, the next President, was the fourth son of Mr. Francis Grant, of Kilgraston, Perthshire. He was born in 1803, became an Associate in 1842, and attained full honours in 1851. He died in 1878, and was succeeded by Sir Frederic (afterwards Lord) Leighton, a son of the late Mr. Frederick Leighton, of Scarborough. Born in 1830, he was admitted an Associate in 1864, elected a Royal Academician in 1868, and died in 1896. Sir John Everett Millais, Bart., who followed him in the Chair, only lived to occupy it a few months, and he in turn was succeeded by Sir E. J. Poynter the Director of the National Gallery.

The inconvenience caused by the building in Trafalgar Square having to afford shelter to both the National Gallery and the Royal Academy taxed the energy of Parliament for years to find a remedy. In 1848 Lord John Russell, Sir Robert Peel, Mr.

Hume, and others forming *one* Committee of the House of Commons, "after careful deliberation, unanimously concurred in the opinion" that the present National Gallery should be enlarged and improved. Two years later Lord John Russell, Sir Robert Peel, Mr. Hume, and others, forming *another* Committee, reported that they could "not recommend that any expenditure should be at present incurred for the purpose of increasing the accommodation of a National Gallery on the present site," and were "not prepared to state that the preservation of the pictures and convenient access for the purpose of study and improvement of taste would not be better secured in a gallery further removed from the smoke and dust of London."

The result of this very negative report was to induce architects and others, year after year, to inflict on the public their views of the vexed question. At one time, indeed, the House of Commons voted £167,000, and the Prince Consort added to that sum the surplus of the Exhibition of 1851, with which was bought the land opposite and outside Hyde Park, at Kensington Gore, the site for which the Government had previously commenced negotiations with the same object, though they had failed to secure it at the time. The House of Commons, however, rejected the plan for removing the National Gallery to this site; and the then notion of rebuilding the Gallery seems now to be finally abandoned. Part of the difficulty has been got over by the removal of the Royal Academy to Burlington House, of which we shall have more to say hereafter, when we come to Piccadilly. The Vernon and Sheepshanks galleries, too, which form part of the national collection, have been removed westward, and found more suitable quarters in the saloons of the South Kensington Museum. Moreover, great enlargements and improvements have been made in the Gallery from time to time, and no expense has been spared to render it fireproof.

To the National Gallery has been added, on the east and north sides, the National Portrait Gallery,* for the reception of the national collection of portraits, which were at one time exhibited at the South Kensington Museum, and afterwards at the Bethnal Green branch of that institution. The site was provided by the Government; the building, begun in 1890 and completed in 1896, was reared at the expense of Mr. W. H. Alexander, who in 1888 undertook to devote a sum of £80,000 to the purpose. Mr. Evan Christian was the architect, and after his decease the supervision of the work was entrusted to Mr. J. H. Christian. The structure is not a particularly effective one, which may be due in part to the general harmony with the older Gallery which the architect appears to have felt himself obliged to maintain; but the east wing, with the main entrance facing St. Martin's Place, is not without elegance, plain and heavy as is the north façade, fronting the Charing Cross Road.

The more ancient portraits of the collection are arranged in chronological order on the top floor. The portraits in the east wing of the upper floor, and most of those on the first floor, are disposed in groups—artists, statesmen, actors, &c. In the east wing of the lower floor are some specimens of the sculptor's art, and in the gallery of the upper basement are large pictures of the Houses of Parliament in session. Among the modern portraits is a fine series from the brush of Mr. G. F. Watts, R.A., the generous gift of the artist.

---

* *See also* Vol. IV., pp. 32–33.

CHAPTER XXII.

ST. MARTIN'S-IN-THE-FIELDS.

"Why, how now, Babell, whither wilt thou build?
I see old Holbourne, Charing Crosse, the Strand,
Are going to St. Giles's-in-the-Field."—*Tom Freeman's Epigrams* (1614).

St. Martin's-in-the-Fields in the Sixteenth and Seventeenth Centuries—The Church built by Henry VIII.—The Church rebuilt—Description of the Edifice—Burial of Sir Edmundbury Godfrey—Notabilities interred in the Churchyard—The Parish Rate-books—Curious Stories about St. Martin's Church—The Royal Society of Literature—Anthropological Institute—National Society for aiding the Sick and Wounded in War—Archbishop Tenison's Library and School—An Ancient Chapel or Oratory—Historic and Artistic Associations of St. Martin's Lane.

IF we could throw ourselves mentally back three centuries, and could take a view of the district lying between St. James's Palace and the villages of Charing and St. Giles's, as it appeared about the year 1560, we should see little more than an open tract of fields. At that time there were only three, or, at the most, four houses towards the eastern end of Pall Mall, and a little further a small church, which has long since disappeared. Still nearer to the Palace, about the centre of what is now St. James's Square, was a well, enclosed in four low walls. The Hay Market and Hedge Lane, as late as the reign of Charles II., were literally lanes, fringed on either side with hedges; and all to the north was open country. In the ancient plans of London the Hay Market is quite clear of buildings, and Windmill Street, when first built, derived its name from a windmill standing in a field on its west side, with a small rural stable in the rear of it.

The parish of St. Martin was originally taken out of that of St. Margaret; and yet so rapid was its

funerals of his liege subjects passing through or past Whitehall, much as Louis XIV. of France resolved to build the Château at Versailles because he could not help seeing the towers of St. Denis from the terrace at Saint-Germain.

The church is so called after the chivalrous Hungarian, St. Martin, who was Bishop of Tours in the fourth century, and in whose honour it is dedicated. It received its surname, "in the fields,"

THE FIRST ROYAL ACADEMY; ABOUT 1740. (*See page* 147.)

growth, that in 1786 it had come to be "one of the most populous within the bills of mortality," being estimated to contain more than 5,000 houses, although the parishes of St. Paul's, Covent Garden; St. Anne's, Soho; St. James's, Piccadilly; and St. George's, Hanover Square, had all been in turn carved out of it.

In very early times it is said that a chapel dedicated to St. Martin was erected near Charing Cross, "for the convenience of the officers of Westminster Abbey and Palace, on their way to Covent Garden;" and this, no doubt, was the original "St. Martin's-in-the-Fields." But this is only a tradition. More trustworthy is the statement that St. Martin's was built by order and at the cost of Henry VIII., who disliked to see the

like its sister church of St. Giles, from its situation outside the City proper, when it was first taken into the bills of mortality, in order to distinguish it from other churches eastwards under the same dedication.

That there was a church on or near this spot as far back as the times of our Norman kings is shown by a dispute, in the year 1222, between William, Abbot of Westminster, and Eustace, Bishop of London, in which the former claimed for it exemption from the bishop's authority—a claim which was decided by the Archbishop of Canterbury in favour of the abbot. This would appear to confirm the tradition that originally it was a chapel for the use of the monks of Westminster, when they visited the convent whose

OLD COCKSPUR STREET.

garden abutted on it to the east. Be this, however, as it may, the endowments of St. Martin's Chapel fell, along with the monks to whom it belonged, under the ruthless paw of Henry VIII., who is said, as already remarked, to have erected in its stead a small parochial church. In 1607 this church was enlarged, at the cost of Prince Henry, son of King James I.

While the Strand was inhabited by the highest titled families, it is no matter of wonder that St. Martin's-in-the-Fields should have been a somewhat fashionable parish in the early Georgian era. In 1721 the church was pulled down, and the present edifice was erected in its place. It was built by Gibbs, the architect of the Radcliffe Library at Oxford, and cost nearly £60,000. George I. took a great interest in the building of the church, and is said to have been so delighted at its completion that he gave £100 to be distributed among the workmen employed on it, and £1,500 more to purchase an organ. The organ, however, was long ago replaced by another.

The portico, of lofty Corinthian columns, is much admired, as, indeed, is the entire west front, to which an ascent is gained up a long flight of steps. In the pediment are seen the royal arms in bas-relief, beneath which is a Latin inscription relating to the foundation of the church. The steeple is stately and elegant, and very lofty, and in the tower is an excellent peal of twelve bells.

"The church of St. Martin," says Mr. Gwynn, "is esteemed one of the best in this city, though far from being so fine as it is usually represented to be. The absurd rustication of the windows, and the heavy sills and trusses under them, are unpardonable blemishes, and very improperly introduced into this composition of the Corinthian order, as it takes away the delicacy which should be preserved in this kind of building. The steeple itself is good, but it is so constructed that it seems to stand upon the roof of the church, there being no appearance of its continuation from the foundation, and consequently it seems to want support; an error of which Gibbs is not alone guilty, but which is very elegantly and judiciously avoided in the turrets in front of St. Paul's; indeed, the spire of the steeple of St. Martin's Church being formed by internal sweeps, makes the angles too acute, which always produces an ill effect. Upon the whole, St. Martin's Church is composed on a grand style of one order, and the portico is truly noble."

Mr. Malton says, "We have in the exterior of this church an excellent example of Roman architecture in its highest style of improvement, without the tawdry and meretricious ornaments with which the Romans frequently disfigured their sacred edifices. It is also the most successful attempt to unite the light and picturesque beauty of the modern steeple to the sober grandeur and square solidity of the Grecian temple. The insulated columns in the recesses at the extremity of the flanks of this church are striking and bold, and once had the merit of novelty, though it is now, by frequent imitation, become less remarkable."

Vast vaults extend from the portico to the east end of the structure: they are light and dry, and contain great numbers of bodies, deposited within separate apartments, and on the floor of the open space. These vaults, however, have for many years been closed up, interments being no longer permitted. The roof of the church is supported by eight pillars, and also by four pilasters and entablatures, which support the ceilings over the aisles. The vaulting of the nave is elaborately ornamented with stucco-work, and the sacrarium commences with a semi-circle and terminates in a recess. The interior decorations are very fine. Mr. Gibbs, the architect, in speaking of the elliptical ceiling, says he found by experience that it is "much better for the voice than the semi-circular, though not so beautiful. It is divided into panels, enriched with fret-work by Signors Artari and Bagutti, the best fret-workers that ever came to England." Slender Corinthian columns, raised on high pedestals, rising to the front of the galleries, serve to support both them and the roof, which, on the sides, rests upon them in a very ornamental arch-work. The east end is richly adorned with fret-work and gilding; and over the altar is a large Venetian window, filled with stained glass.

An allusion to the worshippers in the new church occurs in the "London Spy," published in 1725. "The inhabitants are now supplied with a decent tabernacle, which can produce as handsome a show of white hands, diamond rings, pretty snuff-boxes, and gilt prayer-books, as any cathedral whatever. Here the fair penitents pray in their patches, sue for pardon in their paint, and see their heaven in man." St. Martin's was the royal parish, and in its registers were recorded the births of the princes and princesses born in Westminster, previous to the formation of St. James's parish.

In the vestry-room, on the south-east side of the church, is an admirably-executed model of St. Martin's Church. The vestry walls are adorned with portraits of most of the vicars since the year 1670, many of whom attained high distinction in the Church. There are also half-length portraits of George I., and of Mr. Gibbs, the architect, and one of the unfortunate Sir Edmundbury Godfrey. In one of the windows is a painting of St. Martin dividing his mantle with a beggar, in illustration of the ancient legend.

In the churchyard, which is now covered with flat stones, was buried, "with great solemnity," after having lain in state at Bridewell Hospital for two days, the body of Sir Edmundbury Godfrey. "The pall was supported by eight knights, all justices of the peace; and in the procession were all the city aldermen, together with seventy-two clergymen, in full canonicals, who walked in couples before the body, and a great multitude followed after." The clergyman who preached the sermon on the occasion was supported on either side by a brother divine. A tablet to the memory of Sir Edmundbury Godfrey was erected in the east cloister of Westminster Abbey.

The story of the murder of Sir Edmundbury Godfrey has been often told; but as it belongs specially to the spot which we are now visiting, it shall be told here once more, in the words of Pennant:—"The infamous witnesses against his supposed murderers declared that he was waylaid, and inveigled into the palace under pretence of keeping the peace between two servants who were fighting in the yard : that he was there strangled, his neck broke, and his own sword run through his body; that he was kept four days before they ventured to remove him; at length his corpse was first carried in a sedan-chair to Soho, and then on a horse to Primrose Hill, between Kilburn and Hampstead. There it certainly was found, transfixed with the sword, and his money in his pocket, and his rings on his fingers. The murder, therefore, was not by robbers, but the effect of private revenge. But it is not probable that it was committed within these walls; for the assassins would never have hazarded a discovery by carrying the corpse three miles, when they could have so safely disposed of it into the Thames. The abandoned characters of the evidences, Prance and Bedloe, (the former of whom had been treated with most horrid cruelties to compel him to confess what he declared he never was guilty of), together with the absurd and irreconcilable testimony they gave on the trial, has made unprejudiced times to doubt the whole. That he was murdered there is no doubt; he had been an active magistrate, and had made many enemies. The marks of strangling round his throat, and his broken neck, evince the impossibility of his having put an end to his own existence, as some have insinuated. But the innocence of the three poor convicts would not avail, the torrent of prejudice prevailing against

them; and they were executed, denying the facts in the moment of death. One was a Protestant, the other two Roman Catholics, and belonging to the Chapel; so probably were fixed on by the instigators of the accusation in order to involve the queen in the uncharitable suspicion."

This tragedy became at the time the subject of several medals. On one is the bust of Sir Edmundbury and two hands strangling him; on the reverse the Pope giving his benediction to a man strangling another on the ground. On a second, with the same bust, is the representation of the carrying the magistrate on horseback to Primrose Hill. A third makes him walking with his broken neck, and sword buried in his body; and on the reverse St. Denis with his head in his hand, with this inscription :—

"Godfrey walks up-hill after he was dead ;
Denis walks down-hill carrying his head."

The churchyard contains also the bones of the notorious highwayman, Jack Sheppard. Here, too, lies buried the once famous sculptor, Roubiliac; also the witty, but somewhat licentious, dramatist, Farquhar, author of the *Beau's Stratagem*. Here likewise lies John Hunter, the distinguished anatomist, of whom we have spoken in our account of the museum of the Royal College of Surgeons; as also does the illustrious philosopher, Robert Boyle. Here, too, were buried Sir Theodore Mayerne, Court physician, and the friend of Vandyke; and also Nell Gwynne, whose funeral sermon was preached by Dr. Tenison, incumbent of the parish, and afterwards Archbishop of Canterbury.

The flat pavement on the southern side of the church, facing the "Golden Cross," is called "the Watermen's Burying-ground," from the number of old Thames watermen who were brought thither to their last long rest from Hungerford, York, and Whitehall Stairs.

The rate-books of this parish, which (says Mr. Cunningham) are arranged sheet by sheet, after the manner of a Post Office directory, contain the name of every householder in the parish, from the levying of the first poor-law rate, in the reign of Elizabeth, down to the present time, and the church registers are admirably kept. The rate-books help us to identify the dwellings of very many distinguished persons in the last century.

A curious story about this church is told by Evelyn in his "Diary," under date Good Friday, 1687. "Dr. Tenison preached at St. Martin's. . . . During the service a man came into neere the middle of the church with his sword drawne, with severall others in that posture : in this jealous time it put the congregation into greate confusion;

but it appeared to be one who fled for sanctuary, being pursued by bayliffs."

Mr. Malcolm records an event of a somewhat similar nature which occurred in this church on the 10th of September, 1729. During evening prayers a gentleman abruptly entered, and fired two pistols at the Rev. Mr. Taylor, who was repeating the service ; one of the bullets grazed the surplice, but the other entered the body of Mr. Williams, farrier, of Bedfordbury, who was sitting in a pew near the minister. The congregation fled in alarm from the church, but a sturdy carman resolutely proceeded to secure the offender, which he could not effect without a severe encounter, and much bruising him, particularly on the head. On his examination it was found that this man, named Roger Campaznol, was the son of the Governor of Brest, in France ; that having been cheated by his landlord, a Huguenot, resident near the Seven Dials, of £138, his mind became deranged, so that he was unable to distinguish the victim of his revenge. After his committal to Newgate he made two or three attempts to commit suicide.

In St. Martin's Place, near the church, were the offices of the Royal Society of Literature, and of the Anthropological Institute of Great Britain and Ireland. The Royal Society of Literature was instituted in 1820, and received the royal charter in 1826. It originated in an accidental conversation between Dr. Burgess—afterwards Bishop of St. David's and of Salisbury—and an eminent personage connected with the royal household, in October, 1820, respecting the various institutions which adorn the British nation. It was agreed that a society seemed to be wanting for the encouragement and promotion of general literature ; and that if a society somewhat resembling the French Academy of *Belles Lettres* could be established it might be productive of great advantage to the cause of knowledge. The suggestion was communicated to Sir Benjamin Bloomfield, and by him was mentioned to the king, to whom he had been private secretary during the regency. His Majesty having expressed his approbation, a general outline of the institution was, by command, submitted to the royal perusal. The Bishop of St. David's was shortly afterwards summoned to Carlton House for the purpose of devising the best mode of giving effect to the undertaking, and was entrusted with a full commission to arrange the plan of the society. He accordingly invited a few of his personal friends to assist him, and for some time they had frequent conferences on the subject. Their first meeting took place on the 10th of November, and the title proposed for the Society was "Royal Society of Literature for the Encouragement of Indigent Merit, and the Promotion of General Literature ;" but at a subsequent meeting the objectionable words in this title were expunged, and the title then stood "Royal Society for the Encouragement of Literature." In order to give signs of public life in the Society, a part of the proposed plan was immediately acted on—namely, the offer of prizes for the following subjects :—

1. For the King's Premium, one hundred guineas : "On the age, writings, and genius of Homer; and on the state of religion, society, learning, and the arts during that period. Collected from the writings of Homer."

2. For the Society's Premium, fifty guineas : "Dartmoor; a poem."

3. For the Society's Premium, twenty-five guineas : "On the History of the Greek Language, and the present language of Greece, especially in the Ionian Islands ; and on the difference between ancient and modern Greek." This premium was subsequently increased to fifty guineas, and another of the like sum was proposed for the best poem on "The Fall of Constantinople in the Fifteenth Century."

The first prize awarded by the Society was for the second premium, for which five candidates appeared. Their productions were referred to a sub-committee, who adjudged the prize to the writer of the poem bearing the motto "Come, bright Improvement," which was found to be written by Felicia Hemans.

Among the first members of the Society were the king, two of the royal dukes, several of the bishops, and many other distinguished persons. In its early stages the Society met with some opposition in different quarters ; but by the middle of the year 1823, the constitution and regulations were completed and submitted to the king, and were finally approved of under the royal sign-manual. Stability and importance were given to the Society by a royal charter granted in the sixth year of George IV. in these terms :—"To our right trusty and well-beloved Thomas, by Divine permission Bishop of Salisbury,* and others of our loving subjects who have, under our royal patronage, formed themselves into a Society for the advancement of literature, by the publication of unedited remains of ancient literature, and of such works as may be of great intrinsic value, but not of that popular character which usually claims the attention of publishers ; by the promotion of discoveries in literature ; by endeavouring to fix the

---

* He had recently been translated to this see from St. David's.

standard, as far as practicable, and to preserve the purity of the English language, by the critical improvement of English lexicography; by the reading at public meetings of interesting papers on history, philosophy, poetry, philology, and the arts, and the publication of such of those papers as shall be approved of; by the assigning of honorary rewards to works of great literary merit, and to important discoveries in literature ; and by establishing a correspondence with learned men in foreign countries for the purpose of literary inquiry and information."

In 1826 George IV. made to the Society a grant of the Crown land opposite St. Martin's Church, and the leading and official members voluntarily subscribed £4,300 as a building-fund, with which they erected their original place of meeting. In 1828 the Society adopted the publications of the Egyptian Society, and has since contributed some important researches on the antiquities of Egypt. In rewarding literary men the royal founder enabled the Society to act with princely liberality, by placing at its disposal 1,100 guineas a year, "to be bestowed on the Associates for life, to be elected by the officers and council, each to receive 100 guineas per annum ; and the remaining 100 guineas to be expended on two gold medals, to be bestowed annually upon individuals whose literary merits entitled them to the honour."

In connection with the above gift of 1,100 guineas by the king, Mr. Harford, in his " Life of Dr. Burgess, Bishop of Salisbury " (1840), relates the following anecdote :—" It is a curious fact, which his majesty, George IV., himself mentioned with a smile to the present Dean of Salisbury (Dr. Pearson) that the Bishop, from a misconception of his meaning, at their first interview, committed the king as an *annual* subscriber of £1,000—a sum which he had intended only as a donation to the Society at its outset, while his annual subscription was to have been limited to £100. As, however, his lordship, in his zeal, had immediately proclaimed the king's munificence, and Fame, through the medium of the press, had almost as quickly trumpeted it with her hundred tongues throughout the country, there was no retreat ; and the king not only cheerfully acquiesced, but amused himself with the incident." On the death of George IV., in 1830, this gratifying bequest ceased.

A valuable library has been formed, and greatly enriched by the lexicographical and antiquarian publications presented by Mr. Todd, and by papers furnished by many eminent writers. In 1886 the Society removed to Delahay Street, Westminster ; it is now located in Hanover Square.

Admission to the Royal Society of Literature is obtained by a certificate, signed by three members, and an election by ballot. Ordinary members pay three guineas on admission, and two guineas annually, or compound by a payment of twenty guineas. At the meetings of this Society papers are read by learned men, English and foreigners. The Society, however, incurred considerable ridicule by having admitted a certain M. Cosprons, a few years since, to read a paper, as a French *savant*, under the assumed title of " M. le Duc de Rousillon." The mistake was soon found out, and the " illustrious " *soi-disant* duke was never asked to read a second paper.

The Anthropological Institute of Great Britain and Ireland, whose rooms were in the same building as the above Society, was established in 1863 for the purpose of promoting the study of anthropology in a strictly scientific manner ; it also is now located in Hanover Square. There is an interesting museum, and the publications of the Society are presented to the members. Sir John Lubbock was for long President of this Society, an office now occupied by Dr. Macalister.

In St. Martin's Place were likewise the offices of the Friend of the Clergy Corporation, an institution, under the patronage of the Prince of Wales, " for allowing pensions, not exceeding £40 per annum, to the widows and orphan unmarried daughters of clergymen of the Established Church, and for affording temporary assistance to necessitous clergymen and their families."

St. Martin's Place is worthy of note as having been, during the Franco-Prussian War, the headquarters of the National Society for Aiding the Sick and Wounded, which was founded at a meeting of the English Langue of the Order of St. John held here in July, 1870. During the year and a half of that terrible struggle this Society sent abroad to Germany and France, in nearly equal proportions, money and stores—such as lint, bandages, wine, and surgical appliances—to the value of about half a million, earning thereby the hearty thanks of both the belligerent nations. After the termination of the European struggle the Society resolved not to disband itself, but to continue *en permanence*, so as to be ready for action in case of the outbreak of another war. Its offices, however, are now in Duke Street, Adelphi.

In what used to be Castle Street, behind the National Gallery, a library was founded by Dr. Tenison—afterwards Archbishop of Canterbury— in 1685, for the use of his school, over which it was placed. In 1697, the doctor, who was then vicar of St. Martin's, gave £1,000 towards a fund for the maintenance of his school, and afterwards, by the consent of Dr. Patrick, Bishop of Ely, another sum of £500 which had been left to them jointly, in trust, to be disposed of in charitable uses; these two sums, together with the leasehold messuages, for the term of forty years, he vested in trustees, for the support of his school and library. Out of the profits of these investments the librarian and masters had an annual salary for teaching thirty

him on occasion for frequenting taverns or coffee-houses, told him they would study or employ their time better if they had books. This put the pious Doctor on this design." On the 23rd Evelyn again writes, "Afterwards I went with Sir Christopher Wren to Dr. Tenison, when we made the drawing and estimate of the expense of the library to be begun the next spring near the Mews."

The library was not by any means confined to

WEST VIEW OF THE OLD CHURCH OF ST. MARTIN'S-IN-THE-FIELDS; PULLED DOWN IN 1721.
(*From a Print published by J. T. Smith in* 1808.)

boys, sons of the inhabitants of St. Martin's parish.

This institution was at first situated in Castle Street, at the back of the Mews, which, as we have already shown, afterwards gave place to the National Gallery. Here it stood down to the year 1872, when it was removed to give room for the enlargement of the National Gallery.

The original design of the founder was to supply the clergy and studious persons of Westminster with a place of retirement and study. "He told me," says Evelyn ("Diary," Feb. 15, 1684), "there were thirty or forty young men in orders in his parish, either governors to young gentlemen, or chaplains to noblemen, who, being reproved by

theological subjects, but comprised works of general literature. Amongst the 5,000 volumes of the ordinary staple from which libraries were formed a century and a half ago, were some MSS. of great interest. The library contained a beautiful Sarum Missal of the thirteenth century, and a magnificently illuminated Psalter of a little earlier period. But the gems of the collection, perhaps, were the "Psychomachia of Prudentius," and the "Versarium of Fortunatus," both very rare. The library was dispersed on the removal of the school in 1872.

By a series of misfortunes this institution, it appears, had been reduced, of late years, to the last stage of decay. Its slender endowment was almost entirely lost in the South Sea Bubble, and

ST. MARTIN'S LANE. 1820. (*See page* 158.)

its resources failed altogether on the expiration of a lease, the remainder of which was taken by the Commissioners of Woods and Forests for the improvement of Charing Cross. There were in the end no means of providing salaries for the officers or for any of the expenses incidental to the maintenance of a library, and the fate of an institution which ought to be interesting to all lovers of literature came to be regarded with apprehension and anxiety.

For many years the trustees permitted a society of subscribing members to hold its meetings, to play at chess, and read newspapers in the reading-room; and thus a sort of club or mechanics' institute came to hold its meetings in Archbishop Tenison's Library, and a list of lectures was posted outside the door. A portion even of the shelves of the old library had been appropriated to the books of the new society; and if clergymen and "studious persons," more especially intended by the founder, had resorted to Tenison's Library for purposes of study, they would soon have given up the attempt in despair. A late eminent bookseller bore the following testimony as to the state of the original library a few years previous to its sale by the auctioneer in 1872:—"The books and manuscripts in the library are many of them of great curiosity, rarity, and value, but have suffered injury from dust and neglect; were they properly cleaned and repaired, and the room made comfortable to readers, it would, in my opinion, be much frequented, and accessions be made to the library in the way of books presented." The original intention of the founder having thus been withheld, the interest of the parishioners and others in this library gradually decreased, and it at length became scarcely at all frequented on its own account. The place had altogether a forlorn and miserable appearance; its volumes buried in dust and exposed to the vicissitudes of heat and damp, so that one would be painfully reminded of the day when, under the auspices of the three illustrious men mentioned above, the building was planned, and of the goodly show which Strype tells us the books with their "gilt backs" made in his time.

The Rev. P. Hale, the librarian, some time ago issued a "Plea for Archbishop Tenison's Library," in which he remarked:—"It seems to be a moral law that every institution, in spite of the care and munificence of its founder, should fall short of his aim, in order to give room for the vigilance and charity of his successor."

Notwithstanding the above plea for the preservation of the library, sufficient public interest in it does not appear to have been awakened, and the books and manuscripts were consequently sold and dispersed, the proceeds of the sale being devoted to the erection of the new Archbishop Tenison's School, in Leicester Square.

The clearance effected for the extension of the National Gallery, the erection of the National Portrait Gallery, and the formation of the Charing Cross Road, has greatly improved the aspect of St. Martin's Place. The Charing Cross Road is a handsome thoroughfare which runs northwards through the heart of St. Giles's-in-the-Fields to the point of junction between Oxford Street and New Oxford Street, whence it is continued in a northerly direction by Tottenham Court Road. At its southern end, curving round into St. Martin's Lane, of which we shall speak presently, is the St. Martin's Town Hall and Library. Adjoining this is the Garrick Theatre, built for Mr. John Hare. Farther up are some large blocks of industrial dwellings and a Welsh Presbyterian Chapel; and about half-way between St. Martin's Place and Oxford Street the road intersects the Shaftesbury Avenue at the spot now known as Cambridge Circus, but formerly, when it was but the meeting-place of a number of narrow streets, as the Five Dials.

On the west side of St. Martin's Lane, near Long Acre, is Aldridge's Horse Repository — a middle-class "Tattersall's"—established in 1753.

Newton tells us, in his "London in the Olden Time," that nearly at the end of the Strand a country lane, without habitations, ran northwards between the fields up to St. Giles's hospital. "A small chapel or oratory," he adds, "we know not of what antiquity, stood in the thirteenth century by the east side of this lane in the fields, about a hundred yards from the highway of the Strand." He considers it probable that this chapel was served by the monks of St. Peter's Abbey, to whom the land about the neighbourhood belonged, and who "bestowed their benedictions on, and collected halfpennies from the pilgrims and travellers, passing to and from the north country and the City of Westminster."

This country road, which first obtained the name of St. Martin's Lane about the reign of Charles I., was bounded on the eastern side by the wall of the Convent Garden, and opened into the "Cock and Pie Fields," so called from a house of that name where cakes and ale were sold.

At the bottom of St. Martin's Lane was a nest or rookery of narrow lanes and streets, which rejoiced in slang names, such as "Porridge Island," "The Bermudas," and the "Straits of the Strand," of which mention has already been made. The names constantly imported into the comedies of the time by Ben Jonson and other authors. From the allusions to them which occur, it is clear that they were occupied by a low lot, who indulged in gin, ale, and fighting. Porridge Island, especially, was filled with second-rate cook-shops. In the *World*, of November, 1753, we find an allusion to "a fine gentleman whose lodgings no one is acquainted with," as having his dinner "served up under cover of a pewter plate from the cook-shops in Porridge Island." Part of this rookery was swept away about 1830, and in 1880–81 a further improvement was made by the erection of large blocks of model lodging-houses, occupying nearly all the space between Bedford Street and Bedfordbury.

Many of the houses in St. Martin's Lane have historic and artistic associations, which carry us back to the days of George II. Thus, for instance, Mr. Peter Cunningham informs us that " in a great room on the west side, nearly opposite old 'Slaughter's,' N. Home, the painter, exhibited in 1775 his celebrated ' Conjurer,' intended as a satire on the way in which Sir Joshua Reynolds composed his pictures; and in Cecil Court, in the following year, was born Abraham Raimbach, the engraver."

Smith, too, tells us in his " Nollekens," that the house No. 96, on the west side, " has a large staircase, curiously painted, of figures viewing a procession, which was executed for the famous Dr. Misaubin, about the year 1732, by a painter named Clermont, a Frenchman. Behind the house there is a large room, the inside of which is given by Hogarth in his 'Rake's Progress,' where he has introduced portraits of the doctor and his Irish wife."

St. Martin's Lane, if we except a few houses on the eastern side, at the end near to St. Martin's Church, was built between the years 1610 and 1615. Up to that time it was apparently a really green country lane, known as West Church Lane, with scarcely a single cottage all the way up to St. Giles's. A little before that date we read that Sir Hugh Platt, the most scientific horticulturist of his age, had a garden in St. Martin's Lane. Among its most distinguished inhabitants in its early days were Sir John Suckling, the poet, Sir Kenelm Digby, and D. Mytens, the painter. Here, too, lived at one time the celebrated Earl of Shaftesbury, Dr. (afterwards Archbishop) Thomas Tenison, whilst he was the Vicar of St. Martin's, and the Whig poet, Ambrose Philips. In this street, too, nearly opposite where now are May's Buildings, lived Sir Joshua Reynolds when he first came as a young man to London; and Sir James Thornhill,

who established at the back of his house the artists' school, out of which it is scarcely an exaggeration to say that the Royal Academy took its beginning. Fuseli and Roubilliac, too, in their day had studios here; and those artists who did not actually live in the lane, used to frequent it of an evening, repairing as visitors to "Slaughter's Coffee-house," their accustomed haunt. Here Hogarth was a constant visitor, stepping round from his quarters hard by in Leicester Square; and many of the larger houses, if they have not been tenanted by artists, have been the haunts and homes of extensive picture-dealers.

Allan Cunningham tells us that Roubilliac's first studio was in Peter's Court in this lane, a favourite haunt of artists; " the room," he adds, " has been since pulled down and rebuilt, and its site is now occupied as a meeting-house by the Society of Friends." Roubilliac afterwards removed to a larger studio on the western side of the street, where he died in 1762.

" At the south-west corner of this lane," writes Stow, " there was one house wherein sometimes were distraught and lunatic people; of what antiquity founded, or by whom, I have not heard; neither of its suppression. But it is said that some time a king of England, not liking such a kind of people to remain so near his palace, caused them to be removed further off to Bethlehem, without Bishopsgate; and to that hospital the said house by Charing Cross doth yet remain." The upper part of St. Martin's Lane was originally termed the Terrace, implying probably that it consisted of a number of larger and more imposing edifices built at one time.

Ben Jonson was born in Hartshorn Lane, near Northumberland House, Charing Cross. We learn this from Fuller, who says, " Though I cannot, with all my industrious inquiry, find him in his cradle, yet I can fetch him from his long coats. When a little child he lived in Hartshorn Lane, Charing Cross, when his mother married a bricklayer for her second husband. He was first bred in a private school in St. Martin's Court, then in Westminster School."

Such was St. Martin's Lane in the olden days, before it had become the resort of loose characters, among whom, in the words of Ben Jonson, " the quarrelling lesson was read, and the seconds were bottled ale and tobacco." For, to speak the truth, St. Martin's parish would seem to have been remarkable for tipplers. At all events, that trustworthy authority, the " London Spy," hints that "the malt duty is nowhere better promoted than in this part of the town."

It is to be feared that the narrow gorge by

which to the present day exit is made from St. Martin's Lane into Trafalgar Square, is a standing proof that two hundred years ago the "commissioners for reforming the buildings, ways, and streets, and for regulating the hackney coaches in London," did not do their duty quite as efficiently as our present Metropolitan Board of Works. At all events, John Evelyn tells us, in his "Diary," under date May 25th, 1662, that he and his brother commissioners went from Scotland Yard to the neighbourhood of St. Martin's Church, in order "to view how St. Martin's Lane might be made more passable into the Strand." We fear that, although more than two centuries have passed away since that time, the work has yet to be satisfactorily achieved.

CHAPTER XXIII.

LEICESTER SQUARE AND ITS NEIGHBOURHOOD.

"He made the desert smile."

Leicester Fields—Formation of the Square—Famous Duels fought here—Leicester House—Anecdote of George III.'s Childhood—Sir Ashton Lever's Museum—Saville House—Miss Linwood's Exhibition of Needlework—Destruction of Saville House—Residence of Sir Joshua Reynolds—Hogarth's House—The "Pic-nic Club"—John Hunter's Museum—The Alhambra—Burford's Panorama—The Church of Notre Dame de France—Wyld's "Great Globe"—Downfall of the Statue of George I.—Renovation of the Square by Baron A. Grant—Residence of Sir Isaac Newton—Cranbourn Street and Cranbourn Alley.

THERE are, perhaps, few places in the metropolis remaining at the present day that combine the characteristics of "Old and New London"—rolled into one as it were—to a greater extent than Leicester Square. It dates from the time of the second Charles, to whose reign we are indebted for many of those open spaces in the metropolis which tend so necessarily towards its salubrity. Down to the very last days of the Protectorate, Leicester Fields—as the place was then, and even more recently, termed—was entirely unbuilt upon. The north side of the Leicester Square of to-day was the only place occupied in the vicinity, and this was taken up by Leicester House and its gardens, at the back of which was a large open common, which was used for many years as a place for military exercise.

The history of the square, in fact, begins with Leicester House, which was built between 1632 and 1636, by Robert Sidney, Earl of Leicester, whose voluminous correspondence, preserved among the "Sidney Papers," is a history, in little, of his time, and of whose sons, Philip and Algernon Sidney, Leicester Fields hold many memories.

In Aggas' map there are no houses either north or west of the mews enclosure. St. Martin's Lane is represented with hedgerows, and the site of Leicester Square is a drying-ground for clothes. A woman is laying out sundry garments on the grass, and in the next field are cattle, and a milk-maid carrying her pail. Stow, in his "Survey" of 1598, says of the mews—"And this is the farthest building west on the north side of that High Street." From Faithorne's map, compiled between 1643 and 1647, and published in 1658, we know that, just before the Restoration, St. Martin's was literally "in the fields," a windmill and a few scattered houses stood where Windmill Street now is, and Leicester House was still in grounds not surrounded by buildings.

Of Aggas' map of London, so far as it concerns this region, Mr. Tom Taylor remarks :—"There is so much in the map which brings Shakespeare to mind, that one is surprised not to find the Globe, and the Red Bull, the Fortune, and the Curtain playhouses as conspicuous as the 'Bull and Bear' Gardens."

In this map all the country to the north of Charing Cross and west of Chancery Lane is still entirely devoted to country life and uses, and the Hospital for Lepers, dedicated to St. Giles, stood in the fields, with nothing between it and the spot where now stands Leicester Square. The line of St. Martin's Lane was, however, occupied by buildings on both sides as far as St. Giles's Church. Soon after the Restoration increasing prosperity led to a rapid increase of dwellings. The parish of St. Martin had so enlarged its population that "numerous inhabitants were deprived of an opportunity of publicly celebrating the divine offices," and the result of an application to Parliament was that a separate parish was formed, and a new parish church was built, dedicated to St. Anne, mother of the Virgin. Around this (in what is now known as Dean Street, Soho) buildings clustered, and within fifty years the parish contained 1,337 houses, according to Maitland. He adds the following information about the prosperity of the parish :—"There are of persons that keep coaches seventy-three," and there "is a workhouse for the reception of the poor;" and then he goes on :—"The fields in these parts being lately converted into buildings, I have not discovered anything of antiquity in this parish;" many parts so greatly abound with French that it is an "easy matter for a stranger to fancy himself in France." This is a characteristic of the parish that has not altered. Strype, in 1720, speaks of the "chapels in these parts for the use of the French nation, where our Liturgy turned into French is used, French ministers that are refugees episcopally ordained officiating; several whereof are hereabouts seen walking in the canonical habit of the English clergy. Abundance of French people, many whereof are voluntary exiles for their religion, live in these streets and lanes, following honest trades, and some gentry of the same nation."

From John Overton's map, published in 1706, it is easy to see how the buildings surrounding Leicester Square lay at that time. The grass in the centre is marked as enclosed. Cranbourn Street and Bear Lane give access by the north-east corner, and "Dirty Lane," or Green Street, by the south-east. Panton Street, viâ "Slug Street," opens the south-west corner, but the north-west side is completely closed. Later maps show the communication by way of Sidney Alley, a narrow footway; but the route by which carriages from the west now drive to Drury Lane or Covent Garden was then blocked by a line of houses. Though we cannot trace the building of the square with any accuracy, we have a slight sketch of it by Strype in 1720, which could not have been more than some forty or fifty years after its completion. He says it is "a very handsome square, railed about and gravelled within. The buildings are very good, and well inhabited, and frequented by the gentry. The north and west rows of buildings, which are in St. Anne's parish, are the best; and especially on the north, where is Leicester House, the seat of the Earl of Leicester, being a large building with a fair court before it for the reception of coaches, and a fine garden behind it; the south and east sides being in the parish of St. Martin's."

Rocque's map of 1737 shows how rapidly buildings spread north and west. Leicester House was no longer in the country, as up to Oxford Street the ground was filled with houses. The Country Journal of Craftsmen, under the date of April 16, 1737, contains the following statement :—"Leicester field is going to be fitted up in a very elegant manner : a new wall and rails to be erected all round, and a basin in the middle, after the manner of Lincoln's Inn Fields." Northouck, in 1773, writes :—"This is a handsome square, the inner part of which is enclosed by iron rails, and adorned with grass plats

and gravel walks. In the centre is an equestrian statue of his present Majesty, gilt." This statue was really of George I., modelled by C. Buchard for the Duke of Chandos, and brought hither from Canons, having been purchased by the inhabitants of the square. It was finely gilt, and in 1812 was re-gilt. Of its later history we shall have more to say presently.

Between the Restoration and the Revolution, Leicester Field, as it was then called, had become surrounded by houses and streets, and had assumed nearly its present dimensions. Before the end of the seventeenth century the centre, as shown above, had been railed round, and was as famous for duels as the ground behind Montague House in later times. Here it was that the famous duel occurred, in 1699, between Captains French and Coote, in which Coote was slain on the spot at night, and French and Lord Warwick wounded. In it, too, was implicated Lord Mohun, of duelling notoriety, but who, by all accounts, on this occasion did his best to arrange the difference between the two hot-headed Irishmen. Thackeray has described in "Esmond" how Lord Mohun and Lord Castlewood, with their respective friends, went to the Duke's playhouse and saw Mrs. Bracegirdle in Love in a Wood, then to the "Greyhound" in Charing Cross to sup, where the two lords quarrelled, according to previous arrangement, and it was agreed to take chairs and go to Leicester Field. Colonel Westbury, second to Lord Castlewood, asked, with a low bow to my Lord of Warwick and Holland, second to Lord Mohun, whether he should have the honour of exchanging a pass or two with his lordship. "It is an honour to me," said my Lord of Warwick and Holland, "to be matched with a gentleman who has been at Mons and Namur." Captain Macartney, the second second, if we may so say, of Lord Mohun, asked permission to give a lesson to Harry Esmond, who was then fresh from Cambridge, and destined for holy orders. Chairs were called, and the word was given for Leicester Field, where the gentlemen were set down opposite the "Standard" Tavern. It was moonlight, and the town was abed, and only a few lights shone in the windows of the houses, but the night was bright enough for the purpose of the disputants. All six entered the square, the chairmen standing without the railing and keeping the gate, lest any persons should disturb the meeting. After Harry had been engaged for some two minutes, a cry from the chairmen, who were smoking their pipes, and leaning over the railing as they watched the dim combat within, announced that some catastrophe had occurred. Lord Castlewood had received a mortal wound, and he was carried to the house of Mr. Aimes, surgeon, in Long Acre, where he died.

Besides Leicester House, there were now other great houses in the square. To the west of it stood a mansion belonging to Lord Ailesbury, inhabited in the year 1698 by Lord Carmarthen, the eccentric son of the Duke of Leeds, an enthusiastic amateur sailor and shipbuilder, as well as drinker

Government were just about to patch up. On the 14th of March the Prince left London, having entirely failed in his warlike mission; and the same month brought the Mohocks, "a race of rogues," Swift writes to Stella, "that play the devil about the town every night and slit people's noses— young Davenant telling us at Court how he was set upon by them, and how they ran his chair through with a sword. It is not safe being in the

STATUE OF GEORGE I. AND HOGARTH'S HOUSE, 1790.

and rough customer, to whom William III. confided the care of the Czar Peter. In Lord Carmarthen the latter found a congenial spirit, and his great delight while in England was to sail all day with him in his yacht, the *Peregrine*, and drink brandy spiced with pepper with him all night in Norfolk Street, or Leicester Field. Before going to the theatre, it is recorded that the Czar, besides a pint of brandy and a bottle of sherry, "floored eight bottles of sack after dinner." To the Czar, in January, 1712, succeeded, as a great foreign visitor, Prince Eugene, "a little, ugly, yellow wizened man, with one shoulder higher than the other." He was the hero of the populace, for the English people were eager to carry on the war, and the Prince was against the impending peace which the new Tory

streets at night for them. The Bishop of Salisbury's (Burnet's) son is said to be of the gang. They are all Whigs." Thus writes the great Tory champion of the Whig bishop's son. He, too, had his abode in Leicester Field in 1712, the year of his greatest literary activity.

As we have already mentioned, Leicester House was the first element of the "square," and as buildings gradually grew up around, it formed the boundary on the north side. The house itself stood well back, having a spacious courtyard in front as well as an extensive garden in the rear. Northouck describes the house in 1773 as "a large brick building, with a wide courtyard before." There is extant a drawing of Leicester House by George Virtue, taken in 1748, showing the sentries at the

LEICESTER SQUARE, ABOUT 1750.

gates of Saville and Leicester Houses. Leicester House was of brick, with two storeys, and an attic, and a range of nine windows in front. In 1788 the house was taken down, and maps of 1799, such as Horwood's and Edward Waters', show the building along the north side entirely completed. The enclosure had two rows of trees round it, and was laid out with cross walks ; various maps exhibit different arrangements of trees and walks.

Leicester House was the abode of the Sidneys— that noble family of which, in the sixteenth century, Sir Henry Sidney, "the wisest, greatest, and justest Lord-Deputy Ireland ever had," and his more famous son Philip, were the great ornaments. In the year 1632, Sir Henry's son, Robert, then Earl of Leicester, built Leicester House, having derived the ownership of the Lammas-land of St. Giles's through the grant of Henry VIII. to his ancestor, Lord Lisle. This Lammas-land was the tract of ground lying between Charing Cross and Oxford Road, or St. Giles's Road, and over it the citizens of Westminster had right of common, though the fee-simple was in St. Giles's, St. James's, and other hospitals. Before another century had elapsed those common rights had passed away, before that determined progress from east to west, which building in London has made in generation after generation.

At Leicester House the Sidneys dwelt all through the troublous times of the Commonwealth to the end of the century, their leading spirit being the unhappy Algernon Sidney, the pure patriot and impracticable politician who was persecuted both by Cromwell and Charles II. until he died on the scaffold after the iniquitous trial for the Rye House Plot, in 1683. It was not till near the close of the eighteenth century that the Sidney property of Leicester Fields passed to the Tulk family for £90,000, which went to pay off the incumbrances on Penshurst ; and from the representatives of the Tulks their rights over the enclosure now called the square were in the year 1874 acquired by Mr. Albert Grant for £13,000, and made over to the Board of Works in trust for the public.

Leicester House was for a short time the residence of the Princess Elizabeth, only daughter of James I., the titular Queen of Bohemia, to whom Lord Craven devoted his life and labours, and who, in 1662, here ended her unfortunate life. Besides the Queen of Bohemia—the "Queen of Hearts," as she was called by all who came under the magic of her influence—Leicester House was inhabited in the last century by other royal and noble personages. In 1668 we find lodging in Leicester House the French ambassador, Charles Colbert, Marquis

de Croisay. Pepys tells us in his "Diary," under date October 21st, 1668, that he paid a visit to the French ambassador, Colbert, at Leicester House. Evelyn records a dinner he ate at Leicester House with the grave and gay Anne, Countess of Sunderland, when she sent for Richardson, the famous fire-eater, to exhibit his prowess before them. In 1708, the house was let to the Imperial ambassador, who, in 1712, there received Prince Eugene as his guest, when "on a secret mission to prevent peace from being arranged between Great Britain and France," as we have already noticed.

At Leicester House, in the year 1721, was born William, Duke of Cumberland, the hero of Culloden. There, between 1717 and 1760, lived the Princes of Wales, when a Prince of Wales was always at deadly feud with the head of his house. George II., whilst Prince of Wales, there fed his grudge against his father, which Mr. Taylor, in his "History of Leicester Square," tells us had its deepest root in the sympathy with his hapless mother, Sophia Dorothea, doomed to life-long imprisonment at Zell, on a charge of an intrigue with Count Philip Königsmark, the younger brother of the man who contrived the assassination of Thomas Thynne, of Longleat, of which we shall have more to say hereafter. In his day life in Leicester House was as dull as ditch-water, and not much purer ; and when he succeeded to the throne in 1727, Frederick Prince of Wales (though he lived for a short time in Norfolk House, in St. James's Square, where George III. was born in 1738) became the tenant of Leicester House the year after Sir Robert Walpole's downfall in 1742, and that mansion became again, as Pennant happily called it, "the pouting place of princes" till the somewhat sudden death of Frederick, in 1751. The king never visited his son during his illness, and received the news when playing cards with the Countess Walmoden with the cool expression, "*Fritz ist todt.*"

An amusing story relating to the childhood of George III. is told in connection with Leicester House. A foreigner, named Goupée, an artist of some note in his day, and a favourite with Frederick Prince of Wales, was a frequent visitor there. One day the prince said to him, "Come, sit down, Goupée, and paint me a picture on such a subject. But Goupée perceiving Prince George (afterwards King George III.) a prisoner behind a chair, took the liberty humbly to represent to his royal patron, how impossible it was for him to sit down to execute his royal highness's commands with spirit, while the prince was standing, and under his royal displeasure. "Come out, George, then," said the good-natured prince, "Goupée has released you."

When Goupée was eighty-four years of age, and very poor, he had to nurse and maintain a mad woman, who was the object of his delight when young; he therefore often put himself in the king's sight at Kensington, where he lived. At length the king stopped his coach, and called to him. "How do you do, Goupée?" said the king, and after a few other questions asked him if he had enough to live upon. "Little enough, indeed," replied Goupée; "and as I once took your majesty out of prison, I hope you will not let me go to one." His majesty ordered him a pension of a guinea a week, but he did not live to enjoy it more than a few months.

Here, as we are reminded by Peter Cunningham, the Princess of Wales was waited upon by the wife of the unfortunate Earl of Cromartie, who was so deeply involved in the fatal Scottish rising of 1745. She came leading in her hand her four little children, the sight of whom ought to have roused a feeling of sympathy in a maternal heart. "The princess saw her," says Gray, in one of his letters, "but made her no other answer than by bringing in her own children and by placing them by her."

On the 26th of October, 1760, George III. was proclaimed king before Saville House, in Leicester Square; and on the 29th it was crowded with the mob, assembled to see the courtiers thronging to Leicester House to kiss the hand of the new king. The Dowager Princess of Wales continued to live in Leicester House till 1766, when she removed to Carlton House; and about the same time occurred the last incident connected with royalty in Leicester Fields—the death, at Saville House, of Prince Frederick William, the youngest brother of the king, aged sixteen. While tenanted by the Royal family, the evenings at Leicester House were often enlivened by private theatricals, in which it is recorded that the future king of England and his brothers acted their childish parts with ability and spirit.

Leicester House subsequently became occupied by private persons, and was at one time used by Sir Ashton Lever as a Museum of Natural History. In 1784 Sir Ashton presented a petition to the House of Commons, praying to be allowed to dispose of his museum by a lottery, as Alderman Boydell had done with his gallery. On this occasion it was stated by his manager that it had been brought to London in the year 1775; that it had occupied twelve years in forming, and contained upwards of 26,000 articles; that the money taken for admission amounted, from February, 1775, to February, 1784, to about £13,000, out of which £660 had been paid for house-rent and taxes.

Sir Ashton proposed that his whole museum should go together, and that there should be 40,000 tickets at one guinea each, but of this number only 8,000 tickets were sold. However, the proprietor allowed the lottery to take place, and although he held 28,000 tickets, he lost his museum, which was won by a Mr. Parkinson, who held only two. The house was pulled down shortly afterwards, and the site is now bounded on the west by Leicester Place, a wide thoroughfare leading to Lisle Street. New Lisle Street was built in 1791 on the site of the gardens of Leicester House.

Adjoining Leicester House, on the west, stood, until very recently, a large mansion, called Saville House, formerly the residence of the patriotic Sir George Saville, who was many years Knight of the Shire for the County of York, a relative of the Earls and Marquises of Halifax, and who introduced the Catholic Relief Bill, which led to the Gordon riots in 1780. Saville House, it is well known, occupied nearly the centre of the northern side of the square. It has been, however, as Mr. Timbs remarks in his "Romance of London," frequently confounded with Leicester House, which it adjoined. The latter house, however, stood at the north-eastern extremity, and to this mansion was added Saville House, a communication being made between the two houses for the children of Frederick, Prince of Wales. Saville House was likewise called Ailesbury House, and here Thomas, third Earl of Ailesbury, entertained Peter the Great, when he visited England in the year 1698; and here, too, in all probability, the Czar enjoyed his pet tipple with his boon companion, the Marquis of Carmarthen, as we have already stated. The house passed into the Saville family through the marriage of Lord Ailesbury's son and successor, Charles, third and last Earl of Ailesbury of that creation, who married Lady Ann Saville, eldest daughter and co-heir of Sir William Saville, second Marquis of Halifax. At any rate, Sir George Saville, Bart., M.P., who owned the house in 1780, was the male heir of the Savilles and of the Marquis of Halifax, and the inheritor of the baronetcy. The house, in the Gordon riots, was stripped of its valuable furniture, books, and pictures, which the rioters burnt in the square; and the iron rails were torn from the front of the house and used by the mob as weapons.

Saville House was rebuilt early in the present century, and soon became a sort of " Noah's Ark," for exhibition purposes. Here Miss Linwood exhibited her needlework, from the year 1800 until her death in 1845; and here, too, the National Political Union held its reform meetings, recalling the storms of the previous century. Then came a succession of prodigies of nature and art. Amongst the latter were a large moving panorama of the Mississippi River, and a series of views of New Zealand; concerts and balls, and exhibitions of too questionable a shape for us to detail. "Through some sixty years of the showman's art, flaring by night and by day, Saville House lasted unharmed until the catastrophe of 1865, when the royal baby-house and the cheap pleasure-haunt were burnt in the short space of two hours."

Part of the house, on being refitted after the Gordon riots, was occupied by a carpet manufacturer, and subsequently by Messrs. Stagg and Mantle, drapers and silk mercers; and also by Messrs. Bickers and Bush, extensive booksellers. The eastern wing of it was for many years the show-room of Miss Linwood's exhibition of needle-work, as mentioned above, which enjoyed a popularity second only to that of Madame Tussaud's exhibition of wax-work in Marylebone. This exhibition gave a new name to Saville House, it being known for nearly half a century as the Linwood Gallery. It comprised about sixty copies of the best and finest pictures of the English and foreign schools of art, all executed by the most delicate handicraft with the needle, the tapestry "possessing all the correct drawing, just colouring, and light and shade of the original pictures from which they are copied." The entrance to this exhibition was up a flight of stone steps, leading to a large room.

After enjoying half a century of popularity, the exhibition came to an end in 1844, and the pictures were sold by auction, realising only a comparative trifle. No less than 3,000 guineas had been refused for the chief work, viz., "Salvator Mundi," after Carlo Dolci, and Miss Linwood bequeathed it to the Queen; but so reduced was the value of these works at her death, that when Messrs. Christie and Manson sold the collection by auction, all the pictures, except a few which were reserved, did not realise more than £1,000. The rooms which they occupied were then turned into a concert and ball-room, and made use of for entertainments of a very questionable character; but they were burnt down in February, 1865, the Prince of Wales being among the spectators of the conflagration. The house was presently rebuilt, and in the early part of 1881 was opened for the exhibition of a panorama illustrative of the Charge of Balaclava. The painting, which covered about 1,500 square yards of canvas, was the work of M. Poilpot and Mr. Stephen Jacobs. A part of the building was used as a "Fine Art Gallery."

Underneath Saville House were some extensive apartments, to which access was obtained by a flight of a few steps from the square. The chief room, often called the "theatre," was used for various exhibitions from time to time, including "Miller's Mechanical and Picturesque Representations," consisting of seven views of cities, "the figures of which," says a prospectus in 1814, "are impressed with movements peculiar to each, so as to imitate the operations of nature." The passage leading to this theatre, Mr. Britton tells us, in 1815, "has been lately opened as one of those singular establishments called bazaars."

On the site of this place of entertainment now stands the Empire Theatre, which was opened in the year 1885.

A large house, No. 47, on the western side of the square, was for many years the residence of Sir Joshua Reynolds. Here duchesses and marchionesses, ladies and fair daughters of the aristocracy sat to the monarch of the world of art, to be immortalised by his brush. Here Burke and Foote, Goldsmith and Dr. Johnson, Garrick and Boswell, and most of the celebrated men of the last century, were in the habit of assembling, and of dining almost every week at the hospitable board of the great portrait painter. His house here, we are told, was magnificently proportioned; it possessed one of the finest staircases in London; it was fitted up with exquisite taste, and it was the rendezvous of the literary world. Here Sir Joshua worked with the greatest assiduity until the last, and only ended his laborious toil, which was, however, to him a labour of love, with his life.

Of Sir Joshua Reynolds (who died here in 1792) it would be presumptuous to say a word of praise, beyond quoting the words of Edmund Burke:— "Sir Joshua Reynolds was, on very many accounts, one of the most memorable men of his time. He was the first Englishman who added the praise of his elegant arts to the other glories of his country. In taste, in grace, in facility, in happy invention, and in the richness and harmony of colouring, he was equal to the great masters of the renowned ages. In portrait-painting he was beyond them, for he communicated to that description of the art in which English artists are the most engaged a variety, a fancy, and a dignity derived from the higher branches which even those who professed them in a superior manner did not always preserve, when they delineated individual nature. In painting portraits, he appeared not to be raised upon that platform, but to descend to it from a higher sphere. His paintings illustrate his lessons, and his lessons seem to be derived from his paintings. He possessed the theory as perfectly as the practice of his art. To be such a painter, he was a profound and penetrating philosopher. In full affluence of foreign and domestic fame, admired by the expert in art, and by the learned in science, courted by the great, caressed by sovereign powers, and celebrated by distinguished poets, his native humility, modesty, and candour never forsook him, even on surprise or provocation ; nor was the least degree of arrogance or assumption visible to the most scrutinising eye in any part of his conduct or discourse. His talents of every kind, powerful from nature, and not meanly cultivated by letters, his social virtues in all the relations and all the habitudes of life, rendered him the centre of a very great and unparalleled variety of agreeable societies, which will be dissipated by his death. He had too much merit not to excite some jealousy, too much innocence to provoke any enmity. The loss of no man of his time can be felt with more sincere, general, and unmixed sorrow."

Sir Joshua Reynolds' handsome house was next held by the Earl of Inchiquin ; then by a society known as the Western Literary and Scientific Institution ; it was subsequently taken by Messrs. Puttick and Simpson, the eminent auctioneers, who removed hither from Piccadilly. The actual apartment used as their auction-room was Sir Joshua's studio.

Allan Cunningham, in his "Lives of Painters," gives us the following peep into Sir Joshua Reynolds' painting-room a century ago, and an insight into his regular habits :—

"His study was octagonal, some twenty feet long by sixteen broad, and about fifteen feet high. The window was small and square, and the sill nine feet from the floor. His sitters' chair moved on castors, and stood above the floor about a foot and a half. He held his palettes by the handle, and the sticks of his brushes were eighteen inches long. He wrought standing, and with great celerity ; he rose early, breakfasted at nine, entered his study at ten, examined designs or touched unfinished portraits till eleven brought a sitter, painted till four, then dressed, and gave the evening to company."

The first London residence of Sir Thomas Lawrence, the pupil and successor of Sir Joshua Reynolds as the fashionable portrait painter of the day, was over a confectioner's shop, at No. 4 in the square, a house which was subsequently incorporated in Saville House when the latter building was enlarged.

Bell (afterwards the far-famed Sir Charles Bell) lived in Leicester Square, in the house where Mr. Speaker Onslow had resided. He, in turn, was succeeded by Cruikshank, Sir Joshua Reynolds'

medical attendant, the same who succeeded to Hunter's Medical School.

At the south-eastern corner of the square stood the house in which the inimitable George Hogarth lived and worked for many years. It was in 1733 that Hogarth settled here with his young wife, whom he had carried off from the house of her father, Sir James Thornhill, three years before. The house bore the sign of the "Golden Head," and in it most of Hogarth's finest works were engraved and sold ; and there, after his death, his widow lived till 1789. In April, 1790, "the pictures and prints of the late Mrs. Hogarth" were sold by auction by Mr. Greenwood, at the "Golden Head," Leicester Square. Though the catalogue contained numerous pictures by Hogarth's own hand, by Sir James Thornhill, and a variety of portraits of the artist, his wife, sister, and other relatives, the entire sale realised only £255. It must raise a smile to read that on this occasion a "parcel of Academy figures and studies by Mr. Hogarth" fetched only eleven shillings and sixpence ! After this sale the connection of the Hogarths with Leicester Square ceased.

With reference to the sign of the "Golden Head," Nichols, in his second edition of "Biographical Anecdotes of William Hogarth," says, "Hogarth made one essay in sculpture. He wanted a sign to distinguish his house in Leicester Fields, and thinking none more proper than the "Golden Head," he, out of a mass of cork made up of several thicknesses compacted together, carved a bust of Vandyck, which he gilt and placed over his door. It is long since decayed, and was succeeded by a head in plaster, which has also perished ; and is supplied by a head of Sir Isaac Newton" (since taken down). "Hogarth also modelled another resemblance of Vandyck in clay, which is likewise destroyed." Hogarth's house, or, at all events, part of it, was afterwards converted into the "Sablonnière Hotel," which was kept by an Italian named Pagliano, and largely frequented by foreigners. The building was pulled down in 1870, and on its site was erected the new school-house of Archbishop Tenison, which was removed thither from its old quarters at the back of the National Gallery, to which we have referred in the preceding chapter.

At some public rooms in this square, kept by a foreigner, M. de Texier, as Lord William Lennox tells us, the first " Pic-nic Club" was organised in London, by the aid of Lady Albinia Cumberland, and Colonel (afterwards Sir Charles) Greville. Individuals of either sex belonged to it, and took their chances in a strange lottery, being bound to supply whatever dish, or other eatable or drinkable, they might draw. To this concerts and amateur dramatic entertainments were added; but the club did not prosper, being probably "in advance of the time," and much opposed by parents of the old-fashioned, straight-laced school. It was also attacked by the caricaturists, who, by driving the ladies away, succeeded in slaying it outright. There was a rival Pic-nic Society at the Pantheon in Oxford Street, but it shared a like fate.

already said, in the College of Surgeons. Foote tells us that Hunter held, on Sunday evenings, during the winter months, regular receptions of his friends or public medical levées, for which he sent out cards of invitation; he "regaled them with tea and coffee," and "treated them with medical occurrences." Having raised the science of surgery to a height never believed to be possible, and thus benefited the whole human race, Hunter died of disease of the heart, aggravated by an angry dis-

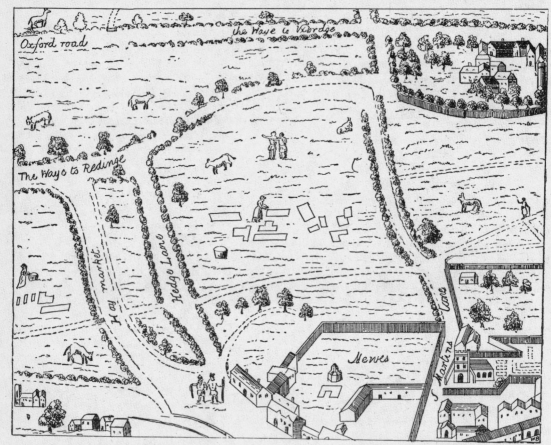

THE SITE OF LEICESTER SQUARE. (*From Aggas' Map.*)

Almost in the centre of the eastern side, nearly on the site of the Alhambra, stood the Anatomical Museum of John Hunter, the celebrated surgeon, where was formed the nucleus of the Hunterian Museum, now at the College of Surgeons, Lincoln's Inn Fields. It was in 1783 that John Hunter became owner of No. 28, immediately south of the present Alhambra, and at the back of it, on ground leading to Castle Street, he built his famous Museum of Comparative Anatomy. In 1785 the erection was complete, and one of the first acquisitions of its owner was the skeleton of O'Brien, the Irish giant, which may still be seen, as we have

cussion in the Board-room of St. George's Hospital, in the sixty-fourth year of his age, "without an equal in the world in his combined character of surgeon and naturalist." He was buried in St. Martin's Church, and his widow would gladly have raised a monument to his memory in Westminster Abbey, but he died poor, and she could not pay the fees. Thus he remained without a statue till Mr. A. Grant selected him as a fit subject for one of the busts in Leicester Square. In 1897 No. 28 came into the builder's hands.

The building now known as the Alhambra Palace of Varieties is a place of amusement where ballet and variety "turns" form the chief features of attraction. It was built in the Moorish or Arabesque style, and opened about 1852-3 as a place of popular instruction, somewhat after the plan of the Polytechnic, and bore at first the name of the "Royal Panopticon of Science and Art." It was burlesque and other pieces requiring scenic effect, Architecturally, it is one of the most elegant places of entertainment of the kind in London. The façade of the building is flat, with lofty minarets at the corners; and the dome in the centre, together with the coloured decoration, make it a striking

THE PANOPTICON, IN 1854.

got up under the auspices of several philanthropic individuals as a joint-stock undertaking. But the speculation did not answer, and after a few years the company broke up. The building was closed for a time, and then re-opened under the name by which it is at present known. It is at once a theatre and a music-hall. It consists of a spacious auditorium, with three tiers of galleries, and a stage particularly adapted for the representation of object. The chief feature of the interior is the rotunda. The great organ, built for the Panopticon, was purchased for St. Paul's Cathedral, but has since been removed to Clifton. The theatre was burnt down in 1882, and rebuilt in 1883-4. In 1897 it was extended to the Charing Cross Road.

In Orange Court, Leicester Fields, the artist, Opie, was living, when discovered by Wyatt.

In this square, towards the close of the last century, Charles Dibdin built and opened a theatre of his own under the name of "Sans Souci."

J. T. Smith tells us, in his "Book for a Rainy Day," that "for many years the back parlour of the 'Feathers' public-house—which stood on the side of Leicester Fields, and which was so called in compliment to its neighbour Frederick, Prince of Wales, who inhabited Leicester House—had been frequented by artists, and several well-known amateurs. Among the former were Stuart, the Athenian traveller; Scott, the marine painter; old Oram, of the Board of Works; Luke Sullivan, the miniature-painter, who engraved Hogarth's picture of 'The March to Finchley,' now in the Foundling Hospital; Captain Grose, the author of 'Antiquities of England,' 'History of Armour,' &c.; Mr. Hearne, the draughtsman of many of England's antiquities, Nathaniel Smith, my father, &c. The amateurs were Henderson, the actor; Mr. Morris, a silver-smith; Mr. John Ireland, then a watchmaker in Maiden Lane, and since editor of Boydell's edition of Dr. Trusler's work, 'Hogarth Moralised;' and Mr. Baker, of St. Paul's Churchyard, whose collection of Bartolozzi's works was unequalled. When this house, the sign of the 'Feathers,' was taken down, to make way for Dibdin's theatre, several of its frequenters adjourned to the 'Coach and Horses' in Castle Street, Leicester Fields; but in consequence of their not proving customers sufficiently expensive for that establishment, the landlord one evening venturing to light them out with a farthing candle, they betook themselves to Gerard Street, and thence to the 'Blue Posts' in Dean Street, where the association dwindled to three members, and died a natural death."

The building known as the "Panorama" stood in the north-east corner of the square, and was an exhibition of ancient reputation. Here Burford's celebrated panoramas were exhibited for several years. Part of the building was subsequently used as a "penny news-room," and as a sort of Red Republicans' Club; but it was finally converted into a Roman Catholic church, dedicated to "Notre Dame de France," under the ministration of the Marist Fathers. The mission was established here in conjunction with *Les Sœurs de Charité Françaises*, or the establishment of the Sisters of Charity in Leicester Place. Some idea of the benefits resulting from this combined force may be gathered from the address of Cardinal Manning at the consecration of the mission in April, 1874. After referring to the manner in which the structure had been raised and embellished, and to the resources for the mission, he said, "With such a church on one side of Leicester Place, and the many establishments of the Sisters of Charity on the other, not only the street itself, but the entire foreign colony around it, enjoys advantages which any other portion of London might envy. We have said 'establishments,' for though there are only eight Sisters of Charity at Leicester Place, they carry on a hospital, a dispensary, a girls' school, an infants' school, a *crèche*, a patronage for young girls, a system of out-door relief, and, with the assistance of a master, a boys' school. Since the foundation of the hospital and the dispensary in 1867, relief has been given to 1,400 in-patients, and 19,000 out-patients; while in relief to the poor souls, 20,000 pounds weight of bread are distributed each year by those 'ministering angels' in human form. In this *crèche* they have an average of twenty-five babies of poor mothers who have to go out and work for their daily bread; in their infant school eighty lisping little ones; in their girls' school seventy pupils; and in their boys' school thirty-six. The patronage numbers from fifty to sixty young girls on its books. If we reflect for a moment on the heterogeneous elements of which the French population of Soho is composed, the work undertaken by the Marist Fathers and the Sisters of Charity will at once appear to be "simply appalling." Other charitable institutions in the square are the Dental Hospital of London and St. John's Hospital for Diseases of the Skin.

We have already referred to the central enclosure of Leicester Square in the early stages of its existence, and it now remains to add that shortly after the commencement of the nineteenth century its glory began to fade. The square gradually became deserted by the gentry who had previously resided within its limits, and in 1851 the area was occupied by a large domed building, in which was exhibited Wyld's "Great Globe." This representation of the world we live in was sixty-five feet in diameter, and comprised a surface of some ten thousand square feet. Galleries encircled the interior of the building at different heights from the ground, by which means visitors were enabled to walk round and inspect every portion of the globe, an attendant, staff in hand, pointing out its principal features; lectures were likewise delivered at intervals during the day. In addition to the "Great Globe," Mr. Wyld introduced, in 1854, a well-executed model of the Crimea, and as this had the positions of the different armies of the Allies and of the Russians correctly laid down from day to day, according as news arrived in England from the seat of war, it was soon the chief object of interest to the thousands who flocked to Leicester Square every day. In 1859 a curious Oriental

Museum was exhibited here, illustrative of life in Turkey, Armenia, and Albania, with life-like models of the interiors of palaces, harems, bazaars, offices of State, and courts of justice, with priests, soldiers, and janissaries, &c., much after the fashion of Madame Tussaud's.

On the removal of Wyld's "Great Globe," after occupying the square for about ten years, the enclosure became exposed once more in all its hideous nakedness. From that time down to the middle of the year 1874, its condition was simply a disgrace to the metropolis. Overgrown with rank and fetid vegetation, it was a public nuisance, both in an æsthetic and in a sanitary point of view; covered with the *débris* of tin pots and kettles, cast-off shoes, old clothes, and dead cats and dogs, it was an eye-sore to every one forced to pass by it. As for the "golden horse and its rider," the effigy of George I., which had been set up in the centre of the enclosure when Leicester House was the "pouting place of princes," besides having suffered all the inclemencies of the weather for years, it had become the subject of every species of practical joke by almost every *gamin* in London. The horse is said to have been modelled after that of Le Sueur at Charing Cross; whilst the statue of George I. was considered a great work of art in its day, and was one of the sights of London, until after a quarter of a century of humiliations, after being the standing butt of ribald caricaturists, and the easy mark of witlings, it gradually fell to pieces. The effigy of his Majesty was the first to be assailed. His arms were first cut off; then his legs followed suit, and afterwards his head; when the iconoclasts, who had doomed him to destruction, at last dismounted him, propping up the mutilated torso against the remains of the once caracolling charger on which the statue had been mounted, and which was in nearly or quite as dilapidated a plight. It would be almost impossible to tell all the pranks that were played upon this ill-starred monument, and how *Punch* and his comic contemporaries made fun of it, whilst the more serious organs waxed indignant as they dilated on the unmerited insults to which it was subjected. One night a party of jovial spirits actually whitewashed it all over, and daubed it ignominiously with large black spots; it was soon after destroyed.

The disgraceful state of Leicester Square became such that it attracted the attention of Parliament, and innumerable were the discussions that took place upon it, with, however, little amelioration in its actual condition. In the year 1869 it was reported that the enterprising proprietors were about to sell the land for building purposes, but upon a communication being sent to the Board of Works, informing them of the fact, it was resolved that the Board would "do all in its power" to prevent the open space from being swallowed up by bricks and mortar. The owners of the fee-simple in the land had all along, in a sort of dog-in-the-manger spirit, not only refused to reclaim the square themselves, but had resisted every effort, or refused every offer of other more beneficent persons, who were willing and eager to undertake a work which it should have been their first duty to accomplish. At length, after an immense amount of litigation, it was finally settled by a decision of the Master of the Rolls, in December, 1873, "that the vacant space in Leicester Square is not to be built over, but will be retained as open ground, for the purposes of ornament and recreation." A "defence committee" was established, and owing to their initiative Mr. Albert Grant was led to make an offer of purchasing the square. Early in 1874 that gentleman set measures on foot which finally resulted in his obtaining possession of the square, on the payment of a large sum for purchase-money to the proprietors. He had determined to present it, as a people's garden, to the citizens of the metropolis; and the purchase having been effected, steps were immediately taken to carry out the intentions of the donor. In laying out the ground, nothing pretentious was attempted. The central space was converted into an ornamental garden, and adorned with statuary, &c. The principal ornament of the new square is a white marble fountain, surmounted by a statue of Shakespeare, also in white marble, the figure being an exact reproduction by Signor Fontana of the statue designed by Kent, and executed by Scheemakers, on the Westminster Abbey cenotaph. The water spouts from jets round the pedestal, and from the beaks of dolphins at each of its corners, into a marble basin. Flower-beds surround this central mass, and the enclosure—so long a squalid and unsightly waste—is now a gay and pleasant garden of flowering shrubs, green plots, inlaid with bright flower-beds and broad gravelled paths. In each angle of the garden is a bust of white marble on a granite pedestal. To the south-east stands Hogarth, by Durham; to the south-west, Newton, by Weekes; to the north-east, John Hunter, by Woolner; and to the north-west, Reynolds, by Marshall.

The ceremony of transferring the ground to the Metropolitan Board of Works for the enjoyment of the public, took place on the 9th of July, 1874. The sum expended by Mr. Grant in purchasing the property and laying out the grounds, &c., amounted to about £30,000.

Close by Leicester Fields in St. Martin's Street, on the east side, lived, in 1710, after his removal from Jermyn Street, Sir Isaac Newton, Master of the Mint and President of the Royal Society, then, perhaps, better known by those titles than by his astronomical works. Though still dingy and dreary, in spite of its having been partly rebuilt, St. Martin's Street in 1710 was good enough for envoys and high officials, and thither Newton drew all that was scientific to his entertainments, while the wits of the day were attracted by the philosopher's clever and charming niece, Catherine Barton, who kept house for him for sixteen years, from 1710 to 1727.

In this famous house in St. Martin's Street afterwards lived Dr. Charles Burney, the author of the "History of Music" and other works, the father of a still more famous daughter, Frances, authoress of "Evelina," the petted friend of all the blues and wits of her generation, and the writer of a diary second only to Boswell's "Life of Johnson" for its vivid pictures of the life and manners of the time of George III. In this house Dr. Burney lived between 1770 and 1789, when he removed to Chelsea Hospital. The house, which adjoins the Orange Street chapel, has been put to various uses since Dr. Burney's days, and is now known as Newton Hall. It is easily to be identified, since it bears one of the tablets of the Society of Arts.

It was here that the antiquary, Dr. Stukely, called one day, by appointment. The servant who opened the door said that Sir Isaac was in his study. No one was permitted to disturb him there; but, as it was near his dinner-time, the visitor sat down to wait for him. In a short time a boiled chicken under a cover was brought in for dinner. An hour passed, and Sir Isaac did not appear. The doctor then ate the fowl, and, covering up the empty dish, desired the servant to get another dressed for his master. Before that was ready, the great man came down. He apologised for his delay, and added, "Give me but leave to take my short dinner, and I shall be at your service. I am fatigued and faint." Saying this, he lifted up the cover, and without emotion, turned about to Stukely with a smile, "See," he said, "what we studious people are! I forgot that I had dined."

In the last century, as now, the neighbourhood of Leicester Fields was the favourite resort of foreigners. Green Street, Bear Street, Castle Street, and Panton Street, formed a district called, as was a purlieu in Westminster too, near the Sanctuary, "Petty France." The dwellers in Leicester Fields' slums, and in the adjoining district of Soho, it would seem, were mainly Catholics, frequenting the Sardinian ambassadors' chapel in Duke Street, Lincoln's Inn Fields. The French hairdressers and perfumers lived mostly under the Piazza in Covent Garden, in Bow Street, and in Long Acre; and very few contrived to live east of Temple Bar.

Cranbourn Street, or, as it was formerly called, Cranbourn Alley, which runs out of Leicester Square at the north-east angle, dates from about 1677, when it was simply a footway for passengers, and named after the family of Cecil, Earl of Salisbury, whose second title was, and is, Viscount Cranbourne. The alley was formed into a street by the pulling down of the whole of one side in 1843-44, thus forming a continuous roadway from Coventry Street, along the top of the Square, into Long Acre. In this alley, Hogarth was apprenticed to a goldsmith named Gamble, in order to learn the art of silver-plate engraving. Mr. Peter Cunningham remarks that "a shop-bill engraved for Gamble by his eminent pupil is the envy of every collector of Hogarth's works." At one time Cranbourn Alley was a celebrated mart for cheap articles in the way of straw bonnets and millinery. To such an extent was this the case, that a Cranbourn Alley article then bore the same

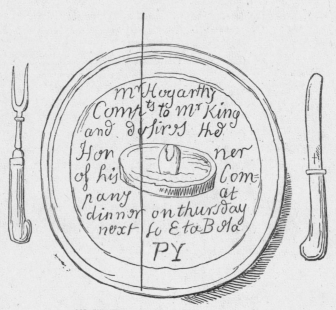

AN INVITATION CARD BY HOGARTH.

meaning which we now are in the habit of affixing to "Brummagem" goods.

Cranbourn Alley, it would seem, was in 1725 a place where the street-songs, broadsides, &c., of the day were hawked and cried. "I never pass through Cranbourn Alley," writes the witty author of the "London Spy," "but I am astonish'd at the remissness and lenity of the magistrates in suffering the Pretender's interest to be carry'd on and promoted in so publick and shameful a manner as it there is. Here a fellow stands eternally bawling out his Pye-Corner Pastorals, in behalf of 'Dear Jemmy, lovely Jemmy,' &c. I have been credibly inform'd that this man has actually in his pocket a commission under the Pretender's great seal, constituting him his Ballad Singer in Ordinary in Great Britain." Of course this is badinage; but no doubt the Jacobite ballad-monger was one of the institutions of the alley, though close to the gates of Denmark House.

A famous shop in old Cranbourn Alley was the silversmith's, Hamlet's—a long, low shop, whose windows seemed to have no end, and not to have been dusted for centuries, with dim vistas of dish-covers, coffee-biggins, and centre-pieces. Hamlet's stock-in-trade is said to have been worth millions. Seven watchmen kept guard over it every night, and half the aristocracy were in his debt. Royalty itself had gone credit for plate and jewellery at Hamlet's. The proprietor of the establishment in the end took to building, and came to grief. His shop is now no more, and his name in the neighbourhood almost forgotten. "Very curious is it to mark," says a well-known writer, "how old trades and old types of inhabitants linger about localities. They were obliged to pull old Cranbourne Street and Cranbourn Alley quite down before they could get rid of the silversmiths, and even now they are seen sprouting forth again round about the familiar haunt."

On the north side of Cranbourn Street, at the Leicester Square end, is Daly's Theatre, a well-appointed house which was built in 1893 for the American company which was the means of introducing Miss Ada Rehan to the notice of theatrical London.

CHAPTER XXIV.

SOHO.

"The lights are fled, the garlands dead."—*Old Song.*

The Situation and Etymology of Soho—Historical Reminiscences—Newport Market—French Refugees—Gerrard Street—The Toxophilite Society—Dryden's House—Edmund Burke—The "Turk's Head" Tavern, and the Literary Club—The "Literary Society"—Macclesfield or Gerard House—The Prince of Wales's Shooting-ground—L'Hôtel de l'Étoile—St. Anne's Church—The Burial-place of Lord Camelford—Vicissitudes of the King of Corsica—The Parish Watch-house and "Sir Harry Dimsdale."

IT has been often remarked—but at the same time, we think, not altogether truthfully—that the past history and character of London cannot be read—like that of Paris, Rome, or Athens—from the appearance of its public buildings and principal thoroughfares. Thus, for instance, Mr. T. Raikes says, in his "Journal," in 1844—"What a difference there is between Paris and London! You may walk through the latter from Hyde Park Corner to Wapping, and, with the exception of a few old churches, the Tower, and the Monument, you see nothing that calls to mind the ancient history of the country. In Paris every street is a *memoria technica* of some anecdote in former times. The one is all poetry, the other is all prose. The Faubourg St. Honoré is now become the residence of the aristocracy in Paris. It is what the Quai des Tournelles and the Quai d'Anjou were in the times of Charles IX., Henri III., and Henri IV.; what the Palais Royal and the Marais were in the times of Louis XIII. and Louis XIV.; what the Faubourg St. Germain was in the times of Louis XV., XVI., and the Restoration. These different migrations of the nobility have left in their former quarters the traces of past splendour, which time has hitherto respected, but which the barbarism of the present age is eager to destroy. One exception to this feeling may be cited. The beautiful old Hôtel Lambert, in the Rue St. Louis, which I visited with Glengall a few years ago, has been purchased by Prince Czartoryski, who has repaired and restored it to its original freshness. Liberty and equality are fine words, but they will leave no monuments behind them, except railroads, barracks, and model prisons."

But, at all events, there is one portion of our metropolis to which this remark will not apply; for we fancy that no city in Europe can more thoroughly tell the story of its own past history, than can Soho testify to the glories of other days, which still surround its decaying and decayed houses as with a halo.

The name Soho, as it is uncertain in its derivation, so also is it loosely applicable to a neighbourhood which it would be impossible to define accurately. It is enough to describe it roughly as lying between St. Martin's and St. Giles'-in-the-Fields, Leicester Square and Oxford Street; but its limits on the western side are very vague. It lies mostly in the district of St. Anne's, which was formed out of the parish of St. Martin's-in-the-Fields, towards the end of the seventeenth century. Pegge mentions the tradition that the name of "Soho"—the watchword at the battle of Sedgemoor, in 1685—was given to a "square" that at that time existed here, called King's Square, in memory of the Duke of Monmouth, whose mansion was upon the south side. Mr. Peter Cunningham, however, negatives this assertion, for he tells us that he has found the name of "Soho" in the rate-books of St. Martin's parish as early as the year 1632. At any rate, people were described as living at the "brick kilns near Soho" as far back as 1636—nearly half a century before the famous battle of Sedgemoor.

"The ruthless hand of historical truth," says a writer in the *Saturday Review*, "has of late years demolished many pretty stories, and has not spared the favourite legend of Soho. In the happy days when we believed in the immaculate purity of Anne Boleyn, when we derived Charing Cross from the *chère reine*, when we attributed the razing of Fotheringay to the filial piety of King James, and had a child-like faith generally in the honour and virtue of crowned heads, there were many tales to be repeated as constantly appropriate to the certain localities. Among them, and involving a singular perversion of facts, is the popular account of the name of this district. 'Soho' was the Duke of Monmouth's watchword at Sedgemoor, and was applied by his party to the square in which his town-house stood. So ran the tale. There is a sediment of truth in it. The Duke did live in a house on the south side of what was then called

King's Square, and his memory was long cherished in that district and elsewhere. But the district was then called, as it is called still, 'Soho,' and King's Square was then, as it is still, in 'Soho.' Monmouth's watchword was derived from the name of the place where his house stood, not exactly from the name of the square, for it was then called generally King's Square, or else Soho Fields, and this name had been known, as Lord Macaulay points out, at least a year before Sedgemoor, and, as he might have pointed out, at least fifty years before that again. Where the name came from is a different question. It is easy to form conjectures about it, and to say it is derived either from the footpad's slang of the sixteenth century, when the fields were lonely at night, and divers persons were robbed in them, and so forth; or else from the cry of the huntsmen in calling off the harriers in the day when all to the west of Holborn and Drury Lane was open country. This sporting derivation of the name will appear the more probable if we remember what Stow says of these parts in 1562, 'The Lord Mayor, aldermen, and many worshipful persons rode to the conduit leads . . . according to the old custom, and then

GAMBLE'S SHOP-BILL. (*After Hogarth.*)

they went and hunted a hare before dinner and killed her; and thence went to dinner at the banqueting-house at the head of the conduit, where a great number were handsomely entertained by the chamberlain. After dinner they went to hunt the fox. There was a great cry for a mile, and at length the hounds killed him at the end of St. Giles', with great hollowing and blowing of horns at his death.' In reality, however, we do not know much about the matter, and had better let it alone; while for those who like associations of the kind, it will be enough to point out that Monmouth's house stood where there is now a hospital for women, and that the narrow alley called Bateman's Buildings is on part of the site. There is still an old-world air about the place. If you dive down into the streets and lanes, you see everywhere evidences of the greatness of former occupants. If a street-door is open, there is a

SOHO SQUARE, ABOUT 1700.

vision of carved oak-panelling, of fretted ceilings, of frescoed walls, of inlaid floors. Squalid as are some of the tenements, their inhabitants do not need to dream that they dwell in marble halls."

"Once on a time," continues the same writer, "even Seven Dials was fashionable; and is not a king buried in St. Giles's? for one Wright, an oil-man in Compton Street, had the body of Theodore of Corsica interred at his own expense, and Horace Walpole pointed the moral of the poor Fleet prisoner's tale in his well-known epitaph. Here and there, at the corners, a little bit of the quaint style now in vogue as Queen Anne's allures the unwary passenger into a noisome alley, and Soho can boast of fully as many smells as Cologne. The paradoxes, in which facts and statistics are so often connected, may receive another example from this densely populated and still more densely per-fumed region, for it has been found that children survive the struggles of infancy better in Soho than in many a high and airy country parish. Paintings by Sir James Thornhill and Angelica Kauffmann are to be seen in some of the houses. Modern cast-iron railings may stand abashed before the finely-wrought work which encloses some of the filthiest areas. There are mantelpieces in marble, heavy with Corinthian columns, and elaborate entabla-tures in many an upper chamber let at so much a week. Visitors to the House of Mercy at the corner of Greek Street have an uncovenanted reward for their charity in seeing how the great Alderman Beckford was lodged when he did *not* make the speech now inscribed on his monument in Guildhall. Art still reigns in the house opposite, where the Royal Academy held its infant meetings; and it was close by, at the corner of Compton Street, that Johnson and Boswell, Reynolds and Burke, kept their literary evenings, and were de-rided by Goldsmith. The more purely scientific associations of the place are almost equally re-markable. In the south-west of the square, in the corner near Frith Street, Sir Joseph Banks and Mr. Payne Knight successively flourished, and the Linnæan Society had here its head-quarters before it was promoted to Burlington House. Since the whole of Soho was more or less fashionable, it is nothing remarkable to find Evelyn and Burnet and Dryden residing within its bounds; but there is some interest in the lying in state there of Sir Cloudesley Shovel, when his body, recovered from the sea at Scilly, was on its way to West-minster Abbey. No doubt an effigy surmounted the pall, and the illustrious foundling appeared in the Roman armour and the full-bottomed wig in which he reposes upon his monument. Half the

sites of the curious scenes in Soho, half the resi-dences of historical characters have, however, been left without identification. When the Society of Arts began some years ago to follow the French example, and to place little tablets on the houses in which great men lived or died, they did well; but of late, for some years, they have slackened their efforts, and the whole district deserves and still needs the signs of their activity. If they are not disposed to carry on the task, they should formally give it up. Here and there among the narrow streets and the crowded passages a shield of arms attached to the front of a house marks the former residence of a great noble, or the name of a corner suggests the scene of some great event; but for the most part the labyrinth is unexplored, and the sites are forgotten or altogether unknown."

In "Burns' Handbook of the Seasons," Soho is described as "an industrial district characterised by several special features of its own. The prin-cipal peculiarity which is most likely to arrest the attention of a stranger here is the display of antique furniture and archæological subjects to be seen in the warehouses of manufacturers, and in the *Dryasdust*-looking curiosity shops. It is worthy of notice that ancient furniture can be manufactured in this locality, of any age, from the tenth century to the nineteenth, and in all manner of styles, from the clumsy Dutch to those in fashion in the reign of Louis XIV. The curiosity shops in Soho are the means of drawing round them numbers of gentlemen, who are continually fishing for relics of a bygone age. Many men with mediæval idiosyn-crasies have added to their stock of archæological stores from this antiquarian storehouse of modern-made furniture. Soho is also the emporium of musical-instrument makers; the square is full of pianoforte manufacturers : these lyres find their way into all parts of the civilised world, and tune the minds of millions of the human family to joy and sadness. This district is also a principal ren-dezvous for foreigners in London, many of whom here ply their avocations as artists and mechanics."

Although, as compared with Belgravia and Tyburnia, the district known as Soho may be called old, yet it has about it none of the poetry of a venerable antiquity. It is a dull, dingy, and dreary part of London, in spite of its proximity to Regent Street and Oxford Street, and it contains little that is picturesque to relieve the monotony of its appearance.

It was laid out for building in the reign of Charles II., and consists almost wholly of straight and narrow streets running at right angles to each other. In many of these streets, however, there are noble and substantial mansions, which were largely occupied by wealthy merchants and members of Parliament, and even by a few peers of the realm, down to the commencement of the present century.

Soho rejoices in a square; but that is of small dimensions and uninviting aspect; and it seems difficult to realise the fact that a century ago, when Mrs. Cornelys' masqued balls were in vogue, it was crowded night after night with the carriages of "the quality," and even of the highest ranks of the nobility; and that, so lately as the first years of her present Majesty's reign, the Duke of Marlborough occupied a residence in it during the Parliamentary session. It is now chiefly occupied by musical and medical publishers, and by other trades which do not depend much on the publicity of a thoroughfare.

We give on page 175 a rare and curious print of the square as it must have been about the year 1700. The view is that of the southern side, in the centre of which, within large iron gates and with a large square courtyard in front, stands Monmouth House. The gardens in the rear are square, and extend as far south as Compton Street; the entrance is flanked by two large houses, the only ones on that side. St. Anne's tower and spire not being built, there is nothing to break the monotony of the square and rectangular streets which cover the ground apparently nearly to Leicester Square. The statue is in the centre, and the whole of the enclosure is laid out after the regular Dutch type. In the original inscription to this print "Frith" Street is called "Thrift" Street, and "Greek" Street figures as "Grig" Street, while what is now Carlisle Street, running into the square from the west, rejoices in the name of "Merry Andrew" Street. The details of the square we shall give in the next chapter.

That the growth of a population and the building of houses in this neighbourhood was looked upon with no favour at Court, and that St. James's already was beginning to growl out its dislike in the direction of St. Giles's, is clear from a royal proclamation, dated in April, 1671, forbidding the erection of small cottages and other tenements in "the Windmill Fields, Dog Fields, and the fields adjoining 'So Hoe,'" on the ground that such buildings "do choak up the air of his Majesty's palaces and parks, and endanger the total loss of the waters which, by expensive conduits, are conveyed from those fields to our palace at White Hall." It is to be feared that this latter ground of alarm was not without foundation, for certainly it would be no longer possible to supply any of the royal residences with water from this neighbour-

hood; though Allen tells us that when the square was first laid out, "a fountain of four showers fell into a basin in the centre."

Commencing on the south side of this district, we find immediately behind Leicester Square a remarkable neighbourhood forming part of Soho, and comprising what used to be known as Newport Market, where Orator Henley held his mock preaching. The father of Horne Tooke was a poulterer here, or, as he is reported to have told his schoolfellows, "a Turkey merchant." In this queer locality a number of genuine French shops were, until recently, to be found much as they were during the emigration after the revocation of the Edict of Nantes. Many of them were cheap cafés and restaurants, like those near "the barrier" in Paris. Most of the French refugees who came to England settled here; and in a work published in 1688, entitled the "Happy Future of England," it is noticed that they had already filled 800 of the new-built and empty houses in London. Maitland, who wrote in 1739, observes that, "Many parts of the parish abound with French, so that it is an easy matter for a stranger to fancy himself in France."

Newport Market was so named from the town-house of the Earl of Newport, which stood close by at its north-west angle. It boasted of no attractiveness in the way of buildings, being neither more nor less than a narrow avenue of shops, occupied chiefly by butchers, the market being established for the sale of butcher's meat.

It had been more than once suggested that it would, perhaps, do much for the improvement of the western portion of the metropolis if the site of Newport Market could be used for some such purposes as for the erection of a block of Peabody buildings, and the suggestion was carried out in 1885-6, and now the aspect of the district has been entirely changed. Here originated the Newport Market Refuge and Industrial School, which has now been removed to Coburg Row, Westminster.

At the back of Leicester House, as we have already seen, were extensive lawns and gardens, where now stands Lisle Street, and "several noblemen residing in Gerrard Street were allowed to have private entrances into the gardens, where there was space for three pairs of targets." In these gardens, in 1781, Sir Ashton Lever, who has already been mentioned in connection with Saville House, in conjunction with Mr. Waring and other friends, started the Toxophilite Society, of which the then Prince of Wales shortly afterwards condescended to become patron. The butts, however, not having sufficient range, the members used to hold their fête-days at Canonbury Tower, at the Artillery Ground, Finsbury, or at Highbury Barn; holding, however, convivial gatherings in the evening in their own quarters here. For about twenty years this society continued to flourish, and its meetings were well supported; but its members dwindled sadly down during the long war against Napoleon, at the end of which they numbered but twenty-five. They afterwards hired a ground at Bayswater, and in 1834 obtained their present grounds in the Regent's Park, where we shall doubtless find the society again, in full plume and feather, when we reach that place.

Gerrard Street took its name from Gerard, Earl of Macclesfield, the owner of the site, and the building of the street was commenced about the year 1677.

In Gerrard Street, on the south side, "the fifth door on the left hand, coming from Newport Street," as he tells his friend Steward in a letter, lived John Dryden. We have Pope's authority, in "Spence's Anecdotes," for the assertion that he used commonly to write in the ground-room next the street. Mr. Peter Cunningham identifies this house with that which is now No. 43, and he quotes Dryden's own dedication of "Don Sebastian" to the Earl of Leicester, in which the poet styles himself "a poor inhabitant of your lordship's garden, whose best prospect is on the garden of Leicester House." Here Dryden died in the year 1700, and here, as John Timbs tells us, took place the disgraceful interference with the poet's funeral procession by a party of drunken Mohocks, headed by Lord Jeffries. The great Edmund Burke, too, in 1787, was a resident in Gerrard Street, at No. 37, which is now an hotel. Mr. J. T. Smith, who was living here at the same time, says of him, "Many a time when I had no inclination to go to bed at the dawn of day, I have looked down from my window to see whether the author of 'Sublime and Beautiful' had left his drawing-room, where I had seen the great orator many a night after he had left the House of Commons, seated at a table covered with papers, attended by an amanuensis who sat opposite to him."

But Burke and Dryden are not the only literary names on which Soho can pride itself. It was at the "Turk's Head," at the corner of Greek Street and Compton Street, and afterwards in Gerrard Street, that the Literary Club—sometimes also called "The Club"—was founded in 1764 by Dr. Johnson and Sir Joshua Reynolds. The "Turk's Head" had already a reputation of its own, having been a kind of head-quarters for the Loyal Association during the Scottish rising of 1745. "The members," says Mr. Peter Cunningham, "met one

evening in every week, at seven, for supper, and generally continued their conversation till a late hour." Sir John Hawkins, Burke, and Goldsmith were among its original members, the latter being admitted in spite of Sir John Hawkins' objection to "Goldy" as a mere literary drudge. At its origin it was composed, or at all events intended to be composed, of representatives of intellectual power in various lines of excellence, Goldsmith gaining admission as "naturalist," on account of his "Animated Nature," whilst Reynolds was, of course, the painter, and Gibbon the historian. In 1772 the supper was changed to a dinner, and the number of members increased from twelve to twenty. In 1783 their landlord died; the original tavern was converted into a private house, and the club removed to Sackville Street. All elections took place by ballot. Johnson himself proposed Boswell, and the last member elected in Johnson's life was Dr. Burney. It was at first called "The Club," but at Garrick's death it was styled the "Literary Club." In 1780 the number of members was raised to forty. After several migrations in the neighbourhood of Dover Street and Sackville Street, in 1799 the club took up its quarters at the "Thatched House" tavern in St. James's Street.

After alluding to a speech of that gruff and sarcastic judge, Lord Chancellor Thurlow, in which his lordship called the "Thatched House" tavern an "alehouse," Mr. Timbs says that "from the time of Garrick's death the club was known as the 'Literary Club,' since which time, however, it has certainly lost its claim to this epithet. It was originally a club of authors by profession; it now numbers few except titled members, which was very far from being the intention of its founders. The name of the club is now 'The Johnson.'" He also states, in the first volume of his "Club Life in London," that "the centenary of the club was celebrated in 1864, at the Clarendon Hotel, the Dean of St. Paul's (then Dr. Milman) being in the chair. Among the members present were—His Excellency M. Sylvain Van de Weyer; Lords Stanhope, Clarendon, Brougham, Stanley, Cranworth, Kingsdown, Hatherley, and Harry Vane; the Bishops of London (Tait) and Oxford (Wilberforce); Sir Edmund Head, Mr. Spencer Walpole, Mr. Robert Lowe, Sir Henry Holland, Sir Charles Eastlake, Sir Roderick Murchison, Dr. Whewell, Professor Owen, Mr. George Grote, Mr. C. Austin, Mr. H. Reeve, and Mr. George Richmond."

In some of these statements, however, as it would seem from information to which we have had access, and which has been placed at our disposal, Mr. Timbs is not strictly accurate. Another association, known as the "Literary Society," has for many years run a parallel course to the "Literary Club," or, as it was formerly styled, "The Club," founded by Johnson and Reynolds. Though running parallel to each other, there is no rivalry or hostility between the two; for, indeed, many distinguished persons belong to both of them. The " Literary Society" is of comparatively recent origin, and one tradition says it is due to the disappointment of one or two of its originators at their non-admission into "The Club," where a single black ball has always excluded a candidate. Perhaps, however, the truer account of its origin may be found in the increase of men of literary, scientific, artistic, and administrative attainments of the grade of those who originally founded "The Literary Club." The latter name was not retained for long after Dr. Johnson's death, because it was too limited to express the real constitution of the association, though possibly it may be urged that the innovators may be held open to blame in choosing the present name of "The" Club, as laying claim to a singular and special excellence. There can be no doubt that generation after generation its members have been elected—not merely from among authors, but among painters, lawyers, statesmen, the only test being that of eminence in a man's own profession. In this way " The Club" has secured a series of "representative men," whose names, if given at length, would go far to justify the apparent conceit of the title. For instance, when Sir Charles Eastlake and Mr. George Richmond were chosen, it was held, no doubt, that they succeeded to the place once held in that circle by Sir Joshua Reynolds; that Grote, Hallam, and Milman were no unworthy successors of Edmund Gibbon; and possibly Professor Owen was at least as great a naturalist as Oliver Goldsmith.

"The Club" dined for many years, as stated by Mr. Timbs, at the "Thatched House" tavern, and afterwards at Grillon's, and at the "Clarendon Hotel." It may also be recorded as a matter of interest that at the centenary dinner Lord Brougham was the "father of the club," and that he came all the way from the south of France in order to be present on the occasion. Mr. John Timbs gives a list of seven absentees from that dinner, including Lords Russell and Carlisle; but one of the members who dined on that day at the "Clarendon" tells us expressly that "it was the only meeting within his memory which included all the then members." Lord Macaulay was very desirous to hold the dinner—not at the "Clarendon," but at the old house where the club had been commenced; but this was found to be impossible.

In 1864 the secretary was Dean Milman, who took a great pride in showing to friends the books and archives of the club, including a valuable collection of autographs. Among the other memorials in the possession of the club is the portrait of Sir Joshua Reynolds with his spectacles, which he painted with his own hand and presented to the society, and which is well known by an engraving.

The "Literary Society," the other association, dates, as we have said, from a far more recent period. Among its members we find the names of the Right Hon. Spencer H. Walpole (president), Lords Coleridge, Chelmsford, Dufferin, Houghton, Lawrence, Cairns, Stratford de Redcliffe, and Selborne; the Archbishop of York and the Bishop of Peterborough; the Dean of Westminster and Professor Partridge; General Sir Edward Sabine, Sir William Boxall, Sir Henry Rawlinson, Sir William Erle, Sir James W. Colvile, Sir John W. Lubbock, and Sir Travers Twiss; Mr. George Richmond, Mr. Henry Reeve, Lord Cranbrook, Sir E. Hamley, Captain Douglas Galton, the Right Hon. William Massey, Sir Charles T. Newton, Mr. J. A. Froude, Rear-Admiral Sherard Osborn, Mr. Kirkman D. Hodgson, and Mr. Matthew Arnold. It may be added that the "Literary Society" meets for dinner once a month on Mondays, at half-past seven, during the season, at Willis's Rooms, from November to July inclusive.

"Of the Literary Club," says Mrs. Piozzi, in her "Johnsoniana," "I have heard Dr. Johnson speak in the highest terms, and with a magnificent panegyric on each member, when it consisted of only a dozen or fourteen friends; but as soon as the necessity of enlarging it brought in new faces, and took off from his confidence in the company, he grew less fond of the meeting, and loudly proclaimed his carelessness as to who might be admitted, when it was become a mere dinner-club."

It was at the "Turk's Head," too, that a Society of Artists met in May, 1753; and another society, numbering among its members West, Chambers, Wilton, Sandby, and others, who, from the "Turk's Head," petitioned George III. to bestow his patronage on a Royal Academy of Art.

In Gerrard Street, just opposite to Macclesfield Street, stood, until recently, Macclesfield or Gerard House, the residence of Charles, first Lord Gerard, afterwards first Earl of Macclesfield. It was a poor, dull-looking structure, dating from about 1680. It was afterwards tenanted by Lord Mohun, the duellist, and also by Lyttelton. The house then became a lamp manufacturer's warehouse; the site is now occupied by offices of the National Telephone Company. To the last it retained many traces of its former magnificence, in the fine ceilings with carved cornices, mantelpieces, and one of the noblest staircases to be seen in London, down which gay ladies swept with their long trains in the days of my Lords Macclesfield and of the gay and profligate Lord Mohun.

was standing at the Restoration; and the site afterwards passed, probably by purchase, into the hands of Lord Gerard, who let out the ground around him on building leases.

Macclesfield Street, we may add, was in the last century popularly known by the abridged name of

DRYDEN'S HOUSE, GERRARD STREET. *From an Original Sketch.* (*See page* 178.)

Before quitting Gerrard Street, we may say that in this street the Linnæan Society held its meetings previous to its establishment in Soho Square.

The neighbourhood of Gerrard and Macclesfield Streets, as appears from a MS. in the British Museum, was originally an enclosure of ground made by Henry Prince of Wales, elder brother of Charles I., for the purpose of "the exercise of arms." Here, it appears, he built a house, which

"Maxfield" Street, but it has since recovered its orthography.

Princes Street, which crossed Gerrard Street at right angles, was built on part of the ground used as the prince's artillery yard. Here, in 1718, lived Halley, the astronomer.

The house in Windmill Street in which the Museum of John Hunter was formed and located before it was transferred to Leicester Square was converted into a foreign restaurant and dining hall, rejoicing in the name of L'Hôtel de l'Étoile.

We learn that as the parish of St. Martin's grew more and more populous, fresh streets being built to the north and west, the inhabitants of the newly-built district applied to the bishop and the legisla-

and no provision had been made for the completion of the tower and steeple, or for building a rectory house, commissioners were appointed to carry out this work; and in March, 1685, the church was consecrated by Dr. Compton, Bishop of London, "and dedicated," says Allen, "to 'the Mother of

ST. ANNE'S, SOHO. (*From a Sketch taken in* 1840.)

ture, by whose joint action a site of land in "Kemp's Field," as it then was called, was granted, though not without difficulty. In 1673, soon after the erection of the new church, it was made into a separate parish, a district cut off from St. Martin's being assigned to it. It was then "discharged from all manner of dependence on the mother church, and ordered to be called the parish church of St. Anne, within the liberty of Westminster." As, however, there was but a slender endowment,

the Blessed Virgin.'" The parish commences at the eastern end of Oxford Street, including Soho Square and all the south side of Oxford Street as far as Wardour Street. Its eastern boundary is formed by Crown Street and West Street, and it extends southwards to about the centre of Leicester Square.

Contrary to the usual custom, the chief front of this church is not to the west, but to the east, abutting on Dean Street. It is a very fair specimen internally of the classical style of the period, and calls for little remark or detail; but its spire may safely be said to rival that of St. George's, Bloomsbury, in ugliness. The name of the architect was Hakewill.

"The church was dedicated to St. Anne," says Allen, "out of compliment to the Princess Anne of Denmark. It is said to have been surmounted at first by a steeple of Danish architecture, which was 'the only specimen of the kind in London.'" But what the Danish style of art may have been in the early part of the eighteenth century, we are not informed.

In the vaults beneath this church is buried the eccentric and unhappy Lord Camelford, who fell in a duel which he fought at Kensington, in the year 1804. He was the only son of Thomas, first Lord Camelford, and was born in 1775. "This young nobleman," says his biographer in the *Gentleman's Magazine*, "was not only inclined to the more enlightened pursuits of literature, but his chemical researches, and his talents as a seaman, were worthy of the highest admiration. His lordship had an idea that his antagonist (Captain Best) was the best shot in England, and he was therefore extremely fearful lest his reputation should suffer, if he made any concession, however slight, to such a person."

It was Lord Camelford's eccentric wish, and, indeed, it was commanded by him in his will, that he should be buried in a lonely spot on an island in a lake in Switzerland; but as at the time of his death the European war was raging, it was impossible for his executors to carry out his instructions at once; and when the peace came, in 1815, he had been too long in his grave for his wishes to be remembered. So his body still lies in a gorgeous coffin, surmounted with his coronet, in the vaults under St. Anne's Church, which have for many years been sealed down and closed.

Among those who lie buried here is the Lady Grace Pierrepont, daughter of the Marquis of Dorchester. A letter published by Sir Henry Ellis in 1686 speaks of the Countess of Dorchester, Sedley's daughter, as furnishing a fine house in St. James's Square, and having just taken a seat (sitting) in the "newly-consecrated St. Anne's Church."

The church also contains the remains of royalty of a certain kind—namely, of a king of Corsica, whose unhappy career and end has been told by Sir Bernard Burke, in his "Vicissitudes of Families;" and before him by Horace Walpole and by Boswell. A tablet in the churchyard to his memory bears the following inscription:—

"Near this place is interred Theodore, King of Corsica, who died in this parish, December 11th, 1756, immediately after leaving the King's Bench Prison by the benefit of the Act of Insolvency; in consequence of which he registered his kingdom of Corsica for the benefit of his creditors.

The grave, great teacher, to a level brings
Heroes and beggars, galley-slaves and kings;
But Theodore this moral learn'd ere dead;
Fate pour'd its lesson on his living head—
Bestow'd a kingdom and denied him bread."

It may interest our readers to know that this fallen monarch was buried at the cost of a small tradesman who had known him in the days of his prosperity, and that the tablet above-mentioned was erected by Horace Walpole, who also wrote the epitaph quoted above.

The King of Corsica was Stephen Theodore, Baron Neuhof of Prussia, and was born at Metz, in 1696. Mr. Cunningham styles him "an adventurer," and certainly in assuming royalty here he went a step further than most other pretenders. He was educated in France, under the care of the Duchess of Orleans. He entered the service of Charles XII. of Sweden, when his name and the distressed state of Corsica induced the inhabitants of the latter island to ask his protection, and in return to offer him their crown. In March, 1736, we are told, he arrived at Aleria in a ship, with two others very richly laden with provisions and ammunition. He was conducted to Corsica, and was elected king amid the acclamations of the people, and was crowned as Theodore I. At this time the Corsicans were in a state of comparative barbarism. Theodore coined money, and maintained an army of 15,000 men at his own cost. The Genoese, in envy and jealousy, published a manifesto filled with falsehoods, and set a price on his head. Finding his life attempted by his own people, he called an assembly, and made them a short speech, which so affected them that they called him their saviour and king. In 1743 he issued a "declaration" calling back to that island all Corsicans in foreign service, under the penalty of confiscation of their estates. His money being now exhausted, he was obliged to seek foreign succour, conferring the regency in his absence on twenty-eight of the nobles. Theodore now went from place to place begging assistance, and in constant fear of assassination. The English sent him to their fleet in the Mediterranean, instructing their admiral to re-establish him on his throne. The admiral, however, told Theodore that the Corsicans meant to oppose his landing. It appears that he was now, in his helpless condition, made the victim of foul play, for on returning soon after to London, money was lent to him by a scheme of the Genoese minister; for this debt he was arrested and sent to prison.

He was arrested by a *ruse*. He lived in a privileged place—probably the Sanctuary at Westminster—and his creditors seized him by making him believe that Lord Grenville wanted to see him on business of importance; he bit at the bait, thinking that he was to be reinstated at once. We may mention that while in England King Theodore distinguished himself, like his humble successor, the *soi-disant* Duc de Roussillon, by his fondness for the fair sex. He fell in love with Lady Lucy Stanhope, sister of the second earl, and even made her an offer of marriage; and another lady, a widow, he all but persuaded to share his shadowy crown.

Horace Walpole describes him as a "comely, middle-sized man, very reserved, and affecting much dignity." A life of him, Walpole tells us, was published, "too big to send but by messenger."

There is a fine portrait of Theodore, taken from life by order of the King of Naples, when under confinement in the castle at Gaeta.

Horace Walpole wrote a paper in the *World*, as he tells us, in order to promote a subscription for King Theodore during his imprisonment. His Majesty's character, however, as Walpole tells us, was so bad, that the sum raised was only fifty pounds; but "though it was much above his deserts, it was so much below his expectation that he sent a solicitor to threaten the printer with a prosecution for having taken so much liberty with his name; and that, too, after he had accepted the money." Well may Horace Walpole add, "I have done with countenancing kings."

It was at Soho that Theodore went "to the place which levels kings and beggars, an unnecessary journey for him," as Walpole says, "who had already fallen from the one to the other."

The story of his actual death is thus related by the gossiping pen of Horace Walpole, who met him at several parties in London in 1749:—"King Theodore recovered his liberty only by giving up his effects to his creditors under the Act of Insolvency; all the 'effects,' however, that he had to give up were his right, such as it was, to the throne of Corsica, which was registered accordingly in due form for the benefit of his creditors. As soon as Theodore was at liberty, he took a (sedan) chair and went to the Portuguese minister; but not finding him at home, and not having a sixpence to pay, he desired the chairmen to carry him to a tailor in Soho, whom he prevailed upon to harbour him; but he fell sick the next day, and died in three more."

"I would have served him if a king, even in jail, could he have been an honest man," said the individual who generously erected his monument.

It may be added that Boswell wrote an account of Theodore, strung together from anecdotes which he picked up from Walpole in Paris.

In the church or churchyard also lie Mr. William Hamilton, a Royal Academician of the last century; Sir John Macpherson; Mr. David Williams, who deserves to be remembered as the founder of the Literary Club; and William Hazlitt, the critic and essayist, over whom the grave closed in 1830.

Adjoining the south-east angle of St. Anne's Church is the parish mortuary. This building was formerly the "watch-house" in the days of the old "Charleys;" and here George Prince of Wales, in his youthful days, was more than once confronted with the ministers of parochial authority, on account of his share in some midnight brawl, but allowed to depart on unbuttoning his coat and showing the "star" on his breast beneath, whilst less well-born marauders were detained, to be brought before the "beak" the next day. Mr. J. T. Smith tells the following amusing anecdote concerning a scene witnessed by him at St. Anne's watch-house during one of those nocturnal rambles he occasionally indulged in whilst lodging in Gerrard Street:—

"Sir Harry Dinsdale, usually called Dimsdale, a short, feeble little man, was brought in to St. Anne's Watch-house, charged by two colossal guardians of the night with conduct most unruly. 'What have you, Sir Harry, to say to all this?' asked the Dogberry of St. Anne. The knight, who had been roughly handled, commenced like a true orator, in a low tone of voice, 'May it please ye, my magistrate, I am not drunk; it is *languor*. A parcel of the bloods of the Garden have treated me cruelly, because I would not treat them. This day, sir, I was sent for by Mr. Sheridan to make my speech upon the table at the Shakespeare Tavern, in *Common* Garden; he wrote the speech for me, and always gives me half-a-guinea when he sends for me to the tavern. You see I didn't go in my royal robes; I only put 'um on when I stand to be member.' Constable: 'Well, but, Sir Harry, why are you brought here?' One of the watchmen then observed, 'That though Sir Harry was but a little *shambling* fellow, he was so *upstroppolus*, and kicked him about at such a rate, that it was as much as he and his comrade could do to bring him along.' As there was no one to support the charge, Sir Harry was advised to go home, which, however, he swore he would not do at midnight without an escort. 'Do you know,' said he, "there's a parcel of *raps* now on the outside waiting for me.' The constable of the night gave orders for him to be protected to the public-house opposite the west end of St. Giles's Church, where he then lodged. Sir Harry, hearing a noise in the street, muttered, 'I shall catch it; I know I shall.' 'See the conquering hero comes' (*cries without*). 'Ay, they always use that tune when I gain my election at Garrett.'"

"Sir Harry Dimsdale," remarks Mr. J. T. Smith, "first came into notice on the death of 'Sir Geoffrey Dunstan,' a dealer in old wigs, who had been for many years returned 'member for Garrett,' on his becoming a candidate. He received mock knighthood, and was ever after known as 'Sir Harry.'" He exercised the itinerant trade of a muffin-man, in the afternoon; he had a little bell, which he held to his ear, smiling ironically at its tingling. His cry was—

"Muffins! muffins! ladies, come buy *me!* pretty, handsome, blooming, smiling maids."

Flaxman, the sculptor, and Mrs. Mathews, of blue-stocking memory, equipped him as a hardwareman, and as such Mr. J. T. Smith made two etchings of him.

This parish has one point in which it differed two centuries ago, and, to a great extent, still differs, from the surrounding districts. To use the words of the "London Spy," in 1725, "King Charles II., of pious memory, was a great benefactor to this parish; for soon after the Plague of London he re-peopled it with ten thousand Protestant families from abroad, who prov'd the most implacable enemies the late French king ever had." The same satirist draws an amusing picture, evidently from life, of one of the "shabby-genteel" households of Soho in his day, where a shopkeeper maintained himself, his wife, and a grown-up daughter, on a limited income. He says, "They were extraordinary economists; brewed their own beer, washed at home; made a joint hold out two days, and a shift three; let three parts of their house ready furnished; and kept paying one quarter's rent under another. . . . The worst the world could say of them was that they liv'd above what they had; that the daughter was as proud a slut as ever clapp'd clog on shoe-leather; and that they entertained lodgers who were no better than they should be." What a picture Charles Dickens could have painted from this description!

CHAPTER XXV.

SOHO SQUARE AND ITS NEIGHBOURHOOD.

"Soho's busy Square."—*Wordsworth.*

Noted Residents in Soho—Appearance of the Square in Queen Anne's Reign—Proposal for the Restoration of the Square—Monmouth House—Lord Bateman—Carlisle House and the celebrated Mrs. Cornelys' Masquerades—St. Patrick's Chapel—Humorous Description of an Irish Wake—The White House and its Fashionable Patrons—Soho Bazaar—The Residence of Sir Joseph Banks—Origin of the Linnæan Society—Frith Street—Sir Samuel Romilly—Compton Street—Dean Street—The New Royalty Theatre—Greek Street—The House of Charity—Wardour Street—"The Mischief" in Oxford Street—Hog Lane (Charing Cross Road) and the Greek Chapel—Hogarth's "Noon."

SOHO SQUARE, as shown in the previous chapter, was originally called the King's Square, and dates from the reign of Charles II. Evelyn, as he tells us in his "Diary," visited at a house in this celebrated vicinity, and spent the winter of 1690 "at Soho, in the great Square." It must not be forgotten, of course, that Sir Roger de Coverley is described, in the beginning of the *Spectator*, as living, when he is in town, at Soho Square. Shadwell, too, in one of his comedies, written in 1691, uses terms which imply that it was a fashionable quarter of the town, for he represents an alderman's wife as having "forced" her husband out of Mark Lane "to live in Soho Square." And no doubt it was the centre of fashion when Grosvenor and Cavendish Squares were not yet in existence.

The building of the Square was only begun in 1681, and at that time it contained no more than nine inhabitants, among whom were the Duke of Monmouth, Colonel Ramsey, Mr. Pilcher, Mr. Broughton, Sir Henry Ingleby, and the Earl of Stamford, as the rate-books of St. Martin's attest.

Pennant says, though erroneously, that its original name was Monmouth Square, but that it came to be called after the king. Mr. Peter Cunningham, with his usual diligence, has sifted the question out by consulting the parish rate-books, ground leases, and other original documents, and so far as it is possible to prove a negative, he shows that it never was called Monmouth Square. It is possible, however that, from the Duke of Monmouth living in it, it may have been called "Monmouth's Square"—*i.e.*, the square in which Monmouth lived—and that this may have misled Pennant. The Duke of Monmouth lived in a large house with two wings on its southern side. It stood back, with a court before it.

This Duke of Monmouth was a natural son of Charles II., by Lucy Walters. His defeat at Sedgemoor, in 1685, and his subsequent execution, are matters of history.

Pennant mentions, as we have noticed before, a tradition to the effect that on the death of the Duke of Monmouth the name of the square was changed by his friends and admirers to Soho, that being the watchword of the day at the battle of Sedgemoor; but Mr. Cunningham has settled this question too in the negative, for he shows, by reference to contemporary documents, that whereas the battle of Sedgemoor was not fought till 1685, this district was called "Sohoe," or "Soho," nearly fifty years previously. For instance, the rate-books of St. Martin's, in 1636, speak of people living at "the Brick-kilns, near Soho;" and in 1650 the Commonwealth Survey describes "Shaver's Hall," or "Piccadilly Hall," as "lying between a roadway leading from Charing Cross to Knightesbridge West, and a highway leading from Charing Cross towards So Hoe." In the face of such evidence, it would seem impossible not to set aside the derivation propounded by Pennant as wholly untenable. It is far more probable that the duke borrowed his "watchword of the day" at Sedgemoor from the neighbourhood in which his home was situated, just as Nelson might have chosen "Burnham" or "Merton" as his watchword at the Nile or Trafalgar. Mr. Peter Cunningham writes—"I never saw it called Monmouth Square in any map, letter, or printed book, or anywhere, indeed, but in Pennant. It was called King Square, certainly, but not Monmouth Square." This, it appears to us, settles the question.

Soho Square is described by Allen, in his "History of London," even so lately as 1839, as presenting a very pleasing and somewhat rural appearance, having in the centre a large area within a handsome iron railing, enclosing several trees and shrubs." We should, however, certainly venture to assert that the expressions are scarcely any longer applicable to the square. "In the centre," adds Allen, "is a pedestrian statue of Charles II., at the feet of which are figures emblematic of the rivers Thames, Trent, Severn, and Humber. They are now," he continues, "in a most wretchedly mutilated state, and the inscriptions on the base of the pedestal are quite illegible."

London was brightened in Queen Anne's reign by numbers of public conduits and fountains. Most of them have been removed or destroyed, but are now in some measure replaced by drinking-fountains, which are certainly of great benefit to thirsty wayfarers. We add a description of the ancient specimen in King's Square, Soho. In the centre was a fountain with four streams. In the middle of the basin was the statue of Charles II., in armour, on a pedestal, enriched with fruit and flowers; on the four sides of the base were figures representing the four chief rivers of the kingdom —Thames, Severn, Trent, and Humber; on the south side were figures of an old man and a young virgin, with a stream ascending; on the west lay the figure of a naked virgin (only nets wrapped about her) reposing on a fish, out of whose mouth flowed a stream of water; on the north, an old man recumbent on a coal-bed, and an urn in his hand whence issues a stream of water; on the east rested a very aged man, with water running from a vase, and his right hand laid upon a shell. The statue became so mutilated and disfigured, and the inscription quite effaced, that it was a difficult matter to distinguish whose it really was; some antiquaries, in fact, are of opinion that it was the effigy of the Duke of Monmouth. It stood originally in the middle of the basin of a fountain, which in its turn was filled up and converted into a somewhat unattractive flower-bed. In or about the year 1880 the centre of the square was "beautified," and the statue was removed.

At different times attempts have been made to obtain power to throw open this square to the general public, but it has been found to be impracticable. A meeting of the inhabitants was convened in 1874, and a committee formed. Mr. Albert Grant, to whom the public are indebted for the transformation of Leicester Square, as described in a preceding chapter, offered to lay out and develop the ground at an estimated cost of £7,000, and to endow it with an annual income of £150 in the names of a committee to be appointed by the inhabitants. But this, like other endeavours to secure the same end, came to nothing, and the use of the square is still confined to a privileged few. To the children of the thickly-populated streets around, the opening of the ground would be an incalculable boon.

Alderman Beckford, whom we have already mentioned as a resident of the square, made here a collection of works of art which subsequently were sold by public auction. This did not, however, deter him from beginning de novo, in order to decorate his new Wiltshire toy, Fonthill, which was destined in the end to share the same fate. Here also the shipwrecked remains of Sir Cloudesley Shovel lay in state in 1707. Bishop Burnet, the historian, lived in Soho Square before his removal to Clerkenwell, and here he had his curiosities, including the supposed "original Magna Charta," with part of the great seal remaining attached to it.

Monmouth House, as shown in an illustration on page 187, was a lofty brick building of three storeys, comprising a centre with slightly projecting wings.

Monmouth, and after his death it was purchased by Lord Bateman, whose family occupied it for a time ; but, as the stream of fashion was setting westwards, they travelled along with it, and, pulling down the mansion, let out the site on building

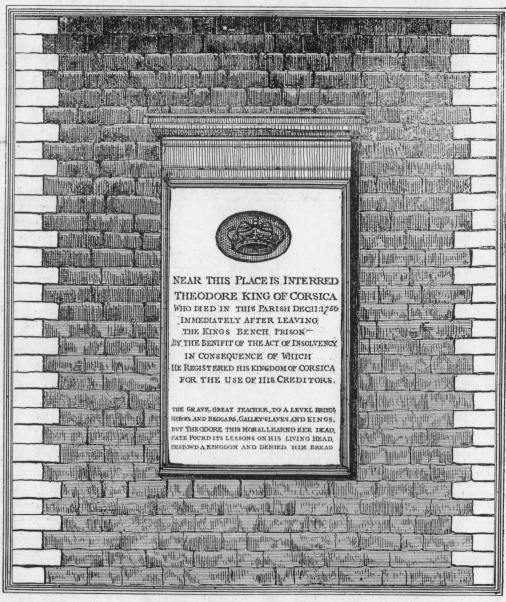

NEAR THIS PLACE IS INTERRED
THEODORE KING OF CORSICA
WHO DIED IN THIS PARISH DEC:11.1756
IMMEDIATELY AFTER LEAVING
THE KINGS BENCH PRISON
BY THE BENIFIT OF THE ACT OF INSOLVENCY
IN CONSEQUENCE OF WHICH
HE REGISTERED HIS KINGDOM OF CORSICA
FOR THE USE OF HIS CREDITORS,

THE GRAVE, GREAT TEACHER, TO A LEVEL BRINGS
HEROES AND BEGGARS, GALLEY-SLAVES AND KINGS,
BUT THEODORE THIS MORAL LEARND ERE DEAD,
FATE POURD ITS LESSONS ON HIS LIVING HEAD,
BESTOWD A KINGDOM AND DENIED HIM BREAD

KING THEODORE'S MONUMENT. (*See page* 182.)

Each wing was adorned with three pilasters, with enriched capitals, rising to the level of the third storey, and each floor was lighted with large semi-circular-headed windows. The doorway in the centre was approached by a broad flight of steps, and protected by an ample porch supported by double columns on each side.

The house was built by Wren for the Duke of

leases. This would seem to be the fate of all the great houses in London sooner or later. The house, in 1717, was converted into auction-rooms, but was demolished in 1793 ; the Hospital for Women now occupies the site. The name of Lord Bateman is kept up by a row of houses called Bateman's Buildings, and by Bateman Street, connecting Dean Street with Greek Street. But the duke has not been so lucky: for a time his name lived on in "Monmouth" Street, St. Giles's; but since it had obtained a bad name as the resort of Jew dealers in rags and old clothes, the thoroughfare was re-christened Dudley Street; the old clothes, however, have not passed away along with the unsavoury name. Of

of the Howards, Earls of Carlisle (a branch of the ducal house of Norfolk), the head of whom was living, in the middle of the last century, in a house on the east side of the square. The mansion, which was built in the reign of James II., originally stood in the midst of a garden, the extent of which

MONMOUTH HOUSE, 1770.

this Lord Bateman, Horace Walpole tells the story that George I. created him an Irish peer to avoid making him a Knight of the Bath; "for," said his majesty, with the wit of Charles II., "I can make him a lord, but I cannot make him a gentleman." Before Lord Bateman's house was pulled down, it was let by him to various persons in the higher ranks of society. Among others, the French ambassador was residing in it in 1791-2.

In Carlisle Street we have perpetuated the name

it would be difficult to define at the present time. The lower walls of the house were of red brick and on the lead-work of the cisterns was the date 1669. The mansion in its original condition must have had a magnificent appearance, with its marble-floored hall, its superbly decorated staircases, and its large and lofty rooms with enriched ceilings.

Towards the close of the last century it was tenanted by the celebrated Mrs. Cornelys, who turned it into a place of resort for masked balls and other fashionable amusements. Her assemblies were at one time the rage of the town, but she was in the end ruined by her extravagance. Hither "the quality" repaired in large numbers, although the morality of the place was rather questionable. Among the lady's chief patrons were the eccentric Duke of Queensberry ("Old Q.") and the notorious Duchess of Kingston, who appeared here in other characters, and especially on one occasion in that of Iphigenia, "in a state almost ready," as Horace Walpole slily remarks, "for the sacrifice." There is a scarce print of the duchess in this character, which shows rather a deficiency of dress. It was at one of Mrs. Cornelys' masquerades that the beautiful daughter of a peer wore the costume of an Indian princess, three black girls bearing her train, a canopy held over her head by two negro boys, and her dress covered with jewels worth £100,000. It was at another that Adam, in flesh-coloured tights and an apron of fig-leaves, was to be seen in company with the Duchess of Bolton as Diana. Death, in a white shroud, bearing his own coffin and epitaph; Lady Augusta Stuart as a Vestal; the Duke of Gloucester, in an old English habit, with a star on his cloak; and the Duke of Devonshire, "who was very fine, but in no particular character"—all these, and others, passed through her rooms; yet before many years had gone by Mrs. Cornelys was selling asses' milk at Knightsbridge, and in 1797 she died in the Fleet Prison, forming schemes to the very last for retrieving her broken fortunes. Attempts were unsuccessfully made to keep up the festivities of Carlisle House; but "Almack's" drew away the great, and the square gradually declined in the world—from fashion to philosophy, from artists to tradesmen, from shops to hospitals—until at length its lowest depth seems to have been reached.

Into the promenades at Mrs. Cornelys' house gentlemen were requested not to enter "with boots;" and in satire the manager of a rival amusement is said to have given this notice :— "THE NEW PARADISE.—No Gentlemen or Ladies to be admitted with nails in their shoes." Of the morality of Mrs. Cornelys and of Carlisle House, Northouck had no high opinion; but he throws the blame on their aristocratic patrons. He says, "Here the nobility of this kingdom long protected Mrs. Cornelys in entertaining their masquerade and gaming assemblies, in violation of the laws, and to the destruction of all sober principles."

It is clear, from the advertisements scattered up and down the files of the London newspapers, that, beginning with the winter of 1762-3, Mrs. Cornelys contrived to secure for some ten or twelve years the almost undivided patronage of the world of fashion, keeping the West End, and especially the neighbourhood of "Soho Fields," alive with a succession of balls, concerts, masquerades, "subscription music meetings," &c., and securing her interest with the families of "quality" by giving balls to their upper servants. Her advertisements are by themselves a study in the art of puffery, and occasionally throw light on the condition of life in London : as, for instance, when she "begs the chairmen and hackney-coach drivers not to quarrel, or to run their poles through each other's windows." On one occasion, when it was rumoured that the enterprising lady was about to open a sister institution in Bishopsgate Street, half the City was up in arms to oppose her on the ground of morality, and the lady was defeated. On several occasions as many as 800 persons of "quality" were present at her masquerades, the Duke of Gloucester, and even the King of Denmark, being of the number. At one time she was threatened with proceedings under the "Alien Act" by a rival in the same line of business; but by a judicious use of "soft sawder" she circumvented her opponents whilst appearing to give way to them, and thus she prolonged her lease of popularity. At length, however, by instituting a harmonic meeting, Mrs. Cornelys placed herself in an attitude of direct hostility to the Italian Opera House, whose managers applied to the magistrates to stop her entertainment. They were so far successful that Sir John Fielding ordered Guardini, the chief singer at Carlisle House, to be arrested. This was the first instalment of ill success which befell her; the next was the establishment of a rival house of entertainment at the Pantheon, in Oxford Street; and in spite of a desperate effort to prop up her falling fortunes by a new amusement, called a "Coterie"—the details of which have not come down to us—in July, 1772, there came a "smash," and in the November following the whole contents of Carlisle House, with its sumptuous decorations, were brought to the hammer. A graphic account of this sale will be found in the *Westminster Magazine* for January, 1773, under the title of "Cupid turned Auctioneer."

But the irrepressible Mrs. Cornelys was not destined to be crushed by a single failure. The "Circe" and "Sultana" of Soho gathered her aristocratic friends and patrons around her; and her name again appears, in 1774, as manager and conductress of a new series of concerts. These, however, would appear to have turned out profitless, for in August, 1775, Carlisle House was advertised for sale by Messrs. Christie "with or without its furniture." She still, however, seems to have fought on against fate, for as late as 1777 we find Mrs. Cornelys still organising masques at Carlisle House, though "the whole company did not exceed three hundred." The exact date of her last effort to amuse the fashionable world on this spot is unknown. In 1779, the establishment appears to have been under the management of a Mr. Hoffmann, who tried a variety of experiments in the way of "masked balls," and "benefit concerts," but with a like result. With the year 1780 we find a great change in the amusements of Carlisle House, for it was devoted to the meetings of a debating society, called the "School of Eloquence:" its meetings being presided over by a clergyman as "moderator;" on other evenings the rooms being devoted to "the reception of company previous to the 'masqued ridotto,'" at the Opera House. On Sunday evenings also there was a "public promenade," the admission to which was by a three-shilling ticket, which included refreshments of "tea, coffee, capillaire, orgeat, and lemonade." These various attractions were held out, but with inferior success, for several years, a Mr. William Wade officiating as master of the ceremonies. In vain did he open a "morning suite of rooms" supplied with the newspapers and periodicals of the day "*gratis* to subscribers;" in vain did he organise courses of "scientific lectures," and advertise concerts by the Polish dwarf, Count Borawlaski, with tickets at half-a-guinea, "entitling the purchaser to see and converse with that extraordinary personage." In 1785 the property was in Chancery, and the house sold under a decree of the court, and Mrs. Cornelys retired into private life at Knightsbridge, where we shall find her again.

What was once the music-room of Lord Carlisle's mansion, and afterwards the grand saloon of Mrs. Cornelys' establishment, was subsequently altered and turned into a Catholic chapel, known as "St. Patrick's, Soho," and largely frequented by the poor Irish of the neighbourhood. The property was purchased in 1792 by the exertions and influence of the celebrated Catholic preacher and controversialist, Dr. O'Leary, who died in 1802. In 1893 the chapel was rebuilt of red brick and Portland stone, in the Late Italian style, with a bell-tower a hundred and twenty-five feet high at the Sutton Street corner.

One of the treasures of St. Patrick's is a painting of the Crucifixion by Vandyke, said to be the finest specimen of a sacred painting by his hand in England, and equal to any in Belgium.

This chapel was formerly much frequented not only by the poor Irish who lived round Soho and St. Giles's, but also by Catholics of the wealthier class residing about Russell and Bedford Squares. It long divided with the Sardinian Chapel in Lincoln's Inn Fields the administration of the chief Roman Catholic charities; and the leading Roman Catholic bishops, Dr. Milner, Cardinal Wiseman, and Cardinal Manning have frequently advocated from its pulpit the cause of charity.

On the north side of the square is another imposing place of worship, the French Protestant Church of London, with a singularly effective façade of red brick and terra-cotta.

Prior to the foundation of St. Patrick's Mission in Sutton Street, mass was said at No. 13 in the Square, in the house of the Neapolitan ambassador, and also, though by stealth and secretly, at a small house in Denmark Street, where some French priests had taken up their abode on the commencement of troubles in France.

The Irish live in various parts of London, apart and amongst themselves, carrying with them the many virtues and vices of their native land, and never becoming absorbed in the nation to which, for years, they may be attached. Swindlers, thieves, and tramps may surround them, but do not in general affect them. Tim Malone still renews upon English ground his feuds with the O'Learys, commencing not within the memory of man; and some Bridget O'Rafferty pays Ellen O'Connor for evidence given by her grandfather against the rebels of '98. "It would be a curious investigation," says Mr. Diprose, in his "Book about London," "for the philosopher, how far the interest and progress of this most gallant and interesting nation have been affected by what, in the absence of a better definition, we shall designate the absence of merging power. Nor is it less curious, that whilst the Irish preserve their national characteristics as steadfastly as do the Jews, they have the quality of absorbing other nations, for we find that the English who settle in Ireland, not merely acquire the brogue, but become more Irish than the Irish themselves. *Ipsis Hibernis Hiberniores* is as true now as it was in the days of the poet Spenser. The 'Irish Hudibras' (1682) thus humorously describes an Irish wake:—

> "'To their own sports (the masses ended)
> The mourners now are recommended.
> Some sit and chat, some laugh, some weep,
> Some sing cronans, and some do sleep;
> Some court, some scold, some blow, some puff,
> Some take tobacco, some take snuff.
> Some play the trump, some trot the hay,
> Some at machan, some at noddy play;
> Thus mixing up their grief and sorrow,
> Yesterday buried, killed to-morrow.'"

The house occupying the northern angle of Sutton Street was celebrated in the last century, and the beginning of the present, as "the White House," and was a place of fashionable dissipation to which only the titled and wealthy classes had the privilege of admission. Its character may be inferred from the fact that it was one of the haunts of the then Prince of Wales, the old Duke of Queensberry, and the Marquis of Hertford; and the ruin of many a female heart may be dated from a visit within its walls. It is said by tradition that its apartments were known as the "Gold," "Silver," "Bronze" Rooms, &c., each being called from the prevailing character of its fittings, and that the walls of nearly every room were inlaid with mirrored panels.

Many of the rooms in this house, too, had a sensational name, as the "Commons," the "Painted Chamber," the "Grotto," the "Coal Hole," and the "Skeleton Room"—the latter so styled on account of a closet out of which a skeleton was made to step forth by the aid of machinery. The "White House," as a scene of profligacy, lived on into the present century, and having been empty for some years, was converted to business uses by the founders of the firm which at present occupies it—Messrs. Crosse and Blackwell, whose enormous premises extend to the Charing Cross Road, which they border for a considerable distance.

We shall not attempt to describe in detail the White House, which enjoyed such an unenviable reputation from the scenes which it witnessed in the days when George III. was King, and George Prince of Wales was living. It was not till 1837-8 that the White House underwent the transformation of which we have just spoken.

No. 21 in this square, which adjoined the "White House," and was afterwards Messrs. D'Almaine's musical repository, is now absorbed into the large warehouse of Messrs. Crosse and Blackwell. Though considerably modernised, it still retains one magnificently-carved mantelpiece and ornamental ceiling; and the grandly-proportioned rooms are the same as when the mansion was the town house of the Lords Fauconberg, and was thronged by beauty and fashion.

In the north-west corner of the square is the celebrated Soho Bazaar, one of the haunts most frequented by sight-seers, especially at Christmas, New Years's Day, and other gift-seasons. It was established in 1815, and for many years was a formidable rival to the Pantheon. It has been a fashionable lounge for ladies and children, and especially attractive to "country cousins." It has now an entrance in Oxford Street also, one of the houses on the south side of that roadway having been added to it. It is scarcely necessary to explain here that the word "bazaar" comes to us from the East, denoting a group of shops in which dealers in some one commodity or class of commodities congregate in one place, much to the gain of both purchasers and sellers. Yet, as Mr. Chambers remarks, "a stranger may do well to bear in mind that in London . . . some approach is made to the system. For instance, coachmakers congregate in considerable numbers in Long Acre, watchmakers and jewellers in Clerkenwell, tanners and leather-dressers in Bermondsey, bird and birdcage sellers in Seven Dials, statuaries in the Euston Road, furniture-dealers and clothiers in Tottenham Court Road, hat-makers in Bermondsey and Southwark, dentists around St. Martin's Lane, and booksellers and publishers in Paternoster Row."

Soho Bazaar, to which belongs the distinction of having been the first of its kind in England, was established, according to Allen, by John Trotter, Esq. It was originally designed by Mr. Trotter as a *depôt* for the sale of articles in aid of the widows and orphans of those who had fallen in the long war against Napoleon; but the Government of the day did not entertain the proposal, and accordingly Mr. Trotter started the bazaar as a private speculation of his own. The institution was opened by Queen Charlotte, in 1816, and was extensively patronised by the royal family. The building, which does not present any architectural features, lies between Soho Square on the south, Oxford Street on the north, and Dean Street on the west, and consists of several rooms, conveniently fitted up with mahogany counters. The bazaar occupies two floors, and has counter accommodation for a large number of tenants. The rent of the counters, which are mostly for the sale of fancy goods, is very moderate. The bazaar has been frequently patronised by royalty; the Queen's eldest daughter, the Princess Victoria, at that time Crown Princess of Prussia, afterwards the Empress Frederick, honoured it with a visit in 1868.

Entering from Oxford Street, the visitor will find an assortment of bicycles of the latest patterns. Farther on are china articles, and stalls for sewing-machines. Up a small staircase to the left is an extensive picture-gallery. Other rooms close by are filled with a variety of fancy goods, or devoted to the purposes of photography. The two principal rooms in the building are about ninety feet long, and in them it is no exaggeration to say that the visitor may find a great variety of trades represented. Connected with the bazaar are spacious and well-appointed refreshment-rooms, and also offices for the registration of governesses and the hire of servants, &c. There is also a school in which the art of cycling is taught—for the bazaar, though intended as an emporium of fancy goods, has not been slow to adapt itself to changing conditions. The bazaar forms the subject of one of the whimsical descriptive ballads of James Catnatch, the founder of the business of which we shall have something to say in our next chapter.

During the latter part of the eighteenth and the earlier years of the present century, Soho Square attained some celebrity as the residence of the learned and accomplished philosopher, Sir Joseph Banks, so bitterly and caustically satirised by "Peter Pindar." He lived at No. 32, now the Hospital for Diseases of the Heart and Paralysis, and here he held his receptions, at which nearly every man eminent in science was a frequent attendant. Sir Joseph Banks, who was descended from an ancient Yorkshire family, was born in Argyle Street, in the parish of St. James's, Westminster, in 1743, and was educated at Harrow and Eton, whence he removed as a gentleman commoner to Christ Church, Oxford. His love of botany increased at the university, and there his mind warmly embraced all the other branches of natural history. In 1766 he was chosen into the Royal Society, and in that year went to Newfoundland, for the purpose of collecting plants. The Royal Society having made a proposition to the Government to effect a general voyage of discovery in those parts of the ocean which were still wholly unknown, or only partially discovered, and especially to observe the transit of Venus at Otaheite in 1769, Banks was appointed, in conjunction with Dr. Solander, naturalist to the expedition, which sailed from Plymouth Sound, under the command of Captain Cook, in August, 1768. After an absence of three years the expedition returned to England, the specimens which Banks had brought, at so much risk and expense, exciting much interest. In 1777, on the retirement of Sir John Pringle from the presidency of the Royal Society, Mr. Banks was elected to the vacant chair. In 1795 he was invested with the Order of the Bath, and he was afterwards sworn a member of the Privy Council, and chosen a member of the National Institute of France. His life was devoted to the prosecution of scientific researches, and the general diffusion of useful knowledge. In fact, he largely anticipated the Humboldts and Owens of a later day. Sir Joseph Banks died in June, 1820.

His house in Soho Square has also had other distinguished inhabitants; Sir J. E. Smith and Mr. Robert Brown, for example, both eminent naturalists. The Linnæan Society was founded in 1788, and held its meetings in Gerrard Street, until its establishment in Soho Square. Here it continued to flourish till its removal to Burlington House, Piccadilly, in 1855.

The Linnæan Society, it would appear, like many another great institution, had its origin in an accident. The late Sir John E. Smith, then a medical student, was breakfasting one day with Sir Joseph Banks, when the latter told him that he just had an offer of the memoranda and botanical collections of the great Linnæus for a thousand pounds, but that he had declined to buy them. Young Smith, whose zeal for botany was great, begged his father to advance to him the money, and at length persuaded him to do so, though not without difficulty. It may appear strange that Sweden should consent to part with the treasures of her far-famed naturalist; and indeed the king, Gustavus III., who had been absent in France, was much displeased, on his return, at hearing that a vessel had just sailed for England with these collections. He immediately dispatched a vessel to the Sound, to intercept it, but was too late. The herbarium, books, MSS., &c., arrived safely in London in 1784, packed in twenty-six cases, and cost the purchaser £1,088 5s. In the following year Smith was elected a Fellow of the Royal Society, and devoted himself more to botanical studies than to his profession as a physician. In 1792 he had the honour of being engaged to teach botany to Queen Charlotte and the princesses, and he was knighted by the Prince Regent in 1814. At his death, in 1828, the celebrated collection, with Sir J. E. Smith's additions, was purchased by the Linnæan Society, and still remains in their possession.

The house of Sir Joseph Banks was kept for many years by his sister, a learned lady, who had as great a passion for collecting coins as her brother had for botanical researches. Her appearance is thus described by the author of a "Book for a Rainy Day:"—"Her dress was that of the old school; her Barcelona quilted petticoat had a hole on either side, for the convenience of rummaging two immense pockets, stuffed with books of all sizes. This petticoat was covered with a deep stomachered gown, sometimes drawn through the pocket-holes, similar to those of many of the ladies of Bunbury's time, which he has produced in his picture. In this dress" (writes Mr. J. T. Smith) "I have frequently seen her walk, followed by a six-foot servant with a cane almost as tall as himself. Miss Banks, I may add, when she wanted to purchase a broadside in the streets, was more than once taken for a member of the ballad-singing confraternity. And yet this same lady, when she was in the prime of life, had been a fashionable whip, and driven a four-in-hand in the Park."

In the south-east corner of the square lived, for many years, the late Mr. Barnes, the responsible editor of the *Times;* and it was here that, when waited upon by some of the leading politicians of

Romilly. He was descended from a Protestant family, who left France after the Revocation of the Edict of Nantes. His father was a jeweller, carrying on business in this street; and he was sent to the French Protestant School close by, where he received but an indifferent education;

SIR SAMUEL ROMILLY.

the time, he laid down the terms on which that paper would support the ministry of the Duke of Wellington, in 1828.

Among the other noted residents of Soho Square we may mention George II., when Prince of Wales; and also Field-Marshal Conway, Walpole's correspondent and friend.

In Frith Street, on the south side of the square, in the year 1757, was born one of our most celebrated advocates and philanthropists, Sir Samuel

but as soon as he had left it he applied himself to self-culture, and his diligence in the acquisition of learning was largely rewarded in after life.

Placed as a lad with a solicitor, whom he left for a merchant's office, which he also resigned, eventually he was articled to one of the sworn clerks of Chancery. At the expiration of his articles he qualified himself for the bar, but had to wait long and patiently ere he was rewarded with any practice. When briefs did at last fall to his lot, it very soon became manifest that they were held by a master, and the result was that a tide of prosperity set in, and "success came upon him like a flood." His income rose to about £9,000 a year, and in his diary he congratulated himself that he did not press his father to buy him a seat in the

1806—the electors of Westminster having returned him to Parliament without the expenditure of a shilling on his part; a great thing in those days of bribery and corruption—and during the short administration of Mr. Grenville he was appointed Solicitor-General, and knighted. Nor was he dis-

THE SIGN OF THE "MISCHIEF." (*See page* 196).

Six Clerks' Office. Romilly now rapidly rose to distinction in the Court of Chancery, where he was distinguished for his profound learning and forcible eloquence; and to him Lord Brougham has paid the following tribute:—"Romilly, by the force of his learning and talents, and the most spotless integrity, rose to the very height of professional ambition. He was beyond question or pretence of rivalry the first man in the courts in this country."

Romilly entered the House of Commons in

tinguished professionally only; but during his political career he was listened to with rapt attention, and a passage in one of his speeches in favour of the abolition of the slave-trade received the singular honour of three distinct rounds of applause from the House.

But Romilly's grand claim to remembrance rests upon his humane efforts to mitigate the Draconic code of English law, in which nearly three hundred crimes, varying from murder to keeping company with a gipsy, were punishable with death. The first bill which he succeeded in getting passed was to repeal a statute of Elizabeth, which made it a capital offence to steal privately from the person of another. He next tried a bolder stroke, and introduced a bill to repeal several statutes which punished with death the crimes of stealing privately in a shop goods to the amount of five shillings; and of stealing to the amount of forty shillings in a dwelling-house; or in vessels in navigable rivers. But this bill was lost. Romilly, however, did not despair, but kept on agitating session after session, and cleared the way for the success which came when he was no more.

In his forty-first year Sir Samuel Romilly married Miss Garbett (a *protégée* of the Marquis of Lansdowne), a lady of rare talents and moral excellence. But after twenty years of happy married life, her health began to decline, and on the 29th of October, 1818, she died. This was a dreadful shock to Romilly, and produced such mental anguish, that delirium followed, and in an unwatched moment he sprang from his bed, cut his throat, and expired almost instantly—and this at a time when worldly honours were being heaped upon him! It is related that the following morning, when Lord Eldon took his seat on the bench and Romilly's place was vacant—iron man though he was—he exclaimed, "I cannot stay here!" and rising in great agitation, broke up the court. The bodies of husband and wife were buried in one grave, at Knill, in Herefordshire.

In Frith Street, too, at No. 6, Hazlitt, the essayist, died of cholera in 1830; he was buried, as we have stated, in St. Anne's Churchyard.

Compton Street was built in the reign of King Charles II., by Sir Francis Compton; and New Compton Street was first called Stiddolph Street, after Sir Richard Stiddolph, the owner of the land on which it was built. Both New Compton and Dean Streets were named after Bishop Compton, Dean of the Chapel Royal, who formerly held the living of St. Anne's, Soho. In Dean Street, on the west side, at No. 75 (now the warehouse of Messrs. Wilson, wholesale tin-plate workers, of Wardour Street), lived Sir James Thornhill, the painter, whose daughter married Hogarth. The house, which is still unaltered in its main features, has several handsome rooms, and a magnificent staircase; and the panels of the walls are adorned with a series of paintings by the hand of its former master.

At No. 33 in this street lived Harlowe, the painter of "The Trial of Queen Katherine." He died here in 1819, at an early age.

The small theatre in this street, now called the Royalty, was built in 1840, by Miss F. Kelly (an actress who had made herself a reputation in light comedy and domestic melodrama on the boards of Drury Lane and the Haymarket) as a school for acting, but she reaped little profit from the enterprise. It was for many years used chiefly for amateur theatricals, but afterwards became popular by its spirited performance of operetta and burlesque entertainments. Miss Kelly, who was the daughter of a retired military officer, was destined for the stage from her birth, and was familiar with the boards of Old Drury at ten years of age as a chorus-singer. Her *début* as an actress was at Glasgow, in 1807, she being then in her seventeenth year. She rose to great eminence in her profession, and was equally successful as a vocalist and an actress, succeeding to many of the parts which had been filled by the celebrated Madame Storace. For several years she was an extraordinary attraction at Drury Lane, and while performing one evening at that theatre, received a striking proof of the power of her charms. A pistol was fired at her from the pit, the ball passing directly over her head; and as the terrified lady fell insensible on the stage, it was at first thought she had been killed, and a scene of wild confusion ensued. The assailant was secured, and proved to be a lunatic who had for some time persecuted Miss Kelly with incoherent letters, expressive of his attachment. A similar attempt was made upon her life in Dublin, but happily with no greater success.

In the fiftieth year of her age, by which time she had acquired a handsome competence, it occurred to Miss Kelly to establish a school for acting, for which purpose she purchased an extensive freehold property in Dean Street, Soho, in the hope of improving the condition of dramatic art. The school was a success. A number of pupils hastened to enrol themselves under the banner of so accomplished a teacher, for few ever equalled Miss Kelly in the art of—

"Making the laugher weep, the weeper smile;
Catching all passion in her craft of wile."

Unfortunately her ambition did not stop here, but inspired her with the wild idea of building a new theatre on her own extensive premises. Encouraged by the lavish promises of support and subscriptions from her numerous patrons among the aristocracy, foremost of whom was the Duke of Devonshire, who especially interested himself in her hazardous undertaking, Miss Kelly converted the large yard and stabling attached to her house into the Theatre Royal, Dean Street, Soho, by which title, however, it was seldom known, generally passing under the name of "Miss Kelly's Theatre." The entrance to all parts of this toy playhouse was through Miss Kelly's private residence, a peculiarity of construction which had, at all events, the advantage of novelty.

Heralded by many a flourish of trumpets on the part of the newspapers, Miss Kelly opened her tiny theatre on the 25th of May, 1840, with a new piece by Mr. Morris Barnett, entitled *Summer and Winter*, in which the author and Miss Kelly sustained the principal parts, supported, as the announcement went, "by an efficient company." The result was as disastrous as it was speedy. The distinguished patronage, from which so much had been expected, proving more select than numerous, the theatre, after being open five nights, on two of which the actors outnumbered the audience, was closed abruptly. In November of the same year Miss Kelly announced herself *At Home*, at the Theatre Royal, Dean Street. The performance was monological, and similar to some entertainments which she had given a few years previously at the Strand, with but moderate success. The result was again a complete failure, and Miss Kelly retired into private life, a loser of more than £7,000 by her unlucky speculation.

In 1850 the little theatre, which had so long languished in obscurity, made a desperate rally, and presented itself to the public as the "New English Opera House," opening with, as the playbills announced, "a grand opera in three acts, entitled *The Last Crusade*, by Alexander Mitchell, the blind composer." This opera had been originally represented with great success at the Grand Ducal Theatre, Brunswick, but, possibly from the inefficiency of the company, proved a total failure at the Soho theatre, and the "New English Opera House" was speedily closed.

In 1861 it was entirely re-constructed, with great improvements, and re-opened on the 12th of November under the name of the "New Royalty," since which time it has enjoyed its fair share of success. In 1866 Miss M. Oliver assumed the management, and under herself and her successors the Royalty kept its *prestige*. It was re-built in 1882–83, when it came under the management of Miss Kate Santley.

Greek Street, which runs from north to south, parallel to Dean Street on the east, dates from the year 1680. Pennant considers that its name is a corruption of "Grig" Street, but it was more probably derived from a colony of merchants from the Levant, for whose use a Greek church was built hard by it in Crown Street.

What used to be the last house on the east side of Greek Street, at the south end, removed to make way for the new Palace Theatre, was occupied by Sir Thomas Lawrence for the first four years of the present century; and during the last century by Josiah Wedgwood. It had previously been a dissecting-room, for Soho Square and the adjoining streets were frequented by the faculty; but Wedgwood, on making it his show-room, named it "Portland House." Here he exhibited the magnificent service which he made for the Empress of Russia, and Queen Charlotte was among those who came hither to inspect it. A great artistic interest belonged to the premises, for, as Miss Meteyard remarks in her "Life of Wedgwood," "it was here that his fame culminated in the greatest of his works—the jasper tablets, the medallion portraits and busts, the cameos, and the Barberini Vase." Time, fire, and alterations, however, had so changed Portland House, that when it was demolished little of what was Wedgwood's Gallery remained except the outer walls; though not many years before it was pulled down the name of the great potter was to be seen here cut with a diamond on a window-pane.

Among the many charitable institutions to be found in Soho, none perhaps are more worthy of public support than one at the corner of the Square and of Greek Street, called "The House of Charity." It occupies the house which formerly belonged to Alderman Beckford, who lived here in princely splendour. The institution, which is under the patronage of the Archbishop of Canterbury, was founded in 1846; but the present building and fitting-up of the premises dates only from 1863, when they were taken at a cost of upwards of £3,000. "It is the only Home in London gratuitously afforded to such distressed persons as are of good character, upon a recommendation from some one who knows them. Thus many deserving persons are saved from the sufferings and privations which precede an application to the casual ward or nightly refuge, as well as from the degradation consequent upon their reception into such promiscuous places of resort. Among the various classes of distress relieved by this House are patients discharged from hospitals before they are sufficiently recovered to take situations; these find here a comfortable lodging and ample diet, and are generally successful in obtaining situations. Orphan or friendless girls who have unadvisedly come to London in search of employment, or have accidentally lost their places, meet here with protection, counsel, and, in general, with situations. Widows, who have been reduced to the necessity of seeking a subsistence for themselves, are here recommended to places of trust or domestic service. Emigrants, while breaking up their homes and converting their effects into money, wait here until they embark. Out-patients of hospitals, excluded, through want of room, or by regulations, from admission into them, are enabled to derive benefit, while here, by attending the hospitals for medical advice and treatment. In short, the House of Charity is," says the Council of the Institution in its report, "a home for every kind of friendlessness and destitution which is not the manifest offspring of vice and profligacy." On the other side of Greek Street is Lincoln House, now one of the centres of the West London Mission (Wesleyan), of which the headquarters are at St. James's Hall ; and adjoining it is the Soho Club and Home for Working Girls.

Wardour Street, which runs from north to south, parallel to Dean Street on its western side, was named after the Lords Arundell of Wardour, one of whom married the daughter and heiress of one of those rare personages, successful gamesters—Colonel Thomas Panton, of St. Martin's-in-the-Fields, a gentleman whose name is still perpetuated in Panton Street, Haymarket.

Wardour Street, as a stone at the corner of Edward Street informs us, was built in 1686. Flaxman was living here in 1784 at No. 27. In this street also lived the once celebrated Tom Hudson, the comic song-writer and singer. He carried on business as a grocer, and every week he wrote a comic song, which he had printed upon his " tea-papers," and presented to his customers on the Saturday.

During the last half-century the name of this street has passed into a by-word and a proverb, as the head-quarters of curiosity-shops, antique and modern, genuine and fictitious. Leigh Hunt tells us in his " Town " that it was a favourite haunt of Charles Lamb, and that he had often heard the author of the " Essays of Elia " expatiate on the pleasure of strolling up Wardour Street on a summer afternoon.

The shops occupied by brokers and dealers in old furniture, pictures, prints, china, &c., are above a score in number, forming thus almost a bazaar or mart, and constituting a class apart from the rest of the locality. Here the late Lord Macaulay might be seen trudging home with a second-hand book, or packet of ballads, or broadsides ; and here Mr. Gladstone himself, even when Prime Minister, would often take a stroll, picking up a

specimen of old-fashioned china for the superb collection he once had in Carlton Terrace.

We read in old documents of " Old Soho, *alias* Wardour Street." To this street, no doubt, Pope really alluded when he wrote, in imitation of Horace :—

> " And when I flatter, let my dirty leaves
> Clothe spice, line trunks, or, fluttering in a row,
> Befringe the rails of Bedlam and Soho."

On the south side of Oxford Street, a few doors to the east of Charles Street, used to be an inn called " The Mischief." In its interior was kept and shown a curious sign which used to hang over the entrance, representing a man with a " load of mischief" on his back ; the said load consisting of a shrewish-looking wife, a monkey or ape ; and hard by are most suspicious-looking pawn-shops and gin-shops. The design, of which we give a copy on page 193, is worthy of Hogarth's pencil.

The narrow, winding lane running southwards from the corner of Oxford Street and Tottenham Court Road, long known as Crown Street, but in former times as Hog Lane, formed the boundary between the parishes of St. Giles and St. Anne, Soho. Its narrowness served to show its antiquity ; and, no doubt, it derived its first name from the pigs that fed along its sides. In 1762 it came to be dignified by its more recent appellation from the " Rose and Crown " tavern. In 1887 it was absorbed in " Charing Cross Road." In it was the Greek church already spoken of, built for the use of " merchants from the Levant," in the time of Charles II. It does not appear, however, to have remained long in the hands of these oriental Christians, but to have been given up to the use of the French Protestants who settled in this neighbourhood in large force. As such it is immortalised by Hogarth.

The poor little chapel which belonged in succession to the Greeks and to the French refugees, stood on the western side of Crown Street, adjoining some almshouses, which are said to have been founded by Nell Gwynne.

In Hog Lane Hogarth has laid the scene of one of the best of his smaller pictures, " Noon." Mr. Peter Cunningham notes a curious fact with respect to this picture, namely, that it is " generally reversed in the engravings, and thus made untrue to the locality, which (he adds) Hogarth never was." The background of the picture gives us a view of the then newly-built church of St. Giles-in-the-Fields.